SAMUEL BUTLER (1612–1680)

Characters

SAMUEL BUTLER
1612-1680

Characters

EDITED WITH AN INTRODUCTION
AND NOTES BY
CHARLES W. DAVES

CLEVELAND / LONDON
THE PRESS OF CASE WESTERN RESERVE UNIVERSITY
1970

TO

Allayne

Contents

Preface

All students of the works of Samuel Butler, particularly of his Characters, are indebted to *Characters and Passages from Note-Books* (Cambridge, 1908), edited by A. R. Waller, which is the standard edition. It is regrettable, however, that Waller's text lacks full editorial apparatus. Therefore the basic tasks which I have undertaken are to provide for the Characters of Butler an introduction, explanatory notes, and textual notes, all of which incorporate the findings of recent scholarship, and to make readily available the Characters discovered since Waller's edition went to press. The wide range of knowledge evidenced by Samuel Butler demands elucidation wherever possible, and the thorough and stimulating work on the Character tradition gives perspective to the critical study which the present edition offers. By careful scrutiny of the available texts I have tried to eliminate the few printing errors in Waller's edition.

The initial 121 Characters in the present edition (pp. 29–247) were first printed in 1759 in *The Genuine Remains in Verse and Prose of Mr. Samuel Butler*, edited in two volumes with notes by Robert Thyer, Keeper of the Public Library at Manchester. In the Preface Thyer writes that *The Genuine Remains* was printed from manuscripts in Samuel Butler's hand formerly held by Butler's friend W. Longueville. Since this manuscript source is no longer extant, I transcribed these Characters directly from Thyer's printing. Some of the Characters, in Thyer's judgment of the manuscript, had evidently been prepared for the press, some perhaps awaited a few revisions, and others remained unfinished. In his edition Robert Thyer follows the common printing conventions of his time: heavy capitalization (of almost all the nouns), frequent use of italics, and the use of long *s*. The explanatory notes in Thyer's volume have been incorporated, where useful, into the notes of this edition.

The next 66 Characters (pp. 247–319) I copied from a microfilm of British Museum Additional Manuscript 32626. The manuscript is generally accepted as a transcription by Robert Thyer of works of Butler which could have been but were not included in *The Genuine Remains*. These Characters are generally in less polished form than the ones in the volume edited by Thyer, for some passages in the British Museum Manuscript have two readings (no final choice is indicated); there are symbols and abbreviations, dashes marking the ends of sentences, and sentences (usually opening ones) beginning with small letters.

Eight Characters (pp. 319–328) I transcribed from the *London Magazine*, their only source. They are among twenty printed in "Butleriana," a series of five articles which appeared in 1825–26. One of the eight, A Self-Conceited Man, shares seven sentences (though in a different order) with the Self Conceited or Singular (pp. 309–310). Josephine Bauer speculates that these eight Characters may have been taken from folios missing from the manuscript when it was purchased by the Museum in 1885.[1] By comparing the twelve Characters that appear both in the British Museum Manuscript and in the series in the *London Magazine*, one can surmise that the eight Characters appearing in the latter only were also altered to conform more closely to nineteenth-century custom—that some capitals were changed to small letters, some contractions were expanded, and some modifications were made in spelling.

The Character of a Schoolmaster, obviously in rough form, which appears in this edition as an appendix, I copied from the unpublished commonplace book of Butler's owned by the Rosenbach Foundation of Philadelphia. Also found in the commonplace book is what seems to be an early, unfinished version of the Character of a Lawyer (pp. 111–115), printed by Thyer. I have not included it, because almost all of the material in it appears in the much longer and rather obviously later version.[2]

Each Character in this edition is copied from the earliest source known to exist and is given in the order found there. In passages where the manuscript offers two readings, I have exercised my judgment to

---

[1] For full information see Josephine Bauer, "Some Verse Fragments and Prose *Characters* by Samuel Butler Not Included in the Complete Works," *Modern Philology*, XLV (1947–48), 160–68.

[2] See Norma E. Bentley, "Another Butler Manuscript," *Modern Philology*, XLVI (1948–49), 132–35.

select the reading for the text which seems most characteristic of Butler. The other choice is recorded in the notes. Except for the correction of obvious printers' errors (such as letters upside-down or repeated words) the only silent emendations are the following: short *s* for long *s*, uniform capitalization in the titles of Characters, capitalization for the beginning words of sentences, periods for full stops, and the writing out of *and* for the frequently used ampersand. For all other changes the version in the copy-text is recorded in the textual notes. Faithful adherence to the copy-text results in a lack of uniformity in spelling, capitalization, and punctuation—which lack I have not attempted to rectify.

Thanks are due to many who have helped in the various stages of preparation of this edition: to Professor Samuel Holt Monk, who encouraged me to undertake the project once I had discovered it; to Professor John D. Hurrell, who supervised the dissertation version; to the Graduate School of the University of Minnesota for a dissertation fellowship; to Anne Young for her expert typing and helpful suggestions on matters of form and style; to the staffs at the libraries of the University of Minnesota and the University of Rochester for many kindnesses; to the secretaries in the Dean's Office at Rochester who typed the final copy of the manuscript; to the Rosenbach Foundation and its director Clive E. Driver for permission to study the Butler commonplace book and to reproduce from it the Character of a Schoolmaster; and to Professor Benjamin Boyce, whose careful readings of my manuscript and his many incisive comments and suggestions helped to turn the dissertation into a book. The errors are, of course, my own.

The primary indebtedness is noted, where it should be, in the dedication.

Rochester, New York   C. W. D.
June, 1968

Introduction

I. LIFE OF BUTLER

Few documentary records exist that confirm the events in the life of Butler, but recent scholarship has sorted out many of the facts, the probabilities, and the possibilities.[1] Samuel Butler, the second son and fifth child of Samuel and Mary Butler, was born probably in the early part of February 1612. Documents record his baptism on February 14, 1612,[2] in Strensham on the Avon, a very small parish in Worcestershire. His father and grandfather, both Anglicans, were well-to-do yeoman farmers.[3] Richard Butler, the author's grandfather, owned a library, to which his son Samuel Butler, senior, after he inherited it, added books in Latin and English in the fields of medicine, philosophy, and logic, as well as the works of Virgil, Ovid, Horace, and Spenser.

In 1622, at the age of nine, Samuel Butler the author began his schooling in Worcester, probably at the King's School,[4] where he

---

[1] My biographical sketch has been reduced to a summary in light of the Introduction to *Hudibras*, edited by John Wilders (Oxford, 1967), Pt. I, "The Life and Ideas of Samuel Butler."

The account which follows of the early life is based, except where noted, on the article by René Lamar, "Du nouveau sur l'auteur d' 'Hudibras': Samuel Butler en Worcestershire," *La Revue Anglo-Américaine*, I (1923–24), 203–27. See also Michael Wilding, "Samuel Butler at Barbourne," *Notes and Queries*, CCXI, N.S. XIII (1966), 15–19.

[2] R. M. Wilding, "The Date of Samuel Butler's Baptism," *Review of English Studies*, N.S. XVII (1966), 174–77. Baptism, which had to be performed within a month of a birth to avoid severe penalty, customarily was performed within a few days.

[3] E. S. de Beer, "The Later Life of Samuel Butler," *Review of English Studies*, IV (1928), 160.

[4] There is some question as to whether Butler attended the King's Cathedral School of Worcester or the Worcester Royal Grammar School, but more sub-

would have studied under Henry Bright. Under the guidance of Bright some two hundred students followed the traditional classical curriculum of grammar, rhetoric, and logic.[5] At the King's School, according to the customs of grammar schools of the time, students kept commonplace books, treasuries for the apprentice in rhetoric and poetry. They kept entries under various heads, such as brief histories, fables, proverbs, hieroglyphs, emblems and symbols, law and ancient customs, exhortations, topics, descriptions of matters of nature and art. The best students were also encouraged to test their skills in the composition of anagrams, epigrams, epitaphs, epithalamiums, eclogues, and acrostics in Greek and Hebrew; and those pupils who stayed into the sixth year (the others commonly having moved on to Oxford or Cambridge) studied the *Copia Verborum* and the *Adagia* of Erasmus. Despite speculations to the contrary, Butler evidently attended neither of the universities.[6]

Following his days of formal schooling, which ended at age fifteen in 1627, Butler is believed to have become a secretary to Leonard Jeffreys, a justice of the peace who lived near Defford at Earle's Croome Court.[7] On the death of his father in the preceding year, Butler had inherited the prized possessions handed down to the most learned of the family, the Greek and Latin books, two large dictionaries, and *The History of Plants* by Rembert Dodoens, a celebrated Dutch botanist.[8]

John Aubrey records that as a young man Butler served in the household of the Countess of Kent for several years, during which time he must have had access to her library. Part of his time was de-

---

stantial evidence exists for the former, and it is now generally accepted that he was educated at the King's School. [See Michael Wilding, "Samuel Butler at Barbourne," 16.]

[5] The account of the King's School is based on the article by René Lamar, "Samuel Butler à l'École du Roi," *Etudes anglaises*, V (1952), 17–24.

[6] When Butler was at the age to go to a university, his father was dead, his mother a widow with eight children; thus it was unlikely that the young man could have afforded Oxford or Cambridge. [See Michael Wilding, "Samuel Butler at Barbourne," 18.]

[7] Note Wilding's questioning of this. [Ibid.]

[8] The will of the elder Samuel Butler read in part as follows, for his son and namesake: " 'two dictionaries, Cooper and Thomasius, and all my lawe and latine books of logicke, rhetorike, philosophy, poetry, physike, my great Dodaneus Herball, and all my other Lattine and greeke bookes whatsoever.' " [Worcestershire Record Office, 008.7 1627/29; quoted in R. M. Wilding, "The Date of Samuel Butler's Baptism," 175.]

voted to the study of painting, drawing, and music, his interest in painting leading to a friendship with Samuel Cooper, "the Prince of Limners of this age."[9] Anthony à Wood notes that Butler became a protégé of one of the most learned men of the time, John Selden.[10]

After the Restoration of the monarchy in England, Butler received an appointment from Richard Vaughan, Earl of Carbery (then Lord President of Wales) to be steward of Ludlow Castle, which appointment he held from January 1661, to January 1662.[11] Recent research supports part of Aubrey's statement that "he [John Cleveland], and Sam Butler, &c. of Grayes Inne, had a club every night" and that Butler "studied the Common Lawes of England, but did not practise."[12]

Parts I and II of *Hudibras* were published anonymously and dated 1662 and 1664, respectively,[13] without the author's annotations and "An Heroical Epistle of Hudibras to Sidrophel," which were added later.[14] The dates for the composition of *Hudibras* are matters for scholarly contention.[15] Tradition has it that Butler gathered material for his major poem while he worked as a secretary to a Puritan country gentleman.

---

9 John Aubrey, *'Brief Lives,'* ed. Andrew Clark (Oxford, 1908), I, 135–36.

10 Anthony à Wood, *Athenae Oxonienses*, ed. Philip Bliss (London, 1813–20), III, 875.

11 The details of Butler's life after the Restoration are drawn, except where noted, from the heavily documented article by E. S. de Beer, "The Later Life of Samuel Butler."

12 Aubrey, *'Brief Lives,'* ed. Clark, I, 175 and 136.

Ricardo Quintana uncovered a letter from Richard Oxenden to his cousin Sir George Oxenden, dated March 30, 1663, which associates Butler's name with Gray's Inn. Quintana believes that his finding supports Aubrey's. ["The Butler-Oxenden Correspondence," *Modern Language Notes*, XLVIII (1933), 1–11.]

13 The edition of the First Part is dated 1663, but Samuel Pepys had bought a copy by December 26, 1662, and another on February 6, 1662/63. The two issues of the Second Part are dated 1664, yet Pepys had purchased a copy on November 28, 1663. *The Intelligencer* ran an advertisement for it on November 30, 1663. [See de Beer, "The Later Life of Samuel Butler," 161.]

14 "Note" in *Hudibras*, ed. A. R. Waller (Cambridge, 1905), p. vi.

15 For the latest detailed consideration of the problem see *Hudibras*, ed. Wilders, xliv–xlviii. See also Hardin Craig, "*Hudibras*, Part I and the Politics of 1647," in *The Manley Anniversary Studies in Language and Literature* (Chicago, 1923), pp. 145–55; Quintana, "The Butler-Oxenden Correspondence"; Joseph T. Curtiss, "Butler's *Sidrophel*," *PMLA*, XLIV (1929), 1066–78; Benjamin Boyce, *The Polemic Character, 1640–1661* (Lincoln, Nebraska, 1955), p. 117, n. 6.

Except for "Lord Roos his Answer . . ." (1660, anon.) the other works of Butler followed the publication of the first parts of *Hudibras*. Robert Thyer states that the Characters, which he published in 1759, had been written largely between 1667 and 1669.[16] Butler had some association with the theater and may have done some writing for the stage.[17] He is credited by Thyer with writing a prologue and an epilogue to *The Queen of Aragon* by William Habington for a performance on the Duke of York's birthday in 1668.[18] Wood includes Butler with Thomas Sprat and Martin Clifford, who are usually mentioned as collaborators with George Villiers, second Duke of Buckingham, in the writing of *The Rehearsal* (1671).[19] Butler in June 1673 (and possibly throughout Buckingham's tenure) held the office of secretary to the Duke, who served as Chancellor of the University of Cambridge from May 11, 1671, to June 11, 1674.

In 1671 Butler published the ode "To . . . Du-Val" and in 1672 the "Two Letters" (represented as being from John Audland and William Prynne). In 1674 a revised version of Parts I and II of *Hudibras* was published, which included the first printing of "An Heroical Epistle of Hudibras to Sidrophel," as well as some notes to the poem, and many changes that had been made in the text. The third part of *Hudibras* is dated 1678.[20] New editions appeared, Part I and II together in 1678 and Part III in 1679. The satire "Upon Critics Who

---

[16] "*As most of these Characters are dated when they were composed, I can inform the curious that they were chiefly drawn up from 1667 to 1669. . . .*" [*The Genuine Remains . . . of Mr. Samuel Butler*, ed. Robert Thyer (London, 1759), II, iv.]

[17] Some support for this speculation lies in the following passage from the anonymous "Session of the Poets," c. 1665:

> Then *Hudibras* boldly demanded the Bays,
>   But *Apollo* bad him not be so fierce;
> And advis'd him to lay aside the making his Plays,
>   Since he already began to write worse and worse.

In "The Later Life of Samuel Butler" de Beer (p. 162) cites as the source for this passage *Poems on Affairs of State*, I, 3d edition (1699), Pt. 1, p. 210.

[18] A Prologue and Epilogue to *The Queen of Aragon*, "acted before the Duke of York, upon his Birthday," are printed in Thyer's *The Genuine Remains . . . of Mr. Samuel Butler*. A performance on the Duke's birthday (October 14) in 1668 is on record; thus it may be assumed that Butler's poems were written for that performance of the play, first acted in 1640.

[19] Butler's association with these men is affirmed by Dr. Johnson in his life of Dryden.

[20] But it was entered at Stationers' Hall August 22, 1677.

Judge of Modern Plays" belongs to the last years of Butler's life.[21]

Samuel Butler is said to have lived in a room in Rose Alley, Covent Garden, and to have been confined to his room by reason of gout from October 1679 to Easter 1680. He died of consumption on September 25, 1680, and was buried on September 27 in the churchyard of Saint Paul's, Covent Garden. Reportedly, he was buried at the expense of Sir William Longueville, who later held some of the author's manuscripts. Longueville's Butler manuscripts were handed down to Robert Thyer,[22] who drew upon them for his edition of Butler's *Genuine Remains in Verse and Prose* (1759), in which he included, along with other works, 121 Characters.

II. THE CHARACTER TRADITION BEFORE BUTLER

Although the description of character types is as old as recorded literature, the Character isolated from the context of a larger literary work and considered as a genre devoted to minute analysis flourished only in seventeenth-century England.[23] This manner of depicting human types became so popular that the courtiers, educators, satirists, and moralists of the time tried their pens on Characters as Elizabethan gentlemen had tested their skill at sonnets a few years earlier.[24]

A seventeenth-century schoolmaster, Ralph Johnson, before outlining for his pupils the rules for making a Character (such rhetorical practices from venerable tradition remained as exercises for boys in grammar schools), defined it as " 'a witty and facetious description of the nature and qualities of some person, or sort of person.' "[25] Appearing under the heading "What a Character Is" in the Overburian collection (discussed later), another seventeenth-century description of the genre concludes with these lines:

---

21 It was written in answer to Thomas Rymer's *Tragedies of the Last Age Considered*, published late in 1677.

22 See Norma E. Bentley, "Another Butler Manuscript," *Modern Philology*, XLVI (1948–49), 132.

23 The standard work on the Character tradition is by Benjamin Boyce, *The Theophrastan Character in England to 1642* (Cambridge, Mass., 1947).

24 In her bibliography of the Characters, published between 1608 and 1700, Gwendolen Murphy lists 1430 Characters in 308 editions. [See *A Cabinet of Characters* (London and Oxford, 1925), p. xxxiv.]

25 Ralph Johnson, *The Scholars Guide* (1665), quoted in Bertram L. Joseph, "A Seventeenth-Century Guide to Character Writing," *Review of English Studies*, N. S. I (1950), 144.

> To square out a Character by our English levell, it is
> a picture (reall or personall) quaintlie drawne in various collours,
> all of them heightned by one shadowing.
> It is a quicke and soft touch of many strings, all shutting
> up in one musicall close: It is wits descant on any plaine song.[26]

The earliest extant examples of the independent Character are the thirty sketches of Theophrastus, who is believed to have lived about 373 to 284 B.C.[27] Called the founder of the science of botany, and thought to have been one of the most prolific writers of the ancient philosophers,[28] Tyrtamus of Lesbos received the name Theophrastus ("the god-like speaker") from his master Aristotle, whom he succeeded in the Academy.[29] Composed in the fourth century B.C., the Characters gently satirize contemporary types in Athenian society in the age of Alexander the Great. Underlying the work is the Aristotelian doctrine of the Mean, the deviations from which are, in modern terms, both social and ethical.[30] The representative men are Boorish, Loquacious, Pretentious, Tactless, but also Arrogant, Cowardly, Mean, Stupid. These pieces are neutral and detached in tone, for Theophrastus allows his personages to "expose their infirmities" through skillfully wrought examples of appearance, speech, and manner. Throughout he is, in Sainte-Beuve's phrase, a " 'botanist of minds.' "[31] Each sketch follows a set pattern: a definition of the type, followed by a catalogue of distinct but unconnected activities and expressions of such persons under certain circumstances, in simple terms, in simple style.[32]

In 1608 Joseph Hall, the first avowed follower of Theophrastus, published *Characters of Vertues and Vices*, the initial English collection of Characters as independent pieces. This collection, however, is but one of the many examples and precedents which gave impetus to, and prepared the reading public for, the outpouring of

---

[26] *The Overburian Characters*, ed. W. J. Paylor (Oxford, 1936), p. 92.

[27] R. C. Jebb, ed., *The Characters of Theophrastus* (London and Cambridge, 1870), p. 15.

[28] G. S. Gordon, "Theophrastus and His Imitators," in *English Literature and the Classics*, collected by G. S. Gordon (Oxford, 1912), p. 49.

[29] R. G. Ussher, ed., *The Characters of Theophrastus* (London, 1960), p. 3.

[30] Ibid., p. 27.

[31] Ernest A. Baker, "The Writers of Charactery," in *The History of the English Novel* (London, 1924–36), II, 229.

[32] See Ussher, *The Characters of Theophrastus*, pp. 20–23, and Gordon, "Theophrastus and His Imitators," pp. 56–58.

Theophrastan Characters in the early seventeenth century. Others include Bacon's *Essays* and the formal word pictures of Ben Jonson which were added in 1600 to the list of Dramatis Personae of *Every Man Out of his Humour* (for example, the sketch of Fastidious Brisk).[33] Isaac Casaubon had published (in Lyons, 1592) the Greek text of twenty-three of the Characters of Theophrastus, accompanied by a Latin translation, a Prolegomena, and annotations. In the editions of 1599 five Characters were added. The time which elapsed between Casaubon's Latin translation of Theophrastus and a conscious English imitator of him may suggest that the time was not ripe for an immediate successor. Hall wrote a bit later when an interest in the analysis of character had come to show itself most in the comedy of humours,[34] but also to some extent in the essay, verse satire (including the work of Hall himself), and epigram, each of which shared some of the qualities of the Character.

Hall's *Characters of Vertues and Vices* contained twenty-four examples, nine exemplary figures and fifteen negative ones. By 1614 two more had been added to the "vertues." In his "Proeme" Hall referred to "that ancient Master of Morality," by whom he meant Theophrastus. Joseph Hall considered himself a moral teacher. Because Hall's work is explicitly moral in tone and didactically Christian in approach, it differs from that of the objective and dramatic Theophrastus, a distinction between "eloquent exhortation" and "disinterested analysis."[35] Not limiting his types to "vices" as did his master, Hall penned a series of "vertuous" types, usually more abstract than the "vices." (Some scholars have thought that Theophrastus himself wrote some exemplary Characters, but none remain.) Joseph Hall expanded the form also by adding a Character of a social or political

[33] See Paylor, *The Overburian Characters*, p. xi, ff. and Elbert N. S. Thompson, "Character Books," in *Literary Bypaths of the Renaissance* (New Haven, 1924), p. 6 ff.

[34] Wendell Clausen argues that the Character and the comedy of humours developed side by side. He believes also that the translation of Theophrastus's *Ethical Characters*, published at a continental Catholic center, did not circulate in England until after 1600, the first tangible allusion being in Jonson's *Volpone* (1605); that the so-called Jonson circle (in which he includes Overbury) set the temper of Overbury's Characters, which could well have been written before those of Hall were published. [See "The Beginnings of English Character-Writing in the Early Seventeenth Century," *Philological Quarterly*, XXV (1946), 32–45 (hereafter cited as "The Beginnings of English Character-Writing").]

[35] Paylor, *The Overburian Characters*, p. viii.

nature, The Good Magistrate, to the moral-psychological figures established in the work of the Greek philosopher.[36]

Moving beyond description and dialogue, Hall supplied his own commentary. The Happy Man may find "his soule is every day dilated to receive that God, in whom hee is; and hath attained to love himselfe for God, and God for his owne sake."[37] Rejecting the plain style of the Characters of Theophrastus, Hall, a true son of his age, injected into his writing the epigram, the pointed expression, and the lively image. The structure of his pieces, however, parallels that of Theophrastus's: first, the quality is defined or a general statement is given; second, detail after detail is enumerated from everyday life or from philosophy (usually a form of neo-stoicism). The following examples are characteristic passages, particularly in style: Of the Faithful Man he says, "The shield that he ever beares before him, can neither be missed, nor pierced; if his hand be wounded, yet his heart is safe: he is often tripped, seldome foyled; and if sometimes foyled, never vanquished." Decidedly Baconian is this excerpt from the Male-content: "Every blessing hath somewhat to disparage and distaste it: Children bring cares, single life is wilde and solitary; eminencie is envious, retiredness obscure; fasting painful; satietie unwieldie; . . . Everything faulteth, either in too much, or too little." Third, unlike Theophrastus's Characters that conclude abruptly, those of Hall typically end in summary and comment.

Many scholars view the collection by Sir Thomas Overbury and "other learned gentlemen his friends" (including John Webster and Thomas Dekker) as the first composed of truly English Characters.[38] The initial ones appeared in a volume with Overbury's poem "A Wife" and numbered twenty-one. A series of additions brought the total to eighty-three. Departing from Theophrastus's defining and illustrating of various deviations from the Mean and from Hall's earnest chastising, the writers of the Overburian Characters realized the nature of their subjects as persons, often by describing manners

---

[36] The example closest to this type in the work of Theophrastus, the Character of An Oligarchy, did not appear in Casaubon's Latin translation nor in Healey's later English version.

[37] Excerpts from Hall are taken from *"Heaven Upon Earth" and "Characters of Vertues and Vices,"* ed. Rudolf Kirk (New Brunswick, N.J., 1948).

[38] One writer contends that they may have been composed earlier than Hall's. See Wendell Clausen, "The Beginnings of English Character-Writing."

and dress in detail, with the air of the town[39] and the flavor of the court and sometimes with a touch of the rural scene. The writers of these Characters at times mixed in samples of speech and behavior as well as some suggestions of appearance. Dealing more with representatives of certain occupations or positions than with moral or psychological types, the Overburian Characters became the most widely imitated by later English writers. In them one can detect, if but slightly, the germ that grew into the controversial Character (discussed below) of mid-century.

At times, the main objective is satire, as in the portraits of the pettifoggers, merchants, and tradesmen, as well as the Jesuit, the Puritan, the Precisian, the Mere Lawyer, and the Mere Scholar. The collection, though, preserves and extends the possibilities in the admirable Character: witness the enduring and appealing sketch of A Fayre and Happy Milk-mayd, whose "excellencies stand in her so silently, as if they had stolne upon her without her knowledge."[40]

That Overbury and his friends exercised their powers as stylists as well as portraitists has led one scholar to think that "each of Overbury's sketches is an exercise in clever phrase and terse expression, in the one respect competing with the ingenuity of the metaphysical poets, in the other, with the compactness of Bacon's *Essays*."[41] They aimed for wit and humour, adding clever phrases and puns to the conceited style used by Hall. The title page labels the Overburian pieces "many witty characters." Sometimes the language is highly figurative. An intruder into Favour is thus described: "His whole body goes all upon *screwes*, and his face is the *vice* that mooves them." The conclusion of the Character of A Mere Scholar illustrates the style and slightly satiric tone to be found in parts of the collection: "In a word, hee is the Index of a man, and the Title-page of a Scholler, or a Puritaine in moralitie, much in profession, nothing in practise."

Clearly the best of the English writers of Theophrastan Characters is John Earle, whose *Micro-cosmography*, consisting of fifty-four Characters, appeared in 1628. In 1629 twenty-three were added. A grand total of seventy-eight made up the 1633 edition. Earle's *Micro-*

---

[39] See Gordon, "Theophrastus and his Imitators," p. 69.

[40] Excerpts from the Overburian Characters are taken from the edition by W. J. Paylor.

[41] Thompson, "Character Books," p. 12.

cosmography surpasses the Overburian Characters in permanent interest because it is "of a deeper insight, a wider sympathy, and a kindlier humour. . . ."[42] About half are "ethical" sketches and the rest are depictions of men in their social or occupational roles. The range of types in Earle, though, narrows to an interest primarily in academic and professional men (Earle was a university don, Overbury a man of the court). He is at his best with the Down-right Scholar and Pretender to Learning, the Grave Divine, and the Young Raw Preacher. From Overbury's precedent of a Character of a place (a prison), Earle penned four: A Tavern, A Bowl Alley, Paul's Walk, and A Prison.

Earle probed deeper into the motives of behavior than did Hall or Overbury. By comparison to him, Earle's English predecessors seem to dwell on the surface of their figures or the ideas which they may suggest, characteristically to spell out the symptoms rather than the causes of behavior.[43] It has often been noted that in spirit Earle seems closer to Theophrastus than does any other English writer, but Earle's gift for Character surpasses even that of the Greek author in "fine delineation," writes one editor of Theophrastus.[44] The gentle humor or wit seems to emerge from the incident rather than from cleverness of phrase. Both Earle and Theophrastus reject overt judgment for objective statement. In each there is the beauty of simplicity.

The style of Earle, though generally free of far-fetched conceits, is not devoid of figurative language. A Young Raw Preacher "is a Bird not yet fledg'd, that hath hopt out of his nest to bee Chirping on a hedge, and will bee straggling abroad at what perill soever."[45] The gentle flow of sentences is at times arrested by epigrammatic phrasing. While sympathetic humor pervades, Earle does not pass up the delight of puns.

John Earle's *Micro-cosmography* marks the high point of achievement in the English Character in the Theophrastan tradition. Following his work and just before mid-century the impulse to engage in charactery pushed into two new directions. One way was into the portrait Character, a sketch of an actual personage set in a larger

---

[42] E. C. Baldwin, "The Relation of the Seventeenth-Century Character to the Periodical Essay," *PMLA*, XIX (1904), 90.

[43] Ibid., 92.

[44] Jebb, *The Characters of Theophrastus*, p. 83.

[45] Excerpts from Earle are taken from *Micro-cosmography*, ed. Gwendolen Murphy (London, 1928).

work, which is superbly illustrated in the portraits in Clarendon's *History of the Rebellion.* Many of the sketches are both accurate and impartial. David Nichol Smith notes that the Theophrastan Character developed and reached its peak in the early seventeenth century when the historical Character was just beginning. The former was on its decline as the latter reached its summit of achievement. "Sometimes," says Nichol Smith, the Theophrastan Character and the historical portrait are "purposely blended, as in Butler's character of 'A Duke of Bucks,' where the satire on a man of pronounced individuality is heightened by describing his eccentricities as if they belonged to a recognized class."[46] But A Duke of Bucks has antecedents also in the second form which Character writing took near the middle of the century, namely, the controversial or polemic or pamphlet Character.

Benjamin Boyce, critic and historian of the Character, emphasizes in his books the changes which took place in the genre. In these changes Boyce finds the seeds of the polemic Character. He writes, in summary:

> The difference between the polemic Characters of the 1640's and 1650's and the earlier, more Theophrastan pieces is one of degree as much as of kind. This truth will be plainer (and more interesting) to the student who begins with Theophrastus, the botanist or simple taxonomer of psychological-moral man, and then reads Hall, the stirring Stoic-Christian moralist, then Sir Thomas Overbury, who vented his spleen and flourished his wit at the expense of his inferiors, and finally John Earle, who studied the hidden natures of curious men and exposed the lamentable motives and ruinous conflicts beneath the surface.[47]

In the 1640's and 1650's the Character became a weapon for the parties in political and religious strife. This adaptation to polemic purposes was easy because the Character, which had obvious connections with the essay, had become more sociological by the 1640's.[48] Often separate Characters that never appeared in collections focused not on general human foibles but rather on the outlining of figures representative of the elements in the current discord, such as A Bishop, an Independent, a Fifth-Monarchy-Man. Only the use of the name "Character" and the borrowing of a few techniques from the

---

[46] David Nichol Smith, *Characters from the Histories & Memoirs of the Seventeenth Century* (Oxford, 1928), pp. xxix–xxx.

[47] *The Polemic Character, 1640–1661,* p. 8.

[48] Ibid., p. 2.

work of such writers of Characters as Overbury and Earle point up the connection to earlier practice.[49] The tradition thus had been extended, even distorted for partisan purposes, to become "sprawling essays and personal diatribes . . . ,"[50] the emphasis on ideas overshadowing the aspects of portraiture.

For fifteen to twenty years anonymous tracts of slight literary importance were penned to attack enemies. By the 1660's the Character book had almost vanished from the publication lists, having been almost completely replaced by the single Character. As political concerns overshadowed religious ones, the subjects for Characters changed, and sketches of typical Puritans and Roman Catholics were replaced by those of Whigs, Tories, and Trimmers. Also in these single Characters occasionally various other contemporary types (similar to ones depicted in the Overburian collection) came to be subjects: the quack astrologer or the quack doctor, the pettifogging lawyer, the prostitute, the fop, the merchant, and others.[51] Single Characters or small collections of them, though overwhelmingly concerned with political and religious and social matters, did not ignore altogether the Theophrastan psychological or moral types. Many of the Characters were but slightly veiled portraits of actual persons, most of them in prose but some in verse.

III. THE CHARACTERS OF BUTLER

Delineating many varieties of human types of the Theophrastan moral or psychological Character and the social or occupational sketches added by the English tradition, Samuel Butler, in his nearly two hundred pieces, scanned the society of his age, which he found wanting. Though none was published before 1759, his Characters are said to have been written largely between 1667 and 1669.[52]

Butler's satiric arrows, found in all his work, strike at immoderation of any kind. Butler lived through an age of extremes. Aubrey reported that even in his youth Butler observed and reflected in a satirical manner.[53] In Butler's time even a mind not nearly so skeptical or

[49] Chester M. Greenough, "The 'Character' as a Source of Information for the Historian," in *Collected Studies* (Cambridge, Mass., 1940), pp. 126–27.

[50] Boyce, *The Polemic Character, 1640–1661*, p. 7.

[51] Anna J. De Armond, "Some Aspects of Character-Writing in the Period of the Restoration," *Delaware Notes*, 16th series (1943), 59.

[52] See the "Life of Butler" in the Introduction to this edition.

[53] '*Brief Lives*,' I, 135.

discerning would have been unsettled by civil warfare, political and religious unrest, and these over such a long period that few men avoided being swept along by one tide or another. Butler was thirty years old when the Civil Wars began; he was forty-eight when the Restoration brought in a new way of life.

His stance is that of the traditional moralist, his immediate intellectual background the Renaissance tradition, specifically the work of the essayists, the satirists in verse, and the writers of Characters of the earlier seventeenth century.[54] It has been argued that his convictions were strongly shaped by his Anglican religion.[55] But the impression that he conveys in his work is that of the complete skeptic, the studied ironist, which makes one wonder without being fully relieved of doubt where is the center of his philosophy or if there is one. Unlike Swift, who resembles him in many ways, Butler does not offer his reader normative patterns even in shadowy outlines. For lack of anything more precise, we must assume the virtue of the mean between extremes and the guidance of right reason.

Butler's Characters presumably project, nevertheless, something of the cast of mind behind them and the way he viewed the life of his age, especially on matters of religion, government and politics, science and pseudo-science, and literature and language. The abiding sin of hypocrisy permeates Butler's sketches. In religious practices it was seen to be most widespread and most heinous. Butler spared neither Puritan nor Roman Catholic, both having the means to lure the credulous, the former largely by the appearance of piety, the latter by the attraction of ritual. His fear of the dissenting sects also stemmed from distrust of the crowd (or mob or rabble), which he saw represented in them. In politics as in religion men ruled for gain, and the mob threatened to disrupt orderly government. Republican schemes clouded the mind. Experiments in government in Butler's lifetime had proved ineffectual.[56] To Butler there was a brand of intellectual folly in science or philosophy, for the experimenters seemed to pursue impossible projects. Their projections resembled in kind those of some political theorists. And, of course, quacks could be found in great abundance among, for example, physicians and astrologers. The

---

[54] The best treatment of Butler's thought is by Ricardo Quintana, "Samuel Butler: A Restoration Figure in a Modern Light," *ELH*, XVIII (1951), 7–31. On this particular point see p. 17.

[55] Ibid., p. 13.

[56] See G. M. Trevelyan, *England Under the Stuarts* (New York, 1949), Chaps. IX and X.

emphasis on the rational, which one sees in Butler's satire on schemes and hypocrisies, holds as well for his observations on literature. He points out, for instance, how certain poetic devices can distort the truth. But the skeptical temperament of Butler works against his propounding any absolute standards of taste and judgment.

To make his observations through the Characters, Butler looked to earlier writers for the means of expression. His skill in the use of so restricted and conventional a form as the Character often is displayed not so much in new departures as in his extension of the number and varying the use of devices found in the work of others.

Butler seems to have owed a debt, for example, to the Overburian Characters. He continues the strong interest found there in occupational and social types, focusing especially on the religious and political groupings into which men of his generation divided themselves, though with less of Overbury's "air of the town" and more of the atmosphere of controversy. Overbury's collection underlines the foibles of men and women, many of whom were assuming new stations in life, but offers for inspection commendable models of certain types, which Butler's never does, and has much wider variations in tone. In the Overburian wit the conceits, which usually replace the Theophrastan opening definition and are scattered throughout a piece, grow pale in the light of Butler's continual application of more flamboyant comparisons.

Butler's Bumpkin, or Country-Squire looks back to Overbury's An Elder Brother, who is a country gentleman.[57] Where Overbury depicts the Elder Brother as one who "lookes like his land, as heavily, and durtily, as stubbornly," Butler makes the Bumpkin an intrinsic part of the soil by a series of figures, saying he is "the Growth of his own Land, a Kind of *Autocthanus*, like the *Athenians*, that sprung out of their own Ground; or Barnacles that grow upon Trees in *Scotland*. . . ." Butler, like Overbury, details the characteristic manner and outlook of a squire in terms commensurate with his environment and upbringing, but also ranges widely to bring in comparisons from that of preachers in conventicles to the tortured seamen at Amboyna. And where Overbury crowds into one sentence references to speech (which he returns to later), smell, and glory ("Hee speaks no language, but smells of dogs or hawkes; and his ambition flies Justice-

---

[57] I am grateful to Professor Benjamin Boyce of Duke University for a list of possible connections between the Characters of Butler and those of his predecessors, which Professor Boyce generously offered for my use.

hight. . . ."), Butler extends the description of each trait and concentrates heavily on each matter in figurative detail, as in the exaggeration of the Bumpkin's movements: "When he salutes a Man, he lays violent Hands upon him, and gripes and shakes him, like a Fit of an Ague: and, when he accosts a Lady, he stamps with his Foot, like a *French* Fencer, and makes a Longee at her, in which he always misses his Aim, too high or too low, and hits her on the Nose or Chin."

Butler's Traveller and Overbury's Affected Traveller exemplify one of the popular objects for satire in the sixteenth and seventeenth centuries because, although the grand tour was *de rigueur* in the education of a gentleman, the continent lay in wait with the vices of Italy and the affectations of France. Overbury describes the attire of the man, his speech, and his actions (including his habitual use of a pick-tooth), while Butler delineates both the external changes in a man wrought by travel, such as a new manner of speech ("He has worn his own Language to Rags, and patched it up with Scraps and Ends of foreign. . . ."), and the alienation of the traveler from his home and his degeneration thereby, which is basically a moral judgment. Where Overbury concludes with an epigrammatic sentence, Butler trails off with no telling point.

Illustrating the uniformity within each Overburian Character is the study A Fine Gentleman, a well-integrated sketch. Figurative language, when used, works to fill out the characterization of the subject: the Gentleman "is somewhat like the *Salamander*, and lives in the flame of love, which paines he expresseth comically. . . ." Butler's Huffing Courtier, very much an Overburian type, is a long Character interspersed with matters not so directly related to the subject as those in Overbury's piece. Butler may well have taken the image of a cinnamon tree "whose bark is worth more than his body" from Overbury's opening sentence but joins to it a second image of the hollowness inside an important exterior, showing once again Butler's manner of developing a description by further figurative example. His imagery calls attention to itself and, on occasion, may be extended to emblem-like dimensions: "His Ribbons are of the true Complexion of his Mind, a Kind of painted Cloud or gawdy Rainbow, that has no Colour of it self, but what it borrows from Reflection."

John Earle's Characters too served as precedents for Butler's. An Antiquary, for instance, would seem to have been a source for some of the ideas and witticisms in Butler's Catholic and his Curious Man. The Antiquary has unnatural appetites and interests in things because they are old, his religion not excepted. He ignores great books in a library while devoting his attention to the antique work of cobwebs. And when he reads manuscripts, as Earle describes in a fine touch, "the dust makes a *Parenthesis* betweene every Syllable." Earle's examples of the antiquarian's preoccupation include his interest in his own agedness (of course to him a virtue) and even in death itself since it will "[gather] him to his Fathers." Butler's Catholic also dotes on his religion because of its vintage quality, the point being intensified by a comparison, perhaps borrowed from Earle, with the love of old cheese for its rottenness. Butler's interest soon shifts, however, away from the man to the institution of the church, to the fallibility of the infallible Pope and other deceptions that demolish the efficacy of the Church and underline the misplaced devotion of its believers. Butler's Curious Man, like Earle's Antiquary, delights in whatever is unusual and rare (though it may be worthless) and in being a rarity himself. Butler is superb in offering examples of odd items less for their particular aptness in depicting a type of man, as is largely true for Earle, and more for the chance to exercise his learning and ingenuity, such as in the depiction of the Curious Man's preference for an iron chain about the neck of a flea rather than the golden chain of an alderman. Earle's generalizing from the details of his piece by a comment on death at the end is strong in contrast to Butler's concluding figure on abstruse knowledge, a further example rather than a capping final judgment. Something more could be added or sentences taken away with little effect.

John Earle begins his depiction of a Self-Conceited Man in paradoxically witty lines: he is a man "that knowes himself so wel, that he does not know himselfe. Two *excellent well dones* have undone him. . . ." There is a psychological acuity in the description of his reliving a moment of glory: "If he have done any thing that ha's past with applause, hee is always re-acting it alone, and conceits the extasie his hearers were in at every period." Such observations penetrate to the essence of the type. In his Proud Man Butler more than usual concentrates on delineating the type. He begins by describing "a Fool in Fermentation, that swells and boils over like a Porridge-Pot. He sets out his Feathers like an Owl, to swell and seem bigger than he is." Butler, however, concerns himself less with the details of the man's psychological makeup and more with the ludicrous way the Proud Man appears to others, by citing outlandish parallels.

Earle's Plain Country Fellow is a man limited in mind and interests, inept in all but the most routine of activities. The references and figures pertain to the land, to animals, and the like. The opening sentence, not very characteristic of Earle's work, is the kind that Butler was to use often for disparagement, where the figure is turned as a weapon against the man, here a man "that manures his ground wel, but lets himself lie fallow and untill'd." This sentence Butler seems to echo in the body of his Character of a Clown, who "manures the Earth like a Dung-hill, but lets himself lye Fallow, for no Improvement will do good upon him." Where Earle cites the activities of the Country Fellow, Butler offers witty comparisons. Earle makes a reference to Nebuchadnezzar which Butler may have borrowed, but he made it into a more cryptic and rich suggestion. Earle writes, "Hee seemes to have the *punishment of Nebuchadnezzar*: for his conversation is among beasts, and his tallons none of the shortest, onely he eats not grasse, because he loves not sallets." Butler's allusion to Nebuchadnezzar is such that it assumes the reader's knowledge of the Biblical source and requires that he fill in the details for himself. Then the figure is extended by a degrading reference to the relationship of the master to his animal: "He is like Nebuchadnezzar after he had been a Month at Grass, but Will never return to be a Man again as he did, if he might; for he despises all Manner of Lives but his own, unless it be his Horse's to whom he is but Valet-de-Chambre."

Other examples can be cited in detail to illustrate the relationship between the Characters of Butler and those of Earle; one can compare the former's Mere Great Man and the latter's Degenerate Noble or in the Character of a Herald of each writer. Butler drew upon the work of Earle for ideas and phrasing. However, Earle, more like the originator of the Character, maintains his interest in the depths of human action as well as in the activity and appearance of certain types. Figurative language and clever phrasing in Earle are seasoning for the main dish. Butler, to the contrary, welcomes the chance wherever possible to exercise his sardonic wit in detail and to display his remarkable figures. In Butler's work there is no example of the "virtuous" Character and certainly no figure bordering on sentimentality, like Earle's rendering of A Child. To whatever he may have borrowed from Earle the later writer gave his peculiar stamp; the differences in temperament and style are readily apparent. Butler may capture less of human nature, which interest is not his sole or central concern, but his writing is more lively and energetic and high keyed than that of Earle, the recognized English master of the Theophrastan Character in its purest form.

To Overbury and Earle, notable practitioners of the art of the

Character, Butler owed much, but it was perhaps to the largely anonymous writers of polemic pieces and to his close contemporaries Richard Flecknoe and John Cleveland that Butler looked for some of the special tendencies in materials, approaches, and attitudes. Flecknoe's Characters (*Enigmaticall Characters* was first published in 1658) anticipate those of Butler in their use of strings of comparisons based on widely scattered materials to develop a trait of a typical person, though Flecknoe's have less of the unbridled exuberance of Butler's. Of a talkative lady Flecknoe writes, "Her tongue runs round like a wheele one spoak after another, there is no end of it: she makes more noice and jangling than the Bels on the fifth of *November*, or a Coronation day; such a wife for *Moroso* had far surpast all the variety of noices invented for tormenting him; and would make a husband wish that either she were dumb or he were deaf. . . ." Flecknoe uses occasionally what Butler employs continually, the degrading image; thus he describes a speaker of commonplaces as using matter that is "like cold meat grown nauseous with often repetition. . . ." On the whole, Flecknoe injects less venom by far than Butler: while the pieces of the latter are consistently satiric, Flecknoe's tone varies with subtle shadings even to light irony. A few would seem to be basically commendable types, the ironic overtones being so gentle or nonexistent. Richard Flecknoe's balanced and epigrammatic style harkens back to earlier Character writers like Hall and to Bacon in the essays, whose manner remained in Overbury and to some extent in John Earle. Of a Lady of excellent conversation Flecknoe writes: "It being *vertue* to know her, *wisdome* to converse with her, *Refinest* breeding to observe her, *joy* to behold her, and a *species* of the beatitude of t'other life, onely to enjoy her Conversation in this." On the subject of wit Flecknoe's earlier comments are suggestive of Butler's treatment of Edward Benlowes in A Small Poet a few years later. Flecknoe writes: ". . . although with the ignorant, he passe for a good companion, tis no pure wit he utters, but only a mingly of clenches, quibbles, and such half-witted stuff he (at best) being rather a *pump* of other jests, Conceits, and Stories, than a *Fountain* of his own. . . ."[58]

John Cleveland wrote three long Characters (which he described as "anatomy lecture[s]"): The Character of A London Diurnal (1645), The Character of A Country Committeeman (1649), and The Character of a Diurnal-Maker (1654).[59] Best known as a poet of the

---

[58] The foregoing quotations are taken from a microfilm of Flecknoe's work.

[59] These Characters are printed in *Character Writings of the Seventeenth Century*, ed. Henry Morley (London, 1891), pp. 298–313.

metaphysical strain, Cleveland carried over that style into his prose Characters. A diurnal-maker's "gloves are the shavings of his hands, for he casts his skin like a cancelled parchment." In Cleveland the reference to living persons, veiled or open, and the use of comic anecdote were joined. He drew from a wide range of sources and he mixed snippets of learning in startling fashion. To the general picture Cleveland added specific and deadly references to his contemporaries, such as a passage on Oliver Cromwell in The Character of A London Diurnal. The usually moderate tone of the Characters of the early seventeenth century had given way to the blistering attack of mid-century animosity.[60]

Butler's Characters show marked resemblance to those of John Cleveland, especially in the kind of figurative allusion employed, and sometimes there is duplication of the very allusion itself. References to the "Iliads in a nutshell," "a Spanish jennet begotten by the wind," and the phrase from the book of Job "corruption, Thou art my Father," all found in Cleveland's A London Diurnal, are effectively used in Butler's A Curious Man, A Fantastic, and An Antiquary, respectively. Cleveland's use of Mahomet's falling sickness in the Character of A Diurnal-Maker is picked up by Butler in A Melancholy Man, and "a chain so thin and light that a flea could trail it" is echoed in A Curious Man. Cleveland's conspicuous employment of miscellaneous, out-of-the-way allusions, which are preeminent in Butler's work, may have suggested or reinforced Butler's procedure of working with diminishing comparisons (which are characteristic of *Hudibras* also) for biting satire. In addition, since Cleveland's Characters are notably longer than earlier ones in the tradition—some exceedingly long for the genre—Butler's extended pieces may have found their model in John Cleveland's practice.

Readers of *Hudibras* will find themselves on familiar terrain in reading Butler's Characters, for the works have many human types in common: the sophistical lawyer, the deceiving astrologer, politicians who work for gain under any regime, and a multitude of religious kinds of every shading and disposition. Ian Jack suggests that if *Hudibras* had been continued, "it seems likely that every type represented in Butler's prose 'Characters' would have found its niche in a comprehensive 'Anatomy of Melancholy.' "[61] The satire in the Characters, however, is less cryptic, more directly and unstintingly realized than in *Hudibras*, because each human type stands under fire,

---

[60] See Thompson, "Character Books," p. 23.
[61] Ian Jack, *Augustan Satire* (Oxford, 1952), p. 18.

singled out for attack. Consideration of *Hudibras* in the light of the Characters underlines the fact that Butler's long poem is not solely or even primarily an attack on a defeated political-religious party so much as a lashing out at the limitless variety of knavery and folly that could be found in his day and time. Many of the qualities attributed to the squire Ralph are the subjects of Butler's Characters. As a figure in the poem Ralph is a ridiculously comic person, whereas the Independent churchmen in the Characters appear as knaves and blockheads. For example, Ralph is said to have gained knowledge directly and the easy way, and by comparison to the knight Hudibras:

> His knowledge was not far behind
> The Knights, but of another kind,
> And he another way came by't,
> Some call it *Gift*, and some *New Light*;
> A liberal Art, that costs no pains
> Of Study, Industry, or Brains.
> His Wits were sent him for a Token,
> But in the Carriage crackt and broken.—[I. i. 479–486.] [62]

The Hypocritical Nonconformist is anatomized as one also naturally gifted with learning. In one of the longest Characters there is ample room for discourse on the subject, and the difference in tone from that of the passage in the poem is readily apparent:

> For it does not only save him the Labour of Study, which he disdains as below his Gifts, but exempts him from many other Duties, and gives his idle Infirmities a greater Reputation among his Followers than the greatest Abilities of the most industrious; while the painful Heavings and Straining, that he uses to express himself, pass for the Agonies of those that deliver Oracles. And this is the Reason why he is so cautious to have all his *Exercises* seem to be done Extempore, that his spiritual Talent may not be thought to receive any Assistance from natural or artificial Means . . . as if Premeditation and Study would but render him, like other False Witnesses, the more apt to contrive and imagine, how to betray and abuse the Truth.

Ralph's access to inner light is similar to that found in A Quaker and other nonconformist types in the Characters. Ralph is, in addition, "A deep occult Philosopher," the very kind of man described in

---

[62] Quotations from *Hudibras* are taken from the edition of A. R. Waller (Cambridge, 1905).

the Character of An Hermetic Philosopher. In fact many of the pointed references used to detail the "mystic Learning" of the companion of Sir Hudibras are found in this piece. Other direct parallels between the Character and the poem's description of the squire can be cited, such as the references in both to Adam's first green britches and the ferocious contentions of ancient Stoics on their porch.[63]

Any comments on the close kinship between *Hudibras* and the Characters should not ignore, of course, the differences between them. As a long narrative poem *Hudibras*, though episodic and in some ways a series of short pieces or fragments, differs in fundamental ways from a miscellaneous series of portraits in prose. The framework of a picaresque narrative and the requirements of the Hudibrastic line with its witty rhyming impose particular demands on the material. Butler varies his tone in the poem so that the scathing, direct diminution in rollicking, energetic verse at times gives way to lyrical passages (see II. i. 903 ff.) and to the mock heroic, as in this invocation, "Thou that with Ale or viler Liquors, / Didst inspire *Withers*, *Prin*, and *Vickars*" [I. i. 645–46].

Like his predecessors Overbury and Earle, Samuel Butler follows the basic Theophrastan model in the structure of each Character. He usually begins with a striking phrase, often by way of tentative definition, many times by running together the title and the opening line. Written in the present tense, the details which illustrate or otherwise extend the definition follow in a series of sentences which have the effect of a string of adjectives rather than a logical progression.[64] Richard Garnett has rightly observed that Butler's Characters tend to be "rather a museum of particulars than a gallery of portraits," to spell out peculiarities, not the personage as a whole.[65]

Typically the Butlerian Character is a witty enumeration of the bad qualities in the type being considered, with a series of similes and metaphors which enliven the piece and engage the reader. Some Characters progress as variations on a theme: A Melancholy Man is developed by a series of symptoms of his malady, and the Character of The Sot is unified by the imagery of moisture throughout. A Character may begin in the usual manner by a description of the subject

---

[63] For these parallels and others see the explanatory notes in the present edition.

[64] See Gwendolen Murphy, *A Cabinet of Characters*, p. viii.

[65] Richard Garnett, *The Age of Dryden* (London, 1897), p. 248.

in the third person but almost imperceptibly shift to the voice of the subject expounding his theories.[66] An Hermetic Philosopher begins with "he" but at a point shifts to "they" as it moves into description of the Brethren of the Holy Cross; but it also depicts, though somewhat obliquely, the hermeticist Thomas Vaughan. Thus in one selection Butler describes a type, a group, and a particular man. An Hermetic Philosopher is replete with all manner of schemes, programs, and lore from alchemists, Rosicrucians, astrologers, and virtuosos. Butler cannot resist adding one more stroke or one more example, but the effect, if one has some knowledge of the background from which he draws, is not deadening but rather the stuff of sheer brilliance little short of Swift in *A Tale of a Tub*. In fact, this Character is Butler's finest supererogation.

Butler pushed the form to its limits and even beyond its limits with a liveliness never before exhibited therein. Because he worked best in short pieces, the restricted form of this genre served him well.[67] Even so, Butler extended the length of the Character, often by the discursive consideration of ideas. Especially conspicuous by reason of their extraordinary length are An Hypocritical Nonconformist, A Modern Politician, An Hermetic Philosopher, and A Small Poet. They are, in effect, theoretical essays, developing Butler's interest in the doctrine or the point of view of groups rather than the personality of typical men. His interest in generalizing and theorizing, though, may be seen throughout the collection. For example, in A Quibbler, Butler states: "There are two Sorts of Quibbling, the one with Words, and the other with Sense, like the Rhetoricians *Figurae Dictonis & Figurae Sententiae*—The first is already cried down, and the other as yet prevails; and is the only Elegance of our modern Poets, which easy Judges call *Easiness*; but having nothing in it but *Easiness*, and being never used by any lasting Wit, will in wiser Times fall to nothing of itself." The long Characters exemplify areas especially significant in Butler's work, representing his outlook on matters important to the Restoration mind. Butler is not, however, immune in his treatment of his subjects to the temptations of other contemporary satirists who smother each victim

---

[66] See the discussion of A Modern Politician in Ricardo Quintana, "Samuel Butler: A Restoration Figure in a Modern Light," 30.

[67] Quintana aptly remarks that Butler's wit first was expressed and characteristically continued in the verse paragraph even in longer poems, and that he is strongest in the epigram and the prose Character. ["The Butler-Oxenden Correspondence," 7.]

with faults without always making sharp distinctions for appropriateness.

Each of the Characters of Butler is replete with samples of his knowledge, from the classics to the Bible, from science to folklore. What Dr. Johnson says of *Hudibras* holds true also for Butler's work in the Characters—that "whatever topick employs his mind he shews himself qualified to expand and illustrate it with all the accessories that books can furnish: he is found not only to have travelled the beaten road, but the bye-paths of literature. . . . If the French boast the learning of Rabelais, we need not be afraid of confronting them with Butler."[68] Dr. Johnson makes mention of the commonplace book which Robert Thyer told him about, in which Butler had gathered material for future use.[69] But he gathered not only from books and lore but from observation of small and ordinary experiences, or secondhand, from travelers and other observers. From all these sources came the most characteristic mark of Butler's style, the witty, allusive comparison.[70] For gentle irony he draws from an uncommon source in making light of a Republican: "If he could but find out a Way to hold Intelligence with *Cardan's Homines aerii*, those subtle Inhabitants of the Air, he might in Probability establish his Government among them, much sooner than here, where so many Experiments have been so lately made to no Purpose." For a marvelously casual touch Butler draws from the Bible to describe The Negligent as "a bird of the air, that neither sows nor reaps, nor gathers into barns." Two images from life around him are typical: In A Traveller he writes, "His Observations are like a Sieve, that lets the finer Flour pass, and retains only the Bran of Things. . ."; and in A Fanatic, "He is but a Puppet Saint, that moves he knows not how, and his Ignorance is the dull leaden Weight that puts all his Parts in Motion."

For the victims of his most scathing invective Butler reserves his lowest comparisons. A rabble is described as "a great Dunghill where all Sorts of dirty and nasty Humours meet, stink, and ferment; for all the Parts are in a perpetual Tumult." In A Lover he asserts that "Love

---

68 Samuel Johnson, "Butler," in *Lives of the English Poets*, ed. G. B. Hill (Oxford, 1905), I, 212.

69 Ibid., 213.

70 Ian Jack rightly points out "that Butler was keenly interested in the analogical uses of language. Like Bacon's indeed, his was 'a mind keenly sensitive to all analogies and affinities . . . spreading as it were tentacles on all sides in quest of chance prey.' If ever a man was haunted by 'the demon of analogy,' it was he." [*Augustan Satire*, p. 31.]

is but a Clap of the Mind, a Kind of running of the Fancy, that breaks out, if it be not stopped in Time, into Botches of heroic Rime. . . ." The passion of An Amorist is "as easily set on Fire as a Fart, and as soon out again." But in less degrading comparisons and less extreme ones we find perceptions that penetrate more surely to the core. A morose man "approves of nothing but in contradiction to other men's opinions, and like a buzzard, delights in nothing more than to flutter against the wind, let it be which way it will." Butler writes of a fool, that "as a little rain makes the streets dirty, and a great deal washes them clean; or as a little wine is apter to pall and grow sour, than a great quantity: So his little understanding inclines him still to the worse; for he mistakes fraud and perfidiousness for wit and wisdom." Samuel Butler can find the image for the idea.

In the broad sweep of satire in the Characters he achieves remarkable effects. Such mocking comparisons rather than analysis and straightforward condemnation usually make the point. Thus, to strike down the Rosicrucians as depicted in An Hermetic Philosopher, Butler intricately follows the details of their legends until by a stroke at the end he cuts away all seriousness: "In this Tabernacle rests the Body of their Prophet or Founder, who dying, as they affirm, hid himself in a Kind of invisible Oven, where after an hundred Years he was discovered by a Kind of Prophesying Door, not overbaked nor cold, but warm, and looking (like a Woodcock's Head stuck in the lid of a Pye) as if he were alive."

By other devices in addition to the diminishing straight comparison Butler makes his point. He fabricates his own mythology. In A Taylor he weaves this legend: "Our *Savior* wore his Coat without Seam, rather than he would have any Thing to do with him; and *Elias*, when he went to Heaven, left his Mantle behind, because it had been polluted by his Fingers." He emphasizes the literal force of a figure: a politician "dissects the Body-politic into Controversies, as Anatomists do the Body of a Man, and mangles every Part, only to find out new Disputes." Combining material from the Bible and from unnatural natural history, he says of an ungrateful man, that "his Mother died in Childbed of him; for he is descended of the Generation of Vipers, in which the Dam always eats off the Sire's Head, and the young ones their Way through *her* Belly."

Butler, like Overbury and Earle, who followed Hall's example, has an addiction to puns. A catchpole "is a man of quick *apprehension*, and very great *judgment*, for it seldom begins or ends without him."

A dueller "is a man of mettle, and his sword and he are of the same family, and very near of kin; but he is chief, and the weapon a poor dependant or hanger-on." However, it should be noted that Butler is less prone to verbal histrionics in the prose Character than in his verse. Yet his wit in both verse and prose is often a potent weapon for serious ends.

By following a practice common in the polemical Characters, Butler departs from the customs of the earlier Theophrastan tradition. Here and there he places two or more lines of verse. The Character of A Lawyer ends with several lines of poetry, and there the departure is most noticeable. Also, like Cleveland, he refers to contemporaries by name. William Prynne may be found in A Small Poet and An Haranguer, Oliver Cromwell (as orator) in A Play-Writer, Hobbes in A Catchpole. A Duke of Bucks is clearly the Second Duke of Buckingham. Edward Benlowes is cited as an example of a Small Poet. Thomas Vaughan as "Anthroposophus"—a name applied to him in a tract by the philosopher Henry More—is the subject of several allusions in An Hermetic Philosopher.

Butler's style is clear, rapid, and vigorous. Its syntax is that of the "speech-based" prose of the Restoration, which is patterned after the unpredictable movements of the conversation of a cultivated speaker, though more heightened, of course, and more rhythmical than that actually met in oral discourse.[71] Butler, like many of the prose writers of his time, especially in the essay and the sermon, had lengthened the compressed Senecan structures. Butler's manner thus contrasts with that of the Character writers of the earlier seventeenth century, who emphasized stylistic wit in terseness of phrase and balanced antitheses. Butler was not, though, a writer who ignored the styles he inherited when he wanted the artistic advantages of turns of phrase. He occasionally penned antithetical lines, but in looser form and with less point than those of his predecessors. For instance, in A Justice of Peace he writes, "His occupation is to keep the Peace but he makes it keep him . . . ," or in A Fanatic, "Saint *Paul* was thought by Festus to be mad with too much Learning; but the *Fanatics* of our Times are mad with too little."

One mark of Butler's style, parallel openings for sentences, is a characteristic of the Ciceronian sentence or period, which was out of

---

[71] For the commentary on Butler's prose style I am indebted to the general remarks by Ian A. Gordon, in *The Movement of English Prose* (London, 1966), Pt. IV: "The Seventeenth Century."

favor when he was writing; it remains as an inheritance from the Character tradition in England. Sentences begin as follows in An Antiquary: He "Is one that has. . . . He despises. . . . He is. . . . He honours. . . . He neglects. . . ." This technique undergirds the description of sentences in Character writing as having the effect of a string of adjectives. Such an effect is achieved not only in the sequence of sentences but also in the parts of a single sentence: the process of adding clauses or phrases is followed, with additions being made as new thoughts occur, the final thought not being anticipated at the beginning of the sentence. Thus a politician "is a State-Empiric, that has Receipts for all the Infirmities of Governments, but knows nothing of their Constitutions, nor how to proportion his Dose." Butler's sentences therefore move with the current of ideas; one is not sure what shape they will take to realize the thought.[72] The following sentences from A Small Poet will provide one sample of his sure concern for the construction of the prose but also the open form that could readily have been ordered and arranged in a more consciously formulated pattern:

> If he understands *Latin* or *Greek* he ranks himself among the Learned, despises the Ignorant, talks Criticisms out of *Scaliger*, and repeats *Martial's* baudy Epigrams, and sets up his Rest wholly upon Pedantry. But if he be not so well qualified, he crys down all Learning as pedantic, disclaims Study, and professes to write with as great Facility, as if his Muse was sliding down *Parnassus*. Whatsoever he hears well said he seizes upon by poetical License; and one Way makes it his own, that is by ill repeating of it—This he believes to be no more Theft, than it is to take that, which others throw away.

Butler uses ordinary vocabulary; there is no straining for unusual words; Latinized diction is rare. His learning is not, however, expressed with ease and lightly carried as in, say, the essays of Cowley. Rather, in Butler remains the Renaissance individualistic display of learning, not through rhetoric or vocabulary but in the daring and sometimes odd references in figures of speech that punctuate his prose style.

The Characters of Butler did not appear in print until the middle of the eighteenth century. The Character was not, in its pure form, a popular genre of the Restoration period. Soon after Charles II

---

[72] F. P. Wilson, *Seventeenth Century Prose* (Berkeley, 1960), p. 13.

came to the throne, the literary and psychological interest for such writing was being absorbed into the drama and the essay, and by the next century into the novel. While he was bringing together many of the subjects and techniques in a form popular in seventeenth-century England, Butler's work strongly anticipated the literary and pictorial caricature of the eighteenth century. Hogarth was a particularly appropriate illustrator for *Hudibras*.

The Characters

A MODERN POLITICIAN

Makes new Discoveries in Politics, but they are, like those
that *Columbus* made of the new World, very rich but barbarous. He
endeavours to restore Mankind to the original Condition, it fell from,
by forgeting to discern between Good and Evil; and reduces all
Prudence back again to its first Author the Serpent, that taught *Adam*
Wisdom;[1] for he was really his Tutor, and not *Samboscor*,[2] as the
Rabbins write. He finds the World has been mistaken in all Ages, and
that Religion and Morality are but vulgar[3] Errors, that pass among the
Ignorant, and are but mere Words to the Wise. He despises all learning as a Pedantic little Thing; and believes Books to be the Business of
Children, and not of Men. He wonders how the Distinction of Virtue
and Vice came into the World's Head; and believes them to be more
ridiculous than any Foppery of the Schools.[4] He holds it his Duty to
betray any Man, that shall take him for so much a Fool as one fit to be
trusted. He stedfastly believes, that all Men are born in the State of
War,[5] and that the civil Life is but a Cessation, and no Peace, nor
Accommodation: And though all open Acts of Hostility are forborn

---

[1] That is, the knowledge of good and evil.

[2] Samboscor has not been identified.

[3] Common; widely held.

[4] The Schoolmen of the Middle Ages and their followers, even in Oxford
and Cambridge in the seventeenth century (see Milton's remarks on his
education), had a reputation for futile discussions and quibbles, for impractical
fine distinctions.

[5] See Hobbes, *Leviathan*, Pt. I, Chap. 13: "During the time men live without
a common power to keep them all in awe, they are in that condition which is
called war; and such a war, as is of every man, against every man." [Ed. Michael
Oakeshott (Oxford, 1946), p. 82.]

by Consent, the Enmity continues, and all Advantages by Treachery or Breach of Faith are very lawful—That there is no Difference between Virtue and Fraud[6] among Friends, as well as Enemies; nor any thing unjust, that a Man can do without Damage to his own Safety or Interest—That Oaths are but Springes[7] to catch Woodcocks withal; and bind none but those, that are too weak and feeble to break them, when they become ever so small an Impediment to their Advantages— That Conscience is the effect of Ignorance, and the same with that foolish Fear, which some Men apprehend, when they are in the dark and alone—That Honour is but the Word, which a Prince gives a Man to pass his Guards withal, and save him from being stopped by Law and Justice the Sentinels of Governments, when he has not Wit nor Credit enough to pass of himself—That to shew Respect to Worth in any Person is to appear a Stranger to it, and not so familiarly acquainted with it as those are, who use no Ceremony; because it is no new Thing to them, as it would appear if they should take Notice of it—That the easiest Way to purchase a Reputation of Wisdom and Knowledge is to slight and undervalue it; as the readiest Way to buy cheap is to bring down the Price: for the World will be apt to believe a Man well provided with any necessary or useful Commodity, which he sets a small Value upon—That to oblige a Friend is but a kind of casting him in Prison, after the old *Roman* Way,[8] or modern *Chinese*, that chains the Keeper and Prisoner together: for he that binds another Man to himself, binds himself as much to him, and lays a restraint upon both. For as Men commonly never forgive those that forgive them, and always hate those that purchase their Estates (tho' they pay dear and more than any Man else would give) so they never

---

[6] "This is a humorous allusion to a line in *Virgil*—Dolus, an Virtus, quis in Hoste requirat?" [Thyer's note.]
The line in the *Aeneid* appears in the following context:
> Mutemus clipeos Danaumque insignia nobis
> aptemus. dolus an Virtus, quis in hoste
> requirat?
> arma dabunt ipsi....

("Change we the shields and don the Danaan emblems; whether deceit or valour, who would ask in warfare? Our foes themselves shall give us weapons.") [*Aeneid*, trans. H. Rushton Fairclough (London and New York, 1920–22), II. 389–391.]

[7] Snares for the woodcocks, foolish birds that were easily caught. Cf. *Hamlet*, I. iii. 115.

[8] "The custom among the Romans was the same as among modern constables, to chain the right hand of the culprit to the left hand of the guard...." [T. R. Nash, ed., *Hudibras* (New York, 1881) III. i. 565 n.]

willingly endure those, that have laid any Engagement upon them, or at what rate soever purchased the least Part of their Freedom—And as Partners for the most Part cheat or suspect one another; so no Man deals fairly with another, that goes the least Share in his Freedom.

To propose any Measure to Wealth or Power is to be ignorant of the Nature of both: for as no Man can ever have too much of either; so it is impossible to determine what is enough; and he, that limits his Desires by proposing to himself the Enjoyment of any other Pleasure, but that of gaining more, shews he has but a dull Inclination, that will not hold out to his Journey's End. And therefore he believes that a Courtier deserves to be beg'd himself, that is ever satisfied with begging: for Fruition without Desire is but a dull Entertainment; and that Pleasure only real and substantial, that provokes and improves the Appetite, and increases in the Enjoyment.[9] And all the greatest Masters in the several Arts of thriving concur unanimously, that the plain downright Pleasure of Gaining is greater and deserves to be prefered far before all the various Delights of Spending, which the Curiosity, Wit, or Luxury of Mankind in all Ages could ever find out.

He believes, there is no Way of thriving so easy and certain as to grow rich by defrauding the Public: for public Thieveries are more safe and less prosecuted than private, like Robberies committed between Sun and Sun, which the County pays, and no one is greatly concerned in.[10] And as the Monster of many Heads has less Wit in them all than any one reasonable Person:[11] so the Monster of many Purses is easier cheated than any one indifferent crafty Fool. For all the Difficulty lies in being trusted; and when he has obtained that, the Business does itself; and if he should happen to be questioned and called to an Accompt,[12] a Baudy Pardon[13] is as cheap as a Paymaster's Fee, not above fourteen Pence in the Pound.

He thinks, that when a Man comes to Wealth or Preferment, and is

---

[9] Apparently an allusion to the popular conception of Epicureanism.

[10] Under an old law, if any parish did not do its duty in the search for a criminal or was not careful in holding him in custody, it had to "make fine" to the king. Also the same parish and the hundred in which it stood had to pay damages to the party who was robbed and "leave his estate harmless." Even after the hue and cry, some constables were heard to say, " 'God restore your loss! I have other business at this time.' " [William Harrison, *Elizabethan England*, ed. Lathrop Withington (London, n.d.), p. 247.]

[11] A being with the power of reason,—*i.e.*, man.

[12] Archaic form of *account*. [*Oxford English Dictionary*; hereafter abbreviated *O.E.D.*]

[13] An unexplained contemporary term.

to put on a new Person, his first Business is to put off all his old Friendships and Acquaintances as Things below him, and no Way consistent with his present Condition; especially such as may have Occasion to make use of him, or have Reason to expect any civil Returns from him: for requiting of Obligations received in a Man's Necessity is the same Thing with paying of Debts contracted in his Minority, when he was under Age, for which he is not accountable by the Laws of the Land. These he is to forget as fast as he can, and by little Neglects remove them to that Distance, that they may at length by his Example learn to forget him: for Men, who travel together in Company, when their Occasions lye several Ways, ought to take leave and part. It is a hard Matter for a Man that comes to Preferment not to forget himself; and therefore he may very well be allowed to take the Freedom to forget others: for Advancement, like the Conversion of a Sinner, gives a Man new Values of Things and Persons, so different from those he had before, that that, which was wont to be most dear to him, does commonly after become the most disagreeable. And as it is accounted noble to forget and pass over little Injuries; so it is to forget little Friendships, that are no better than Injuries when they become Disparagements, and can only be importune and troublesome, instead of being useful, as they were before. All Acts of Oblivion[14] have, of late Times, been found to extend, rather to loyal and faithful Services done, than Rebellion and Treasons committed.[15] For Benefits are like Flowers, sweet only and fresh when they are newly gathered, but stink when they grow stale and wither; and he only is ungrateful, who makes returns of Obligations; for he does it merely to free himself from owing so much as Thanks. Fair Words are all the Civility and Humanity, that one Man owes to another; for they are obliging enough of themselves, and need not the Assistance of Deeds to make them good: for he that does not believe them has already received too much, and he that does, ought to expect no more. And therefore promises ought to oblige those only to whom they are made, not those who make them; for he that expects a Man should bind himself is worse than a Thief, who does that Service for him, after he has

---

[14] Cf. the Act of Indemnity and Oblivion (1660) "pardoning all those who had taken part in the rebellion or the subsequent republican governments except some fifty named individuals." [G. N. Clark, *The Later Stuarts*, 2d edition (Oxford, 1955), p. 4.]

[15] Some Cavaliers suggested that the Act of Indemnity and Oblivion meant Indemnity for the enemies of the King and Oblivion for his friends. [G. M. Trevelyan, *England Under the Stuarts* (New York, 1949), p. 277.]

robbed him on the High-way—Promises are but Words, and Words Air, which no Man can claim a Propriety in, but is equally free to all, and incapable of being confined; and if it were not, yet he who pays Debts, which he can possibly avoid, does but part with his Money for nothing, and pays more for the mere Reputation of Honesty and Conscience than it is worth.

He prefers the Way of applying to the Vices and Humours[16] of great Persons before all other Methods of getting into Favour: for he that can be admitted into these Offices of Privacy and Trust seldom fails to arrive at greater; and with greater Ease and Certainty than those, who take the dull Way of plain Fidelity and Merit. For Vices, like Beasts, are fond of none but those that feed them; and where they once prevail, all other Considerations go for nothing. They are his own Flesh and Blood, born and bred out of him; and he has a stronger natural Affection for them than all other Relations whatsoever—And he, that has an Interest in these, has a greater Power over him than all other Obligations in the World. For though they are but his Imperfections and Infirmities, he is the more tender of them; as a lame Member, or diseased Limb is more carefully cherished than all the rest, that are sound and in perfect Vigour. All Offices of this kind are the greatest Endearments, being real Flatteries enforced by Deeds and Actions, and therefore far more prevalent than those, that are performed but by Words and Fawning; though very great Advantages are daily obtained that Way—And therefore he esteems Flattery as the next most sure and successful Way of improving his Interests. For Flattery is but a kind of civil Idolatry, that makes Images it self of Virtue, Worth, and Honour in some Person, that is utterly void of all, and then falls down, and worships them. And the more dull and absurd these Applications are, the better they are always received: for Men delight more to be presented with those Things they want, than such as they have no need nor use of. And though they condemn the Realities of those Honours and Renowns, that are falsely imputed to them, they are wonderfully affected with their false Pretences. For Dreams work more upon Men's Passions, than any waking Thoughts of the same Kind; and many, out of an ignorant Superstition, give more Credit to them, than the most rational of all their vigilant Conjectures, how false soever they prove in the Event—No wonder then

---

[16] Fancies or whims; disposition or bent, as determined by the proportions of the four major fluids (humours) in the body: melancholy, phlegm, blood, and choler.

if those, who apply to Men's Fancies and Humours, have a stronger Influence upon them than those, that seek to prevail upon their Reason and Understandings, especially in things so delightful to them as their own Praises, no Matter how false and apparently incredible: for great Persons may wear counterfeit Jewels of any Caract,[17] with more Confidence and Security from being discovered, than those of meaner Quality; in whose Hands the Greatness of their Value (if they were true) is more apt to render them suspected. A Flatterer is like *Mahomet's* Pigeon,[18] that picks his Food out of his Master's Ear, who is willing to have it believed, that he whispers Oracles into it; and accordingly sets a high Esteem upon the Service he does him, though the Imposter only designs his own Utilities[19]—For Men are for the most Part better pleased with other Men's Opinions, though false, of their Happiness, than their own Experiences; and find more Pleasure in the dullest Flattery of others than all the vast Imaginations they can have of themselves, as no Man is apt to be tickled with his own fingers; because the Applauses of others are more aggreeable to those high Conceits, they have of themselves, which they are glad to find confirmed, and are the only Music, that sets them a dancing, like those that are bitten with a Tarantula.

He accounts it an Argument of great Discretion, and as great Temper, to take no Notice of Affronts and Indignities put upon him by great Persons. For he that is insensible of Injuries of this Nature can receive none; and if he lose no Confidence by them, can lose nothing else; for it is greater to be above Injuries, than either to do, or revenge them; and he, that will be deterred by those Discouragements from prosecuting his Designs, will never obtain what he proposes to himself. When a Man is once known to be able to endure Insolencies easier than others can impose them, they will raise the Siege, and leave him as impregnable; and therefore he resolves never to omit the least Opportunity of pressing his Affairs, for Fear of being baffled and affronted; for if he can at any Rate render himself Master of his Purposes, he would not wish an easier, nor a cheaper Way, as he knows

---

[17] Carat (confused with *charact*): worth, value; estimate. [*O.E.D.*]

[18] "Mahomet had a tame Dove that used to pick Seeds out of his Ear, that it might be thought to whisper and Inspire him." [Butler's note to *Hudibras*, I. i. 232.] Reginald Scott remarked that many people thought, on seeing the pigeon "pick a pease" out of Mahomet's ear, that the Holy Ghost was speaking to him. [*The Discovery of Witchcraft*, 3d edition (London, 1665), p. 143.]

[19] Purposes or ends.

how to repay himself, and make others receive those Insolencies of him for good and current Payment, which he was glad to take before—And he esteems it no mean Glory to shew his Temper of such a Compass, as is able to reach from the highest Arrogance to the meanest, and most dejected Submissions. A Man, that has endured all Sorts of Affronts, may be allowed, like an Apprentice that has served out his Time, to set up for himself, and put them off upon others; and if the most common and approved Way of growing rich is to gain by the Ruin and loss of those, who are in necessity, why should not a Man be allowed as well to make himself appear great by debasing those, that are below him? For Insolence is no inconsiderable Way of improving Greatness and Authority in the Opinion of the World. If all Men are born equally fit to govern,[20] as some late Philosophers affirm, he only has the Advantage of all others, who has the best Opinion of his own Abilities, how mean soever they really are; and, therefore, he stedfastly believes, that Pride is the only great, wise, and happy Virtue that a Man is capable of, and the most compendious and easy Way to Felicity—For he, that is able to persuade himself impregnably, that he is some great and excellent Person, how far short soever he falls of it, finds more Delight in that Dream than if he were really so; and the less he is of what he fancies himself to be, the better he is pleased, as Men covet those things, that are forbidden and denied them, more greedily than those, that are in their Power to obtain; and he, that can enjoy all the best Rewards of Worth and Merit without the Pains and Trouble that attend it, has a better Bargain than he, who pays as much for it as it is worth. This he performs by an obstinate implicit believing as well as he can of himself, and as meanly of all other Men; for he holds it a kind of Self-Preservation to maintain a good Estimation of himself: And as no Man is bound to love his Neighbour better than himself; so he ought not to think better of him than he does of himself; and he, that will not afford himself a very high Esteem, will never spare another Man any at all. He who has made so absolute a Conquest over himself (which Philosophers say is

---

[20] "Our author here has his Eye upon *Harrington*, who by his scheme of *Rotation*, admits all by turns into the Government, and must consequently suppose all fit." [Thyer's note.]

The Rota was a debating club founded by James Harrington (1611–77) in 1659–60 which advocated republican ideas, including a scheme of rotation for the representatives of government, such that a third would "rote out" by ballot each year and be ineligible for reelection for three years following; thus every ninth year the Senate would be completely changed.

the greatest of all Victories) as to be received for a Prince within himself, is greater and more arbitrary within his own Dominions, than he that depends upon the uncertain Loves or Fears of other Men without him—And since the Opinion of the World is vain, and for the most Part false, he believes it is not to be attempted but by Ways as false and vain as it self; and therefore to appear and seem is much better and wiser, than really to be, whatsoever is well esteemed in the general Value of the World.

Next Pride he believes Ambition to be the only generous and heroical Virtue in the World, that Mankind is capable of. For as Nature gave Man an erect Figure,[21] to raise him above the groveling Condition of his fellow Creatures the Beasts: so he, that endeavours to improve that, and raise himself higher, seems best to comply with the Design and Intention of Nature.[22] Though the Stature of Man is confined to a certain Height, yet his Mind is unlimited,[23] and capable of growing up to Heaven:[24] And as those, who endeavour to arrive at that Perfection, are adored and reverenced by all; so he, that endeavours to advance himself as high as possibly he can in this World, comes nearest to the Condition of those holy and divine Aspirers. All the purest Parts of Nature always tend upwards, and the more dull and heavy downwards:[25] so in the little World[26] the noblest Faculties of Man, his Reason and Understanding, that give him a Prerogative

---

[21] The belief in man's upright stature as a symbol of his superiority to the beasts and of his kinship with God may be found in classical literature: Plato, *Timaeus*, 90.a; Cicero, *On the Nature of the Gods*, II. lvi; Ovid, *Metamorphoses*, I. 76–86. Cf. *Paradise Lost*, VII. 505–11.

[22] Suggestive of the idea that in the "great chain of being" man's tendency is to move toward the angels and God and away from the animals, which are below him in the chain.

[23] For an expression of the view that man's possibilities are limitless see Pico della Mirandola (1463–94), *Oration on the Dignity of Man*, written in the full flower of the Renaissance.

[24] This reference to the mind's soaring upward is similar to the description of Neoplatonic trances (such as Plotinus is said to have enjoyed), in which the soul separates from the body, and to the characteristic teaching of Neoplatonists that he who soars above the flesh to converse with divine objects will become little less than a God.

[25] The natural movement of the elements air and fire is upward in a straight line; that of earth and water is downward.

[26] Widely held and referred to in the seventeenth century was the idea of man as a microcosm, or little world, comprising in himself all the elements found in the great world. Cf., for example, John Earle's title *Micro-cosmography* for his collection of Characters.

above all other earthly Creatures,[27] mount upwards—And therefore he, who takes that Course and still aspires in all his Undertakings and Designs, does but conform to that which Nature dictates—Are not the Reason and the Will, the two commanding Faculties of the Soul, still striving which shall be uppermost? Men honour none but those that are above them, contest with Equals, and disdain Inferiors. The first Thing that God gave Man, was Dominion over the rest of his inferior Creatures; but he, that can extend that over Man, improves his Talent to the best Advantage. How are Angels distinguished but by *Dominions, Powers, Thrones,* and *Principalities?*[28] Then he, who still aspires to purchase those, comes nearest to the Nature of those heavenly Ministers, and in all Probability is most like to go to Heaven—No Matter what Destruction he makes in his Way, if he does but attain his End: for nothing is a Crime, that is too great to be punished; and when it is once arrived at that Perfection, the most horrid Actions in the World become the most admired and renowned. Birds, that build highest are most safe; and he, that can advance himself above the Envy or Reach of his Inferiors, is secure against the Malice and Assaults of Fortune. All Religions have ever been persecuted in their primitive Ages, when they were weak and impotent; but, when they propagated and grew great, have been received with Reverence and Adoration by those, who otherwise had proved their cruellest Enemies; and those, that afterwards opposed them, have suffered as severely as those, that first profest them. So Thieves, that rob in small Parties, and break Houses, when they are taken are hanged: but, when they multiply and grow up into Armies, and are able to take Towns, the same things are called heroic Actions, and acknowledged for such by all the World. *Courts of Justice,* for the most Part, commit greater Crimes than they punish, and do those that sue in them more Injuries than they can possibly receive from one another; and yet they are venerable, and must not be told so, because they have Authority and Power to justify what they do, and the Law (that is, whatsoever they

---

[27] These faculties of man, not shared by the lower animals, were to make him strive to be a little lower than the angels rather than just above the other beings of the earth.

[28] Butler lists the four orders of angels also found in the Epistle of Paul to the Colossians (I. 16) but not in the same sequence.

Traditionally the full complement of angels is in three hierarchies, each consisting of three orders, for a total of nine orders which range from highest to lowest as follows: seraphim, cherubim, thrones; dominions, virtues, powers; principalities, archangels, angels.

please to call so) ready to give Judgment for them. Who knows, when a *Physician* cures or kills? and yet he is equally rewarded for both, and the Profession esteemed never the less worshipful—And therefore he accounts it a ridiculous Vanity in any Man to consider, whether he does right or wrong in any Thing he attempts; since the Success is only able to determine, and satisfy the Opinion of the World, which is the one, and which the other. As for those Characters and Marks of Distinction, which *Religion*, *Law*, and *Morality* fix upon both, they are only significant and valid, when their Authority is able to command Obedience and Submission; but when the greatness, Numbers, or Interest of those, who are concerned, out-grows that, they change their Natures; and that, which was Injury before, becomes Justice, and Justice Injury. It is with Crimes, as with Inventions in the Mechanics, that will frequently hold true to all Purposes of the Design, while they are tried in little; but, when the Experiment is made in great, prove false in all Particulars, to what is promised in the Model: So Iniquities and Vices may be punished and corrected, like Children while they are little and impotent; but when they are great and sturdy, they become incorrigible, and Proof against all the Power of Justice and Authority.

Among all his Virtues there is none, which he sets so high an Esteem upon as Impudence, which he finds more useful and necessary than a Vizard is to a Highwayman. For he, that has but a competent Stock of this natural Endowment, has an Interest in any Man he pleases, and is able to manage it with greater Advantages than those, who have all the real Pretences imaginable, but want that dextrous Way of solliciting, by which, if the worst fall out, he is sure to lose Nothing, if he does not win. He that is impudent is shot-free, and if he be ever so much overpowered can receive no hurt; for his Forehead is impenetrable and of so excellent a Temper, that nothing is able to touch it, but turns Edge and is blunted. His Face holds no Correspondence with his Mind,[29] and therefore whatsoever inward Sense or

---

[29] The notion, which Elizabethans commonly held, that the character of a person shows in his face, that the quality of soul is reflected in the visage, is challenged by the words of Duncan in *Macbeth*, I. iv. 11–12: "There's no art / To find the mind's construction in the face."

For a discussion of rendering the emotions by outward signs, a subject in the criticism of the arts in the late seventeenth and the eighteenth centuries, see Brewster Rogerson, "The Art of Painting the Passions," *Journal of the History of Ideas*, XIV (1953), 68–94.

Conviction he feels, there is no outward Appearance of it in his Looks, to give Evidence against him; and in any Difficulty, that can befal him, Impudence is the most infallible Expedient to fetch him off, that is always ready, like his Angel Guardian, to relieve and rescue him in his greatest Extremities; and no outward Impression, nor inward neither (though his own Conscience take Part against him) is able to beat him from his Guards. Though Innocence and a good Conscience be said to be *a brazen Wall*,[30] a *brazen Confidence* is more impregnable, and longer able to hold out; for it is a greater Affliction to an innocent Man to be suspected, than it is to one, that is guilty and impudent, to be openly convicted of an apparent Crime. And in all the Affairs of Mankind, a brisk Confidence, though utterly void of Sense, is able to go through Matters of Difficulty with greater Ease, than all the Strength of Reason less boldly inforced; as the *Turks* are said by a small slight handling of their Bows, to make an Arrow without a Head pierce deeper into hard Bodies, than Guns of greater Force are able to do a Bullet of Steel.[31] And though it be but a Cheat and Imposture, that has neither Truth nor Reason to support it, yet it thrives better in the World than Things of greater Solidity; as Thorns and Thistles flourish on barren Grounds, where nobler Plants would starve: And he, that can improve his barren Parts by this excellent and most compendious Method, deserves much better, in his Judgment, than those, who endeavour to do the same thing by the more studious and difficult Way of downright Industry and Drudging. For Impudence does not only supply all Defects, but gives them a greater Grace than if they had needed no Art; as all other Ornaments are commonly nothing else, but the Remedies, or Disguises of Imperfections—And therefore he thinks him very weak, that is unprovided of this excellent and most useful Quality, without which the best natural or acquired Parts are of no more use, than the *Guanches* Darts,

---

[30] "A joking Allusion to Horace.
      —Hic murus aeneus esto,
    Nil conscire sibi, nulla pallescere Culpa." [Thyer's note.]
("Be this our wall of bronze, to have no guilt at heart, no wrongdoing to turn us pale.") [*Epistles*, I. i. 60–61, in *Satires, Epistles and Ars Poetica*, trans. H. Rushton Fairclough (London and New York, 1932).]

[31] See Samuel Purchas, *Hakluytus Posthumus, or Purchas His Pilgrimes* (1625), (Glasgow, 1905), VIII, 143: "I have seene their [the Turks'] Arrowes shot by our Embassadour through Targets of Steele, pieces of Brasse two inches thicke; and through wood, with an Arrow headed with wood, of eight inches."

which, the Virtuosos say,[32] are headed with Butter hardned in the Sun. It serves him to innumerable Purposes, to press on and understand no Repulse, how smart or harsh soever; for he, that can sail nearest the Wind, has much the Advantage of all others; and such is the Weakness or Vanity of some Men, that they will grant that to obstinate Importunity, which they would never have done upon all the most just Reasons and Considerations imaginable; as those, that watch Witches, will make them confess that, which they would never have done upon any other Account.[33]

He believes a Man's Words and his Meaning should never agree together: For he, that says what he thinks, lays himself open to be expounded by the most ignorant; and he, who does not make his Words rather serve to conceal, than discover[34] the Sense of his Heart, deserves to have it pulled out, like a Traytor's, and shewn publicly to the Rabble.[35] For as a King, they say, cannot reign without dissembling; so private Men, without that, cannot govern themselves with any Prudence or Discretion imaginable—This is the only politic Magic, that has Power to make a Man walk invisible, give him access into all Men's Privacies, and keep all others out of his; which is as great an Odds, as it is to discover, what Cards those he plays with have in their Hands, and permit them to know nothing of his. And therefore he

---

[32] "What Butler refers to is recorded by *Sprat* in his History of the Royal Society." [Thyer's note.]

In a small section of the *History* based on a study of the Island of Tenariffe, whose inhabitants are called Guanchios, Sprat's words are as follows: "For embalming they took butter of goat's milk and in this boiled certain herbs. Having no knowledge of iron they made lances of wood in the same way." [See *Reproduction of 1667*, ed. Jackson I. Cope and Harold W. Jones (St. Louis, 1958), pp. 210–13.]

[33] Reference to witch trials where the only real witness was the accused witch herself, since Satan could not be called for testimony. The crime of being a witch brought the death penalty, so the accused would not confess except under torture, which almost inevitably brought a confession, usually one that conformed to the stereotyped idea of witchcraft that had been elaborated by theologians, inquisitors, lawyers, and judges. [See Rossell Hope Robbins, *The Encyclopedia of Witchcraft and Demonology* (New York, 1959).]

[34] Reveal, show; make known.

[35] The punishment for high treason was as follows: the traitor was placed upon a hurdle or sledge and drawn to the gallows; there he was hanged by the neck, then cut down alive. His entrails were suddenly pulled out of his belly, and burned before the criminal's eyes. Following this was decapitation, drawing, and quartering. [Edward Chamberlayne, *Angliae Notitia: or The Present State of England* (London, 1677), I, 43.]

never speaks his own Sense, but that which he finds comes nearest to
the Meaning of those he converses with; as Birds are drawn into Nets
by Pipes that counterfeit their own Voices.[36] By this means he possesses Men, like the *Devil*, by getting within them before they are
aware, turns them out of themselves, and either betrays, or renders
them ridiculous, as he finds it most agreeable either to his Humour,[37]
or his Occasions.

As for Religion, he believes a wise Man ought to possess it, only
that he may not be observed to have freed himself from the Obligations of it, and so teach others by his Example to take the same Freedom: For he, who is at Liberty, has a great Advantage over all those,
whom he has to deal with, as all Hypocrites find by perpetual Experience—That one of the best Uses, that can be made of it, is to take
Measure of Men's Understandings and Abilities by it, according as
they are more or less serious in it; for he thinks, that no Man ought to
be much concerned in it but Hypocrites, and such as make it their
Calling and Profession; who, though they do not *live by their Faith*,
like the Righteous, do that which is nearest to it, get their living by it;
and that those only take the surest Course, who make their best Advantages of it in this World, and trust to Providence for the next, to
which purpose he believes it is most properly to be relied upon by
all Men.

He admires good Nature as only good to those who have it not,
and laughs at Friendship as a ridiculous Foppery, which all wise Men
easily outgrow; for the more a Man loves another, the less he loves
himself. All Regards and civil Applications should, like true Devotion,
look upwards, and address to those that are above us, and from whom
we may in Probability expect either Good or Evil; but to apply to
those, that are our Equals, or such as cannot benefit or hurt us, is a
far more irrational Idolatry than worshipping of Images or Beasts. All
the Good, that can proceed from Friendship, is but this, that it puts
Men in a Way to betray one another. The best Parents, who are commonly the worst Men,[38] have naturally a tender Kindness for their
Children, only because they believe they are a Part of themselves,
which shews, that Self-love is the Original of all others, and the Foun-

---

[36] "The art of netting and luring birds by innumerable devices, was then much
practiced by gentlemen. . . ." [Trevelyan, *England Under the Stuarts*, p. 7.]

[37] See p. 33, n. 16.

[38] Probably Butler's own expression. For a similar idea and phrasing see the
Character of A Lawyer: "*as the best Laws are made of the worst Manners*, even
so are the best Lawyers of the Worst Men."

dation of that great Law of Nature, Self-Preservation; for no Man ever destroyed himself wilfully, that had not first left off to love himself—Therefore a Man's Self is the proper Object of his Love, which is never so well employed, as when it is kept within its own Confines, and not suffered to straggle. Every Man is just so much a Slave as he is concerned in the Will, Inclinations, or Fortunes of another, or has any thing of himself out of his own Power to dispose of; and therefore he is resolved never to trust any Man with that Kindness, which he takes up of himself, unless he has such Security as is most certain to yield him double Interest: For he that does otherwise, is but a *Jew*[39] and a *Turk*[40] to himself, which is much worse than to be so to all the World beside. Friends are only Friends to those who have no need of them, and when they have, become no longer Friends; like the Leaves of Trees, that clothe the Woods in the Heat of Summer, when they have no need of Warmth, but leave them naked when cold Weather comes; and since there are so few that prove otherwise, it is not Wisdom to rely on any.

He is of Opinion, that no Men are so fit to be employed and trusted as Fools, or Knaves; for the first understand no Right, the others regard none; and whensoever there falls out an Occasion, that may prove of great Importance, if the Infamy and Danger of the Dishonesty be not too apparent, they are the only Persons, that are fit for the Undertaking. They are both equally greedy of Employment, the one out of an Itch to be thought able, and the other honest enough to be trusted, as by Use and Practice they sometimes prove: For the general Business of the World lies, for the most Part, in *Rotines*[41] and Forms, of which there are none so exact Observers, as those, who understand nothing else to divert them; as Carters use to blind their Fore-horses on both Sides, that they may see only forward, and so keep the Road the better; and Men, that aim at a Mark, use to shut one Eye, that they may see the surer with the other. If Fools are not notorious, they have far more Persons to deal with of their own Elevation (who understand one another better) than they have of those, that are above them, which renders them fitter for many Businesses than wiser Men,

---

[39] A term applied to any grasping or extortionate usurer, or a trader who drove hard bargains or dealt craftily.

[40] Applied to anyone having qualities attributed to the Turks: a cruel, savage, rigorous, or tyrannical man.

[41] Routines: set forms of speech; a regular set or series (of phrases, etc.). [*O.E.D.*]

and they believe themselves to be so for all: For no Man ever thought himself a Fool, that was one, so confident does their Ignorance naturally render them; and Confidence is no contemptible Qualification in the Management of human Affairs—And as blind Men have secret Artifices and Tricks to supply that Defect, and find out their Ways, which those, who have their Eyes and are but hoodwinked, are utterly unable to do: so Fools have always little Crafts and Frauds in all their Transactions, which wiser Men would never have thought upon; and by those they frequently arrive at very great Wealth, and as great Success, in all their Undertakings—For all Fools are but feeble and impotent Knaves, that have as strong and vehement Inclinations to all Sorts of Dishonesty as the most notorious of those Engineers, but want Abilities to put them in Practice; and as they are always found to be the most obstinate and intractable People to be prevailed upon by Reason or Conscience; so they are as easy to submit to their Superiors, that is Knaves, by whom they are always observed to be governed, as all Corporations are wont to choose their Magistrates out of their own Members. As for Knaves, they are commonly true enough to their own Interests; and while they gain by their Employments, will be careful not to disserve those, who can turn them out when they please, what Tricks soever they put upon others; and therefore such Men prove more useful to them, in their Designs of Gain and Profit, than those, whose Consciences and Reason will not permit them to take that Latitude.

And since Buffoonery is, and has always been so delightful to great Persons, he holds him very improvident, that is to seek in a Quality so inducing, that he cannot at least serve for want of a better; especially since it is so easy, that the greatest Part of the Difficulty lyes in Confidence, and he, that can but stand fair, and give Aim to those that are Gamesters, does not always lose his Labour, but many times becomes well esteemed for his generous and bold Demeanor; and a lucky Repartee hit upon by Chance may be the making of a Man. This is the only modern Way of running at Tilt, with which great Persons are so delighted to see Men encounter one another, and break Jests, as they did Lances heretofore; and he that has the best Beaver to his Helmet, has the greatest Advantage; and as the former past upon the Account of Valour, so does the latter on the Score of Wit, though neither, perhaps, have any great Reason for their Pretences, especially the latter, that depends much upon Confidence, which is commonly a great Support to Wit, and therefore believed to be its betters, that

ought to take place of it, as all Men are greater than their Dependents
—So pleasant it is to see Men lessen one another, and strive who shall
shew himself the most ill-natured and ill-mannered. As in Cuffing all
Blows are aimed at the Face; so it fares in these Rencounters,[42] where
he, that wears the toughest Leather on his Visage, comes off with
Victory, though he has ever so much the Disadvantage upon all other
Accounts—For a Buffoon is like a Mad-Dog, that has a Worm in his
Tongue,[43] which makes him bite at all that light in his Way; and as
he can do nothing alone, but must have somebody to set him that he
may throw at, he that performs that Office with the greatest Freedom,
and is contented to be laughed at, to give his Patron Pleasure, cannot
but be understood to have done very good Service, and consequently
deserves to be well rewarded; as a Mountebank's *Pudding*,[44] that is
content to be cut, and slashed, and burnt, and poisoned, without
which his Master can shew no Tricks, deserves to have a considerable
Share in his Gains.

As for the Meanness of these Ways, which some may think too base
to be employed to so excellent an End, that imports nothing: for what
Dislike soever the World conceives against any Man's Undertakings,
if they do but succeed and prosper, it will easily recant its Error, and
applaud what it condemned before; and therefore all wise Men have
ever justly esteemed it a great Virtue to disdain the false Values, it
commonly sets upon all Things, and which it self is so apt to retract—
For as those, who go up Hill, use to stoop and bow their Bodies forward, and sometimes creep upon their Hands; and those, that descend,
to go upright: so the lower a Man stoops and submits in these endear-
ing Offices, the more sure and certain he is to rise; and the more upright he carries himself in other Matters, the more like in probability
to be ruined—And this he believes to be a wiser course for any Man
to take than to trouble himself with the Knowledge of Arts or Arms:
For the one does but bring a Man an unnecessary Trouble, and the
other an[a] unnecessary Danger; and the shortest and more easy Way to
attain to both, is to despise all other Men, and believe as stedfastly in
Himself as he can, a better and more certain Course than that of Merit.

---

[42] Encounters or engagements between two opposing forces, especially a
contest in wit or argument. [*O.E.D.*]

[43] To have "a worm in one's tongue" is a proverbial expression for one who
is cantankerous.

[44] I.e., a Jack-pudding: a buffoon, clown or merry-andrew, especially, as
indicated here, one who attends on a mountebank. [*O.E.D.*]

[a] an] as

What he gains wickedly he spends as vainly; for he holds it the greatest Happiness, that a Man is capable of, to deny himself nothing, that his Desires can propose to him, but rather to improve his Enjoyments by glorying in his Vices: for Glory being one End of almost all the Business of this World, he who omits that in the Enjoyment of himself and his Pleasures, loses the greatest Part of his Delight. And therefore the Felicity, which he supposes other Men apprehend that he receives in the Relish of his Luxuries, is more delightful to him than the Fruition itself.

AN HYPOCRITICAL NONCONFORMIST[a/1]

Is an Embassador Extraordinary of his own making, not only from *God Almighty* to his *Church*, but from his Church to him; and pretending to a plenipotentiary Power from both, treats with himself, and makes what Agreement he pleases; and gives himself such Conditions as are conducible to the Advantage of his own Affairs. The whole Design of his Transaction and Employment is really nothing else, but to procure fresh supplies for the *good old Cause*[2] *and Covenant*,[3] while they are under Persecution; to raise Recruits of new Proselites, and deal with all those, who are, or once were, good Friends to both; to unite and maintain a more close and strict Intelligence among themselves against the common Enemy, and preserve their general Interest alive, until they shall be in a Condition to declare more

---

[a] "This Character, though fairly transcribed by our Author, by lying in too damp a Place has received some little Damage, which will account for several Hiatus's, which appear in it. . . ." [Thyer's note.]

[1] Nonconformist: a term applied originally to a person who, while adhering to the Church of England, refused to conform in discipline and practice. Especially after the Restoration and the Clarendon Code it was applied to those Puritans separated from the Established Church.

[2] The *good old Cause* was, in general, that of the sectaries. More precisely, the term was used by Republicans for their constitution, founded on the death of Charles I and lasting until the dissolution of the Rump by Cromwell on April 20, 1653. Cromwell's Dictatorship and Protectorate, the Republicans felt, disrupted the natural course of events. Now that Cromwell was dead and his greatness gone, it was time to reinstate the old Commonwealth. [See David Masson, *The Life of Milton* (London, 1871–94), V, 444–45.]

[3] *Covenant* means the Solemn League and Covenant (concluded in 1643), an agreement reached between the Scots and the parties in England against the king in the Civil Wars, the Scots supplying troops and the Parliamentarians working to establish Presbyterianism (the national religion of Scotland) in England.

openly for it; and not out of Weakness to submit perfidiously to the Laws of the Land, and rebelliously endure to live in Peace and Quietness under the present Government: In which, though they are admitted to a greater Share of rich and profitable Employments than others, yet they will never be able to recover all their Rights which they once enjoyed, and are now unjustly deprived of, but by the very same Expedients and Courses, which they then took.

The Wealth of his Party, of which he vapours[4] so much to startle his Governors, is no mean Motive to enflame his Zeal, and encourage him to use the Means, and provoke all Dangers, where such large Returns may infallibly be expected. And that's the Reason why he is so ready and forward to encounter all appearing Terrors, that may acquire the Reputation of Zeal and Conscience; to despise the Penalties of the Laws, and commit himself voluntarily to Prison, to draw the Members of his Church into a more sensible fellow-feeling of his Sufferings, and a freer Ministration. For so many and great have been the Advantages of this thriving Persecution, that the Constancy and Blood of the primitive Martyrs did not propagate the Church more, than the Money and good Creatures earned by these profitable Sufferings have done the Discipline of the modern Brethren.

He preaches the Gospel in despite of[5] it self; for though there can be no Character so true and plain of him, as that which is there copied from the *Scribes* and *Pharisees*,[6] yet he is not so weak a Brother to apply any Thing to himself, that is not perfectly agreeable to his own Purposes; nor so mean an Interpreter of Scripture,[7] that he cannot relieve himself, when he is prest Home with a Text, especially where his own Conscience is Judge: For what Privilege have the *Saints*[8]

---

[4] I.e., brags, blusters, speaks, or writes in pompous, inflated, or extravagant manner.

[5] In contempt or open defiance of. [*O.E.D.*]

[6] In the Bible the Scribes and Pharisees are often coupled as upholders of ceremonial tradition. The Scribes were members of the class of professional interpreters of the Law after the return of the Israelites from captivity. The Pharisees were members of an ancient Jewish sect especially distinguished by strict observance of traditional and written law and by pretensions to superior sanctity.

[7] The Protestant movement in general and the dissenting sects in particular placed emphasis on individual interpretation of the Bible for religious guidance and the determination of salvation.

[8] *Saints* was the name by which many Puritans, especially Independents, liked to call themselves. The Independents saw the true church or congregation con-

more than the *Wicked*, if they cannot dispense with themselves in such Cases? This Conscience of his, (like the Righteousness of the *Scribes* and *Pharisees*, from whom it is descended) is wholly taken up with such slight and little Matters, that it is impossible, it should ever be at Leisure to consider Things of greater Weight and Importance. For it is the Nature of all those, that use to make great Matters of Trifles, to make as little of Things of great Concernment—And therefore he delights more to differ in Things indifferent; no Matter how slight and impertinent, they are weighty enough, in Proportion to his Judgment, to prevail with him before the Peace and Safety of a Nation. But he has a further Artifice in it; for little petulant Differences are more apt and proper to produce and continue Animosities among the Rabble of Parties, than Things of weightier Consideration, of which they are utterly uncapable, as Flies and Gnats are more vexatious in hot Climates, than Creatures that are able to do greater Mischiefs. And they, that are taught to dislike the indifferent Actions of others must of Necessity abominate the greater. And as Zeal is utterly lost, and has no Way to shew it self but in Opposition; nor Conscience to discover its Tenderness[9] but in seeking Occasions to take Offence perpetually at something, and the slighter and more trivial the better; so that Conscience, that appears strict and scrupulous in small Matters, will be easily supposed by the erroneous Vulgar to be more careful and severe in Things of Weight, though nothing has been more false upon all Experience.

  for[a] violating the Laws of God, as the Laws of the Land, and takes more care[b]   upon his Conscience, than to give it any just Satisfaction; for as it is apt to quarrel upon small and trivial Occasions, so it is as easily appeased with slight and trivial Pretences, and in great Matters with none at all; but rather,

---

sisting of Christ at the head and the saints under him. The congregation of saints was not to be dependent on any agency but Christ. [See Masson, *Life of Milton*, II, 591–92 and 595.]

  [9] Tender conscience: a conscience susceptible to moral or spiritual influence; impressionable, sympathetic; sensitive to pious emotions.

  1660: Charles II: *Declaration from Breda*: We do declare a liberty to tender consciences.

  1788: Wesley, *Works* (1872): One of a tender conscience is exact in observing any deviation from the word of God, whether in thought, or word, or work. [*O.E.D.*]

  [a] A blank space precedes this word in Thyer's edition. See p. 45, note a.

  [b] A blank space follows in Thyer's edition.

like the *Devil*, tempts him to commit all Manner of Wickedness: for we do not find, that any Possessions[10] of the *Devil* ever produced such horrid Actions, as some Men have been guilty of by being only possest with their own Consciences. And therefore, ever since the Act of Oblivion[11] reprieved him from the Gallows, he endeavours to supplant all Law and Government for being partial to him in his own Case; as bad Men never use to forgive those, whom they have injured, or received any extraordinary Obligation from: For he cannot endure to think upon Repentance, as too great a Disparagement for a *Saint* to submit to, that would keep up the Reputation of Godliness. And because the Scripture says, *Obedience is better than Sacrifice*,[12] he believes the less of it will serve: For he is so far from being sensible of *God's* Mercy and the *King's*, for his Pardon and Restoration to a better Condition than he was in before he rebelled,[13] that his Actions make it plainly appear that he accounts it no better than an Apostacy and *Backsliding*; and he expects a Revolution of Rebellion as obstinately, as the *Turk*[14] does *Mahomet's* Coming. For it is just with him as with other impenitent Malefactors, whom a Pardon or unexpected Deliverance from suffering for the first Crime does but render more eager to commit the same over again: For like a loosing Gamester he cannot endure to think of giving over, as long as he can by any Means get Money or Credit to venture again. And as the most desperate of those People, after they have lost all, use to play away their Cloaths, he offers to stake down his very Skin; and not only (as some barbarous

---

[10] Dominations or influences.

[11] See p. 32, n. 14.

[12] I Samuel, XV. 22.

[13] Many Nonconformists did not fare badly after the Restoration. The regicides, sentenced to death in 1660, became scapegoats for the other rebels. The Convention Parliament, made up largely of men from Roundhead families, took care of the safety and financial interests of their fellows, while Charles II and his advisor Hyde judiciously worked to create an aura of security for all persons and goods. The Roundheads who had bought land on a fallen market and who, for their benefit and protection, turned Anglican (at least in public observance) fared well. [Trevelyan, *England Under the Stuarts*, pp. 277–78.]

[14] *Turk* was often used by European writers to mean Mahometans of all nationalities (see the Book of Common Prayer, Collect for Good Friday).

"In their observed gestures, they [Mahometans] hold a regard unto Mecha and Medina Talnabi, two Cities in Arabia faelix; where their Prophet was born and buried; whither they perform their pilgrimages; and from whence they expect he should return again." [Sir Thomas Browne, *Pseudodoxia Epidemica*, in *Works*, ed. Geoffrey L. Keynes (London and New York, 1928–31), III, 213.]

People use) set[15] his Wife and Children, but his Head and four Quarters[16] to the Hangman, if he chance once more to throw out.[17] And yet, as stubborn and obstinate as he is to obey his lawful Sovereign, of whose Grace and Mercy he holds his Life, he has always appeared true and faithful to all tyrannical Usurpations, without the least Reluctancy of Conscience: for though he was fool'd and cheated by them, yet they were more agreeable to his own Inclination, that does not care to have any thing founded in Right, but left at large to *Dispensations* and *Out-goings* of Providence,[18] as he shall find Occasion to expound them to the best Advantage of his own Will and Interest.

He crys down the Common-Prayer,[19] because there is no Ostentation of Gifts[20] to be used in the reading of it, without which he esteems it no better than mere loss of Time, and Labour in Vain, that brings him in no Return of Interest and Vain-Glory from the Rabble; who have always been observed to be satisfied with nothing but what they do not understand; and therefore the Church of *Rome* was fain (to comply with their natural Inclinations) to enjoin them to serve *God* in a Language of which they understood not one Word; and though they abominate that, yet they endeavour to come as near it as they can, and serve *God* in an unknown Sense, which their own godly Teacher has as great a Care to prepare equal and suitable to their wonderful Capacities. And therefore, as the *Apostles* made their divine Calling appear plainly to all the World by speaking Languages,

---

[15] To stake at play: to offer a wager at dice to another. [Samuel Johnson, *A Dictionary of the English Language*, 8th edition (London, 1799).]

[16] Reference to the decapitation, drawing, and quartering which followed hanging.

[17] To throw out: in the dice game of hazard (see p. 110 and 110, n. 7), to make a losing cast. [*O.E.D.*]

[18] Special dealing or covenant with a group by the grace of God, not from good works. Religious order or system divinely instituted, or as a stage in a progressive revelation.
1643–47 *Westminster Confession of Faith*, VII. 6 (1877): There are not therefore two covenants of grace, differing in substance, but one and the same under various dispensations. [*O.E.D.*]

[19] The Book of Common Prayer, largely the work of Archbishop Thomas Cranmer in the sixteenth century, was written to aid popular devotion and the desire to use the vernacular in the services of the Church of England. The Nonconformists rejected the Book because it was a part of the Episcopal service and because it prescribed set prayers.

[20] Faculties, powers, or qualities bestowed miraculously, here in the sense of inspiration.

which they never understood before;[21] he endeavours to do the same Thing most preposterously by speaking that which is no Language at all, nor understood by any Body, but a Collection of affected and fantastic Expressions, wholly abstract from Sense, as *Nothingness, Soul Damningness and Savingness*, &c. in such a fustian Stile[22] as the *Turks* and *Persians* use; that signify nothing but the Vanity and want of Judgment of the Speaker; though they believe it to be the true Property of the Spirit, and highest Perfection of all Sanctity. And the better to set this off, he uses more artificial Tricks to improve his Spirit of Utterance either into Volubility or Dullness, that it may seem to go of it self, without his Study or Direction, than the old Heathen Orators knew, that used to liquor their Throats, and harrangue to Pipes. For he has fantastic and extravagant Tones, as well as Phrases, that are no less agreeable to the Sense of[a] . . . . in a Kind of *stilo recitativo*[23] between singing and braying; and abhors the . . . . . Liturgy, lest he should seem to conform to it. But as it is a Piece of Art to conceal Art, so it is by artificial Dullness to disguise that which is natural; and as his Interest has always obliged him to decry human Learning, Reason, and Sense;[24] he and his Brethren have with long and diligent Practice found out an Expedient to make that Dullness, which would become intolerable, if it did not pretend to something above Nature, pass for *Dispensations*, *Light*, *Grace*, and *Gifts*.[25] For in the Beginning of the late unhappy civil War, the greatest Number

---

[21] See Acts, II, esp. 3–4.

[22] Thomas Babington Macaulay, in *History of England* (New York, 1880), I, 182, discusses matters associated with the Puritans in theology, manners, and dialect, and he includes "speech interspersed with quaint texts," which made for a cant or jargon.

[a] See p. 45, note a.

[23] "In the style of recitative"—*i.e.*, musical declamation, intermediate between singing and ordinary speech, commonly employed in the dialogue and narrative parts of operas and oratorios. Thus, speaking in a pompous, recitative cadence. [*O.E.D.*]

[24] "The Independents and Anabaptists were great enemies to all human learning: they thought that preaching as every thing else was to come by inspiration." [Nash, ed., *Hudibras*, I. iii. 1340 n.]

[25] Dispensations: religious orders or systems, conceived as stages in a progressive revelation, expressly adapted to particular nations or ages.

Light: inner Light; specifically among Quakers, the inward revelation of Christ in the Soul.

Grace: the free and unmerited favor of God.

Gifts: faculties, powers, or qualities miraculously bestowed, occasionally in the sense of inspiration. [*O.E.D.*]

of those of the Clergy, who by the means of their Parts, or Friends, or Honesty had no Hopes to advance themselves to Preferment in the *Church*,[26] took Part with the *Parliament* against it, who were very willing to give a kind Reception and Encouragement to all those, that offered themselves to promote the *Cause of Reformation*, which they found to be the best Disguise they could possibly put upon *Rebellion*; and then this heavy Dullness, being a public Standard of the common Talents of their Teachers, became (for want of a better) a Mode, and afterwards a Character of the *Power of Godliness*, in Opposition to the Ingenuity[27] and Learning of the other Clergy; and whosoever was not naturally endued with it, or so much Hypocrisy as would serve to counterfeit it, was held unable, or suspected unfit to be confided in. And upon this account it has continued ever since among the Party, where it passes for a Mark of Distinction to discover who are gifted, and who not; as among the Antient *Pagans*, when Monsters and Prodigies[28] had gained the Reputation of divine Presages, the more unnatural and deformed they appeared, they were received with the more devout and pious Regard, and had Sacrifices accordingly appointed for their Expiation. And this he finds useful to many Purposes; for it does not only save him the Labour of Study, which he disdains as below his Gifts, but exempts him from many other Duties, and gives his idle Infirmities a greater Reputation among his Followers than the greatest Abilities of the most industrious; while the painful Heavings and Strainings, that he uses to express himself, pass for the Agonies of those that deliver Oracles. And this is the Reason why he is so cautious to have all his *Exercises* seem to be done Extempore, that his spiritual Talent may not be thought to receive any Assistance

---

[26] There was, in fact, a scarcity of orthodox and learned ministers. The Civil War disrupted education at the universities; and some ministers were silenced for refusing the Covenant, some were scattered, and others were killed in the Wars. The Independents, little concerned about clerical orders, gained many lay preachers, believing that when necessary "pious men with some natural gifts" could serve. Many enthusiasts obtained leadership, even some undesirables. [Daniel Neal, *History of the Puritans* (London, 1738), III, 476–77.]

[27] High intellectual capacity; genius, talent, wit. [*O.E.D.*]

[28] In Latin, *prodigium*: the name for an unnatural or, at least, unusual and inexplicable phenomenon, which was treated as requiring expiation. If such was seen on the State grounds, the Senate, taking the advice of the Pontiffs, set forth particular sacrifices, even to specific deities, or a public intercession. [*A Dictionary of Classical Antiquities, Mythology, Religion, Literature and Art*, from the German of Dr. Oskar Seyffert, revised and edited with additions by Henry Nettleship and J. E. Sandys (London and New York, 1891).]

from natural or artificial Means, but to move freely of it self, without any Care or Consideration of his; as if Premeditation and Study would but render him, like other false Witnesses, the more apt to contrive and imagine, how to betray and abuse the Truth. And to propagate this Cheat among his Hearers, he omits no little Artifice, that he thinks will pass unperceived: As, when he quotes a Text of Scripture, he commonly only names the Chapter, and about the Beginning, Middle, or End of it, or about such or such a Verse, and then turns over the Leaves of his Book to find it, to shew that he had not so much Preparation as to do it before; but was always surprized with his Gifts, and taken tardy before he was aware; and when he happens to be out, which is not seldom, will steal a Look, and squint into his Notes as cunningly as a Schoolboy does into his Lesson that he is to repeat without Book, that he may not be observed to need the same Means, which all those, that are ungifted, are necessitated to make use of: Although his Concordance supplies him with all the Gifts he has to cap Texts, and his Adversaries Writings, with all the Doctrine and Use he has, except that which is factious and seditious, which is always his own, and all that, beside Nonsense, he can justly pretend to.

The Contribution, which he receives from his Congregation, serves him, like a Scale, to take a just Measure of the Zeal and Godliness of every particular Member of it; and by computing what their Offerings amount to, in proportion to their Abilities, cast up exactly how much Grace and spiritual Gifts every Man is endued with. This, like auricular[29] Confession, lets him into the darkest Secrets of their Hearts, and directs him how to apply his Remedies according to their several Constitutions; and by finding out by Observation or Enquiry the particular Sins, that any[a] . . . . with a Particular of his Estate . . . . plant all his Batteries against them, and deliver them over . . . . until he . . . . ransom, and be converted to an equal Contribution and . . . . . . of them all. As Charity is said to cover a Multitude of Sins; so does charitable Contributions; and if that is wanting, it is his Duty to lay them open, and impose such Penances as he judges fitting, as well as dispose of Indulgences,[30] though he does not like the Word, to the best Advantage. And therefore he is an implacable Enemy to all ecclesiastical Judges and Officers in the Church,

---

[29] Addressed to the ear; told privately in the ear. [*O.E.D.*]

[a] See p. 45, note a.

[30] Obviously suggestive of Catholic practice, and the Roman Catholic Church was anathema to any Puritan.

and would trust no Creature living with the Conduct and Management of Men's Sins, but himself and the *Devil*, who is the only secular Power that he can confide in to deliver them over to, or redeem them back again at his own Rates. For he is a spiritual Interloper, that steals a Trade underhand, and by dealing in prohibited Commodities can undersell, and allow better Bargains of Sins and Absolution, than those that deal fairly and openly can afford. As for the *Bishops*, he is rather a Rival than an Enemy to them, and therefore becomes the more jealous of them: For all the Illwill he bears them is only, whatever he pretends, for their Authority and their Lands, with which he is most passionately in Love, but cannot possibly get the Consent of both Parties to the Match; and therefore, like Solomon's Harlot, had rather divide the Child, than let the right Owner have it.[31] For his Church Members have the keeping of his Conscience, as well as he has of theirs, and both sealed and delivered, like a Pair of Indentures, to one another's Uses; so that he cannot, though he would, alter his Judgment without their Consent, or such a valuable Consideration, as will secure him against all Damages, that he may receive by renouncing them and his own Opinion, when he finds it most convenient to satisfy all his Scruples, and conform. For as he parted with his Benefice, like a Gamester that discards and throws out a suit that is dealt him to take in a better out of the Pack, and mend his Hand: so he can as easily by the same light and Revelation, be converted, and change his Conventicle for a better spiritual Improvement, when a good Occasion is offered him. For how is it possible that he, who cannot conform to himself, should do so to any thing else; or he that plants all Improvements of Piety in spiritual Novelties should be constant to any Thing? For he that can endure nothing that is settled, only because it is so, can never possibly settle in any Thing; but must, as he outgrows himself in Grace, at length outgrow Grace too, as the most refined of his Disciples have done Ordinances and Government. For he differs no less from his own Doctrine and Discipline, than from that of the Church, and is really made up of nothing but Contradictions; denies free Will,[32] and yet will endure Nothing but his own Will in all the Practice of his Life; is transported with Zeal for Liberty of Conscience, and yet is the severest Imposer upon all other Men's Consciences in the whole World; is a profest Enemy to all Forms in

---

[31] I Kings, III. 16 ff.

[32] The denial of free will was a Calvinistic doctrine espoused by many dissenting sects.

Godliness, and yet affects nothing more than a perpetual Formality in all his Words and Actions; makes his Devotions rather Labours than Exercises, and breaks the Sabbath by taking too much Pains to keep it, as he does the Commandments of God, to find out new Ways for other Men to keep them; calls his holding forth[33] taking of great Pains, and yet pretends to do it by the Spirit without any Labour or Study of his own. And although *Christ* says, *blessed be the Peacemakers*, he will have none so but the Peacebreakers; and because the first *Christians* were commanded to be obedient for Conscience Sake, he commands his Brother *Christians* to be disobedient for the same Reason; makes longer Prayers than a Pharisee;[34] but, if the Treason, Sedition, Nonsense, and Blasphemy were left out, shorter than a Publican;[35] for he is no Friend to the Lords-Prayer, for the Power and full Sense of it, and because it is a Form, and none of his own, nor of the Spirit because it is learnt; and therefore prefers the pharisaical Way of Tediousness and Tautology. This he calls the *Gift of Prayer*, which he highly values himself upon, and yet delivers in a Tone that he steals from the Beggars; blames the *Catholics* for placing Devotion in the mere Repetition of Words, and yet makes the same the Character of spiritual Gifts and Graces in himself; for he uses the old Phrases of the *English* Translation of the Bible from the *Jewish* Idiom, as if they contained in them more Sanctity and Holiness than other Words, that more properly signify the same Thing. He professes a mortal Hatred to Ceremonies, and yet has more Punctilios than a *Jew*; for he is of too rugged and churlish a Nature to use any respect at all to any Thing. And though Ceremonies are Signs of Submission, and very useful in the public Service of God, yet they do not turn to any considerable Accompt, nor acquire any Opinion of Gifts from the People to those that use them; and he pretends to a nearer Familiarity with his Maker than to need any Ceremonies, like a Stranger; and indeed they are nothing agreeable to that audacious Freedom that he assumes in his Applications to him. So he condemns Uniformity in the public Service of God, and yet affects nothing else in his own *Doctrines* and *Uses*, and *Cap* and *Beard*,[36] which are all of the same Stamp. He denounces against all those that are given over to a reprobate Sense, but

---

[33] Preaching.

[34] See p. 46, n. 6.

[35] In Roman history a tax-gatherer, often mentioned in the New Testament.

[36] Many Presbyterians and Independents swore not to cut their beards until the monarchy and the Church of England were put down. [Nash, ed., *Hudibras*, I. i. 256 n.]

takes no Notice of those, that are given over to a reprobate Nonsense. He is an implacable Enemy to Superstition and Profaneness, and never gives it quarter, but is very tender of meddling with Hypocrisy,[37] though it be far more wicked, because the Interests of it are so mixt with his own, that it is very difficult to touch the one without disordering the other: For though Hypocrisy be but a *Form of Godliness* without Power, and he defies Forms above all Things, yet he is content to allow of it there, and disclaim it in all Things else.

A REPUBLICAN[1]

Is a civil Fanatic,[2] an *Utopian* Senator; and as all Fanatics cheat themselves with Words, mistaking them for Things;[3] so does he with the false Sense of Liberty. He builds Governments in the Air, and shapes them with his Fancy, as Men do Figures in the Clouds. He is a great Lover of his own Imaginations, which he calls his Country; and is very much for Obedience to his own Sense, but not further. He is a nominal Politician, a faithful and loyal Subject to notional Governments, but an obstinate Rebel to the real.[4] He dreams of a Republic waking; but as all Dreams are disproportionate and imperfect; so are his Conceptions of it: For he has not Wit enough to

---

[37] Macaulay notes that some men during the reign of Charles II imitated what were taken to be signs of Puritans—the sombre dress, sour look, straight hair, nasal whine, speech from quaint texts. The true Puritans were lost among men of the world of the worst sort, who feigned piety but were practicing "fraud, rapacity, and secret debauchery." The estimate of the whole group suffered from the actions of the hypocrites. [*History of England*, I, 182.]

[1] "This and the following Character were visibly intended for *Harrington* and his Followers. . . ." [Thyer's note.]

See p. 35, n. 20.

[2] Fanatic: affected by excessive and mistaken enthusiasm, especially in religious matters; a very common term to designate dissenters in the latter half of the seventeenth century. It was used by Archbishop Maxwell as early as 1644 and by Thomas Fuller in his *Mixt Contemplations* (1660): "a new word coined within a few months, called fanatics seemeth well . . . proportioned to signify . . . the sectaries of our age." [*O.E.D.*]

[3] The classical association of *words* and *things* and the seventeenth-century employment of them, notably by Bacon, Hobbes, and Bishop Sprat, are discussed by A. C. Howell in "*Res et Verba*: Words and Things," *ELH*, XIII (1946), 131–42.

[4] Perhaps a hit at James Harrington, who was on the Presbyterian side at the beginning of the Civil War.

understand the Difference between Speculation and Practice. He is so much a Fool, that, like the Dog in the Fable, he loses his real Liberty, to enjoy the Shadow of it:[5] For the more he studies to dislike the Government, he lives under, the further he is off his real Freedom. While he is modelling of Governments, he forgets that no Government was ever made by Model: For they are not built as Houses are, but grow as Trees do. And as some Trees thrive best in one Soil, some in another; so do Governments, but none equally in any, but all generally where they are most naturally produced; and therefore 'tis probable, the State of *Venice* would be no more the same in any other Country, if introduced, than their Trade of Glass-making.[6] To avoid this he calculates his Model to the Elevation of a particular Clime, but with the same Success (if put in Practice) as Almanac-Makers do, to serve only for a Year; and his Predictions of Success would be according, but nothing so certain as their fair and foul Weather. He has not Judgment enough to observe, that all Models of Governments are merely *Utopian*, that have no Territory but in Books, nor Subjects but in hot Heads and strong Fancies; that *Plato*'s is much wiser than any of his[7] Size, and yet it has been a long while in the World quite out of Employment, and is like to continue so, at least till his *great Year*,[8] a sad Discouragement to a State-Projector[9] —But his is like to have a harder Province; for without a previous Rebellion nothing is to be expected, and then that is to prosper, or else all is lost: Next the Nation is to fall into Ruin and Confusion just in the Order as he has designed it, otherwise it will be to no Purpose —Then nothing is to intervene; but after so many Alterations the same Persons are to outlive all, and continue still in the same Mind they were in, especially those in Power, and their Interests to be the very same they are at present, else nothing is to be done. After all this, if nothing else interpose, but the Will of God, a Model of a Republic may (if the Times will bear it) be proposed, and if it be

---

[5] An allusion to the well-known fable of the dog who dropped his bone in the stream because he opened his mouth to take hold of the reflection of it.

[6] Venice, especially well known for its artistry in clear, colorless glass, had begun its glass industry by the eleventh century.

[7] Its.

[8] The Platonic year, the time required for a complete revolution of the entire machine of the world, is a conception from the *Timaeus*. The time for the cycle has been estimated at thousands of years, at the end of which the universe was to be renewed.

[9] Projector: a schemer; speculator.

thought fit it should go no further, the Proposers shall be ordered to have Thanks, and be told, that it shall be taken into Consideration, or is so already; and then it will be just where it is now. And this is all the possible *Rotation*[10] our speculative State-Botcher can in Reason promise to himself to make those, that have any Sense of his Party to believe. This is much more probable than any Dream of the State-Quack, that used to mount his Bank[11] in a Coffee-House, and foretold *Oliver Cromwel* should live so many Years after he was hanged, and after dying leave the *Republicans* his Heirs;[12] tho' that has been partly performed in some, who have since taken upon them to be his Administrators, and in due Time is like to befall the rest. He has a Fancy, for 'tis no more, to a Commonwealth, because he has seen the Picture of it, no Matter whether true or false, it pleases his Humour, though it be nothing but a great Corporation; for 'tis but calling the Bailiffs of a good Town *Consuls*, the Aldermen *Senators*, the Churchwardens *Ædiles*,[13] and the Parson *Pontifex Maximus*,[14] and the Thing is done. Most that I know of this Sort are Haranguers, that will hold any Argument rather than their Tongues, and like this Government before any other, because every Man has a Voice in it, and the greatest Orators prove the ablest Statesmen. He catched this Itch at the *Rota*, where a State Charletan seduced him with Coffee and Sedition by promising his Abilities great Advancements in *Oceana*.[15] Ever since he has a mind to be a Piece of a Prince, tho' his own whole Share of *Highness* will not amount to the Value of *a Pepper Corn yearly if it be demanded*: Howsoever it will serve to entitle him to a Share in the Government, which he would fain be at, and believes himself right able to manage, though that be an ill Sign; for commonly those, that desire it most, are the most unfit

---

10 See p. 35, n. 20.

11 Bench. Also a play on *mountebank,* a quack who stands on a bench at fairs to advertise his nostrums. See the Character of a Mountebank.

12 Cf. "A Vision, Concerning his late Pretended Highnesse Cromwell, the Wicked . . ." (London, 1661), in Abraham Cowley, *The Essays and Other Prose Writings,* ed. Alfred B. Gough (Oxford, 1915), pp. 45–98.

13 Magistrates in ancient Rome, who had charge of public buildings, shows, police, etc. Also, municipal officers. [*O.E.D.*]

14 Chief Priest of the principal college of priests in ancient Rome. [*O.E.D.*]

15 *Oceana* is a work (published 1656) in which James Harrington outlined his conception of an ideal government, one quite in contrast to the state advocated by Hobbes a few years earlier. Elected officials were to lead a state of people free and equal, with the amount of property owned by an individual to be limited, so that no one could overpower the people as a whole. See also p. 35, n. 20.

for it. He follows his Inclination to a *Republic*, as a Bowler does his Bowl,[16] when he mistakes his Ground, and screws his Body that Way he would have it run, and to as much Purpose, but more dangerous; for if he run too far, he may, before he is aware, run his Neck into a Halter. Of all State-Fanatics he is the most foolish, and furthest off any of his Ends, unless it be the Gallows. Sure 'tis a very politic Thing to wish, and great Wisdom is required to fancy properly, and contrive judiciously what might be, if all Things would but fall out as they ought, and *Fate* were but as wise as it should be.

If he could but find out a Way to hold Intelligence with *Cardan*'s *Homines aerii*,[17] those subtle[18] Inhabitants of the Air, he might in Probability establish his Government among them, much sooner than here, where so many Experiments have been so lately made to no Purpose.[19] For *Oceana* is but a kind of a floating Island, like the *Irish O Brian*,[20] that never casts Anchor; and those that have been upon

---

[16] In the game of bowls a small ball (or bowl), which is called the *jack* or *mistress*, was set as a mark at one end of the green. The players, at the other end, rolled their bowls toward the jack, and the player whose bowl rested nearest the jack scored highest. Not perfectly spherical, the bowl was made with one side protruded (the protrusion being called the *bias*), which made the ball roll erratically. The game was played on greens and in bowling alleys; the former were not smooth but instead had lumps (called *rubs*) in the turf that diverted the bowls. [G. B. Harrison, ed., *Shakespeare: The Complete Works* (New York, 1952), Appendix 13.]

[17] Jerome Cardan (Girolomano Cardano, 1501–76): Italian physician and writer on medicine and occult sciences. He recorded that as a child resting quietly, under his father's orders to do so, he "used to vision, at is were, divers images of airy nothingness of body," which he described in some detail. [See Chapter 37 of *De Vita Propria Liber* (1557), English translation from the Latin by Jean Stoner (New York, 1930), as *The Book of My Life*. Quotation from p. 147.]

Reginald Scott states that "Fascuis Cardan had (as he himself and his son *Hierone Cardanus* report) a familiar Devil, consisting of the fiery Element. . . . He came not always alone, but sometimes some of his fellows with him." [*A Discourse Concerning the Nature and Substance of Devils and Spirits*, 3d Impression (London, 1665), p. 4.]

[18] Immaterial; rarefied.

[19] During the 1640's and 1650's various kinds of governments, some of them strongly democratic, were proposed and some of them attempted after the death of Charles I in 1649. [See especially Trevelyan, *England Under the Stuarts*, Chaps. IX and X.]

[20] This is perhaps an island from one of the many medieval legends about fabulous islands, such as Saint Brendan's Island (long sought by sailors and sometimes believed to have been sighted), that "became a fixed geographical

it know not where to find it again, nor what to make on't: For there is no Account of it in the Map, nor any where else, but in the Globe of an empty Noddle. Democracy is but the Effect of a crazy Brain; 'tis like the Intelligible World,[21] where the Models and Ideas of all Things are, but no Things; and 'twill never go further. They are State-Recusants, politic Nonconformists,[22] that out of Tenderness of Humour cannot comply with the present Government, nor be obedient to the Laws of the Land with a safe Fancy. They were all Freeborn in *Fairy-Land*, but changed in the Cradle;[23] and so being not Natives here, the Air of the Government does not agree with them. They are silenced Ministers[24] of State, that hold forth Sedition in Conventicles,[25] and spread new Governments erroneous both in Doctrine and Discipline. They mold Governments, as Children do Dirt-Pyes, only to busy and please themselves, tho' to no Purpose. He derives the Pedigree of Government from Universals, that produce nothing; and supposes the Right of it to be only in those, that are incapable of the Use of it, that is *all Men*, which is all one with *no Man*; for that which is every where is no where. He will undertake to prevent civil Wars by proving, that Mankind was born to

---

concept and appears on many 15th century maps of the Atlantic." [See "Saint Brendan" in *Chambers's Encyclopædia* (New York, 1950).]

[21] Reference to Plato's world of Ideas or Forms. "Ideas . . . are not in the soul, but in a superior intelligible nature, wherein the soul only beholds and contemplates them. And so they are only objectively in the soul, or tanquam in cognoscente, but really elsewhere, even in the intelligible world . . . that Plato speaks of, to which the soul is united and where she beholds them." [Nash, ed., *Hudibras*, I. i. 535 n.]

See John Norris, *An Essay Towards the Theory of the Ideal or Intelligible World* (1701, 1704).

[22] Recusants and Nonconformists: Here Butler uses, for political matters, terms usually applied to religious dissent.

[23] A changeling is a peevish or sickly child. The notion was that the fairies took a healthy child and left in its place a starveling elf which could not thrive. [See Shakespeare, *A Midsummer-Night's Dream*, II. i. 18 ff.]

[24] Preachers silenced by the Act of Uniformity, May, 1662, when every beneficed clergyman was ordered to give his "unfeigned consent and assent" to everything in the Prayer Book. Rather than conform nearly two thousand ministers went forth from their cures on Sunday, August 24, 1662, Saint Bartholomew's Day. Other Acts of the Clarendon Code also held the Nonconformist ministers in check. See the Character of a Silenc'd Presbyterian.

[25] In 1664 a Conventicle Act, part of what became known as the Clarendon Code, established punishments for attendance at meetings for religious observances other than those of the Established Church.

nothing else, and reduce them to Subjection and Obedience by maintaining, that Nature made them all equal. He pretends to secure the Right of Princes by proving, that whosoever can get their Power from them has Right to it, and persuade them and their Subjects to observe imaginary Contracts, because they are invalid as soon as made. He has as wise Disputes about the Original of Governments, as the *Rosicrucians* have about the Beginning of the World;[26] when it would puzzle both him and them to find out, how the first Hammer was made; but he would fain have them made by Laws, because Laws are made by them, as if the Child begot the Parent. His Pedigree of Power and Right are as obscure, as a Herald's genealogical Tree, that is hung with Matches,[27] like several Pair of Spectacles, and you may see as far into Truth with them. He is a State-Quack, that mounts his Bank[28] in some obscure Nook, and vapours what Cures he could do on the Body politic; when all the Skill he has will not serve to cure his own Itch of Novelty and Vainglory. All his Governments are Ideots, and will never be admitted to the Administration of their own Estates, nor come to Years of discretion.

A POLITICIAN

Is a speculative Statesman, Student in the liberal Art of free Government, that did all his Exercises in the late Times of cursed Memory at the *Rota*, but is not yet admitted to practise. He is a State-Empiric,[1] that has Receipts for all the Infirmities of Governments, but knows nothing of their Constitutions, nor how to proportion his Dose. He dissects the Body-politic into Controversies, as Anatomists do the Body of a Man, and mangles every Part, only to find out new Disputes. He weighs every Thing in the Ballance of

---

[26] On the Rosicrucians see the Character of An Hermetic Philosopher. I have not found that the Rosicrucians exhibited particular interest in "the Beginning of the World," a subject speculated on by many thinkers.

[27] The herald's concern with genealogies stemmed from his interest in proving (especially for evidence in law courts) the lines of descent of baronial or knightly families, whose members held lands by feudal tenure. For his support of titles to lands the herald was rewarded with a fee.

Genealogical tree: a table exhibiting the relation of ancestors to descendants in the form of a tree with spreading branches. [*O.E.D.*]

Match: a matrimonial alliance as represented heraldically. [*O.E.D.*]

[28] See p. 57, n. 11.

[1] Empiric: quack or charlatan.

Property, which at first would turn with the fortieth Part of a Grain, but since by Use is worn so false, that it inclines one Way more than the other most abominably. He shapes dirty Governments on his *Rota*[2] like Pipkins,[3] that never prove without some Crack or Flaw. He is always finding out of Expedients, but they are such as light in his Way by Chance, and nobody else would stoop to take up. The harder he charges his Head with Politics, the more it recoils and is nearer cracking; for, though in Matters of Action the more Experience a Man has the more he knows, it fares otherways,[4] with Speculations, in which an Error is seldom discovered, until it be reduced to Practice; and if but one of these creep in among his Contemplations, it makes Way for others to follow, and the further he pursues his Thoughts, the further he is out of his Way. He derives the Pedigree of Government from its first Original, and makes it begotten on the Body of a Woman by the first Father, and born with the first Child, from whom all that are at present in the World are lineally descended. He is wonderfully enamoured of a *Commonwealth* because it is like a common Whore, which every one may have to do with; but cannot abide *Monarchy*, because it is honest and confined to one. He despises the present Government, let it be what it will, and prefers the old *Greek* and *Roman*, like those that wear long Beards, Trunk-Hose, and Ruffs,[5] but never considers, that in that they are more fantastic than those, that affect the newest Fashions.

A STATE-CONVERT[1]

Is a thrifty Penitent, that never left Rebellion until it left him. He has always appeared very faithful and constant to his Prin-

---

[2] Latin for *wheel*, here in the image of a potter's wheel. Also, a reference to Harrington's Rota Club. See p. 35, n. 20.

[3] Small earthen pots.

[4] Otherwise.

[5] Beards, trunk-hose, and ruffs had been worn c. 1550–1610 (roughly the Elizabethan period) and thus were out of fashion.

Trunk-Hose: upper portion of male leg-wear, from the waist round the seat, and joined to the stockings. The Trunk-Hose was usually padded and thus distended. [Cecil W. Cunnington and Phyllis Cunnington, *Handbook of English Costume in the Sixteenth Century* (London, 1954).]

[1] A Presbyterian or follower of Cromwell (Independent, etc.) who turned Royalist. Many such converts could be found at the beginning of the Restoration period in 1660.

ciples to the very last: For as he first engaged against the Crown for
no other Reason but his own Advantages; so he afterward faced
about, and declared for it for the very same Consideration; and when
there was no more to be made of it, was thoroughly convinced, and
renounced it from the Bottom of his Heart. He espoused the *good
old cause,*[2] like an old Whore that had Money in her Purse, and
made her an honest Woman; but, when all was spent and gone, turned
her out of Doors to shift for her self, and declared her to be no better
than she should be. He was very much unsatisfied in his Conscience
with the Government of the Church, as long as Presbytery bore the
Bag, and had Money to receive for betraying *Christ*; but as soon as
those Saints were gulled and cheated of all, and that the Covenant
began to be no better than a beggarly Ceremony, his Eyes were presently opened, and all his Scruples vanished in a Moment. He did
his Endeavour to keep out the King as long as he could possibly; but
when there was no Hopes left to prevail any longer, he made a Virtue
of Necessity, and appeared among the foremost of those, that were
most earnest to bring him in: and, like *Lipsius*'s Dog,[3] resolved to
have his Share in that which he was able to defend no longer. What
he gained by serving against the King he laid out to purchase profitable Employments in his Service; for he is one that will neither obey
nor rebel against him for nothing; and though he inclines naturally to
the latter, yet he has so much of a Saint left as to deny himself, when
he cannot have his Will, and denounce against *Self-seeking*, until he
is sure to find what he looks for. He pretends to be the only Man
in the World that brought in the King, which is in one Sense very
true; for if he had not driven him out first, it had been impossible
ever to have brought him in. He endures his Preferment patiently

---

[2] See p. 45, n. 2.

[3] Thyer refers to a story related by Sir Kenelm Digby. Digby, writing on
the cunning and obedience of dogs, reports on Lipsius's dog who would bring
from the market as much meat as he carried money to the butcher to pay for.
Dogs, Digby assures his readers, are cunning by reason of training, which calls
on sense and memory but not discourse or reason. His story in illustration is
that Lipsius's dog, one day plagued by dogs snatching at the meat that hung
out of the basket he carried in his mouth, sat down to ward one off; then others
took advantage of the opportunity and got some of the meat until chased off by
him. Then Lipsius's dog himself ate the rest of the meat. Thus, once the pattern
of training in his memory was disturbed by the fighting, the dog followed his
natural bent, and ate what he had fought for. [See *Of Bodies and of Man's Soul*
(London, 1679), Chap. 37, pp. 404–6.]

(tho' he esteems it no better than a Relapse) merely for the Profit he receives by it; and prevails with himself to be satisfied with that and the Hopes of seeing better Times, and then resolves to appear himself again, and let the World see he is no Changeling: And therefore he rejoices in his Heart at any Miscarriages of State-Affairs, and endeavours to improve them to the uttermost, partly to vindicate his own former Actions, and partly in Hope to see the Times come about again to him, as he did to them.

A RISKER

Exposed himself to very great Hazards, when he had no other Way in the World to dispose of himself so well. He ventured very hard to serve the King in doing the Duty of his Place, that is, in putting him to Charges,[1] when he had nothing for himself. He never forsook him in his greatest Extremities, but eat and drunk truly and faithfully upon him, when he knew not how to do so any where else: For all the Service he was capable of doing his Master was the very same with that of *Bel* and the *Dragon's*[2] Clerks, to eat up his Meat, and drink up his Drink for him. He was very industrious to promote his Affairs to as high a Rate as he could, and improved his Revenue by increasing his Expences to the uttermost of his Power. 'Tis true he ventured all he had, that is himself, in the King's Service: for he left nothing behind him but his Debts, and to avoid these and Persecution he was glad to fly to him for Protection. He served him freely, as Soldiers are said to be Volunteers, that take up Arms because they know not how to live otherwise. He forsook his native Country because it forsook him before, and cast himself upon the King, who knew as little what to do with him, as he did with himself. As for neglecting his own Affairs, nobody knows what that means, unless it be that he did not betray the King, when he might have gotten Money to do it, as some others of his Fellows did. And these are all

---

[1] Employment, office; also accusations or impeachments.

[2] Bel and the Dragon: one of the apocryphal books of the Old Testament, removed from the Book of Daniel. The Babylonians worshiped Bel (or Baal), and the story relates how Daniel convinced their King Astyages that the idol was merely a brass image. The dragon, a living animal, was worshiped also. Daniel, to undercut the idea of its being divine, gave it pieces of fat, pitch, and hair to eat, and the animal burst open.

the great and meritorious Services he has done, for which he believes
the King is so far behind hand with him, that he will never be able
to come out of his Debt: For all Men are apt to set very high Rates
upon ever so little that they do for Kings, as if they were to be over-
reckoned by their Prerogatives; or that it were the Mark of Majesty
and Power to make Men Thieves, and give them leave to cheat; that
it were a Flower of the Crown to be first served with all Sorts of
Cheats and Impostors, for the Management of the Royal Revenue,
before the Subjects[a] can be admitted to furnish themselves for their
necessary Occasions. He is persuaded that he deserved so well of the
King in being a Burthen to him in his Necessities, that he ought to be
allowed to be one to the Nation for ever after. He is as confident that
he contributed as much as any Man to the King's Restoration, which
is very true; for he did what he could, and though that were nothing,
yet no Man can do more. The most desperate of all his Risks was to
venture over the Sea by Water, with private instructions or privy
Seals to borrow Money for the King's Use, and venture it in Play[b]
for his own, in which he often miscarried; for the Plot being discovered, all the Money was lost, except some small Sums, that he laid
out for his necessary Charges of Whores, Fidlers, and Surgeons—In
tender Consideration of all which great Services and Sufferings, he
believes the King is obliged in Honour and Conscience to grant him
a Brief[3] to beg of him all the Days of his Life, and deny him nothing
that he shall demand according to the Rules of the Court, and in case
of Refusal to prosecute his Suit, till he recover it against him by main
Importunity.

A MODERN STATESMAN

Owns his *Election* from *Free-Grace*[1] in Opposition to *Merits*
or any Foresight of *good Works*:[2] For he is *chosen*, not for his Abilities or Fitness for his Employment, but, like a *Tales*[3] in a Jury, for

---

[a] Subjects] Subject

[b] venture it in Play] venture it Play

[3] Writ or royal mandate.

[1] Free and unmerited favor of God. [*O.E.D.*]

[2] *Merits or . . . good Works*: such means to salvation were rejected by strict
Calvinists.

[3] A person added to a jury to make up any deficiency in the available number
of jurors regularly summoned.

happening to be near in *Court*—If there were any other Consideration in it (which is a hard Question to the wise) it was only because he was held able enough to be a *Counsellor extraordinary* for the Indifference and Negligence of his Understanding, and consequently Probability of doing no Hurt, if no Good; for why should not such prove the safest Physicians to the Body politic, as well as they do to the natural? Or else some near Friend, or Friend's Friend helped him to the Place, that engaged for his Honesty and good Behaviour in it—Howsoever he is able to sit still, and look wise *according to his best Skill and Cunning*; and, though he understand no Reason, serve for one that does; and be most stedfastly of that Opinion, that is most like to prevail. If he be a great Person he is chosen, as *Aldermen* are in the City, for being rich enough; and fines to be taken in, as those do to be left out; and Money being the Measure of all Things, it is sufficient to justify all his other Talents, and render them, like it self, good and current. As for Wisdom and Judgment with those other out-of-fashioned Qualifications, which have been so highly esteemed heretofore, they have not been found to be so useful in this Age, since it has invented Scantlings for Politics, that will move with the Strength of a Child, and yet carry Matters of very great Weight; and that Raillery and Fooling is proved by frequent Experiments to be the more easy and certain Way. For as the *Germans* heretofore were observed to be wisest when they were drunk, and knew not how to dissemble: so are our modern Statesmen, when they are mad, and use no reserved Cunning in their Consultations. And as the Church of *Rome* and that of the *Turks* esteem ignorant Persons the most devout, there is no Reason why this Age, that seems to incline to the Opinions of them both, should not as well believe them to be the most prudent and judicious: For heavenly Wisdom does by the Confession of Men far exceed all the Subtlety and Prudence of this World. The *Heathen* Priests of old never delivered Oracles but when they were drunk, and mad or distracted, and who knows why our modern Oracles may not as well use the same Method in all their Proceedings—Howsoever he is as ably qualified to govern as that Sort of Opinion that is said to govern all the World, and is perpetually false and foolish; and if his Opinions are always so, they have the fairer Title to their Pretensions. He is sworn to advise no further than his Skill and Cunning will enable him, and the less he has of either, the sooner he dispatches his Business; and Dispatch is no mean Virtue in a Statesman.

A DUKE OF BUCKS[1]

Is one that has studied the whole Body of Vice. His Parts are disproportionate to the whole, and like a Monster he has more of some, and less of others than he should have. He has pulled down all that Fabric[2] that *Nature* raised in him, and built himself up again after a Model of his own. He has dam'd up all those Lights, that Nature made into the noblest Prospects of the World, and opened other little blind Loopholes backward, by turning Day into Night, and Night into Day. His Appetite to his Pleasures is diseased and crazy, like the Pica in a Woman, that longs to eat that, which was never made for Food, or a Girl in the Green-sickness,[3] that eats Chalk and Mortar. Perpetual Surfeits of Pleasure have filled his Mind with bad and vicious Humours[4] (as well as his Body with a Nursery of Diseases) which makes him affect new and extravagant Ways, as being sick and tired with the Old. Continual Wine, Women, and Music put false Values upon Things, which by Custom become habitual, and debauch his Understanding so, that he retains no right Notion nor Sense of Things. And as the same Dose of the same Physic has no Operation on those, that are much used to it; so his Pleasures require a larger Proportion of Excess and Variety, to render him sensible of them. He rises, eats, and goes to Bed by the *Julian* Account,[5] long after all others that go by the *new Stile*;[6] and keeps the same Hours with Owls and the *Anti-*

---

[1] Cf. Dryden's portrait of Zimri (George Villiers, second Duke of Buckingham) in ll. 543–62 of *Absalom and Achitophel*.

[2] Structure, pattern.

[3] An anemic disease, found mostly in young women near the age of puberty, which causes the complexion to appear pale or greenish. There are frequent references in the literature of the time to these strange cravings. For example, in Thomas Shadwell's *The Scowrers* (V. 1): " 'Green-Sickness maids now dream of Clay and Lime.' "

[4] See p. 33, n. 16.

[5] I.e., the Julian Calendar: introduced by Julius Caesar in 46 B.C., known as *Old Style* after the Gregorian Calendar was introduced.

[6] I.e., the Gregorian Calendar: a modification of the Julian Calendar, introduced by Pope Gregory XIII in 1582 and adopted soon thereafter by Catholic countries but not officially by Great Britain until 1752. Until that time there was some confusion brought on by concurrent use of both Old Style and New Style. Butler's "long after all others" is, presumably, to point up the slowness of the Julian Calendar by comparison to the Gregorian.

podes. He is a great Observer of the *Tartars* Customs, and never eats, till the great *Cham*[7] having dined makes Proclamation, that all the World may go to Dinner. He does not dwell in his House, but haunt it, like an evil Spirit, that walks all Night to disturb the Family, and never appears by Day. He lives perpetually benighted, runs out of his Life, and loses his Time, as Men do their Ways in the Dark; and as blind Men are led by their Dogs, so is he governed by some mean Servant or other, that relates to his Pleasures. He is as inconstant as the Moon, which he lives under; and altho' he does nothing but advise with his Pillow all Day, he is as great a Stranger to himself, as he is to the rest of the World. His Mind entertains all Things very freely, that come and go; but, like Guests and Strangers they are not welcome, if they stay long—This lays him open to all Cheats, Quacks, and Impostors, who apply to every particular Humour while it lasts, and afterwards vanish. Thus with St. *Paul,* tho' in a different Sense, he *dies daily,*[8] and only lives in the Night. He deforms Nature, while he intends to adorn her, like *Indians,* that hang Jewels in their Lips and Noses. His Ears are perpetually drilled with a Fiddlestick. He endures Pleasures with less Patience, than other Men do their Pains.

A DEGENERATE NOBLE:
or,
One that is proud of his Birth,

Is like a Turnep, there is nothing good of him, but that which is under-ground, or Rhubarb a contemptible Shrub, that springs from a noble Root.[1] He has no more Title to the Worth and Virtue of his Ancestors, than the Worms that were engendred in their dead Bodies,[2] and yet he believes he has enough to exempt him-

---

[7] Obsolete form of *Khan.*

[8] See I Corinthians, XV. 31.

[1] Dried roots of rhubarb were used for pharmaceutical purposes, being "good to purge choler and phlegm." [Nathan Bailey, *An Universal Etymological Dictionary,* 4th edition (London, 1730).]

[2] Pliny writes that worms are born in the flesh of dead bodies, and other insects are generated out of dirt by the rays of the sun. [*Natural History,* trans. H. Rackham (Cambridge, Mass., and London, 1938–63), XI. xxxix.] Still widely held was the belief from antiquity that living beings were generated spontaneously from putrescent matter.

self and his Posterity from all Things of that Nature for ever. This makes him glory in the Antiquity of his Family, as if his Nobility were the better, the further off it is in Time, as well as Desert, from that of his Predeccessors. He believes the Honour, that was left him, as well as the Estate, is sufficient to support his Quality, without troubling himself to purchase any more of his own; and he meddles as little with the Management of the one as the other, but trusts both to the Government of his Servants, by whom he is equally cheated in both. He supposes the empty Title of Honour sufficient to serve his Turn, though he has spent the Substance and Reality of it, like the Fellow that sold his Ass, but would not part with the Shadow of it;[3] or *Apicius*, that sold his House, and kept only the Balcony, to see and be seen in.[4] And because he is privileged from being arrested for his Debts,[5] supposes he has the same Freedom from all Obligations he owes Humanity and his Country, because he is not punishable for his Ignorance and want of Honour, no more than Poverty or Unskilfulness is in other Professions, which the Law supposes to be Punishment enough to it self. He is like a *Fanatic*,[6] that contents himself with the mere Title of a Saint,[7] and makes that his Privilege to act all manner of Wickedness; or the Ruins of a noble Structure, of which there is nothing left but the Foundation, and that obscured and buried under

---

[3] The tale told by Demosthenes is that a man hired an ass to take him on a trip to Megara; at the heat of midday the man dismounted and sat in the shadow of the animal. The owner, who happened by, claimed that he had the right to the shady spot, with the statement that he hired out the ass but not the shadow of the ass. A fight ensued, during which the ass ran away, leaving both men to the heat of the sun. [E. Cobham Brewer, *Brewer's Dictionary of Phrase and Fable*, new edition (Philadelphia, 1929).]

[4] "What suggested to *Butler* this piece of Wit is a story told by *Asconius Paedianus* of one *Menius*, who sold his House, but reserved one Pillar of it to Build a Balcony upon, from Whence he might view the Combats of the Gladiators." [Thyer's note.]

Thyer wonders whether Butler made a mistake in applying it to *Apicius*, whose name is proverbial for gluttony from his extravagance in the time of Tiberius, or thought the change more suitable to his purpose.

For the story of Menius and the pillar reserved to himself and his heirs see Suetonius, "Annotations Upon Caius Caesar Caligula," 18a, in *History of Twelve Caesars*, trans. Philemon Holland (London, 1899), II, 261.

[5] Many nobles stood upon their rank and looked upon themselves as exempt from the laws that applied to others. [See Wallace Notestein, *The English People on the Eve of Colonization* (New York, 1954), pp. 38–39.]

[6] See p. 55, n. 2.

[7] See p. 46, n. 8.

the Rubbish of the Superstructure. The living Honour of his Ancestors is long ago departed, dead and gone, and his is but the Ghost and Shadow of it, that haunts the House with Horror and Disquiet, where once it lived. His Nobility is truly *descended* from the Glory of his Forefathers, and may be rightly said to *fall* to him; for it will never rise again to the Height it was in them by his means; and he succeeds them as Candles do the Office of the Sun. The Confidence of Nobility has rendered him ignoble, as the Opinion of Wealth makes some Men poor; and as those that are born to Estates neglect Industry, and have no Business, but to spend; so he being born to Honour believes he is no further concerned, than to consume and waste it. He is but a Copy, and so ill done, that there is no Line of the *Original* in him, but the *Sin* only. He is like a Word, that by ill Custom and Mistake has utterly lost the Sense of that, from which it was derived, and now signifies quite contrary: For the Glory of noble Ancestors will not permit the good or bad of their Posterity to be obscure. He values himself only upon his Title, which being only verbal gives him a wrong Account of his natural Capacity; for the same Words signify more or less, according as they are applied to Things, as *ordinary* and *extraordinary*[8] do at Court; and sometimes the greater Sound has the less Sense, as in Accompts though four be more than three, yet a third in Proportion is more than a fourth.

A HUFFING COURTIER

Is a Cypher, that has no Value himself, but from the Place he stands in. All his Happiness consists in the Opinion he believes others have of it. This is his Faith, but as it is heretical and erroneous, though he suffer much Tribulation for it, he continues obstinate, and not to be convinced. He flutters up and down like a Butterfly in a Garden; and while he is pruning of his Peruque takes Occasion to contemplate his Legs, and the Symmetry of his Britches. He is part of the Furniture of the Rooms, and serves for a walking Picture, a moving Piece of Arras. His Business is only to be seen, and he performs it with admirable Industry, placing himself always in the best Light, looking wonderfully Politic, and cautious whom he mixes withal. His Occupation is to show his Cloaths, and if they could but walk themselves, they would save him the Labour, and do his Work

---

[8] The distinction between regular magistrates and those added for temporary purposes.

as well as himself. His Immunity from Varlets[1] is his Freehold,[2] and he were a lost Man without it. His Cloaths are but his Taylor's Livery, which he gives him, for 'tis ten to one he never pays for them. He is very careful to discover[3] the Lining of his Coat, that you may not suspect any Want of Integrity or Flaw in him from the Skin outwards. His Taylor is his Creator, and makes him of nothing; and though he lives by Faith in him, he is perpetually committing Iniquities against him. His Soul dwells in the Outside of him, like that of a hollow Tree; and if you do but pill[4] the Bark off him he deceases immediately. His Carriage of himself is the wearing of his Cloaths, and, like the Cinamon Tree, his Bark is better than his Body. His looking big is rather a Tumor, than Greatness. He is an Idol, that has just so much Value, as other Men give him that believe in him, but none of his own. He makes his Ignorance pass for Reserve, and, like a Hunting-nag, leaps over what he cannot get through. He has just so much of Politics, as Hostlers in the University have *Latin*. He is as humble as a Jesuit to his Superior; but repays himself again in Insolence over those, that are below him; and with a generous Scorn despises those, that can neither do him good, nor hurt. He adores those, that may do him good, though he knows they never will; and despises those, that would not hurt him, if they could. The Court is his Church, and he believes as that believes, and cries up and down every Thing, as he finds it pass there. It is a great Comfort to him to think, that some who do not know him may perhaps take him for a Lord; and while that Thought lasts he looks bigger than usual, and forgets his Acquaintance; and that's the Reason why he will sometimes know you, and sometimes not. Nothing but want of Money or Credit puts him in mind that he is mortal; but then he trusts Providence that somebody will trust him; and in Expectation of that hopes for a better Life, and that his Debts will never rise up in Judgment against him. To get in debt is to labour in his Vocation; but to pay is to forfeit his Protection; for what's that worth to one that owes Nothing? His Employ-

---

[1] In the sense of *bumbailiff* (a bailiff of the meanest kind; one that is employed in arrests [*O.E.D.*]). See also p. 115 for the reference for which Thyer made the following note: "The word *varlet*, *Butler* uses in another place for a Bumbailif, in which it must be here taken; though I don't find that our Dictionary-writers ever give it that Signification."

[2] A tenure by which an estate . . . is held in fee-simple [in absolute possession], fee-tail [in limited fee], or for terms of life. [*O.E.D.*]

[3] Expose; display.

[4] Peel.

ment being only to wear his Cloaths, the whole Account of his Life and Actions is recorded in Shopkeepers Books, that are his faithful Historiographers to their own Posterity; and he believes he loses so much Reputation, as he pays off his Debts; and that no Man wears his Cloaths in Fashion, that pays for them, for nothing is further from the Mode. He believes that he that runs in Debt is beforehand with those that trust him, and only those, that pay, are behind. His Brains are turned giddy, like one that walks on the Top of a House; and that's the Reason it is so troublesome to him to look downwards. He is a Kind of Spectrum, and his Cloaths are the Shape he takes to appear and walk in; and when he puts them off he vanishes. He runs as busily out of one Room into another, as a great Practiser does in *Westminster*-Hall[5] from one Court to another. When he accosts a Lady he puts both Ends of his Microcosm[6] in Motion, by making Legs at one End, and combing his Peruque at the other. His Garniture[7] is the Sauce to his Cloaths, and he walks in his Portcannons[8] like one, that stalks in long Grass. Every Motion of him crys *Vanity of Vanities, all is Vanity*, quoth the Preacher. He rides himself like a well-managed Horse, reins in his Neck, and walks *Terra Terra*.[9] He carries his elbows backward, as if he were piniored like a trust-up Fowl, and moves as stiff as if he was upon the Spit. His Legs are stuck in his great voluminous Britches, like the Whistles in a Bagpipe, those abundant Britches, in which his nether Parts are not cloathed, but packt up. His Hat has been long in a Consumption of the Fashion, and is now almost worn to Nothing; if it do not recover quickly it will grow too little for a Head of Garlick. He wears Garniture on the Toes of his Shoes to justify his Pretensions to the Gout,[10] or such

---

[5] Part of old Westminster Palace and principal seat of justice from the time of Henry III until the nineteenth century, as well as scene of many trials including those of Strafford and Charles I.

[6] Humorous use of a popular concept. See p. 36, n. 26.

[7] Embellishment, trimming.

[8] Ornamented rolls laid in a set like sausages round the ends of the legs of breeches. [W. W. Skeat and A. L. Mayhew, *A Glossary of Tudor and Stuart Words* (Oxford, 1914).]

[9] Terra a terra: an artificial gait taught to horses, resembling a low curvet (i.e., a leap of a horse in which the fore-legs are raised together and equally advanced, and the hind-legs raised with a spring before the fore-legs reach the ground.) Also, any frisking motion. [*O.E.D.*]

[10] Since gout was supposed to settle in the big toe, perhaps the "garniture" here is an enlargement or extra piece put on the front of the shoe to help alleviate the malady and to advertise the fashionable disease.

other Malady, that for the Time being is most in Fashion or Request. When he salutes a Friend he pulls off his Hat, as Women do their Vizard-Masques. His Ribbons[11] are of the true Complexion of his Mind, a Kind of painted Cloud or gawdy Rainbow, that has no Colour of it self, but what it borrows from Reflection. He is as tender of his Cloaths, as a Coward is of his Flesh, and as loth to have them disordered. His Bravery[12] is all his Happiness; and like *Atlas* he carries his Heaven on his Back. He is like the golden Fleece, a fine Outside on a Sheep's Back. He is a Monster or an *Indian* Creature,[13] that is good for nothing in the World but to be seen. He puts himself up into a Sedan, like a Fiddle in a Case, and is taken out again for the Ladies to play upon, who when they have done with him, let down his treble-String, till they are in the Humour again. His Cook and Valet de Chambre conspire to dress Dinner and him so punctually together, that the one may not be ready before the other. As Peacocks and Ostridges have the gaudiest and finest Feathers, yet cannot fly; so all his Bravery is to flutter only. The Beggars call him *my Lord*, and he takes them at their Words, and pays them for it. If you praise him, he is so true and faithful to the Mode, that he never fails to make you a Present of himself, and will not be refused, tho' you know not what to do with him when you have him.

A COURT-BEGGAR

Waits at Court, as a Dog does under a Table, to catch what falls, or force it from his Fellows if he can. When a Man is in a fair Way to be hanged that is *richly* worth it, or has hanged himself, he puts in to be his Heir and succeed him[a] and pretends as much Merit as another, as, no doubt, he has great Reason to do, if all Things were rightly considered. He thinks it vain to deserve well of his Prince, as long as he can do his Business more easily by begging; for the same idle Laziness possesses him that does the rest of his Fraternity, that had rather take an Alms than work for their Livings; and therefore he accounts Merit a more uncertain and tedious Way of rising, and

---

[11] Huge bows, ribbons, or points were popularly used to decorate the breeches at the garter.

[12] Display, show; splendor. Here, specifically, fine clothes.

[13] Creature: an instrument or puppet. [*O.E.D.*]

[a] succeed him] succeed, him

sometimes dangerous. He values himself and his Place not upon the Honour or Allowances of it, but the convenient Opportunity of begging, as King *Clause*'s Courtiers[1] do when they have obtained of the superior Powers a good Station where three Ways meet, to exercise the Function in—The more ignorant, foolish, and undeserving he is, provided he be but impudent enough, which all such seldom fail to be, the better he thrives in his Calling, as others in the same Way gain more by their Sores and broken Limbs, than those that are sound and in Health. He always undervalues what he gains, because he comes easily by it; and how rich soever he proves is resolved never to be satisfied, as being like a *Friar Minor*,[2] bound by his Order to be always a Beggar. He is, like King *Agrippa*, almost a Christian;[3] for though he never begs any Thing of God, yet he does very much of his Vice-gerent the King that is next him. He spends lavishly what he gets, because it costs him so little Pains to get more, but pays Nothing; for, if he should, his Privilege would be of no use at all to him, and he does not care to part with any Thing of his Right. He finds it his best Way to be always craving, because he lights many Times upon Things that are disposed of or not beggable; but if one hit, it pays for twenty that miscarry; even as those Virtuosos[4] of his Profession at large ask as well of those that give them nothing, as those few that out of Charity give them something. When he has past almost all Offices, as other Beggars do from Constable to Constable, and after meets with a Stop, it does but encourage him to be more industrious in watching the next Opportunity, to repair the Charge he has been at to no Purpose. He has his Emissaries, that are always hunting out for Discoveries, and when they bring him in any Thing, that he judges too heavy for his own Interest to carry, he takes in others to join with him (like blind Men and Cripples that beg in Consort) and if they prosper they share, and give the Jackal some small Snip for his Pains in questing, that is, if he has any further use of him, otherwise he leaves him like Virtue to reward himself; and because he deserves well, which he does by no means approve of, gives him that, which he believes to be the fittest Recompense of all Merit, just nothing. He believes, that the King's Restoration being upon his Birth-Day, he is

---

[1] Christmas mummers.

[2] A Franciscan. Franciscans were also called *Minorities* or *Grey Friars*.

[3] See Acts, XVI, esp. 28.

[4] Persons with special knowledge or skill or particular adeptness. The term is here used, of course, sarcastically.

bound to observe it all the Days of his Life, and grant, as some other Kings have done upon the same Occasion, whatever is demanded of him, though it were the one half of his Kingdom.

A BUMPKIN,
or
COUNTRY-SQUIRE

Is a Clown[1] of Rank and Degree. He is the Growth of his own Land, a Kind of *Autocthanus*,[a]/[2] like the *Athenians*, that sprung out of their own Ground;[3] or Barnacles that grow upon Trees in *Scotland*:[4] His homely Education has rendered him a Native only of his own Soil, and a Foreigner to all other Places, from which he differs in Language, Manner of Living, and Behaviour, which are as rugged as the Coat of a Colt that has been bred upon a Common. The Custom of being the best Man in his own Territories has made him the worst every where else. He assumes the upper End of the Table at an Ale-House, as his Birthright; receives the Homage of his Company, which are always subordinate, and dispenses Ale and Communication, like a Self-conforming Teacher in a Conventicle.[5] The chief Points, he treats on, are the Memoirs of his Dogs and Horses, which he repeats as often as a Holder-forth,[6] that has but two Sermons; to which if he adds the History of his Hawks and Fishing, he is very painful and laborious. He does his endeavour to appear a Drole, but his Wit being,

---

[1] A country man, peasant, or rustic.

a Autocthanus] Antocthanus

[2] *Autochthonous*: (from the Greek word for aborigines), one sprung from the soil he inhabits; a "son of the soil." [*O.E.D.*]

Sir Thomas Browne's use of the term: "There was . . . never *autochthon*, or man arising from the earth, but Adam; for the woman being formed out of the rib, was once removed from earth, and framed from that Element under incarnation." [*Pseudodoxia Epidemica*, VI. 1, in *Works*, ed. Keynes, II, 160.]

[3] Reference to the myth of Cadmus and the sowing of dragon's teeth, out of which armed men grew up from the ground. See Ovid, *Metamorphoses*, Bk. III.

[4] Barnacles: tree geese. It was believed, even by serious botanists, that from the barnacles, which grew on rotten wood immersed in sea water, emerged creatures which grew into birds like geese. [John Brand, *Popular Antiquities of Great Britain* (London, 1905).]

[5] See p. 59, n. 25.

[6] A preacher.

like his Estate, within the Compass of a Hedge, is so profound and obscure to a Stranger, that it requires a Commentary, and is not to be understood without a perfect Knowledge of all Circumstances of Persons, and the particular Idiom of the Place. He has no Ambition to appear a Person of civil Prudence or Understanding, more than in putting off a lame infirm Jade for sound Wind and Limb; to which Purpose he brings his Squirehood and Groom to vouch; and, rather than fail, will outswear an Affidavit-Man.[7] The Top of his Entertainment is horrible strong Beer, which he pours into his Guests (as the *Dutch* did Water into our Merchants, when they tortured them at *Amboyna*[8]) till they *confess* they can drink no more; and then he triumphs over them as subdued and vanquished, no less by the Strength of his Brain, than his Drink. When he salutes a Man, he lays violent Hands upon him, and gripes and shakes him, like a Fit of an Ague: and, when he accosts a Lady, he stamps with his Foot, like a *French* Fencer, and makes a Longee at her, in which he always misses his Aim, too high or too low, and hits her on the Nose or Chin. He is never without some rough-handed Flatterer, that rubs him, like a Horse, with a Curry-Comb, till he kicks and grunts with the Pleasure of it. He has old Family Stories and Jests, that fell to him with the Estate, and have been left from Heir to Heir time out of Mind: With these he entertains all Comers over and over, and has added some of his own Times, which he intends to transmit over to Posterity. He has but one Way of making all Men welcome, that come to his House, and that is, by making himself and them drunk; while his Servants take the same Course with theirs, which he approves of as good and faithful Service, and the rather, because, if he has Occasion to tell a strange improbable Story, they may be in a Readiness to vouch with the more Impudence, and make it a Case of Conscience to lye, as well as drink for his Credit. All the heroical Glory he aspires to, is but to be reputed a most potent and victorious Stealer of Deer, and beater-up of Parks, to which Purpose he has compiled Commentaries of his own great Actions, that treat of his dreadful Adventures in the Night,

---

[7] A professional witness ready to swear to anything for pay.

[8] After English traders invaded territory which the Dutch considered part of their monopoly, in 1619 at Amboyna in the Spice Islands ten English settlers were tortured and put to death. The massacre at Amboyna was taken very hard by the English populace and was a cause of bitterness for many years, so that English-Dutch relations were adversely affected. [Godfrey Davies, *The Early Stuarts*, 2d edition (Oxford, 1959), p. 53.]

of giving Battle in the Dark, discomfiting of Keepers, horsing the deer on his own Back, and making off with equal Resolution and Success. He goes to Bawdy-Houses, to see Fashions; that is, to have his Pocket pick't, and the Pox into the Bargain.

AN ANTIQUARY

Is one that has his Being in this Age, but his Life and Conversation is in the Days of old. He despises the present Age as an Innovation, and slights the future; but has a great Value for that, which is past and gone, like the Madman, that fell in Love with *Cleopatra*.[1] He is an old frippery-Philosopher, that has so strange a natural Affection to worm-eaten Speculation, that it is apparent he has a Worm in his Skull.[2] He honours his Forefathers and Fore-mothers, but condemns his Parents as too modern, and no better than Upstarts. He neglects himself, because he was born in his own Time, and so far off Antiquity, which he so much admires; and repines, like a younger Brother,[3] because he came so late into the World. He spends the one half of his Time in collecting old insignificant Trifles, and the other in shewing them, which he takes singular Delight in; because the oftener he does it, the further they are from being new to him. All his Curiosities take place of one another according to their Seniority, and he values them not by their Abilities, but their Standing. He has a great Veneration for Words that are stricken in Years, and are grown so aged, that they have out-lived their Employments— These he uses with a Respect agreeable to their Antiquity, and the good Services they have done. He throws away his Time in enquiring after that which is past and gone so many Ages since, like one that shoots away an Arrow, to find out another that was lost before. He fetches things out of Dust and Ruins, like the Fable of the chymical Plant raised out of its own Ashes.[4] He values one old Invention, that is

---

[1] I have found no possible identification for this reference.

[2] A proverbial expression.

[3] Because by primogeniture he loses the property or title which descends to the eldest son.

[4] Sir Thomas Browne, *Religio Medici*, I. 48, in *Works, ed. Keynes,* I, 60, writes: "A plant or vegetable consumed to ashes to a contemplative and school-Philosopher seems utterly destroyed, and the form to have taken his leave for ever; but to a sensible Artist the forms are not perished, but withdrawn into their incombustible part, where they lie secure from the action of

lost and never to be recovered, before all the new ones in the World, tho' never so useful. The whole Business of his Life is the same with his, that shows the Tombs at *Westminster*, only the one does it for his Pleasure, and the other for Money. As every Man has but one Father, but two Grand-Fathers and a World of Ancestors; so he has a pro-portional Value for Things that are antient, and the further off the greater.

He is a great Time-server, but it is of Time out of Mind, to which he conforms exactly, but is wholly retired from the present. His Days were spent and gone long before he came into the World, and since his only Business is to collect what he can out of the Ruins of them. He has so strong a natural Affection to any Thing that is old, that he may truly *say to Dust and Worms you are my Father, and to Rotten-ness thou art my Mother.*[5] He has no Providence nor Fore-sight; for all his Contemplations look backward upon the Days of old, and his Brains are turned with them, as if he walked backwards. He had rather interpret one obscure Word in any old senseless Discourse, than be Author of the most ingenious new one; and with *Scaliger* would sell the Empire of *Germany* (if it were in his Power) for an old Song.[6] He devours an old Manuscript with greater Relish than Worms and Moths do, and, though there be nothing in it, values it above any Thing printed, which he accounts but a Novelty. When he happens to cure a small Botch in an old Author, he is as proud of it, as if he had got the Philosophers Stone, and could cure all the Diseases of Mankind. He values things wrongfully upon their Antiquity, forget-ting that the most modern are really the most ancient of all Things in the World, like those that reckon their Pounds before their Shillings and Pence, of which they are made up. He esteems no Customs but such as have outlived themselves, and are long since out of Use; as the

---

that devouring element. This is made good by experience, which can from the Ashes of a Plant revive the plant, and from its cinders recall it into stalk and leaves again."

Cf. also Joseph Glanvill, *The Vanity of Dogmatizing*, Chap. V (p. 47 of *Facsimile Text* of 1661 edition, New York, 1931). Glanvill mentions the hypo-thesis with some confirmation of "the artificial *resurrection* of *Plants* from their *ashes*, which Chymists are so well acquainted with. . . ."

5 Job, XVII. 14.

6 "*Julius Scaliger* [*Poetices*] was so much affected with Poetry, that he brake out into a pathetical protestation, he had rather be the Author of 12 verses in *Lucan*, or such an ode in *Horace* [Lib. 3. Ode 9. (I. ii.) Donec gratus eram tibi, etc.] than Emperor of *Germany*." [Robert Burton, *The Anatomy of Melancholy*, ed. A. R. Shilleto (London, 1912–13), II, 104.]

Catholics allow of no Saints, but such as are dead, and the *Fanatics*, in Opposition, of none but the Living.[7]

A PROUD MAN

Is a Fool in Fermentation, that swells and boils over like a Porridge-Pot. He sets out his Feathers like an Owl, to swell and seem bigger than he is. He is troubled with a Tumour and Inflammation of Self-Conceit, that renders every Part of him stiff and uneasy. He has given himself Sympathetic Love-Powder, that works upon him to Dotage, and has transformed him into his own Mistress. He is his own Gallant, and makes most passionate Addresses to his own dear Perfections. He commits Idolatry to himself, and worships his own Image; though there is no Soul living of his Church but himself, yet he believes as the Church believes, and maintains his Faith with the Obstinacy of a *Fanatic*. He is his own Favourite, and advances himself not only above his Merit, but all Mankind; is both *Damon* and *Pythias* to his own dear self, and values his Crony above his Soul. He gives Place to no Man but himself, and that with very great Distance to all others, whom he esteems not worthy to approach him. He believes whatsoever he has receives a Value in being his; as a Horse in a Nobleman's Stable will bear a greater Price than in a common Market. He is so proud, that he is as hard to be acquainted with himself as with others; for he is very apt to forget who he is, and knows himself only superficially; therefore he treats himself civilly as a stranger with Ceremony and Compliment, but admits of no Privacy. He strives to look bigger than himself, as well as others, and is no better than his own Parasite and Flatterer. A little Flood will make a shallow Torrent swell above its Banks, and rage, and foam, and yield a roaring Noise, while a deep silent Stream glides quietly on. So a vainglorious insolent proud Man swells with a little frail Prosperity, grows big and loud, and over-flows his Bounds, and when he sinks, leaves Mud and Dirt behind him. His Carriage is as glorious and haughty, as if he were advanced upon Men's Shoulders, or tumbled over their Heads like Knipperdolling.[1] He fancies himself a Colosse, and so he

---

[7] See p. 46, n. 8.

[1] Bernhard Knipperdolling, a leader of the Münster Anabaptists in 1533–35; an Anabaptist and hence a religious fanatic. Knipperdolling was executed, with fearful tortures (perhaps alluded to in this passage), on January 22, 1536.

is, for his Head holds no Proportion to his Body, and his foundation is lesser than his upper Stories. We can naturally take no view of our selves, unless we look downwards, to teach us how humble Admirers we ought to be of our own Values. The slighter and less solid his Materials are, the more Room they take up, and make him swell the bigger; as Feathers and Cotton will stuff Cushions better than Things of more close and solid Parts.

A FIFTH-MONARCHY-MAN[1]

Is one, that is not contented to be a Privy-Counsellor of the Kingdom of Heaven, but would fain be a Minister of State of this World, and translate the Kingdom of Heaven to the Kingdom of Earth. His Design is to make *Christ* King, as his Forefathers the *Jews* did, only to abuse and crucify him, that he might share his Lands and Goods, as he did his Vice-gerents here. He dreams of a Fool's Paradise without a Serpent in it, a golden Age all of Saints, and no Hypocrites, all *holy-Court* Princes, and no Subjects but the Wicked; a Government of *Perkin Warbec* and *Lambert Simnel*[2] Saints, where every Man, that had a Mind to it, might make himself a Prince, and claim a Title to the Crown. He fancies a *fifth-Monarchy* as the Quintessence of all Governments, abstracted from all Matter, and consisting wholly of Revelations, Visions, and Mysteries. *John of Leyden*[3] was the first

---

[1] A member of the sect of persons in the seventeenth century that expected the immediate second coming of Christ and repudiated all government but his kingdom. It was the duty of the Christian to be prepared to assist in the establishment of that reign by force.

The belief that Christ would reign on earth a thousand years grew out of the idea of the five monarchies, as set forth by many theologians of the middle ages, based on the Book of Daniel, II, esp. 44-45, and foreshadowed in Revelation, XX. 1-5.

These fervent Independents seized on the idea of the millenium being near at hand and even worked to accelerate its coming. [See Masson, *Life of Milton*, V, 16-17.]

[2] Warbec and Simnel: Pretenders, under the guidance of other men, to the throne of Henry VII. Warbec claimed to be Richard, son of Edward IV, and tried to gain the kingship by force but was defeated and hanged. Simnel claimed to be the Earl of Warwick but was stopped and demeaned by being made a turnspit in the royal kitchen.

[3] John of Leyden (1509-36): an Anabaptist fanatic (see the Character of An Anabaptist) who, when he became the leader of the sect in 1534, revolutionized

Founder of it, and though he miscarried, like *Romulous* in a Tempest,[4] his Posterity have Revelations every full Moon, that there may be a Time to set up his Title again, and with better Success; though his Brethren, that have attempted it since, had no sooner quartered his Coat with their own, but their whole outward Men were set on the Gates of the City; where a Head and four Quarters stand as Types and Figures of the *fifth-Monarchy*.[5] They have been contriving (since Experiments, that cost Necks are too chargeable) to try it in little, and have deposed King *Oberon*, to erect their Monarchy in *Fairy-Land*, as being the most proper and natural Region in the whole World for their Government, and if it succeed there to proceed further. The *Devil*'s Prospect of all the Kingdoms of the Earth, and the Glory of them,[6] has so dazzled their Eyes, that they would venture their Necks to take him at his Word, and give him his Price. Nothing comes so near the Kingdom of Darkness as the *fifth-Monarchy*, that is no where to be found, but in dark Prophesies, obscure Mythologies, and mystical Riddles, like the Visions *Æneas* saw in Hell[7] of the *Roman* Empire. Next this it most resembles *Mahomet*'s Coming to the *Turks*,[8] and King *Arthur*'s Reign over the Britons in *Merlin*'s Prophesies;[9] so near of Kin are all fantastic Illusions, that you may discern the same Lineaments in them all. The poor Wicked are like to have a very ill time under them, for they are resolved upon arbitrary Government, according to their ancient and fundamental Reve-

the city of Leyden and established a theocracy or Kingdom of Zion, of which he was crowned king. Apparently there was no direct connection between John of Leyden and the Fifth-Monarchy-Men in England. Butler's point, however, is obvious.

[4] Perhaps a reference to the mysterious death of Romulus, one of the legendary founders of Rome, and his disappearance during a storm.

[5] Reference to the result of the insurrection of Thomas Venner and his Fifth-Monarchy-Men in London near St. Paul's, beginning January 6, 1660/61. They began to destroy "Babylon" and human monarchy and to institute the reign of King Jesus. By the fourth day the men were subdued. Sixteen were condemned to be hanged, drawn, and quartered; thirteen, including Venner, actually received that punishment. [See Masson, *Life of Milton*, VI, 120.]

[6] See Luke, IV, Matthew, IV, and Milton's *Paradise Regained* (1671).

[7] *Aeneid*, Bk. VI.

[8] See p. 48, n. 14.

[9] Merlin, the magician in the Arthurian romances, displayed his knowledge of the past and the future—especially as depicted in the version by the French poet Robert de Boron (in the late twelfth or thirteenth century)—and connects the early history of the Grail with the days of King Arthur.

lations, and to have no Subjects but Slaves, who between them and the *Devil* are like to suffer Persecution enough to make them as able Saints, as their Lords and Masters. He gathers Churches on the Sunday, as the *Jews* did Sticks on their Sabbath, to set the State on Fire. He humms and hahs[10] high Treason, and calls upon it, as Gamesters do on the Cast they would throw. He groans Sedition, and, like the *Pharisee*, rails, when he gives Thanks. He interprets Prophesies, as *Whittington* did the Bells,[11] to speak to him, and governs himself accordingly.

THE HENPECT MAN

Rides behind his Wife and lets her wear the Spurs and govern the Reins. He is a Kind of preposterous Animal, that being curbed in goes with his Tail forwards. He is but subordinate and ministerial to his Wife, who commands in chief, and he dares do nothing without her Order. She takes Place of him, and he creeps in at the Bed's Feet, as if he had married the *Grand Seignor*'s[1] Daughter, and is under Correction of her Pantofle. He is his Wife's Villain, and has nothing of his own further than she pleases to allow him. When he was married he promised to worship his Wife with his Soul instead of his Body, and endowed her among his worldly Goods with his Humanity. He changed Sexes with his Wife, and put off the old Man to put on the new Woman. She sits at the Helm, and he does but tug like a Slave at the Oar. The little Wit he has being held *in capite*[2] has rendered all the rest of his Concernments liable to Pupilage and Wardship,[3] and his Wife has the Tuition of him during his or her Life; and he has no Power to do any Thing of himself, but by his Guardian. His Wife manages him and his Estate with equal Authority, and he lives under her arbitrary Government and Command as his superior

---

[10] Hems and haws.

[11] In the famous legend of Dick Whittington and his cat, Whittington imagined the tolling of the bells to say:

> Turn again, Whittington
> For thou in time shalt grow
> Lord Mayor of London. . . .

[1] Grand signior: the Sultan of Turkey.

[2] A kind of tenure—land held immediately of the king, who was spoken of as "lord paramount."

[3] Pupilage and wardship: under guardianship as a minor.

Officer. He is but a kind of Messuage and Tenement[4] in the Occupation of his Wife. He and she make up a Kind of Hermaphrodite, a Monster, of which the one half is more than the whole; for he is the weaker Vessel, and but his Wife's Helper. His wife espoused and took him to Husband for better or worse, and the last Word stands. He was meant to be his Wife's Head, but being set on at the wrong End she makes him serve (like the Jesuits Devil)[5] for her Feet. He is her Province, an Acquisition that she took in, and gives Laws to at Indiscretion; for being overmatched and too feeble for the Encounter, he was forced to submit and take Quarter. He has inverted the Curse, and turned it upon himself; for his Desire is towards his Wife, and she reigns over him, and with *Esau* has sold his Birthright for a Mess of Matrimony. His Wife took his Liberty among his wordly Goods, to have and to hold till Death them do part. He is but Groom of his Wife's Chamber, and her menial Husband, that is always in waiting, and a Slave only in the Right of his Wife.

A SMALL POET

Is one, that would fain make himself that, which *Nature* never meant him; like a *Fanatic*,[1] that inspires himself with his own Whimsies. He sets up Haberdasher of small Poetry, with a very small Stock, and no Credit. He believes it is Invention enough to find out other Men's Wit; and whatsoever he lights upon either in Books, or Company, he makes bold with as his own. This he puts together so untowardly, that you may perceive his own Wit has the Rickets, by the swelling Disproportion of the Joints. Imitation is the whole Sum of him; and his Vein is but an Itch or Clap, that he has catched of others; and his Flame like that of Charcoals, that were burnt before: But as he wants Judgment to understand what is best, he naturally takes the worst, as being most agreeable to his own Talent. You may know his Wit not to be natural, 'tis so unquiet and troublesome in him: For as those, that have Money but seldom, are always shaking

---

[4] Messuage: the portion of land intended to be occupied or actually occupied as a site for a dwelling-place and its appurtenances. [*O.E.D.*]

Tenement: land or real property which is held of another by any tenure; a holding. [*O.E.D.*]

[5] I have seen no reference elsewhere to this Devil.

[1] See p. 55, n. 2.

their Pockets, when they have it; so does he, when he thinks he has got something, that will make him[2] appear. He is a perpetual Talker; and you may know by the Freedom of his Discourse, that he came lightly by it, as Thieves spend freely what they get. He measures other Men's Wits by *their* Modesty, and his own by *his* Confidence. He makes nothing of writing Plays, because he has not Wit enough to understand the Difficulty. This makes him venture to talk and scribble, as Chowses[3] do to play with cunning Gamesters, until they are cheated and laughed at. He is always talking of Wit, as those, that have bad Voices, are always singing out of Tune; and those, that cannot play, delight to fumble on Instruments. He grows the unwiser by other Men's Harms; for the worse others write, he finds the more Encouragement to do so too. His Greediness of Praise is so eager, that he swallows any Thing, that comes in the Likeness of it, how notorious and palpable soever, and is as Shot-free against any Thing, that may lessen his good Opinion of himself—This renders him incurable, like Diseases, that grow insensible.

If you dislike him it is at your own Peril; he is sure to put in a Caveat beforehand against your Understanding; and, like a Malefactor in Wit, is always furnished with Exceptions against his Judges. This puts him upon perpetual Apologies, Excuses, and Defences, but still by Way of Defiance, in a Kind of whiffling Strain, without Regard of any Man, that stands in the Way of his Pageant. Where he thinks he may do it safely, he will confidently own other Men's Writings; and where he fears the Truth may be discovered, he will by feeble Denials and feigned Insinuations give Men Occasion to suppose so.

If he understands *Latin* or *Greek* he ranks himself among the Learned, despises the Ignorant, talks Criticisms out of *Scaliger*,[4] and repeats *Martial's* baudy Epigrams,[5] and sets up his Rest wholly upon Pedantry. But it he be not so well qualified, he crys down all Learning as pedantic, disclaims Study, and professes to write with as great Facility, as if his Muse was sliding down *Parnassus*. Whatsoever he

---

[2] It (i.e., wit).

[3] Chouses: gulls, dupes.

[4] Probably J. J. Scaliger (1540–1609), son of J. C. Scaliger (1484–1558), also a very learned man. J. J. Scaliger, considered to be the greatest scholar of the Renaissance, was the founder of historical criticism and the critical editor of many classical authors.

[5] In his epigrams the Latin poet (c. A.D. 40–104) describes in realistic details various characters of contemporary Rome.

hears well said he seizes upon by poetical Licence;[6] and one Way makes it his own, that is by ill repeating of it—This he believes to be no more Theft, than it is to take that, which others throw away. By this means his Writings are, like a Taylor's Cushion, of mosaic Work, made up of several Scraps sewed together. He calls a slovenly nasty Description *great Nature*, and dull Flatness *strange Easiness*.[7] He writes down all that comes in his Head, and makes no Choice, because he has nothing to do it with, that is Judgment.[8] He is always repealing the old Laws of Comedy, and like the *long Parliament* making *Ordinances*[9] in their Stead; although they are perpetually *thrown out* of Coffee-Houses, and come to Nothing. He is like an *Italian* Thief, that never robs, but he murthers, to prevent Discovery; so sure is he to cry down the Man from whom he purloins, that his petty Larceny of Wit may pass unsuspected. He is but a Copier at best, and will never arrive to practise by the Life: For bar him the Imitation of something he has read, and he has no Image in his Thoughts. Observation and Fancy, the Matter and Form of just Wit,[10] are above his Philosophy. He appears so over concerned in all Men's Wits, as if they were but Disparagements of his own; and crys down all they do, as if they were Encroachments upon him. He takes Jests from the Owners and breaks them, as *Justices* do false Weights, and Pots that want Measure. When he meets with any Thing, that is very good, he changes it into small Money, like three Groats for a Shilling,

---

6 "In this *Butler* alludes to *Martial's* Epigram to Fidentinus." [Thyer's note.]
Quem recitas meus est, o Fidentine, libellus:
sed male cum recitas, incipit esse tuus.
("That book you recite, O Fidentinus, is mine. But your vile recitation begins to make it your own.") [Martial, *Epigrams*, trans. Walter C. A. Ker (London and New York, 1919–20), I. xxxviii.]

7 *Great Nature* and . . . *Easiness*: terms much in use in the developing concern for "good sense" in the neoclassic age.

8 An intellectual control by the poet and critic, especially over the "fancy," in favor of "decorum." *Judgment* was an important term for neoclassic critics, and it figures prominently in the critical discussions of Butler's contemporaries Dryden and Hobbes.

9 The Long Parliament sat from November, 1640, to April, 1653, when dissolved by Cromwell, but a small part of it, called "The Rump, continued until 1660. In its contentions with the King, the Parliament by 1641 began to use unprecedented means for joint work by the Houses, proclaiming ordinances without his consent, as they assumed administrative power.

10 For an admirable, concise summation of the changing conceptions of wit see George Williamson, *The Proper Wit of Poetry* (London, 1961).

to serve several Occasions. He disclaims Study, pretends to take Things in Motion, and to shoot flying, which appears to be very true by his often missing of his Mark. His Wit is much troubled with Obstructions; and he has Fits as painful as those of the Spleen.[11] He fancies himself a dainty spruce Shepherd, with a Flock and a fine silken Shepherdess, that follows his Pipe, as Rats did the Conjurers in *Germany*.[12]

As for *Epithets*, he always avoids those, that are near akin to the Sense. Such matches are unlawful, and not fit to be made by a *Christian* Poet;[13] and therefore all his Care is to chuse out such, as will serve, like a wooden Leg, to piece out a maim'd Verse, that wants a Foot or two; and if they will but rhime now and then into the Bargain, or run upon a Letter,[14] it is a Work of Supererrogation.[15]

For *Similitudes*, he likes the hardest and most obscure best: For as Ladies wear black Patches, to make their Complexions seem fairer than they are; so when an Illustration is more obscure than the Sense that went before it, it must of Necessity make it appear clearer than it did: For Contraries are best set off with Contraries.

He has found out a Way to save the Expence of much Wit and Sense: For he will make less than some have prodigally laid out upon five or six Words serve forty or fifty Lines. This is a thrifty Invention, and very easy; and, if it were commonly known, would much increase the Trade of Wit, and maintain a Multitude of small Poets in constant Employment. He has found out a new Sort of poetical *Georgics*, a Trick of sowing Wit like clover-grass on barren Subjects, which would Yield nothing before. This is very useful for the Times, where-

---

[11] The *vapours*, the *hypo*, the *spleen*—all three terms were used to describe a moribund condition ranging from depression and "nerves" to melancholia. The symptoms would seem to indicate maladies now called nervous disorders. For a description of manifestations of these disorders see Pope's Cave of the Spleen in Book IV of *The Rape of the Lock*. See also an excellent study, "The English Malady," in C. A. Moore, *Backgrounds of English Literature, 1700–1760* (Minneapolis, 1953).

[12] For example, the Pied Piper of Hamlin in Westphalia.

[13] A hit at the extravagant style of much religious poetry in the late sixteenth and early seventeenth centuries.

[14] To dwell upon, or be occupied with, a subject.

[15] Supererrogation: in Roman Catholic theology the performance of good works beyond what God commands or requires, which are held to constitute a store of merits that the church may dispense to others to make up for their deficiencies. Thus, also, performance of more than duty or circumstances require. [*O.E.D.*]

in, some Men say, there is no Room left for new Invention. He will take three Grains of Wit like the Elixir, and projecting it upon the *Iron-Age* turn it immediately into *Gold*—[16] All the Business of Mankind has presently vanished, the whole World has kept Holiday; there has been no Men but Heroes and Poets, no Women but Nymphs and Shepherdesses; Trees have born Fritters, and Rivers flowed Plum-Porrige.

We read that *Virgil* used to make fifty or sixty Verses in a Morning, and afterwards reduce them to ten.[17] This was an unthrifty Vanity, and argues him as well ignorant in the Husbandry of his own Poetry, as *Seneca* says he was in that of a Farm;[18] for in plain *English* it was no better than bringing a Noble to Ninepence.[19] And as such Courses brought the *prodigal Son* to eat with Hogs: So they did him to feed with Horses,[20] which were not much better Company, and may teach us to avoid doing the like. For certainly it is more noble to take four or five Grains of Sense, and, like a Gold-Beater, hammer them into so many Leaves as will fill a whole Book; than to write nothing but Epitomies, which many wise Men believe will be the Bane and Calamity of Learning.

When he writes, he commonly steers the Sense of his Lines by the Rhime that is at the End of them, as Butchers do Calves by the Tail. For when he has made one Line, which is easy enough; and has found out some sturdy hard Word, that will but rhime, he will hammer the Sense upon it, like a Piece of hot Iron upon an Anvil, into what Form he pleases.

---

[16] The Golden Age: according to Hesiod and others, an age of innocent happiness, without injustice, and where the earth gave up its fruits abundantly of its own accord.

[17] "This alludes to a Passage in the life of *Virgil* ascribed to *Donatus*." [Thyer's note.]

[18] Thyer refers the reader to Seneca's Eighty-sixth Epistle, where Seneca finds fault with Virgil's handling, in the *Georgics*, of matters of husbandry and adds:
> [Virgilius] qui non quid verissime, sed
> quid decentissime diceretur aspexit nec
> agricolas docere voluit, sed legentes delectore.

("Virgil who sought not what was nearest to the truth, but what was most appropriate, and aimed, not to teach the farmer, but to please the reader.") [*The Epistles of Seneca*, trans. Richard M. Gummere (London and New York, 1925), LXXXVI. 15.]

[19] Proverbial for idle dissipation of money.

[20] Thyer again refers to the "Life" by Donatus, in which he relates Virgil's experience in the stables of Augustus.

There is no Art in the World so rich in Terms as Poetry; a whole Dictionary is scarce able to contain them: For there is hardly a Pond, a Sheep-walk, or a Gravel-pit in all *Greece*, but the antient Name of it is become a Term of Art in Poetry. By this means small Poets have such a Stock of able hard Words lying by them, as *Dryades, Hamadryades, Aonides, Fauni, Nymphae, Sylvani, &c.* that signify nothing at all; and such a World of pedantic Terms of the same Kind, as may serve to furnish all the new Inventions and *thorough*[21]-*Reformations*, that can happen between this and *Plato*'s great Year.[22]

When he writes he never proposes any Scope or Purpose to himself, but gives his Genius all Freedom: For as he, that rides abroad for his Pleasure, can hardly be out of his Way; so he that writes for his Pleasure, can seldom be beside his Subject. It is an ungrateful Thing to a noble Wit to be confined to any Thing—To what Purpose did the Antients feign *Pegasus* to have Wings, if he must be confined to the Road and Stages like a Pack-Horse, or be forced to be obedient to Hedges and Ditches? Therefore he has no Respect to Decorum and Propriety of Circumstance; for the Regard of Persons, Times, and Places is a Restraint too servile to be imposed upon poetical Licence; like him that made *Plato* confess *Juvenal* to be a Philosopher,[23] or *Persius*, that calls the *Athenians Quirites*.[24]

For *Metaphors*, he uses to chuse the hardest, and most far-fet that he can light upon—These are the Jewels of Eloquence, and therefore the harder they are, the more precious they must be.[25]

He'll take a scant Piece of coarse Sense, and stretch it on the Tenter-hooks of half a score Rhimes, until it crack that you may see through it, and it rattle like a Drum-Head. When you see his Verses hanged

---

21 Perhaps a reference to the policy of "thorough," the stringent and thorough-going action and policy of the Earl of Stafford in the reign of Charles I. [See Trevelyan, *England Under the Stuarts*, pp. 155–57.]

22 See p. 56, n. 8.

23 I have found no source for this anachronism.

24 In Satire IV, Persius has Socrates address the multitude as *quirites*, the name for Roman citizens in their civil capacity.

25 Reminiscent of this is the quotation given by John Dennis from Father Dominique Bouhours (1628–1702), Jesuit grammarian and critic, who said of wit, *C'est un solide qui brille*: " 'Tis a shining Solid, like a Diamond, which the more solid it is, is always the more glittering; and derives its height of Lustre from its perfect Solidity.' " [Edward N. Hooker, ed., *The Critical Works of John Dennis* (Baltimore, 1939–43), I, 405.]

up in Tobacco-Shops, you may say, in defiance of the Proverb, *that the weakest does not always go to the Wall*; for 'tis well known the Lines are strong[26] enough, and in that Sense may justly take the Wall of any, that have been written in our Language. He seldom makes a Conscience of his Rhimes; but will often take the Liberty to make *preach* rhime with *Cheat*, *Vote* with *Rogue*, and *Committee-Man* with *Hang*.

He'll make one Word of as many Joints, as the Tin-Pudding,[27] that a Jugler pulls out of his Throat, and chops in again—What think you of *glud-fum-flam-hasta-minantes*?[28] Some of the old *Latin* poets bragged, that their Verses were tougher than Brass,[29] and harder than Marble; what would they have done, if they had seen these? Verily they would have had more reason to wish themselves an hundred Throats, than they then had, to pronounce them.

There are some, that drive a Trade in writing in praise of other Writers, (like Rooks, that bet on Gamesters Hands) not at all to celebrate the learned Author's Merits, as they would shew, but their own Wits, of which he is but the Subject. The Letchery of this Vanity has spawned more Writers than the *civil Law*: For those, whose Modesty must not endure to hear their own praises spoken, may yet publish of themselves the most notorious Vapours imaginable. For if the Privilege of Love be allowed—*Dicere quae puduit, scribere jussit Amor*,[30] why should it not be so in Self-Love too? For if it be Wisdom to conceal our Imperfections, what is it to discover our Virtues? It is not like, that *Nature* gave Men great Parts upon such Terms, as the

---

[26] Strong lines: in essence "strong lines" belong to what we have come to know as metaphysical poetry, though not exclusively. The term indicated obscurity, compression, or extravagance. [See George Williamson, "Strong Lines," *English Studies*, XVIII (1936), 152–59.]

[27] Obviously some instrument used to show the ability of the juggler to perform as does a sword swallower.

[28] *Glad(ius)-fum(us)-flam(ma)-hasta-minantes*: sword-smoke-flames-spear-threatening.

[29] Thyer points to Horace:
        Exigi monumentum aere perennius
        regalique situ pyramidum altius. . . .
("I have finished a monument more lasting than bronze / and loftier than the Pyramids' royal pile. . . ." [*Odes*, III. xxx. 1–2, in Horace, *The Odes and Epodes*, trans. C. E. Bennett (Cambridge, Mass., and London, 1934).]

[30] "With me, what modesty forbade to say, love has commanded me to write." [Ovid, *Heroides*, in *Heroides and Amores*, trans. Grant Shaverman (London and New York, 1914), IV. 10.]

Fairies use to give Money, to pinch and leave them[31] if they speak of it. They say—*Praise is but the Shadow of Virtue*; and sure that Virtue is very foolish, that is afraid of its own Shadow.

When he writes *Anagrams*, he uses to lay the Outsides of his Verses even (like a Bricklayer) by a Line of Rhime and Acrostic, and fill the Middle with Rubbish—In this he imitates *Ben. Johnson*,[32] but in nothing else.

There was one, that lined a Hat-Case[33] with a Paper of *Benlowse's*[34] Poetry—*Prynne*[35] bought it by Chance, and put a new Demi-Castor[36] into it. The first Time he wore it he felt only a singing in his Head, which within two Days turned to a Vertigo—He was let Blood in the Ear by one of the State-Physicians, and recovered; but before he went abroad he writ a Poem of Rocks and Seas, in a Stile so proper and natural, that it was hard to determine, which was ruggeder.

There is no Feat of Activity, nor Gambol of Wit, that ever was performed by Man, from him that vaults on *Pegasus*, to him that tumbles through the Hoop of an Anagram, but *Benlows* has got the Mastery in it, whether it be high-rope Wit, or low-rope Wit. He has all Sorts of *Echoes, Rebus's, Chronograms*, &c. besides *Carwitchets, Clenches*,[37] and *Quibbles*—As for *Altars* and *Pyramids* in

---

[31] Fairy money: found money, said to be placed by a good fairy at the spot where it was picked up. Fairy money is liable to be transformed into leaves; thus Butler makes a pun on "leave."

[32] Thyer reminds the reader that Ben Jonson "was intended for" a bricklayer and did for a time work as one.

[33] Hat-box. [*O.E.D.*]

[34] Edward Benlowes (1602-76), best known for his metaphysical religious poem *Theophila* (1652). He has been termed by Douglas Bush (*English Literature in the Earlier Seventeenth Century*) as "the Cleveland—or the Urquhart— of 'divine and Christian Poesie.' " He is known also as a borrower of phrases and lines, with little or no change, from other writers.

In his introduction to Benlowes in Volume I of *Minor Poets of the Caroline Period* (Oxford, 1905) George Saintsbury refers frequently to Butler's Character of A Small Poet.

Benlowes' reputation had so faded by the middle of the eighteenth century that Robert Thyer had not heard of him. He suggests that the name *Benlowes* "is a cant word for some one that he [Butler] did not choose to name" and then proceeds to make a case for the person's being John Denham!

[35] William Prynne (1600-1669), Puritan pamphleteer and author of *Histrio-mastix*, a large work written in opposition to the drama.

[36] A hat made of beaver's and other fur. [*O.E.D.*]

[37] Carwitchets (also, carwickets, carwhitchets): jests; puns, quibbles, conundrums.

Clenches: plays upon words.

Poetry, he has out-done all Men that Way; for he has made a *Gridiron*, and a *Frying-Pan* in Verse,[38] that, beside the Likeness in Shape, the very Tone and Sound of the Words did perfectly represent the Noise, that is made by those Utensils, such as the old Poet called *sartago loquendi*.[39] When he was a Captain, he made all the Furniture of his Horse, from the Bit to the Crupper, in beaten Poetry, every Verse being fitted to the Proportion of the Thing, with a moral Allusion of the Sense to the Thing; as the *Bridle of Moderation, the Saddle of Content*, and *the Crupper of Constancy*; so that the same Thing was both Epigram and Emblem, even as a Mule is both Horse and Ass.

Some Critics are of Opinion, that Poets ought to apply themselves to the Imitation of *Nature*,[40] and make a Conscience of digressing from her; but he is none of these. The antient Magicians could charm down the Moon, and force Rivers back to their Springs by the Power of Poetry only;[41] and the Moderns will undertake to turn the Inside of the Earth outward (like a Jugler's Pocket) and shake the *Chaos*[42] out of it, make *Nature* shew Tricks like an Ape, and the Stars run on Errands; but still it is by dint of Poetry. And if Poets can do such noble Feats, they were unwise to descend to mean and vulgar: For where the rarest and most common Things are of a Price (as they

---

[38] Poems in typographical shapes are found from the sixteenth century in English and are discussed in Puttenham's *Art of English Poesie* (1589). See Margaret Church, "The First English Pattern Poems," *PMLA*, LXI (1946), 636–50. See especially Addison's essays on True and False Wit in *Spectator* Papers 58–63.

[39] Jargon, of obsolete and modern words.

"*Sartago* literally signifies a frying-pan; and the poet, perhaps, calls the mixture or jargon of old words and new, *sartago loquendi*, in allusion to the mixture of ingredients of which they made their fried cakes, as bran, fat, honey, seeds, cheese, and the like." See Persius, *Satires* I. 80 and note to that line in *Juvenal and Persius*, trans. M. Madan (London, 1829).

[40] Although *nature* is a word with many different meanings and shades of meaning, to the contemporaries of Butler and the following age the term suggested the fundamental qualities in man and the ideal qualities in works of art best represented in the great compositions of the ancients; hence "truth," especially general truth. See Pope, *An Essay on Criticism* (1711).

[41] Orpheus, mythical poet of Thrace, who, having been presented with a lyre by Apollo, charmed all animate and inanimate things with it, even turning back a river.

[42] The original unordered matter of the universe, here conceived of as remaining as the core of the earth.

are all one to Poets) it argues Disease in Judgment not to chuse the most curious. Hence some infer, that the Account they give of things deserves no Regard, because they never received any Thing, as they find it, into their Compositions, unless it agree both with the Measure of their own Fancies, and the Measure of their Lines, which can very seldom happen: And therefore when they give a Character of any Thing or Person, it does commonly bear no more Proportion to the Subject, than the Fishes and Ships in a Map do to the Scale. But let such know, that Poets, as well as Kings, ought rather to consider what is fit for them to give, than others to receive; that they are fain to have regard to the Exchange of Language, and write high or low, according as that runs: For in this Age, when the smallest Poet seldom goes below more the most,[43] it were a Shame for a greater and more noble Poet not to out-throw that cut a Bar.

There was a *Tobacco-Man*, that wrapped *Spanish* Tobacco in a Paper of Verses, which *Benlows* had written against the Pope,[44] which by a natural Antipathy, that his Wit has to any Thing that's Catholic, spoiled the Tobacco; for it presently turned Mundungus.[45] This Author will take an *English* Word, and, like the *Frenchman*, that swallowed Water and spit it out Wine,[46] with a little Heaving and Straining would turn it immediately into *Latin*, as *plunderat ille Domos*—Mille *Hocopokiana*,[47] and a thousand such.

There was a young Practitioner in Poetry, that found there was no good to be done without a Mistress: For he, that writes of Love before he hath tried it, doth but travel by the Map; and he, that makes Love without a Dame, does like a Gamester, that plays for Nothing. He thought it convenient therefore, first to furnish himself with a Name for his Mistress beforehand, that he might not be to seek, when his Merit or good Fortune should bestow her upon him: for every Poet is his mistresse's Godfather, and gives her a new Name,

---

43 "There is an apparent Defect or Error in these words. . . ." [Thyer's note.]
44 *Papa Perstrictus* (1645), which illustrates Benlowes' "forcefulness in juggling with words." [See H. Jenkins, *Edward Benlowes* (Cambridge, Mass., 1952), pp. 151–53.] Although brought up a Roman Catholic or converted to Catholicism, Benlowes became, in his mature years, a "zealous Protestant" who was antagonistic toward Catholics and the beliefs of Catholics and openly expressed his views. [*Dictionary of National Biography*; hereafter abbreviated *D.N.B.*]
45 Offensive-smelling tobacco.
46 Evidently proverbial.
47 "Assailing the dwellings—a thousand hocus pocuses [incantations]."

like a Nun that takes Orders. He was very curious to fit himself with a handsome Word of a tunable Sound; but could light upon none, that some Poet or other had not made use of before. He was therefore forced to fall to coining, and was several Months before he could light on one, that pleased him perfectly. But after he had overcome that Difficulty, he found a greater remaining, to get a Lady to own him. He accosted some of all Sorts, and gave them to understand, both in Prose and Verse, how incomparably happy it was in his Power to make his Mistress, but could never convert any of them. At length he was fain to make his Landress supply that Place as a Proxy, until his good Fortune, or somebody of better Quality would be more kind to him, which after a while he neither hoped nor cared for; for how mean soever her Condition was before, when he had once pretended to her, she was sure to be a Nymph and a Goddess. For what greater Honour can a Woman be capable of, than to be translated into precious Stones and Stars? No Herald in the World can go higher. Besides he found no Man can use that Freedom of Hyperbole in the Character of a Person commonly known (as great Ladies are) which we can in describing one so obscure and unknown, that nobody can disprove him. For he, that writes but one Sonnet upon any of the public Persons, shall be sure to have his Reader at every third Word cry out—What an Ass is this to call *Spanish paper and Ceruse*[48] *Lilies and Roses*, or *claps Influences*—To say, *the Graces are her waiting Women*, when they are known to be no better than her Bawdes—that *Day breaks from her Eyes*, when she looks asquint—Or that *her Breath perfumes the Arabian Winds*, when she puffs Tobacco?

It is no mean Art to improve a Language, and find out Words, that are not only removed from common use, but rich in Consonants, the Nerves and Sinews of Speech, to raise a soft and feeble Language like ours to the Pitch of *High-Dutch*, as he did, that writ

Arts rattling Foreskins shrilling Bagpipes quell.[49]

This is not only the most elegant, but most politic Way of Writing, that a Poet can use; for I know no Defence like it to preserve a Poem from the Torture of those that lisp and stammer. He that wants Teeth may as well venture upon a Piece of tough horny Brawn as such a Line, for he will look like an Ass eating Thistles.

He never begins a Work without an Invocation of his *Muse*; for

---

[48] Cosmetics, the former a fine rouge, the latter originally made of white lead.
[49] Thyer notes, "This, if I mistake not, is a Line of *Howard's* in his *British Princes.*" But I have not found the line in that poem or elsewhere.

it is not fit that she should appear in public, to shew her Skill before she is entreated, as Gentlewomen do not use to sing, until they are applied to, and often desired.

I shall not need to say any Thing of the Excellence of Poetry, since it has been already performed by many excellent Persons, among whom some have lately undertaken to prove, that the civil Government cannot possibly subsist without it,[50] which, for my Part, I believe to be true in a poetical Sense, and more probable to be received of it, than those strange Feats of building Walls, and making Trees dance, which Antiquity ascribes to Verse.[51] And though *Philosophers* are of a contrary Opinion, and will not allow Poets fit to live in a Commonwealth, their Partiality is plainer than their Reasons; for they have no other Way to pretend to this Prerogative themselves, as they do, but by removing Poets, whom they know to have a fairer Title; and this they do so unjustly, that *Plato*, who first banished Poets from his Republic,[a] forgot that that very Commonwealth was poetical. I shall say nothing to them, but only desire the World to consider, how happily it is like to be governed by those, that are at so perpetual a civil War among themselves, that if we should submit ourselves to their own Resolution of this Question, and be content to allow them only fit to rule if they could but conclude it so themselves, they would never agree upon it—Mean while there is no less Certainty and Agreement in Poetry than the Mathematics; for they all submit to the same Rules without Dispute or Controversy. But whosoever shall please to look into the Records of Antiquity shall find their Title so unquestioned, that the greatest Princes in the whole World have been glad to derive their Pedigrees, and their Power too, from Poets. *Alexander* the great had no wiser a Way to secure that Empire to himself by *Right*, which he had gotten by *Force*, then by declaring him-

---

[50] *Hudibras*, I. ii. 399–400:
> To government, which they suppose
> Can never be upheld in prose. . . .

"A ridicule on Sir William Davenant's preface to *Gondibert*, where he endeavours to show, that neither *Divines*, *leaders of Armies*, *Statesmen*, nor *Ministers of the law*, can uphold the Government, without the aid of poetry. . . ." [Zachary Grey, ed. (London, 1744), I, 134.]

[51] Amphion and Zethus, twin sons of Zeus, visited Thebes, where they constructed the lower city, Amphion's stones moving to the sounds of his lyre and falling into place. Orpheus (see p. 90, n. 41) made trees and rocks move from their places to follow the sounds of his music.

[a] banished Poets from his Republic] banished Poets his Republic

self the Son of Jupiter;[52] and who was *Jupiter* but the Son of a Poet?[53] So *Caesar* and all *Rome* was transported with Joy, when a Poet made *Jupiter* his Colleague in the Empire;[54] and when *Jupiter* governed, what did the Poets, that governed Jupiter?

A PHILOSOPHER

Seats himself as Spectator and Critic on the great Theater of the World, and gives Sentence[1] on the Plots, Language, and Action of whatsoever he sees represented, according to his own Fancy. He will pretend to know what is done behind the Scene, but so seldom is in the Right, that he discovers nothing more than his own Mistakes. When his Profession was in Credit in the World, and Money was to be gotten by it, it divided itself into Multitudes of Sects, that maintained themselves and their Opinions by fierce and hot Contests with one another; but since the Trade decayed and would not turn to Account, they all fell of themselves, and now the World is so unconcerned in their Controversies, that three Reformado Sects joined in one, like *Epicuro-Gassendo-Charltoniana*,[2] will not serve to maintain one Pedant. He makes his Hypotheses himself, as a Taylor does a Doublet without Measure, no Matter whether they fit *Nature*, he can make *Nature* fit them, and, whether they are too strait or wide, pinch or stuff out the Body accordingly. He judges of the Works of *Nature*, just as the Rabble do of State-Affairs: They see things done, and every Man according to his Capacity guesses at the Reasons of them, but knowing nothing of the Arcana or secret Movements of either, they seldom or never are in the Right; howsoever they please themselves, and some others, with their Fancies, and the further they are off Truth, the more confident they are they are near it; as those,

---

[52] Ammonian Jove (African Jove) in legend was said to have been, in the form of a serpent, the father of Alexander. To foster the belief in his divinity Alexander undertook, while he was in Egypt, a hazardous expedition to the temple of Jove Ammon in the desert.

[53] I.e., a creation of early Greek poets, a figment of their imaginations.

[54] I have found no helpful suggestion about this allusion.

[1] Passes judgment.

[2] "*Butler* in this sneeringly alludes to Dr. *Charlton*, who published a Book under the following Title, Physiologia Epicuro-Gassendo-Charltoniana. *Or a Fabrick of natural Science erected upon the most ancient Hypothesis of Atoms* Lond. 1653." [Thyer's note.]

that are out of their Way, believe, the further they have gone, they are nearer their Journey's End, when they are furthest of all from it. He is confident of immaterial Substances, and his Reasons are very pertinent, that is, *substantial* as he thinks, and *immaterial* as others do. Heretofore his Beard was the Badge of his Profession, and the Length of that in all his Polemics was ever accounted the Length of his Weapon; but when the Trade fell, that fell too. In *Lucius*'s time they were commonly called *Beard-Wearers*;[3] for all the Strength of their Wits lay in their Beards, as *Sampson*'s did in his Locks: But since the World began to see the Vanity of that *Hair-brained* Cheat, they left it off, to save their Credit.

A FANTASTIC

Is one that wears his Feather on the Inside of his Head.[1] His Brain is like Quicksilver, apt to receive any Impression, but retain none. His Mind is made of changeable Stuff, that alters Colour with every Motion towards the Light. He is a Cormorant, that has but one Gut, devours every Thing greedily, but it runs through him immediately. He does not know so much as what he would be, and yet would be every Thing he knows. He is like a Paper-Lanthorn, that turns with the Smoak of a Candle. He wears his Cloaths, as the antient Laws of the Land have provided, according to his Quality,[2] that he may be known what he is by them; and it is as easy to decipher him by his Habit as a *Pudding*.[3] He is rigg'd with Ribbon, and his Garni-

---

[3] In ancient Greece the wearing of long beards was associated with philosophers. For example in the Works of Lucian, satirist and Sophist of the second century, Hermotimus, on giving up the life of a philosopher, vows to do away with his "big, shaggy beard." Cf. also Plutarch: ". . . having a beard and wearing a coarse look does not make philosophers. . . ." ["Isis and Osiris," in *Plutarch's Moralia*, trans. Frank Cole Babbitt (London and New York, 1927–61), 352. c.]

[1] Recall the term *featherbrained*.

[2] "In keeping with the doctrine that everyone was born to a certain station ordained by heaven and should content himself with his lot, however humble, sumptuary laws . . . traditionally prescribed the degrees of luxury permissible to each class." But due to the increase of power and wealth in the middle class during the reign of Elizabeth, earlier regulations had to be relaxed. [Virginia A. LaMar, "English Dress in the Age of Shakespeare," in *Life and Letters in Tudor and Stuart England*, ed. Louis B. Wright and Virginia A. LaMar (Ithaca, New York, 1962), p. 385.]

[3] See p. 44, n. 44.

ture[4] is his Tackle; all the rest of him is Hull.[5] He is sure to be the earliest in the Fashion, and lays out for it like the first Pease and Cherries. He is as proud of leading a Fashion, as others are of a Faction, and glories as much to be in the Head of a Mode, as a Soldier does to be in the Head of an Army. He is admirably skilful in the Mathematics of Cloaths; and can tell, at the first View, whether they have the right Symmetry. He alters his Gate[6] with the Times, and has not a Motion of his Body, that (like a Dottrel)[7] he does not borrow from somebody else. He exercises his Limbs, like the Pike and Musket, and all his Postures are practised—Take him all together, and he is nothing but a Translation, Word for Word, out of *French*, an Image cast in Plaister of *Paris*, and a Puppet sent over for others to dress themselves by. He speaks *French*, as Pedants do *Latin*, to shew his Breeding; and most naturally, where he is least understood. All his non-Naturals, on which his Health and Diseases depend, are *stile novo*. *French* is his Holiday-Language, that he wears for his Pleasure and Ornament, and uses *English* only for his Business and necessary Occasions. He is like a *Scotchman*, though he is born a Subject of his own Nation, he carries a *French* faction within him.

He is never quiet, but sits as the Wind is said to do, when it is most in Motion. His Head is as full of Maggots as a Pastoral Poet's Flock. He was begotten, like one of Pliny's Portuguese Horses,[8] by the Wind—The Truth is he ought not to have been reared; for being calved in the Increase of the Moon, his Head is troubled with a——.[a]/[9]

A MELANCHOLY MAN

Is one, that keeps the worst Company in the World, that is, his own; and tho' he be always falling out and quarrelling with him-

---

[4] Trimming.

[5] A mere shell.

[6] Gait; way, manner, or method of doing or behaving. [*O.E.D.*]

[7] A silly person.

[8] "It is known that in Lusitania in the neighborhood of the town of Lisbon and the river Togus mares when a west wind is blowing stand facing towards it and conceive the breath of life and that this produces a foal, and this is the way to breed a very swift colt, but it does not live more than three years." [Pliny, *Natural History*, trans. Rackham, VIII. lxvii. 166.]

[a] "N. B. The last Word not legible." [Thyer's note.]

[9] [Mola]? See p. 275 and p. 302.

self, yet he has not power to endure any other Conversation. His Head is haunted, like a House, with evil Spirits and Apparitions, that terrify and fright him out of himself, till he stands empty and forsaken. His Sleeps and his Wakings are so much the same, that he knows not how to distinguish them, and many times when he dreams, he believes he is broad awake and sees Visions. The Fumes and Vapours that rise from his Spleen[1] and Hypocondries have so smutched and sullied his Brain (like a Room that smoaks) that his Understanding is blear-ey'd, and has no right Perception of any Thing. His Soul lives in his Body, like a Mole in the Earth, that labours in the Dark, and casts up Doubts and Scruples of his own Imaginations, to make that rugged and uneasy, that was plain and open before. His Brain is so cracked, that he fancies himself to be Glass, and is afraid that every Thing he comes near should break him in Pieces. Whatsoever makes an Impression in his Imagination works it self in like a Screw, and the more he turns and winds it, the deeper it sticks, till it is never to be got out again. The Temper of his Brain being earthy, cold, and dry,[2] is apt to breed Worms, that sink so deep into it, no Medicine in Art or Nature is able to reach them. He leads his Life, as one leads a Dog in a Slip that will not follow, but is dragged along until he is almost hanged, as he has it often under Consideration to treat himself in convenient Time and Place, if he can but catch himself alone. After a long and mortal Feud between his inward and his outward Man, they at length agree to meet without Seconds, and decide the Quarrel, in which the one drops, and the other slinks out of the Way, and makes his Escape into some foreign World, from whence it is never after heard of. He converses with nothing so much as his own Imagination, which being apt to misrepresent Things to him, makes him believe, that it is something else than it is, and that he holds Intelligence with Spirits, that reveal whatsoever he fancies to him, as the antient rude People, that first heard their own Voices repeated by Echoes in the Woods, concluded it must proceed from some invisible Inhabitants of those solitary Places, which they after believed to be Gods, and called them *Sylvans*, *Fauns*, and *Dryads*. He makes the Infirmity of his Temper pass for Revelations, as *Mahomet* did by his falling

---

[1] See p. 85, n. 11.

[2] In the set of correspondences that made up the contemporary "world picture" the counterparts to *Melancholy* were the element *Earth* and the qualities *cold* and *dry*.

Sickness,[3] and inspires himself with the Wind of his own Hypocondries. He laments, like *Heraclitus*[4] the Maudlin Philosopher, at other Men's Mirth, and takes Pleasure in nothing but his own un-sober Sadness. His Mind is full of Thoughts, but they are all empty, like a Nest of Boxes. He sleeps little, but dreams much, and soundest when he is waking. He sees Visions further off than a second-sighted Man in *Scotland*, and dreams upon a hard Point with admirable Judgment. He is just so much worse than a Madman, as he is below him in Degree of Frenzy; for among Madmen the most mad govern all the rest, and receive a natural Obedience from their Inferiors.

AN HARANGUER

Is one, that is so delighted with the sweet Sound of his own Tongue, that *William Prynne*[1] will sooner lend an Ear, than he, to any Thing else. His Measure of Talk is till his Wind is spent; and then he is not silenced, but becalmed. His Ears have catched the Itch of his Tongue, and though he scratch them, like a Beast with his Hoof, he finds a Pleasure in it. A *silenced Minister*,[2] has more Mercy on the Government in a secure Conventicle, than he has on the Company, that he is in. He shakes a Man by the Ear, as a Dog does a Pig, and never looses his Hold, till he has tired himself, as well as his Patient. He does not talk to a Man, but attack him, and whomsoever he can get into his Hands he lays violent Language on. If he can he will run a Man up against a Wall, and hold him at a Bay by the Buttons, which

---

[3] Mahomet claimed to receive messages from the other world. When such revelations came in public, he, in a way common to many prophets, would fall into a frenzied state. There is some reason to believe that Mahomet had epileptic fits, and what came with the fits he may have adapted for effect on other occasions. [D. S. Margoliouth, *Mohammed and the Rise of Islam* (New York, 1905), pp. 85–86.] Thomas Heywood in *Hierarchie of the Blessed Angels* (1635), p. 320, makes reference to the falling sickness of Mahomet, whom he considered an impostor.

[4] Because he saw life and the external world as constantly changing and fleeting, Heraclitus of Ephesus became known as the "weeping philosopher." His major work is *Concerning Nature* (c. 500 B.C.).

[1] See p. 89, n. 35. Prynne, accused of making disparaging remarks about Charles I and the queen, was sent to prison for life by the Court of the Star Chamber in 1634, fined £5,000, and lost both ears in the pillory. Later he was fined again and deprived of the remaining portion of his ears for violent attacks on the Bishops. [Trevelyan, *England Under the Stuarts*, p. 149.]

[2] See p. 59, n. 24.

he handles as bad as he does his Person, or the Business he treats upon. When he finds him begin to sink, he holds him by the Cloaths, and feels him as a Butcher does a Calf, before he kills him. He is a walking Pillory, and crucifies more Ears[3] than a dozen standing ones. He will hold any Argument rather than his Tongue, and maintain both sides at his own Charge; for he will tell you what you will say, though, perhaps, he does not intend to give you leave. He lugs Men by the Ears, as they correct Children in *Scotland*, and will make them tingle, while he talks with them, as some say they will do, when a Man is talked of in his Absence. When he talks to a Man, he comes up close to him, and like an old Soldier lets fly in his Face, or claps the Bore of his Pistol to his Ear, and whispers aloud, that he may be sure not to miss his Mark. His Tongue is always in Motion, tho' very seldom to the Purpose, like a Barber's Scissars, which are always snipping, as well when they do not cut, as when they do. His Tongue is like a Bagpipe Drone, that has no Stop, but makes a continual ugly Noise, as long as he can squeeze any Wind out of himself. He never leaves a Man until he has run him down, and then he winds a Death over him. A Sow-Gelder's Horn is not so terrible to Dogs and Cats, as he is to all that know him. His Way of Argument is to talk all, and hear no Contradition. First he gives his Antagonist the Length of his Wind, and then, let him make his Approaches if he can, he is sure to be beforehand with him. Of all dissolute Diseases the Running of the Tongue is the worst, and the hardest to be cured. If he happen at any time to be at a Stand, and any man else begins to speak, he presently drowns him with his Noise, as a Water-Dog makes a Duck dive: for when you think he has done he falls on, and lets fly again, like a Gun, that will discharge nine Times with one Loading. He is a Rattlesnake, that with his Noise gives Men warning to avoid him, otherwise he will make them wish they had. He is, like a Bell, good for nothing but to make a Noise. He is like common Fame,[4] that speaks most and knows least, Lord *Brooks*,[5] or a Wildgoose always cackling when he is upon

---

[3] Punishment by standing in the pillory could be accompanied by whipping and sometimes by the nailing of one or both ears to the pillory or the cutting off of ears. [See Chamberlayne, *Angliae Notitia,* p. 46.]

[4] Public report or rumor.

[5] Probably Robert Greville, second Lord Brooke (1609–43), parliamentary general, who supported the impeachment of Laud and Strafford and is noted by Clarendon in 1641 as the only "positive enemy" to the whole establishment of church and state besides Lord Saye and Sele in the House of Lords. [*D.N.B.*]

William Haller says that "Brooke writes the grave, elaborate style of a

the Wing. His Tongue is like any Kind of Carriage, the less Weight it bears, the faster and easier it goes. He is so full of Words, that they run over, and are thrown away to no Purpose; and so empty of Things, or Sense, that his Dryness has made his Leaks so wide, whatsoever is put in him runs out immediately. He is so long in delivering himself, that those that hear him desire to be delivered too, or dispatched out of their Pain. He makes his Discourse the longer with often repeating *to be short*, and talks much of *in fine*, but never means to come near it.

A POPISH PRIEST

Is one that takes the same Course, that the *Devil* did in Paradise, he begins with the Woman. He despises all other *Fanatics* as Upstarts, and values himself upon his Antiquity. He is a Man-Midwife to the Soul, and is all his Life-time in this World deluding it to the next. *Christ* made St. *Peter* a Fisher of Men; but he believes it better to be a Fisher of Women, and so becomes a Woman's Apostle. His Profession is to disguise himself, which he does in Sheep's-Cloathing, that is, a Lay Habit; but whether, as a Wolf, a Thief, or a Shepherd, is a great Question; only this is certain, that he had rather have one Sheep out of another Man's Fold, than two out of his own. He gathers his Church as *Fanatics* do, yet despises them for it, and keeps his Flock always in Hurdles, to be removed at his Pleasure; and though their Souls be rotten or scabby with Hypocrisy, the Fleece is sure to be sound and orthodox. He tars their Consciences with Confession and Penance, but always keeps the Wool, that he pulls from the Sore, to himself. He never makes a Proselyte, but he *converts* him to his very Shirt, and *turns* his Pockets into the Bargain; for he does nothing unless his Purse prove a good *Catholic*. He never gets within a Family, but he gets on the Top of it, and governs all down to the Bottom of the Cellar—He will not tolerate the Scullion unless he be orthodox, nor allow of the turning of the Spit, but *in ordine ad Spiritualia*.[1] His *Dominion is not founded in*

---

seventeenth-century grandee, sowing his pages thick with quotations from the classics. . . . When moved to eloquence he is not always able to keep firm hold upon his sentence. But there is nothing archaic or confused in his thought." [*The Rise of Puritanism* (New York, 1957), Harper Torchbooks), p. 333.]

[1] "Toward spiritual matters."

Grace, but Sin; for he keeps his Subjects in perfect Awe by being acquainted with their most sacred Iniquities, as *Juvenal* said of the Greeks.

Scire volunt secreta domus, atque inde timeri.[2]

By this means he holds Intelligence with their own Consciences against themselves, and keeps their very Thoughts in Slavery; for Men commonly fear those that know any Evil of them, and out of Shame give Way to them. He is very cautious in venturing to attack any Man by Way of Conversion, whose Weakness he is not very well acquainted with, and like the Fox, weighs his Goose, before he will venture to carry him over a River.[3] He fights with the *Devil* at his own Weapons, and strives to get ground on him with Frauds and Lies—These he converts to pious Uses. He makes his Prayers (the proper Business of the Mind) a Kind of Manufacture, and vents them by Tale,[4] rather than Weight; and while he is busied in numbring them, forgets their Sense and Meaning. He sets them up as Men do their Games at *Picquet*,[5] for fear he should be misreckoned; but never minds whether he plays fair or not. He sells Indulgences, like *Lockier's* Pills,[6] with Directions how they are to be taken. He is but a Copyholder[7] of the *Catholic* Church, that claims by Custom. He believes the *Pope*'s Chain is fastened to the Gates of Heaven, like King *Harry*'s in the Privy-Gallery.[8]

---

[2] "*They wish to know the family secrets and thus make themselves feared.*" [Juvenal, *Satires*, III. 113, in *Juvenal and Persius*, trans. G. G. Ramsay (London and New York, 1918).] Spoken with reference to persons in Rome, who, introduced into the families as slaves and thus gaining possession of the family secrets, asked for money as blackmail.

[3] In a discussion of the inventiveness of foxes and other beasts Sir Kenelm Digby relates a tale of a fox who killed a goose on one side of a river and wished to swim to the other side to carry the goose to his den. He weighed the goose with a piece of wood; then he swam over with the wood. Thus predicting his success with the goose, he went back and got the bird itself. [*Of Bodies and of Man's Soul*, p. 390.]

[4] A count or enumeration. Cf. French *taille* or English *tally*.

[5] A card game played by two persons.

[6] Lionel Lockyer was famous in the reign of Charles II for his pill, which had a great reputation and vogue. He died April 26, 1672, but the pills were still being sold in the eighteenth century in St. Paul's Churchyard. [J. Granger, *A Biographical History of England* (London, 1769), Vol. II, Pt. II, pp. 323–24.]

[7] One who holds land by the right of being recorded as a holder in the court of the manor.

[8] I have found no definitive information on this point. Perhaps the reference is to a private gallery in a royal chapel.

A TRAVELLER

Is a Native of all Countries, and an Alien at Home. He flies from the Place where he was hatched, like a Wildgoose, and prefers all others before it. He has no Quarrel to it, but because he was born in it, and like a Bastard, he is ashamed of his Mother, because she is of him. He is a Merchant, that makes Voyages into foreign Nations, to drive a Trade in Wisdom and Politics, and it is not for his Credit to have it thought, he has made an ill Return, which must be, if he should allow of any of the Growth of his own Country. This makes him quack and blow up himself with Admiration of foreign Parts, and a generous Contempt of Home, that all Men may admire, at least, the means he has had of Improvement, and deplore their own Defects. His Observations are like a Sieve, that lets the finer Flour pass, and retains only the Bran of Things; for his whole Return of Wisdom proves to be but Affectation,[1] a perishable Commodity, which he will never be able to put off. He believes all Men's Wits are at a stand, that stay at Home, and only those advanced, that travel; as if Change of Pasture did make great Politicians, as well as fat Calves. He pities the little Knowledge of Truth which those have, that have not seen the World abroad, forgetting, that at the same time he tells us, how little Credit is to be given to his own Relations and those of others, that speak and write of their Travels. He has worn his own Language to Rags, and patched it up with Scraps and Ends of foreign —This serves him for Wit; for when he meets with any of his foreign Acquaintance, all they smatter passes for Wit, and they applaud one another accordingly. He believes this Raggedness of his Discourse a great Demonstration of the Improvement of his Knowledge; as *Inns-of-Court* Men[2] intimate their Proficiency in the Law by the Tatters of their Gowns. All the Wit he brought Home with him is like foreign Coin, of a baser Alloy than our own, and so will not pass here without great Loss. All noble Creatures, that are famous in any one Coun-

---

[1] Although travel was looked upon as a necessary part of a gentleman's education, a trip on the continent might have ill effects: from Italy notorious vices, from France exaggerated manners.

[2] Lawyers. The Inns of Court were four sets of buildings which legal societies owned. These societies had the right to admit men to practice at the bar. Each of the societies at Lincoln's Inn, the Inner Temple, the Middle Temple, and Gray's Inn were made up of benchers, barristers, and students.

try, degenerate by being transplanted; and those of mean Value only improve—If it hold with Men, he falls among the Number of the latter, and his Improvements are little to his Credit. All he can say for himself is, his Mind was sick of a Consumption, and change of Air has cured him: For all his other Improvements have only been to eat in[a] . . . . and talk with those he did not understand; to hold Intelligence with all Gazettes,[3] and from the Sight of Statesmen in the Street unriddle the Intrigues of all their Councils, to make a wondrous Progress into Knowledge by riding with a Messenger, and advance in Politics by mounting of a Mule, run through all Sorts of Learning in a Waggon, and sound all Depths of Arts in a Felucca, ride post[4] into the Secrets of all States, and grow acquainted with their close Designs in Inns and Hostleries; for certainly there is great Virtue in Highways and Hedges to make an able Man, and a good Prospect cannot but let him see far into Things.

A CATHOLIC

Says his Prayers often, but never prays, and worships the Cross more than *Christ*. He prefers his Church merely for the Antiquity of it, and cares not how sound or rotten it be, so it be but old. He takes a liking to it as some do to old Cheese, only for the blue Rottenness of it. If he had lived in the primitive Times he had never been a *Christian*; for the Antiquity of the *Pagan* and *Jewish* Religion would have had the same Power over him against the *Christian*, as the old *Roman* has against the modern Reformation. The weaker Vessel he is, the better and more zealous Member he always proves of his Church; for Religion, like Wine, is not so apt to leak in a leathern Boraccio[1] as a great Cask, and is better preserved in a small Bottle stopped with a light Cork, than a vessel of greater Capacity, where the Spirits being more and stronger are the more apt to fret.

---

[a] Ellipses appear here in Thyer's edition.

[3] News-sheets or periodicals giving accounts of current events; also, the official organ of any government. By 1665 there were, for example, in Great Britain three official Journals: the London *Gazette*, the Edinburgh *Gazette*, and the Belfast *Gazette*, appearing twice a week. They contained legal and governmental notices.

[4] To serve as courier of the king's packet as well as to transmit letters by means of horses stationed at intervals along a fixed route.

[1] A goatskin bag.

He allows of all holy Cheats, and is content to be deluded in a true, orthodox, and infallible Way. He believes the *Pope* to be infallible, because he has deceived all the World, but was never deceived himself, which was grown so notorious, that nothing less than an Article of Faith in the Church could make a Plaster big enough for the Sore. His Faith is too big for his Charity, and too unwieldy to work Miracles; but is able to believe more than all the Saints in Heaven ever made. He worships Saints in Effigie, as *Dutchmen* hang absent Malefactors;[2] and has so weak a Memory, that he is apt to forget his Patrons, unless their Pictures prevent him. He loves to see what he prays to, that he may not mistake one Saint for another; and his Beads and Crucifix are the Tools of his Devotion, without which it can do nothing. Nothing staggers his Faith of the *Pope*'s Infallibility so much, as that he did not make away the Scriptures, when they were in his Power, rather than those that believed in them, which he knows not how to understand to be no Error. The less he understands of his Religion, the more violent he is in it, which, being the perpetual Condition of all those that are deluded, is a great Argument that he is mistaken. His Religion is of no Force without Ceremonies, like a Loadstone that draws a greater Weight through a Piece of Iron, than when it is naked of it self. His Prayers are a kind of Crambe[3] that used to kill Schoolmasters; and he values them by Number, not Weight.[4]

A CURIOUS MAN[1]

Values things not by their Use or Worth, but Scarcity. He is very tender and scrupulous of his Humour, as *Fanatics* are of their Consciences, and both for the most part in Trifles. He cares not how

---

[2] I have no further information on this practice.

[3] A wearying repetition of words or ideas. Originally "cabbage" (Greek *krambe*), used by Juvenal (*Satires*, VII. 154) in the phrase *crambe repetita*, cabbage repeated or served up again. [See Joseph T. Shipley, *Dictionary of World Literature*, revised edition (New York, 1953).]

[4] Cf. p. 101: "[a Popish Priest] makes his Prayers . . . a Kind of Manufacture, and vents them by Tale, rather than Weight. . . ."

[1] One who collects "curiosities." In *The London-Spy* Ned Ward makes reference to the various "curiosities" of the Old Sophister in a coffee-house, such as his nail from the ark, Diogenes' lamp, a toothpick of Epicurus, etc. [Casanova Society edition (London, 1924), Pt. I, pp. 13–14.]

unuseful any Thing be, so it be but unusual and rare. He collects all the Curiosities he can light upon in Art or Nature, not to inform his own Judgment, but to catch the Admiration of others, which he believes he has a Right to, because the Rarities are his own. That which other Men neglect he believes they oversee, and stores up Trifles as rare Discoveries, at least of his own Wit and Sagacity. He admires subtleties above all Things, because the more subtle they are, the nearer they are to nothing; and values no Art but that which is spun so thin, that it is of no Use at all. He had rather have an iron Chain hung about the Neck of a Flea, than an Alderman's of Gold,[2] and *Homer*'s Iliads in a Nutshel[3] than *Alexander*'s Cabinet.[4] He had rather have the twelve Apostles on a Cherry-Stone, than those on St. *Peter*'s Portico,[5] and would willingly sell *Christ* again for that numerical Piece of Coin, that *Judas* took for him. His perpetual Dotage upon Curiosities at length renders him one of them, and he shews himself as none of the meanest of his Rarities. He so much affects Singularity, that rather than follow the Fashion, that is used by the rest of the World, he will wear dissenting Cloaths with odd fantastic Devices to distinguish himself from others, like Marks set upon Cattle. He cares not what Pains he throws away upon the meanest Trifle, so it be but strange, while some pity, and others laugh at his illemployed Industry. He is one of those, that valued *Epictetus*'s Lamp[6]

---

[2] I.e., the chain of office. Such chains were "flat and broad in the link, and at times very highly decorated." [Percy Macquoid, "Costume," in *Shakespeare's England: An Account of the Life and Manners of his Age* (Oxford, 1917), II, 115.]

[3] Pliny, *Natural History*, trans. Rackham, VII, xxi. 85: "Cicero records that a parchment copy of Homer's poem *The Iliad* was enclosed in a nutshell." Cf. also Rabelais, *Pantagruel*, V. xx.

[4] Alexander the Great loved learning and loved reading. Believing the *Iliad* to be "a viaticum" of the military art, he carried with him always the "Iliad of the Casket," the name of which resulted from the following episode: A small coffer was brought to Alexander as the most precious item among the effects of Darius. Unable to gather any consensus on what to put in it, Alexander himself decided to place the *Iliad* there. [See Plutarch, "Alexander," in *Plutarch's Lives*, trans. Bernadotte Perrin (London and New York, 1914–26), VIII and XXVI.]

[5] Surmounting the facade of St. Peter's church are statues of Christ and each of the apostles.

[6] The earthen lamp of Epictetus was sold sometime after his death for 3,000 drachmas. [John Lemprière, *A Classical Dictionary* (London, 1801).] Epictetus, Stoic philosopher (c. A.D. 60–140), actually left no writing. His short work *Enchiridion* was compiled from his discourses by his pupil Arrian.

above the excellent Book he writ by it. If he be a Bookman he spends all his Time and Study upon Things that are never to be known. The *Philosopher's Stone* and *universal Medicine* cannot possibly miss him, though he is sure to do them. He is wonderfully taken with abstruse Knowledge, and had rather hand to Truth with a Pair of Tongs wrapt up in Mysteries and Hieroglyphics, than touch it with his Hands, or see it plainly demonstrated to his Senses.

A RANTER[1]

Is a *Fanatic* Hector,[2] that has found out by a very strange Way of new Light, how to transform all the *Devils* into *Angels of Light*; for he believes all Religion consists in Looseness, and that Sin and Vice is *the whole Duty of Man*.[3] He puts off the *old Man*, but puts it on again upon the *new one*, and makes his *Pagan* Vices serve to preserve his *Christian* Virtues from wearing out; for if he should use his Piety and Devotion always it would hold out but a little while. He is loth that Iniquity and Vice should be thrown away, as long as there may be good Use of it; for if that, which is wickedly gotten, may be disposed to pious Uses, why should not Wickedness itself as well? He believes himself Shot-free against all the Attempts of the *Devil*, the *World*, and the *Flesh*,[4] and therefore is not afraid to attack them in their own Quarters, and encounter them at their own Weapons. For as strong Bodies may freely venture to do and suffer that, without any Hurt to themselves, which would destroy those that are feeble: So a Saint, that is strong in Grace, may boldly engage himself in those great Sins and Iniquities, that would easily damn a weak

---

[1] The Ranters were a wild sect which defamed and denied the church, the Scriptures, worship, and ordinances. Their doctrine of libertinism was bound up in their claim that God cared only for the heart, not at all for the actions of the outer man. [See Masson, *Life of Milton*, V, 17–18.]

[2] Hector: a member of a group of dissolute young men in the second half of the seventeenth century who "swagger[ed] by night about [London], breaking windows, upsetting sedans, beating quiet men, and offering rude caresses to pretty women." [Macaulay, *History of England*, I, 396.] See the Character of An Hector.

[3] Perhaps an allusion to *The Whole Duty of Man*, now generally ascribed to Richard Allestree, a devotional book published in 1658 anonymously, in which the duties of man with respect to God and his fellow man are fully analyzed and discussed. It remained very popular for over a century.

[4] See *The Litany* (Book of Common Prayer).

Brother, and yet come off never the worse. He believes Deeds of Darkness to be only those Sins that are committed in private, not those that are acted openly and owned. He is but an *Hypocrite* turned the wrong Side outward; for, as the one wears his Vices within, and the other without, so when they are counter-changed the *Ranter* becomes an *Hypocrite*, and the *Hypocrite* an able *Ranter*. His Church is the *Devil's* Chappel; for it agrees exactly both in Doctrine and Discipline with the best reformed Baudy-Houses. He is a Monster produced by the Madness of this latter Age; but if it had been his Fate to have been whelped in old *Rome* he had past for a Prodigy,[5] and been received among raining of Stones and the speaking of Bulls, and would have put a stop to all public Affairs, until he had been expiated. *Nero* cloathed *Christians* in the Skins of wild Beasts;[6] but he wraps wild Beasts in the Skins of *Christians*.

A CORRUPT JUDGE

Passes Judgment as a Gamester does false Dice. The first Thing he takes is his Oath and his Commission, and afterwards the strongest Side and Bribes. He gives Judgment, as the Council at the Bar are said to give Advice, when they are paid for it. He wraps himself warm in Furs,[1] that the cold Air may not strike his Conscience inward. He is never an upright Judge, but when he is weary of sitting and stands for his Ease. All the Use he makes of his Oath is to oppose it against his Prince, for whose Service he first took it, and to bind him with that, which he first pretended to bind himself with; as if the King by imparting a little of his Power to him gave him a Title to all the rest, like those who holding a little Land in *Capite*[2] render all the rest liable to the same Tenure. As for that which concerns the People, he takes his Liberty to do what he pleases; this he maintains with Canting, of which himself being the only Judge, he can give it what arbitrary Interpretation he pleases; yet is a great

---

[5] See p. 51, n. 28.

[6] Christians were covered with the skins of beasts and torn by dogs, which caused the death of many persons. [See Tacitus, *Annals*, XV. xliv, in *The Histories*, trans. Clifford H. Moore; *The Annals*, trans. John Jackson (Cambridge, Mass., and London, 1937.]

[1] Gowns of various kinds were worn by members of the learned professions and by officials.

[2] Held directly from the king or crown; a kind of feudal tenure.

Enemy to arbitrary Power, because he would have no Body use it but himself. If he have Hopes of Preferment he makes all the Law run on the King's Side; if not, it always takes part against him; for as he was bred to make any Thing right or wrong between Man and Man, so he can do between the King and his Subjects. He calls himself *Capitalis*,[3] &c. which Word he never uses but to Crimes of the highest Nature. He usurps unsufferable Tyranny over Words; for when he has enslaved and debased them from their original Sense, he makes them serve against themselves to support him, and their own Abuse. He is as stiff to Delinquents, and makes as harsh a Noise as a new Cart-wheel, until he is greased,[4] and then he turns about as easily. He calls all necessary and unavoidable Proceedings of State, without the punctual Formality of Law, arbitrary and illegal, but never considers, that his own Interpretations of Law are more arbitrary, and, when he pleases, illegal. He cannot be denied to be a very impartial Judge; for right or wrong are all one to him. He takes Bribes, as pious Men give Alms, with so much Caution, that his right Hand never knows what his left receives.

AN AMORIST

Is an Artificer, or Maker of Love, a sworn Servant to all Ladies, like an Officer in a Corporation. Though no one in particular will own any Title to him, yet he never fails, upon all Occasions, to offer his Services, and they as seldom to turn it back again untouched. He commits nothing with them, but himself to their good Graces; and they recommend him back again to his own, where he finds so kind a Reception, that he wonders how he does fail of it every where else. His Passion is as easily set on Fire as a Fart, and as soon out again. He is charged and primed with Love-Powder like a Gun, and the least Sparkle of an Eye gives Fire to him, and off he goes, but seldom, or never, hits the Mark. He has common Places and Precedents of Repartees and Letters for all Occasions; and falls as readily into his Method of making love, as a Parson does into his Form of Matrimony. He converses, as Angels are said to do, by Intuition,[1] and expresses

---

[3] First, chief, distinguished. As a legal term: that which imperils a man's life.
[4] Recall the expression "to grease a palm."

[1] This reference is to the scholastic distinction between the discursive or deliberative reason of man and angelic intuition. See Aquinas, *Summa Theologica*, Pt. I. lxxxv. i, and Richard Hooker, *Of the Laws of Ecclesiastical Polity*, I. vi.

himself by Sighs most significantly. He follows his Visits, as Men do their Business, and is very industrious in waiting on the Ladies, where his Affairs lie; among which those of greatest Concernment are *Questions and Commands, Purposes*,[2] and other such received Forms of Wit and Conversation; in which he is so deeply studied, that in all Questions and Doubts, that arise, he is appealed to, and very learnedly declares, which was the most true and primitive Way of proceeding in the purest Times. For these Virtues he never fails of his Summons to all Balls, where he manages the Country-Dances with singular Judgment, and is frequently an Assistant at L'hombre;[3] and these are all the Uses they make of his Parts, beside the Sport they give themselves in laughing at him, which he takes for singular Favours, and interprets to his own Advantage, though it never goes further; for all his Employments being public, he is never admitted to any private Services, and they despise him as not Woman's Meat: For he applies to too many to be trusted by any one; as Bastards by having many Fathers, have none at all. He goes often mounted in a Coach as a Convoy, to guard the Ladies, to take the Dust in *Hyde-Park*;[4] where by his prudent Management of the Glass Windows he secures them from Beggars, and returns fraught with China-Oranges[5] and Ballads. Thus he is but a Gentleman-Usher General, and his Business is to carry one Lady's Services to another, and bring back the others in Exchange.

AN ASTROLOGER

Is one that expounds upon the Planets, and teaches to construe the *Accidents* by the *due joining of Stars in Construction*.[1] He

---

[2] Parlor games.

[3] A card game played by three persons that was very popular in the seventeenth and eighteenth centuries. See especially *The Rape of the Lock* and, for the history and rules, Appendix C in the Twickenham Edition of Pope's *Rape of the Lock*, ed. Geoffrey Tillotson (London, 1940), pp. 361–68.

[4] The dust in Hyde Park was stirred up by the horses and carriages which followed the circular road when men and women of fashion in fine weather "took the air."

[5] The sweet orange was originally brought from China.

[1] "Astrology, which had a recondite jargon, was professionally divided into three branches, called, respectively, horary, judicial, and natural. The heavens were in each case examined by a different method and for a different purpose. By means of horary astrology questions about business of the moment were

talks with them by dumb Signs, and can tell what they mean by their twinckling, and squinting upon one another, as well as they themselves. He is a Spy upon the Stars, and can tell what they are doing, by the Company they keep, and the Houses[2] they frequent. They have no Power to do any Thing alone, until so many meet, as will make a *Quorum*. He is Clerk of the Committee to them, and draws up all their Orders, that concern either public or private Affairs. He keeps all their Accompts for them, and sums them up, not by *Debtor*, but *Creditor* alone, a more compendious Way. They do ill to make them have so much Authority over the Earth, which, perhaps, has as much as any one of them but the Sun, and as much Right to sit and vote in their Councils, as any other: But because there are but seven Electors of the *German* Empire, they will allow of no more to dispose of all other; and most foolishly and unnaturally depose their own Parent of its Inheritance; rather than acknowledge a Defect in their own Rules. These Rules are all they have to shew for their Title; and yet not one of them can tell whether those they had them from came honestly by them. *Virgil's* Description of *Fame*, that reaches from Earth to the Stars, *tam ficti pravique tenax*,[3] to carry Lies and Knavery, will serve Astrologers without any sensible Variation. He is a Fortune-Seller, a Retailer of Destiny, and petty Chapman to the Planets. He casts Nativities[4] as Gamesters do false Dice, and by slurring and palming *sextile, quartile*, and *trine*,[5] like *size, quater, trois*,[6] can throw what chance he pleases. He sets a Figure, as Cheats do a Main at Hazard;[7] and Gulls throw away their Money at it. He fetches the Grounds of his Art so far off, as well from Reason, as the Stars,

---

answered; judicial astrology foretold human affairs; natural astrology, in which the horoscope was cast, disclosed the destiny of persons from the configuration of the planets at their birth." [E. B. Knobel, "The Sciences: Astronomy and Astrology," in *Shakespeare's England*, I, 456.]

[2] A "house" is one of the twelve divisions of the circle representing the zodiac. Here suggested also, an inn or tavern.

[3] "As tenacious of falsehood and wrong." [*Aeneid*, trans. Fairclough, IV. 188. For a description of Fame, or Rumor, see ll. 173–97.]

[4] Horoscopes. The casting of horoscopes by astrologers necessitated calculation of planetary positions, in this case (for a nativity) at the moment of birth.

[5] Terms in astrology to describe "aspects" of the planets when they are, respectively, sixty degrees, ninety degrees, and one hundred and twenty degrees apart.

[6] Dicing terms: *six, four, three*, respectively.

[7] Hazard: a very popular dice game, the *main* being the number called by the caster before the dice are thrown.

that, like a Traveller, he is allowed to lye by Authority.[8] And as Beggars, that have no Money themselves, believe all others have, and beg of those, that have as little as themselves: So the ignorant Rabble believe in him, though he has no more Reason for what he professes, than they.

A LAWYER

Is a Retailer of Justice, that uses false Lights, false Weights, and false Measures—He measures Right and Wrong by his retaining Fee, and, like a *French* Duelist, engages on that Side that first bespeaks him, tho' it be against his own Brother, not because it is right, but merely upon a Punctilio of Profit, which is better than Honour to him, because Riches will buy Nobility, and Nobility nothing, as having no intrinsic Value. He sells his Opinion, and engages to maintain the Title against all that claim under him, but no further. He puts it off upon his Word, which he believes himself not bound to make good, because when he has parted with his Right to it, it is no longer his. He keeps no Justice for his own Use, as being a Commodity of his own Growth, which he never buys, but only sells to others: and as no Man goes worse shod than the Shoemaker; so no Man is more out of Justice than he that gets his Living by it. He draws Bills, as Children do Lots at a Lottery, and is paid as much for Blanks as Prizes. He undoes a Man with the same Privilege as a Doctor kills him, and is paid as well for it, as if he preserved him, in which he is very impartial, but in nothing else. He believes it no Fault in himself to err in Judgment, because that part of the *Law* belongs to the Judge, and not to him. His best Opinions and his worst are all of a Price, like good Wine and bad in a Tavern, in which he does not deal so fairly as those, who, if they know what you are willing to bestow, can tell how to fit you accordingly. When his Law lies upon his Hands, he will afford a good Penyworth, and rather pettyfog[1] and turn common Barreter,[2] than be out of Employment. His opinion is one Thing while it is his own, and another when it is paid for; for

---

[8] Proverbial. A traveler may lie with authority (i.e., he has the privilege or leave to lie).

[1] Pettifog: get up [prepare] or conduct minor cases, especially by a lawyer of minor status who employs mean, caviling practices. [*O.E.D.*] See the Character of A Pettifogger.

[2] One who vexatiously raises, or incites to, litigation. [*O.E.D.*]

the Property being altered, the Case alters also. When his Council is not for his Client's Turn, he will never take it back again, though it be never the worse, nor allow him any Thing for it, yet will sell the same over and over again to as many as come to him for it. His Pride encreases with his Practice, and the fuller of Business he is, like a Sack, the Bigger he looks. He crouds to the Bar like a Pig through a Hedge; and his Gown is fortified with Flankers about the Shoulders, to guard his Ears from being galled with Elbows. He draws his Bills more extravagant and unconscionable than a Taylor; for if you cut off two thirds in the Beginning, Middle, or End, that which is left will be more reasonable and nearer to Sense than the whole, and yet he is paid for all: For when he draws up a Business, like a Captain that makes false Musters, he produces as many loose and idle Words as he can possibly come by, until he has received for them, and then turns them off, and retains only those that are to the Purpose—This he calls drawing of *Breviates.* All that appears of his Studies is in short Time converted into Waste-Paper, Taylor's Measures, and Heads for Children's Drums. He appears very violent against the other Side, and rails to please his Client, as they do Children, *give me a Blow and I'll strike him, ah naughty, &c.*—This makes him seem very zealous for the good of his Client, and, though the Cause go against him, he loses no Credit by it, especially if he fall foul on the Council of the other Side, which goes for no more among them than it does with those virtuous Persons, that quarrel and fight in the Streets, to pick the Pockets of those that look on. He hangs Men's Estates and Fortunes on the slightest Curiosities and feeblest Niceties imaginable, and undoes them like the Story of breaking a Horse's Back with a Feather, or sinking a Ship with a single Drop of Water; as if Right and Wrong were only notional,[3] and had no Relation at all to practice (which always requires more solid Foundations) or Reason and Truth did wholly consist in the right Spelling of Letters, when, as the subtler Things are, the nearer they are to nothing; so the subtler Words and Notions are, the nearer they are to Nonsense. He overruns *Latin* and *French* with greater Barbarism, than the *Goths* did *Italy* and *France,* and makes as mad a Confusion of Language by mixing both with English. Nor does he use *English* much better, for he clogs it so with Words, that the Sense becomes as thick as Puddle, and is utterly lost to those, that have not the Trick

---

[3] Abstract concepts.

of skipping over, where it is impertinent. He has but one Termination for all *Latin* Words, and that's a Dash.[4] He is very just to the first Syllables of Words, but always bobtails the last, in which the Sense most of all consists, like a Cheat, that does a Man all Right at the first, that he may put a Trick upon him in the End. He is an *Apprentice* to the Law without a Master, is his own Pupil, and has no Tutor but himself, that is a Fool. He will screw and wrest Law as unmercifully as a Tumbler does his Body, to lick up Money with his Tongue. He is a *Swiss*, that professes mercenary Arms,[5] will fight for him, that gives him best Pay, and, like an *Italian* Bravo,[6] will fall foul on any Man's Reputation, that he receives a retaining Fee against. If he could but maintain his Opinions as well as they do him, he were a very just and righteous Man; but when he has made his most of it, he leaves it, like his Client, to shift for itself. He fetches Money out of his Throat, like a Jugler: and as the Rabble in the Country value Gentlemen by their Housekeeping and their Eating; so is he supposed to have so much Law as he has kept Commons, and the abler to deal with Clients by how much the more he has devoured of *Inns o' Court*[7] Mutton; and it matters not, whether he keep his Study, so he has but kept Commons. He never ends a Suit, but prunes it, that it may grow the faster, and yield a greater Increase of Strife. The Wisdom of the Law is to admit of all the petty, mean, real Injustices in the World, to avoid imaginary possible great ones, that may perhaps fall out. His Client finds the Scripture fulfilled in him, that *it is better to part with a Coat too, than go to Law for a Cloke*;[8] for *as the best Laws are made of the worst Manners*, even so are the best Lawyers of the worst Men. He humms about *Westminster-Hall*,[9] and returns Home with his Pockets, like a Bee with his Thighs laden; and that which *Horace* says of an Ant, *Ore trahit quodcunque potest, atque addit acervo*,[10]

---

[4] I.e., he is unsure of inflectional endings.

[5] Swiss professional soldiers traditionally served in foreign armies for hire.

[6] Desperado or hired assassin.

[7] Cf. p. 102, n. 2.

[8] Matthew, V. 40: "And if any man will sue thee at the law, and take away thy coat, let him have *thy* cloke also."

[9] See p. 71, n. 5.

[10] *Satires*, I. l. 33.

> parvola, nam exemplo est, . . . sicuit magni formica laboris
> Ore trahit quodcunque potest atque addit acervo
> quem struit; haud ignara ac non incauta futuri.

("Even as the tiny, hardworking ant (for she is their model) drags all she can

is true of him; for he gathers all his Heap with the Labour of his Mouth, rather than his Brain and Hands. He values himself, as a Carman does his Horse, by the Money he gets, and looks down upon all that gain less as Scoundrels. The Law is like that double-formed ill-begotten Monster,[11] that was kept in an intricate Labyrinth, and fed with Men's Flesh; for it devours all that come within the Mazes of it, and have not a Clue to find the Way out again. He has as little Kindness for the Statute Law, as *Catholics* have for the Scripture, but adores the common Law as they do Tradition, and both for the very same Reason: For the statute Law being certain, written and designed to reform and prevent Corruptions and Abuses in the Affairs of the World (as the Scriptures are in Matters of Religion) he finds it many Times a great Obstruction to the Advantage and Profit of his Practice; whereas the common Law being unwritten, or written in an unknown Language, which very few understand but himself, is the more pliable and easy to serve all his Purposes, being utterly exposed to what Interpretation and Construction his Interest and Occasions shall at any Time incline him to give it; and differs only from arbitrary Power in this, that the one gives no Account of itself at all, and the other such a one as is perhaps worse than none, that is implicit, and not to be understood, or subject to what Construction he pleases to put upon it.

> Great Critics in a *noverint universi,*[12]
> *Know all Men by these Presents* how to curse ye;
> Pedants of *said and foresaid* and both *Frenches*
> Pedlars, and Pockie,[13] may those rev'rend Benches
> Y' aspire to be the Stocks, and may ye be
> No more call'd to the Bar, but Pillory;
> Thither in Triumph may ye backward ride,
> To have your Ears most justly crucify'd,[14]
> And cut so close, until there be not Leather
> Enough to stick a Pen in left of either;

with her mouth, and adds it to the heap she is building, because she is not unaware and not heedless of the morrow.") [In *Satires, Epistles and Ars Poetica,* trans. Fairclough.]

[11] The Minotaur of mythology, offspring of Pasiphaë with a bull, that was killed by Theseus.

[12] "Let all men know": the opening phrase of writs.

[13] One who is pock-marked. Sometimes used to express dislike or used as an intensive. [*O.E.D.*]

[14] See p. 99, n. 3.

Then will your Consciences, your Ears, and Wit
Be like Indentures Tripartite cut fit:
May your Horns[15] multiply, and grow as great
As that which does blow Grace before your Meat:
May Varlets[16] be your Barbers now, and do
The same to you, they have been done unto;
That's Law and Gospel, too, may it prove true,
Then they shall do Pump-Justice[17] upon you;
And when y' are shav'd and powder'd you shall fall
Thrown o'er the Bar, as they did o'er the Wall,
Never to rise again, unless it be
To hold your Hands up for your Roguery;
And when you do so, may they be no less
Sear'd by the Hangman, than your Consciences:
May your Gowns swarm, until you can determine
The Strife no more between yourselves and Vermin,
Than you have done between your Clients purses—
Now kneel, and take the last and worst of curses—
May you be honest, when it is too late,
That is, undone the only Way you hate.

AN HERALD[1]

Calls himself a *King*, because he has Power and Authority
to *hang*, *draw*, and *quarter*[2] Arms; for assuming a Jurisdiction over
the distributive Justice of Titles of Honour, as far as Words extend,
he gives himself as great a Latitude that Way, as other Magistrates
use to do, where they have Authority, and would enlarge it as far as
they can. 'Tis true he can make no Lords nor Knights of himself, but

---

[15] The traditional sign of a cuckold.

[16] See p. 70, n. 1.

[17] Pump: to duck under the pump, especially as treatment applied to bailiffs,
constables, and pickpockets. [Eric Partridge, *A Dictionary of Slang and Unconventional English*, 4th edition (New York, 1951).]

[1] A herald granted (and invented) coats of arms, recorded and traced pedigrees, and supervised funerals. The College of Heralds included six heralds
among other officials. Coats of arms, being the symbols of gentility, were in
great demand by the ambitious who, all too frequently, paid for their honours
(as the Character suggests).

[2] Note that the use of terms for traditional punishment for serious crimes
are applied to coats of arms that can be hung up, are sketched or drawn, and
are divided into four parts or areas.

as many Squires and Gentlemen as he pleases, and adopt them into what Family they have a Mind. His Dominions abound with all Sorts of Cattle, Fish, and Fowl, and all manner of Manufactures, besides whole Fields[3] of Gold and Silver, which he magnificently bestows upon his Followers, or sells as cheap as Lands in *Jamaica*.[4] The Language they use is barbarous, as being but a Dialect of Pedlar's *French*, or the *Ægyptian*,[5] though of a loftier Sound, and in the Propriety affecting Brevity, as the other does Verbosity. His Business is like that of all the Schools, to make plain Things hard with perplexed Methods and insignificant Terms, and then appear learned in making them plain again. He professes Arms not for use, but Ornament only, and yet makes the basest Things in the World, as Dogs-Turds and Women's Spindles, Weapons of good and worshipful Bearings. He is wiser than the Fellow that sold his Ass, but kept the Shadow for his own Use;[6] for he sells only the Shadow (that is the Picture) and keeps the Ass himself. He makes Pedigrees as 'Pothecaries do Medicines, when they put in one Ingredient for another that they have not by them: by this means he often makes incestuous Matches, and causes the Son to marry the Mother. His chief Province is at Funerals, where he commands in chief, marshals the *tristitiae irritamenta*,[7] and like a Gentleman-Sewer to the Worms serves up the Feast with all punctual Formality. He will join as many Shields together as would make a *Roman* Testudo,[8] or *Macedonian* Phalanx, to fortify the Nobility of a new made Lord, that will pay for the impresting of them, and allow him Coat and Conduct Money. He is a kind of a Necromancer,[9] and can raise the Dead out of their Graves, to make them marry and beget

---

[3] Backgrounds for heraldic devices.

[4] Jamaica was captured from Spain by the British fleet in 1655, while Cromwell was ruler, and he artificially planted Englishmen on this island, which was thinly populated with Spaniards. Often settlers were offered free land in the West Indian Islands as well as Virginia, and they were encouraged by pamphlets circulated from companies promoting emigration from England. [See Trevelyan, *England Under the Stuarts*, pp. 267–69, and Trevelyan, *Illustrated English Social History* (London, 1950), II, 69.]

[5] Gipsy?

[6] See p. 68, n. 3.

[7] Incitements to grief.

[8] A cover or screen formed by a body of troops in close formation whose shields overlapped above their heads.

[9] In general a conjurer but more specifically one who predicted events by means of communication with the dead.

those they never heard of in their Life-time. His Coat is like the King of *Spain*'s Dominions[10] all Skirts; and hangs as loose about him; and his Neck is the Waste,[11] like the Picture of *Nobody*[12] with his Breeches fastened to his Collar. He will sell the Head or a single Joint of a Beast or Fowl[13] as dear as the whole Body, like a Pig's Head in *Bartlemew*-Fair,[14] and after put off the rest to his Customers at the same Rate. His Arms being utterly out of Use in War, since Guns came up, have been translated to Dishes and Cups, as the Ancients used their precious Stones according to the Poet—*Gemmas ad pocula transfert a Gladiis, &c.*[15] and since are like to decay every Day more and more; for since he gave Citizens Coats of Arms, Gentlemen have made bold to take their Letters of Mark[16] by way of Reprisal. The Hangman has a Receipt to mar all his Work in a Moment; for by nailing the wrong End of a Scutcheon upwards upon a Gibbet, all the Honour and Gentility extinguishes of itself, like a Candle that's held

---

[10] A reference to the heterogeneous empire of Charles Hapsburg, who by 1519 as Charles I of Spain and Charles V, Holy Roman Emperor, ruled over the Netherlands, Spain, Naples, Sardinia, Sicily, the Holy Roman Empire, the Hapsburg holdings in eastern Europe, and a vast colonial empire overseas.

Unlike the rulers of England and France, where the monarchy drew its strength from a compact national domain, Charles V (despite the immense resources of his holdings) confronted a variety of disparate problems from scattered lands, which in some ways weakened each other.

[11] Waist.

[12] A woodcut of No-Body precedes the text of the play *Nobody and Somebody* (printed 1606). He is a chubby man, all breech and no body. The original cut may be seen reproduced in later printings, for example, "[Glasgow] Printed for private circulation [by R. Anderson], 1877."

[13] I.e., the parts of animals that appear on coats of arms.

[14] Bartholomew Fair: A fair held for centuries after its beginnings in 1133 at Smithfield, London, on Saint Bartholomew's Day. Originally the fair was a market for cloth and other goods, but it continued until the mid-nineteenth century as a pleasure-fair. Ben Jonson's *Bartholomew Fair* gives a picture of the fair in the seventeenth century.

[15] Juvenal, *Satires*, V. 43 ff.

> Virro, ut multi, gemmas ad pocula transfert
> a digitis, quas in vaginae fronte solebat
> ponere zelotypo invenis praelatus Iarbae.

("Virro, like so many others, transfers from his fingers to his cups the jewels with which the youth [who was] preferred to the jealous Iarbas used to adorn in front of his scabbard.") [In *Juvenal and Persius*, trans. Ramsay.]

[16] Small charges (devices) added to coats of arms as signs of distinction. [*O.E.D.*]

with the Flame downwards. Other Arms are made for the spilling of Blood; but his only purify and cleanse it like Scurvy-grass;[17] for a small Dose taken by his Prescription will refine that which is as base and gross as Bull's Blood (which the *Athenians* used to poison withal) to any Degree of Purity.

A LATITUDINARIAN

Gives himself the more Scope, because he that has the largest Conscience is most like, in all Probability, to keep within Compass of it: for one that is strait is uneasy, apt to pinch, and will not do half the Service that a wider will endure. He does not greatly care to live within the Pale of the Church, but had rather have the Church live within his Pale. He believes the Way to Heaven is never the better for being strait, and if it could be made wider it would be much more convenient; for there being so many that undertake that Journey, how few soever arrive at the End of it, they must of Necessity justle, croud and fall foul upon one another, as we find they do, and therefore he thinks it best, both for himself and the Ease of his Fellow-Travellers, to get out of the common Road, and leave the more Room for those that cannot leap Ditches,[1] and if they could, when they are once out, do not know how to get in again so well as he does. He is but a Kind of a modest Ranter,[2] that believes *Christian* Liberty and *natural* Liberty may very well consist together; for being Things of the same Kind there can be no possible Difference between them, but only in Degree, which can never cause the one to destroy the other; and natural Liberty being of the elder House, if there be any Precedency, ought to have a Right to it. He believes Obedience is nothing but a civil Complacence, that obliges a Man no further than saying—*I am your humble Servant*; and that Uniformity[3] is too like

---

[17] A cress, especially one from arctic regions, used as a remedy for scurvy.

[1] In the seventeenth century adequate roads were lacking, for the highways were not much different from what they had been in the Middle Ages. The roads were not even clearly defined, winding across the open country. Wheels of coaches made the surfaces worse than ever. In winter even main roads became bogs of mud and so impassable the traveler would be forced to go through adjacent fields. Usually in the spring parish authorities plowed up the ruts. [Arthur Bryant, *The England of Charles II* (London, 1935), pp. 150–51.]

[2] See the Character of A Ranter.

[3] Conformity by all Englishmen to the Church of England. In particular, a

a Thing made and complotted to be true. He believes Laws are made to punish those only, that do not understand how to break them discreetly, and to do no Man right, that has not Money or Interest to compel them to it; that like foolish Magistrates require Respect in public, but will endure all Manner of Affronts in private, especially among Friends.

A MATHEMATICIAN

Shews as many Tricks on the Outside of Body,[1] as *Philosophers* do on the Inside of it, and for the most Part to as little Purpose; the only Difference is, that the one begins in Nonsense and ends in Sense, and the other quite contrary begins in Sense and ends in Nonsense: For the Mathematician begins with Body abstract, which was never found in Nature, and yet afterwards traces it to that which is real and practical; and the Philosopher begins with Body as it is really in Nature, and afterwards wears it away with much handling into thin Subtilties that are merely notional.[2] The Philosopher will not endure to hear of Body without Quantity, and yet afterwards gives it over, and has no Consideration of it any further: And the Mathematician will allow of Being without Quantity, and yet afterwards considers nothing else but Quantity. All the Figures he draws are no better, for the most Part, than those in Rhetoric, that serve only to call certain Rotines[3] and Manners of Speech by insignificant Names, but teach nothing. His Art is only instrumental, and like others of the same Kind, when it outgrows its Use becomes merely a Curiosity; and the more it is so, the more impertinent it proves; for Curiosities are impertinent to all Men but the Curious,[4] and they to all the rest of the World. His Forefathers past among the Ancients for Conjurers, and carried the Credit of all Inventions, because they had the Luck to stand by when they were found out, and cry'd *half's ours*. For though

reference to the Act of Uniformity (1662), by which "2,000 Puritan clergy were expelled from livings in the Established Church, for refusing to assert their 'unfeigned consent and assent' to everything in the Prayerbook." [Trevelyan, *England Under the Stuarts*, p. 283.]

[1] Substance?

[2] Abstract; purely speculative.

[3] See p. 42, n. 41.

[4] I.e., those interested in the strange or rare. Cf. the Character of A Curious Man.

the Mechanics have found out more excellent Things, than *they* have Wit enough to give names to, (though the greatest Part of their Wit lies that Way) yet they will boldly assume the Reputation of all to themselves, though they had no Relation at all to the Inventions; as Great Persons use to claim kindred (though they cannot tell how it comes about) with their Inferiors when they thrive in the World. For certainly Geometry has no more right to lay Claim to the Inventions of the Mechanics than Grammar has to the original of Language, that was in Use long before it; and when that Use and Custom had prevailed, some Men by observing the Construction, Frame, and Relations that Words have to one another in Speech drew them into Rules, and of these afterwards made an Art; and just so and no more did Geometry by the Dimensions, Figures, and Proportions of Things that were done long before it was in being; nor does the present Use of one or the other extend further than this, to teach Men to speak, and write, and proportion things regularly, but not to contrive or design at all. Mathematicians are the same Things to Mechanics, as Markers in Tennis Courts are to Gamesters;[5] and they that ascribe all Inventions to Mathematics are as wise as those that say, no Man can play well that is not a good Marker; as if all the Skill of a Goldsmith lay in his Balance, or a Draper in his Yard; or that no Man can play on a Lute that is not a good Fiddle-Maker.

When his Art was in its Infancy, and had by Observation found out the Course of the Sun and Moon and their Eclipses (though imperfectly) and could predict them, which the rest of the World were ignorant of, he went further, and would undertake upon that Account to foretel any Thing, as Liars that will make one Truth make Way for a hundred Lies. He believes his Art, or rather Science, to be wholly practical, when the greatest Part of it, and as he believes the best, is merely contemplative, and passes only among Friends to the Mathematics and no further, for which they flatter and applaud one another most virtuously.

AN EPIGRAMMATIST

Is a Poet of small Wares, whose Muse is short-winded, and quickly out of Breath. She flies like a Goose, that is no sooner upon

---

5 Players.

the Wing, but down again. He was originally one of those Authors, that used to write upon white Walls,[1] from whence his Works being collected and put together pass in the World, like single Money among those that deal in small Matters. His Wit is like Fire in a Flint,[2] that is nothing while it is in, and nothing again as soon as it is out. He treats of all Things and Persons that come in his Way, but like one that draws in little, much less than the Life.

> *His Bus'ness is t' inveigh and flatter*
> *Like parcel Parasite and Satyr.*

He is a Kind of Vagabond Writer, that is never out of his Way; for nothing is beside the Purpose with him, that proposes none at all. His Works are like a running Banquet, that have much Variety but little of a Sort; for he deals in nothing but Scraps and Parcels like a Taylor's Broker. He does not write, but set his Mark upon Things, and gives no Accompt in Words at length, but only in Figures. All his Wit reaches but to four Lines, or six at the most; and if he ever venture further it tires immediately like a Post-Horse, that will go no further than his wonted Stages. Nothing agrees so naturally with his Fancy as Bawdery, which he dispenses in small Pittances to continue his Reader still in an Appetite for more.

A VIRTUOSO[1]

Is a Well-willer to the Mathematics—He persues Knowledge rather out of Humour than Ingenuity, and endeavours rather to seem,

---

[1] From the earliest times the Greeks would carve sentences (usually in verse) upon their tombs and public monuments; these inscriptions were later collected. For poems in the meter used for monuments and gravestones see *The Greek Anthology*.

[2] Note the use of a similar expression (the Latin *Silex Scintillans*) by Henry Vaughan for his volume of poetry first issued in 1650.

[1] The term *virtuoso* came into use in the earlier seventeenth century and was originally applied to one whom we now call an *antiquarian*, who was interested in statues, coins, inscriptions. The term could be used as either a compliment or a pejorative word—i.e., for either a connoisseur or a mere dabbler. The term was used also by Boyle and others for men interested in science and came to be applied to men of the Royal Society. See Thomas Shadwell, *The Virtuoso* (1676), and for a full analysis and brief history see Walter E. Houghton, "The English Virtuoso in the Seventeenth Century," *Journal of the History of Ideas*, III (1942), 51-73, 190-219.

than to be. He has nothing of Nature but an Inclination, which he strives to improve with Industry; but as no Art can make a Fountain run higher than its own Head; so nothing can raise him above the Elevation of his own Pole. He seldom converses but with Men of his own Tendency, and wheresoever he comes treats with all Men as such, for as Country-Gentlemen use to talk of their Dogs to those that hate Hunting, because they love it themselves; so will he of his Arts and Sciences to those that neither know, nor care to know any Thing of them. His Industry were admirable, if it did not attempt the greatest Difficulties with the feeblest Means: for he commonly slights any Thing that is plain and easy, how useful and ingenious soever, and bends all his Forces against the hardest and most improbable, tho' to no Purpose if attained to; for neither knowing how to measure his own Abilities, nor the Weight of what he attempts, he spends his little Strength in vain, and grows only weaker by it—And as Men use to blind Horses that draw in a Mill, his Ignorance of himself and his Undertakings makes him believe he has advanced, when he is no nearer to his End than when he set out first. The Bravery[2] of Difficulties does so dazzle his Eyes, that he prosecutes them with as little Success, as the Taylor did his Amours to *Queen Elizabeth*.[3] He differs from a Pedant, as *Things* do from *Words*;[4] for he uses the same Affectation in his Operations and Experiments, as the other does in Language. He is a Haberdasher of small Arts and Sciences, and deals in as many several Operations as a baby-Artificer[5] does in Engines. He will serve well enough for an Index, to tell what is handled in the World, but no further. He is wonderfully delighted with Rarities, and they continue still so to him, though he has shown them a thousand Times; for every new Admirer, that gapes upon them, sets him a gaping too. Next these he loves strange natural Histories; and as those, that read Romances, though they know them to be Fictions, are as much affected as if they were true, so is he, and will make hard

---

[2] Fine show or display.

[3] Isaac D' Israeli discusses the private anecdotes which mention the encouragement given by Queen Elizabeth to almost all who were near her. She coquettishly encouraged all persons of eminence to fall in love with her. Courtiers, following her lead, feigned passion for her. She ranked many among her suitors, including Henry III of France, and "there was also a *taylor* who died for love of her majesty." [*Curiosities of Literature* (London, 1794), I, 441–42.]

[4] See p. 55, n. 3.

[5] Perhaps a novice who presented some new device to the Royal Society.

Shift to tempt himself to believe them first to be possible, and then he's sure to believe them to be true, forgetting that *Belief upon Belief is false Heraldry*.[6] He keeps a Catalogue of the Names of all famous Men in any Profession, whom he often takes Occasion to mention as his very good Friends, and old Acquaintances. Nothing is more pedantic than to seem too much concerned about Wit or Knowledge, to talk much of it, and appear too critical in it. All he can possibly arrive to is but like the Monkies dancing on the Rope, to make Men wonder, how 'tis possible for *Art* to put *Nature* so much out of her Play.

His Learning is like those Letters on a Coach, where many being writ together no one appears plain. When the King happens to be at the University, and Degrees run like Wine in Conduits at public Triumphs, he is sure to have his Share; and though he be as free to chuse his Learning as his Faculty, yet like St. *Austin's* Soul *creando infunditur, infundendo creatur*.[7] *Nero* was the first Emperor of his Calling, tho' it be not much for his Credit.[8] He is like an Elephant that, though he cannot swim, yet of all Creatures most delights to walk along a River's Side; and as in Law, *Things that appear not, and things that are not, are all one*; so he had rather not be than not appear. The Top of his Ambition is to have his Picture graved in Brass, and published upon Walls, if he has no Work of his own to face with it. His want of Judgment inclines him naturally to the most extrav-

---

[6] An analogy to the solecism in heraldry of placing color on color, metal on metal, or fur on fur. Cf. the phrasing in Zachary Grey's note to *Hudibras*, I. i, 545: "Gold upon Gold would have been false Heraldry. . . ."

[7] "Infused in the process of creation, and in being infused is created." Butler may well have drawn upon Sir Thomas Browne's discussion of opposing beliefs on the creation of man's soul, in which he writes of "that Rhetorical sentence and *Antimetathesis* of Augustine; *creando infunditur, infundendo creatur*." [*Religio Medici*, I. 36, in *Works*, ed. Keynes, I, 45. See also Hobbes, *Leviathan*, Pt. 4, Chap. 46.] The phrase originated not in the works of Augustine but rather in Peter Lombard's summary, in *Sententiarum* (c. 1150), Lib. II, dist. XVII, of the opinion of St. Augustine, especially as set forth in *De Genesi ad litteram* (c. 26), Lib. VII. Lombard's phrase was "*creando infundit animas Deus et infundendo creat*." Franz Delitsch writes that the saying of Lombard became "an authentic formula" used in the Roman Catholic Church. [*A System of Biblical Psychology*, trans. R. E. Wallis (Edinburgh, 1867), p. 130.]

[8] Nero appears to have been a man of many talents: he drew, painted, modeled, and composed verses, and he demonstrated some ability in music. But to the contrary was his reputation for cruel and unrestrained brutality and for spectacular display.

agant Undertakings,[9] like that of *making old Dogs young*,[10] *telling how many Persons there are in a Room by knocking at a Door*,[11] *stopping up of Words in Bottles*, &c. He is like his Books, that contain much Knowledge, but know nothing themselves. He is but an Index of Things and Words, that can direct where they are to be spoken with, but no further. He appears a great Man among the ignorant, and like a Figure in Arithmetic, is so much the more, as it stands before Ciphers that are nothing of themselves. He calls himself an *Antisocordist*[12] a Name unknown to former Ages, but spawned by the Pedantry of the present. He delights most in attempting Things beyond his Reach, and the greater Distance he shoots at, the further he is sure to be off his Mark. He shows his Parts, as Drawers do a Room at a Tavern, to entertain them at the Expence of their Time and Patience. He inverts the Moral of that Fable of him, that caressed his Dog for fawning and leaping up upon him, and beat his Ass for doing the same Thing;[13] for it is all one to him, whether he be applauded by an Ass, or a wiser Creature, so he be but applauded.

A JUSTICE OF PEACE

Is one that has a Patent for his Wit, and understands by Commission, in which his Wife and his Clerk are of the *Quorum*.[1]

---

[9] Beginning in 1665 *The Philosophical Transactions* of the Royal Society, which each month recorded the observations and inquiries of the Society, provided ample material for the wits of the time, by reason of the impractical, even ludicrous experiments and plans of men who took all knowledge for their province.

[10] Allusion to the transfusion of blood from a young dog to an old one. Grey in his edition of *Hudibras* ["An Heroical Epistle," ll. 59–60, n.] cites instances from *The Philosophical Transactions*.

[11] See Butler's "Virtuoso," in *Samuel Butler: Satires and Miscellaneous Poetry and Prose*, ed. René Lâmar (Cambridge, 1928) p. 167:
    . . . our Modern Curious Virtuosos,
    By only knocking at the Doores of Houses,
    Will, by the Sound, unriddle the Just Sum
    How many persons are in the Roome.

[12] In Butler's sense a *virtuoso*. See p. 121, n. 1. Cf. also the Character of An Antisocordist.

[13] This fable told by Aesop concerns an ass who, jealous of a lap-dog, sought to frolick like the dog and climb upon his master. After completely upsetting the household, the ass was tied down with sticks and staves. Then the ass reflected on the stupidity of trying to change his natural position by imitating a mere puppy.

[1] Certain justices of the peace, usually of special qualifications, whose pres-

He is Judge of the Peace, but has nothing to do with it until it is broken; and then his Business is to patch it up again. His Occupation is to keep the Peace, but he makes it keep him; and lives upon the Scraps of it, as those he commits do on the common Basket.[2] The Constable is his Factor, and the Jaylor the Keeper of his Warehouse, and Rogues, Bawds, and Thieves his Goods. He calls taking of Pigs and Capons taking of Bail; and they pass with him for *substantial House-keepers*. Of these he takes Security, that the Delinquent shall answer it before the Sessions, that is before the Court sits next, otherwise Forfeiture of Recognizance is sure to rise up in Judgment. He binds Men over, as Highwaymen do, to unty their Purses, and then leaves them to unbind themselves again, or rather as Surgeons do, to let their Purses Blood. He makes his Commission a Patent, that no Man shall set up any Sin without Licence[3] from him. He knows no Virtue, but that of his Commission, for all his Business is with Vice, in which he is so expert, that he can commit one Sin instead of another, as *Bribery* for *Bawdery*, and *Perjury* for *Breach of the Peace*. He uses great Care and Moderation in punishing those, that offend regularly, by their Calling, as residentiary Bawds, and incumbent Pimps, that pay Parish Duties—Shopkeepers, that use constant false Weights and Measures, these he rather prunes, that they may grow the better, than disables; but is very severe to Hawkers and Interlopers, that commit Iniquity on the Bye. He interprets the Statutes, as *Fanatics* do the Scripture, by his own Spirit; and is most expert in the Cases of light Bread, Highways, and getting of Bastards. His whole Authority is like a *Welsh*-Hook;[4] for his Warrant is a *Puller to her*, and his Mittimus[5] a *thrust-her from her*. He examines bawdy Circumstances with singular Attention, and files them up for the Entertainment of his Friends, and Improvement of the Wit of the Family. Whatsoever he is else, he is sure to be a Squire, and bears Arms the first Day he bears Office; and has a more indubitate and apparent

---

ence was necessary to constitute a bench. [*O.E.D.*] Those of the "quorum" were men who had some special knowledge of the law and may have attended one of the Inns of Court.

[2] Probably a reference to the dependence of the lowest grade of poor prisoners (those in the "hole") for their sustenance on what passers-by put in the basket for them.

[3] Justices of the Peace licensed alehouses.

[4] I.e., a bill hook: a heavy, thick knife or chopper with a hooked end, used for pruning, etc.

[5] A warrant of commitment to prison.

Title to *worship*, than any other Person. If he be of the long Robe[6] he is more busy and pragmatical on the Bench, than a secular Justice; and at the Sessions, by his Prerogative, gives the Charge, which puts him to the Expence of three *Latin* Sentences, and as many Texts of Scripture; the rest is all of Course. He sells good Behaviour, and makes those, that never had any, buy it of him at so much a Dose, which they are bound to take off in six Months or longer, as their Occasions require. He is apt to mistake the Sense of the Law, as when he sent a zealous Botcher to Prison for *sewing* Sedition, and committed a Mountebank for *raising* the Market, because he set up his Bank in it. Much of his Business and Ability consists in the distributive Justice of disposing of Bastards, before they are born, to the right Proprietors, that no Parish[7] may be wronged, and forced to pay for more Fornication, than they have had Occasion for. Next this he does his Country signal Service in the judicious and mature Legitimation of tipling Houses,[8] that the Subject be not imposed upon with illegal and arbitrary Ale. At the Sessions his Recognisances appear, or hide their Heads, according as his Wife and Clerk have found the Bill; for Delinquents, like Aldermen, that fine for't, are excused, otherwise they must stand and bear Office in the Court, tho' it be but to be whipped, or set in the Pillory. If he be of the *Quorum*[9] he is a double Justice, and ought, like a double Jugg, to hold as much as two simple ones; but if he hap to be empty and out of Justice in any Business, he is not at Home; or not at Leisure, and so the Matter is transmitted to the next in Capacity. His Conscience is never troubled for his own Sins, especially those of Commission (which he takes to be but the Privilege of his Place) for he finds it is Business enough for one Man, to have to do with those of others.

A FANATIC[1]

Saint *Paul* was thought by *Festus* to be mad with too much Learning;[2] but the *Fanatics* of our Times are mad with too little. He

---

[6] A lawyer.

[7] The Parliaments of Elizabeth had instituted the legal obligation of every parish to maintain the system of charity for its own inhabitants.

[8] See p. 125, n. 3.

[9] See p. 124, n. 1.

[1] See p. 55, n. 2.

[2] Acts, XVI, esp. 24. Festus was the Roman Procurator of Judea, c. A.D. 60–62, before whom the apostle Paul was brought.

chooses himself one of the *Elect*,[3] and packs a Committee of his own Party to judge the twelve Tribes of *Israel*. The *Apostles* in the primitive Church worked Miracles to confirm and propagate their Doctrine; but he thinks to confirm his by working at his Trade. He assumes a Privilege to impress what Text of Scripture he pleases for his own Use, and leaves those that make against him for the Use of the Wicked. His Religion, that tends only to Faction and Sedition, is neither fit for Peace nor War, but Times of a Condition between both; like the Sails of a Ship, that will not endure a Storm, and are of no Use at all in a Calm. He believes it has enough of the primitive Christian, if it be but persecuted as that was, no Matter for the Piety or Doctrine of it; as if there were nothing required to prove the Truth of a Religion but the Punishment of the Professors of it; like the old Mathematicians, that were never believed to be profoundly knowing in their Profession, until they had run through all Punishments, and just 'scaped the Fork.[4] He is all for suffering for Religion, but nothing for acting; for he accounts *good Works* no better than Encroachments upon the Merits of *free believing*, and a good Life the most troublesome and unthrifty Way to Heaven. He canonizes himself a Saint[5] in his own Life-time, as the more sure and certain Way, and less troublesome to others. He outgrows Ordinances, as a 'Prentice that has served out his Time does his Indentures, and being a Freeman supposes himself at Liberty to set up what Religion he pleases. He calls his own supposed Abilities *Gifts*, and disposes of himself like a Foundation designed to pious Uses, although, like others of the same Kind, they are always diverted to other Purposes. He owes all his *Gifts* to his Ignorance, as Beggars do the Alms they receive to their Poverty. They are such as the *Fairies* are said to

---

[3] One chosen by God in his grace for eternal life, a Calvinistic tenet held by many of the nonconforming sects.

[4] *Mathematici*: fortune tellers and astrologers. In post-Augustan Latin *mathematicus* meant an astrologer. (Note the use of *mathematics* in Ben Jonson's *The Alchemist*, IV. i. 83–84.) The forks: the gallows, Latin *furca*. *Furca* also means a yoke to which the hands of criminals are fastened.

Tiberius for one banished the astrologers. [Cf. Suetonius, "Tiberius," in *The Lives of the Caesars*, trans. J. C. Rolfe (London and New York, 1924), Bk. III. See also Tacitus, *The Histories*, trans. Clifford H. Moore (London and New York, 1925), I. xxii, on the astrologers, "a tribe of men untrustworthy for the powerful, deceitful towards the ambitious, a tribe which in our state will always be both forbidden and retained. . . ."]

[5] See p. 46, n. 8.

drop in Men's Shoes, and when they are discovered to give them over and confer no more; for when his Gifts are discovered they vanish, and come to nothing. He is but a Puppet[6] Saint, that moves he knows not how, and his Ignorance is the dull leaden Weight that puts all his Parts in Motion. His outward Man is a Saint, and his inward Man a Reprobate; for he carries his Vices in his Heart, and his Religion in his Face.

AN INTELLIGENCER

Would give a Peny for any Statesman's Thought at any Time. He travels abroad to guess what Princes are designing by seeing them at Church or Dinner; and will undertake to unriddle a Government at first Sight, and tell what Plots She goes with, male or female; and discover, like a Mountebank, only by seeing the public Face of Affairs, what private Marks there are in the most secret Parts of the Body politic. He is so ready at Reasons of State, that he has them, like a Lesson, by Rote: but as Charlatans make Diseases fit their Medicines, and not their Medicines Diseases; so he makes all public Affairs conform to his own established Reason of State, and not his Reason, though the Case alter ever so much, comply with them. He thinks to obtain a great Insight into State-Affairs by observing only the outside Pretences and Appearances of Things, which are seldom or never true; and may be resolved several Ways all equally probable; and therefore his Penetrations into these Matters are like the Penetrations of Cold into natural Bodies, without any Sense of itself, or the Thing it works upon—For all his Discoveries in the End amount only to Entries and Equipages, Addresses, Audiences, and Visits, with other such politic Speculations, as the Rabble in the Streets is wont to entertain itself withal. Nevertheless he is very cautious not to omit his Cipher, though he writes nothing but what every one does, or may safely know; for otherwise it would appear to be no Secret. He endeavours to reduce all his Politics into Maxims, as being most easily portable for a travelling Head, though, as they are for the most Part of slight Matters, they are but, like Spirits drawn out of Water, insipid and good for nothing. His Letters are a Kind of Bills of Exchange, in which he draws News and Politics upon all his Correspondents, who place it to Accompt, and draw it back again upon him; and though

---

[6] Notice Milton's use in *Areopagitica* of an Adam "in the motions"—i.e., in puppet shows.

it be false, neither cheats the other, for it passes between both for good and sufficient Pay. If he drives an inland Trade, he is Factor to certain remote Country *Virtuosos*,[1] who finding themselves unsatisfied with the Brevity of the *Gazette*[2] desire to have Exceedings of News, besides their ordinary Commons.[3] To furnish those he frequents Clubs and Coffee-Houses,[4] the Markets of News, where he engrosses all he can light upon; and, if that do not prove sufficient, he is forced to add a Lye or two of his own making, which does him double Service; for it does not only supply his Occasions for the present, but furnishes him with Matter to fill up Gaps the next Letter with retracting what he wrote before, and in the mean-time has served for as good News as the best; and, when the Novelty is over it is no Matter what becomes of it, for he is better paid for it than if it were true.

A PROSELITE

A Priest stole him out of the Craddle, like the Fairies, and left a Fool and Changeling[1] in his Place. He new dyes his Religion, and commonly into a sadder and darker Colour than it was before. He gives his Opinion the Somer-Salt, and turns the wrong Side of it outwards. He does not mend his Manners, but botch them with Patches of another Stuff and Colour. Change of Religion being for the most Part used by those, who understand not why one Religion is better than another, is like changing of Money two Sixpences for a Shilling; both are of equal Value, but the Change is for Convenience or Humour. There is nothing more difficult than a Change of Religion for the better; for as all Alterations in Judgment are derived from a precedent confest Error, that Error is more probably like to produce another, than any Thing of so different a Nature as Truth. He imposes upon himself in believing the Infirmity of his Nature to be the Strength of his Judgment, and thinks he changes his Religion when he changes himself, and turns as naturally from one thing to another,

---

[1] See p. 121, n. 1.

[2] See p. 103, n. 3.

[3] Rations or daily fare.

[4] After early dinner, the members of the literary and political society went to the coffee-house or club. The host of the coffee-house had all the town gossip, which each person, on entering, asked for, and the host related. [H. D. Traill, ed., *Social England* (London, 1895), IV, 482–83.]

[1] See p. 59, n. 23.

as a Maggot[2] does to a Fly. He is a Kind of Freebooty and Plunder, or one Head of Cattle driven by the Priests of one Religion out of the Quarters of another; and they value him above two of their own:[3] for beside the Glory of the Exploit they have a better Title to him, (as he that is conquered is more in the Power of him that subdued him, than he that was born his Subject) and they expect a freer Submission from one that takes Quarter, than from those that were under Command before. His Weakness, or Ignorance, or both, are commonly the chief Causes of his Conversion; for if he be a Man of a Profession, that has no Hopes to thrive upon the Accompt of mere Merit, he has no Way so easy and certain, as to betake himself to some forbidden Church, where, for the common Cause's Sake, he finds so much brotherly Love and Kindness, that they will rather employ him than one of another Persuasion though more skilful; and he gains by turning and winding his Religion as Tradesmen do by their Stocks.[4] The Priest has commonly the very same Design upon him; for he that is not able to go to the Charges of his Conversion may live free enough from being attacked by any Side. He was troubled with a Vertigo in his Conscience, and nothing but Change of Religion, like Change of Air, could cure him. He is like a Sick-man, that can neither lye still in his Bed, nor turn himself but as he is helped by others. He is like a Revolter in an Army; and as Men of Honour and Commanders seldom prove such, but common Soldiers Men of mean Condition frequently to mend their Fortunes: So in Religion Clergymen, who are Commanders, seldom prevail upon one another, and, when they do, the Proselyte is usually one, who had no Reputation among his own Party before, and after a little Trial finds as little among those, to whom he revolts.

A CLOWN

Is a Centaur, a Mixture of Man and Beast, like a Monster engendred by unnatural Copulation, a Crab engrafted on an Apple. He was neither made by Art, nor Nature, but in Spight of both, by evil Custom. His perpetual Conversation with Beasts has rendered him one of them, and he is among Men but a naturalized Brute. He

---

[2] The worm-like larva.

[3] See the Character of A Popish Priest for similar wording.

[4] A bitstock or brace, the handle by which bits are held in boring.

appears by his Language, Genius and Behaviour to be an Alien to Mankind, a Foreigner to Humanity, and of so opposite a Genius, that 'tis easier to make a *Spaniard* a *Frenchman*, than to reduce him to Civility. He disdains every Man that he does not fear, and only respects him, that has done him Hurt, or can do it. He is like *Nebuchadnezzar* after he had been a Month at Grass,[1] but will never return to be a Man again as he did, if he might; for he despises all Manner of Lives but his own, unless it be his Horse's to whom he is but Valet de Chambre. He never shews himself humane or kind in any Thing, but when he pimps to his Cow, or makes a Match for his Mare; in all Things else he is surly and rugged, and does not love to be pleased himself, which makes him hate those that do him any Good. He is a *Stoic* to all Passions but Fear, Envy, and Malice; and hates to do any Good, though it cost him nothing. He abhors a Gentleman because he is most unlike himself, and repines as much at his Manner of Living, as if he maintained him. He murmurs at him as the Saints do at the Wicked, as if he kept his Right from him; for he makes his Clownery a Sect, and damns all that are not of his Church. He manures the Earth like a Dung-hill, but lets himself lye Fallow, for no Improvement will do good upon him. *Cain* was the first of his Family, and he does his Endeavour not to degenerate from the original Churlishness of his Ancestor. He that was fetched from the Plough to be made Dictator[2] had not half his Pride and Insolence; nor *Caligula*'s Horse, that was made Consul.[3] All the worst Names that are given to Men are borrowed from him, as *Villain, Deboyse,*[4] *Peasant,* &c. He wears his Cloaths like a Hide, and shifts them no oftener than a Beast does his Hair. He is a Beast, that *Gesner*[5] never thought of.

---

[1] Daniel, IV, 32.

[2] L. Quintus Cincinnatus: hero of the old Roman republic, who cultivated his land himself until 458 B.C., when he was called from the plough to the dictatorship to free the Roman consul and the army from the interference of the Aequians. Cincinnatus bolstered up the army of Rome, defeated the enemy, and, after being dictator but sixteen days, went back to the farm.

[3] Suetonius in "Gaius Caligula" writes that Caligula built for Incitatus, a chariot-horse, a stable of marble and a manger of ivory and, in addition, placed jewels on his harness. Caligula had a house and family of servants for the horse, and guests were invited in his name. It is also reported that Caligula intended to prefer Incitatus into a consulship. [*Lives of the Caesars,* trans. Rolfe, Bk. IV.]

[4] A by-form of *debosh:* debauch. [*O.E.D.*]

[5] Conrad Gesner (1516–65): Swiss naturalist and scholar, who practiced medicine at Zurich. His *History of Animals* (*Historiae Animalium*) is probably the work from which he gained his most lasting reputation.

A QUIBBLER

Is a Jugler of Words, that shows Tricks with them, to make them appear what they were not meant for, and serve two Senses at once, like one that plays on two *Jews* Trumps.[1] He is a Fencer of Language, that falsifies his Blow, and hits where he did not aim. He has a foolish Slight of Wit, that catches at Words only, and lets the Sense go, like the young Thief in the Farce, that took a Purse, but gave the Owner his Money back again.[2] He is so well versed in all Cases of Quibble,[3] that he knows when there will be a Blot upon a Word, as soon as it is out. He packs his Quibbles like a Stock of Cards, let him but shuffle, and cut where you will, he will be sure to have it. He dances on a Rope of Sand, does the *Somerset, Strapado,* and *half-strapado*[4] with Words, plays at all manner of Games with *Clinches, Carwickets,*[5] and *Quibbles,* and talks *under-Leg.*[6] His Wit is left-handed, and therefore what others mean for right, he apprehends quite contrary. All his Conceptions are produced by equivocal Generation,[7] which makes them justly esteemed but Maggots. He rings the Changes upon Words, and is so expert, that he can tell at first Sight, how many Variations any Number of Words will bear. He talks with a *Trillo,* and gives his Words a double Relish. He had rather have them bear two Senses in vain and impertinently, than one to the Purpose, and never speaks without a Lere-Sense.[8] He talks nothing but Equivocation and mental Reservation, and mightily affects to give a Word a double Stroke, like a Tennis-Ball against two Walls at one Blow, to defeat the Expectation of his Antagonist. He commonly slurs every fourth or fifth Word, and seldom fails to throw Doublets. There are two Sorts of Quibbling, the one with Words, and the other

---

[1] Jews' harps.
[2] I am not able to identify the farce mentioned here.
[3] Play on words; punning.
[4] Somerset: somersault.
Strapado: a torture in which the victim is hoisted by a rope and let fall to the length of the rope.
[5] See p. 89, n. 37.
[6] With double meanings or hidden meanings?
[7] See p. 67, n. 2.
[8] "A *Lere-Sense* is a second or supernumerary Sense. . . ." [Thyer's note.]

with Sense, like the Rhetoricians *Figuræ Dictonis* & *Figuræ Sententiæ*[9] —The first is already cried down, and the other as yet prevails; and is the only Elegance of our modern Poets, which easy Judges call *Easiness*; but having nothing in it but *Easiness*, and being never used by any lasting Wit, will in wiser Times fall to nothing of itself.

A WOOER

Stands Candidate for Cuckold, and if he miss of it, it is none of his Fault; for his Merit is sufficiently known. He is commonly no Lover, but able to pass for a most desperate one, where he finds it is like to prove of considerable Advantage to him; and therefore has Passions lying by him of all Sizes proportionable to all Women's Fortunes, and can be indifferent, melancholy, or stark-mad, according as their Estates give him Occasion; and when he finds it is to no Purpose, can presently come to himself again, and try another. He prosecutes his Suit against his Mistress as Clients do a Suit in Law, and does nothing without the Advice of his learned Council, omits no Advantage for want of soliciting, and, when he gets her Consent, overthrows her. He endeavours to match his Estate, rather than himself, to the best Advantage, and if his Mistress's Fortune and his do but come to an Agreement, their Persons are easily satisfied, the Match is soon made up, and a Cross Marriage between all four is presently concluded. He is not much concerned in his Lady's Virtues, for if the Opinion of the *Stoics* be true, *that the virtuous are always rich*,[1] there is no doubt, but she that is rich must be virtuous. He never goes

---

[9] *Figurae Dictonis*: figures of sound.
Figurae Sententiae: figures of thought.
Cf. Dryden, "A Discourse Concerning the Original and Progress of Satire" (1693), in *Essays of John Dryden*, ed. W. P. Ker (Oxford, 1926), II, 108: "Had I time, I could enlarge on the beautiful turns of words and thoughts. . . . With these beautiful turns I confess myself to have been unacquainted, till about twenty years ago, in a conversation which I had with . . . Sir George Mackenzie, he asked me why I did not imitate in my verses the turns of Mr. Waller and Sir John Denham. . . . I have often read with pleasure, and some profit, these two fathers of our English poetry, but had not seriously enough considered those beauties which gave the last perfection to their works."
[1] The virtuous man puts away worldly things and has a true perspective on the universe. Indifferent to riches as to poverty, to pleasure as to pain, the stoic is rich in that he has all that he needs or wishes. Lucretius (who held many of the ideas of Epicurus) put it thus: " ' Divitiae grandes Romini sunt vivere parcè /

without a List in his Pocket of all the Widows and Virgins about the Town, with Particulars of their Jointures,[2] Portions, and Inheritances, that if one miss he may not be without a Reserve; for he esteems *Cupid* very improvident, if he has not more than two Strings to his Bow. When he wants a better Introduction, he begins his Addresses to the Chamber-maid, like one that sues the Tenant to eject the Landlord, and according as he thrives there makes his Approaches to the Mistress. He can tell readily what the Difference is between Jointure with Tuition[3] of Infant, Land, and Money of any Value, and what the Odds is to a Penny between them all, either to take or leave. He does not so much go a wooing as put in his Claim, as if all Men of Fortune had a fair Title to all Women of the same Quality, and therefore are said to demand them in Marriage. But if he be a Wooer of Fortune, that designs to raise himself by it, he makes wooing his Vocation, deals with all Matchmakers, that are his Setters, is very painful in his Calling, and, if his Business succeed, steals her away and commits Matrimony with a felonious Intent. He has a great desire to beget Money on the Body of a Woman, and as for other Issue is very indifferent, and cares not how old she be, so she be not past Money-bearing.

AN IMPUDENT MAN

Is one, whose want of Money and want of Wit have engaged him beyond his Abilities. The little Knowledge he has of himself being suitable to the little he has in his Profession has made him believe himself fit for it. This double Ignorance has made him set a Value upon himself, as he that wants a great deal appears in a better Condition, than he that wants a little. This renders him confident, and fit for any Undertaking, and sometimes (such is the concurrent Ignorance of the World) he prospers in it, but oftener miscarries, and becomes ridiculous; yet this Advantage he has, that as nothing can make him see his Error, so nothing can discourage him that Way; for he is fortified with his Ignorance, as barren and rocky Places are

---

Æquo animo.'" ("Great wealth it is in man to be content / To live on little.") [*De Rerum Natura*, V. 1118–19, quoted by Robert Burton in *Anatomy of Melancholy*, ed. Shilleto, II, 182.]

[2] The holding of property to the joint use of husband and wife for life or in tail, as a provision for the latter during widowhood. [*O.E.D.*]

[3] Protection or custody.

by their Situation, and he will rather believe that all Men want Judgment, than himself. For as no Man is pleased, that has an ill Opinion of himself, Nature, that finds out Remedies herself, and his own Ease render him insensible of his Defects—From hence he grows impudent; for as Men judge by Comparison, he knows as little what it is to be defective, as what it is to be excellent. Nothing renders Men modest, but a just Knowledge how to compare themselves with others; and where that is wanting; Impudence supplies the Place of it; for there is no *Vacuum* in the Minds of Men, and commonly, like other Things in Nature, they swell more with Rarefaction than Condensation. The more Men know of the World, the worse Opinion they have of it; and the more they understand of Truth, they are better acquainted with the Difficulties of it, and consequently are the less confident in their Assertions, especially in matters of Probability, which commonly is squint-ey'd, and looks nine Ways at once. It is the Office of a just Judge to hear both Parties, and he that considers but the one Side of Things can never make a just Judgment, though he may by Chance a true one. Impudence is the Bastard of Ignorance, not only unlawfully, but incestuously begotten by a Man upon his own Understanding, and laid by himself at his own Door, a Monster of unnatural Production; for Shame is as much the Propriety of human Nature (though overseen by the Philosophers) and perhaps more than Reason, laughing, or looking asquint, by which they distinguish Man from Beasts; and the less Men have of it, the nearer they approach to the Nature of Brutes. Modesty is but a noble Jealousy of Honour, and Impudence the Prostitution of it; for he, whose Face is proof against Infamy, must be as little sensible of Glory. His Forehead, like a voluntary Cuckold's,[1] is by his Horns made Proof against a Blush. Nature made Man barefaced, and civil Custom has preserved him so; but he that's impudent does wear a Vizard more ugly and deformed than Highway Thieves disguise themselves with. Shame is the tender moral Conscience of good Men. When there is a Crack in the Skull, Nature herself with a tough horny Callus repairs the Breach; so a flaw'd Intellect is with a brawny Callus Face supplied. The Face is the Dial of the Mind;[2] and where they do not go together, 'tis a Sign, that one or both are out of Order. He that is impudent is like a Merchant, that trades upon his Credit without a Stock, and if his Debts were known, would break immediately. The Inside of his

---

[1] See the Character of A Wittal.
[2] See p. 38, n. 29.

Head is like the Outside; and his Peruke as naturally of his own Growth, as his Wit. He passes in the World like a Piece of Counterfeit Coin, looks well enough until he is rubbed and worn with Use, and then his Copper Complexion begins to appear, and nobody will take him, but by Owl-light.[3]

AN IMITATER

Is a counterfeit Stone, and the larger and fairer he appears the more apt he is to be discovered, whilst small ones, that pretend to no great Value, pass unsuspected. He is made like a Man in Arras-Hangings, after some great Master's Design, though far short of the Original. He is like a Spectrum or walking Spirit, that assumes the Shape of some particular Person, and appears in the Likeness of something that he is not, because he has no Shape of his own to put on. He has a Kind of Monkey and Baboon Wit, that takes after some Man's Way, whom he endeavours to imitate, but does it worse than those Things that are naturally his own; for he does not learn, but take his Pattern out, as a Girl does her Sampler.[1] His whole Life is nothing but a Kind of Education, and he is always learning to be something that he is not, nor ever will be: For Nature is free, and will not be forced out of her Way, nor compelled to do any Thing against her own Will and Inclination. He is but a Retainer to Wit, and a Follower of his Master, whose Badge he wears every where, and therefore his Way is called *servile Imitation*. His Fancy is like the innocent Lady's, who by looking on the Picture of a *Moor* that hung in her Chamber conceived a Child of the same Complexion;[2] for all his Conceptions are produced by the Pictures of other Men's Imaginations, and by their Features betray whose Bastards they are. His Muse is not inspired but infected with another Man's Fancy; and he catches his Wit, like the Itch, of somebody else that had it before, and when he writes he does but scratch himself. His Head is, like his Hat, fashioned upon a Block, and wrought in a Shape of another Man's Invention. He melts down his Wit, and casts it in a Mold: and as metals melted and cast are not so firm and solid, as those that are

---

[3] Twilight, dusk. Also, the dark.

[1] A piece of needlework made to preserve a pattern or as a sample of skill, showing embroidered letters or verses.

[2] This story is attributed to Quintilian when retold by John Baptista Porta. [*Natural Magick* (London, 1669), p. 51.]

wrought with the Hammer; so those Compositions, that are founded and run in other Men's Molds, are always more brittle and loose than those, that are forged in a Man's own Brain. He binds himself Prentice to a Trade, which he has no Stock to set up with, if he should serve out his Time, and live to be made free. He runs a whoring after another Man's Inventions (for he has none of his own to tempt him to an incontinent Thought) and begets a Kind of Mungrel Breed, that never comes to good.

A TIME-SERVER

Wears his Religion, Reason, and Understanding always in the Mode; and endeavours as far as he can to be one of the first in the Fashion, let it change as oft as it can. He makes it his Business, like a politic *Epicure*,[1] to entertain his Opinion, Faith, and Judgment, with nothing but what he finds to be most in Season; and is as careful to make his Understanding ready according to the present Humour of Affairs, as the Gentleman was, that used every Morning to put on his Cloathes by the Weather-Glass.[2] He has the same reverend Esteem of the modern Age, as an Antiquary has for venerable Antiquity; and like a Glass receives readily any present Object, but takes no Notice of that which is past, or to come. He is always ready to become any Thing as the Times shall please to dispose of him, but is really nothing of himself; for he that sails before every Wind can be bound for no Port. He accounts it Blasphemy to speak against any Thing in present Vogue, how vain or ridiculous soever, and Arch-Heresy to approve of any Thing, though ever so good and wise, that is laid by; and therefore casts his Judgment and Understanding upon Occasion, as Bucks do their Horns, when the Season arrives to breed new against the next, to be cast again. He is very zealous to shew himself, upon all Occasions, a true Member of the Church for the Time being, that

---

[1] *Epicure* was used in the sense of *libertine*. For an enlightening discussion of Epicureanism in seventeenth-century England see Dale Underwood, *Etherege and the Seventeenth-Century Comedy of Manners* (New Haven, 1957), especially Pt. I, Chap. 2.

[2] A kind of thermometer, used to ascertain the temperature of the air and also to prognosticate changes in the weather. [*O.E.D.*] The first thermometers of modern times were invented and developed in the seventeenth century, beginning with work attributed to Galileo. [See Abraham Wolf, *A History of Science, Technology, and Philosophy in the 16th and 17th Centuries* (New York, 1935), pp. 82–92.]

has not the least Scruple in his Conscience against the Doctrine or Discipline of it, as it stands at present, or shall do hereafter, unsight unseen: for he is resolved to be always for the Truth, which he believes is never so plainly demonstrated as in that Character, that says —*It is great and prevails*, and in that Sense only fit to be adhered to by a prudent Man, who will never be kinder to Truth than she is to him; for suffering is a very *evil Effect*, and not like to proceed from a *good Cause*. He is a Man of a right public Spirit, for he resigns himself wholly to the Will and Pleasure of the Times; and, like a zealous implicit Patriot, believes as the State believes, though he neither knows, nor cares to know, what that is.

A PRATER

Is a common Nusance, and as great a Grievance to those that come near him as a Pewterer is to his Neighbours. His Discourse is like the braying of a Mortar, the more impertinent the more voluble and loud, as a Pestle makes more Noise when it is rung on the Sides of a mortar, than when it stamps downright and hits upon the Business. A Dog that opens upon a wrong Scent will do it oftner than one that never opens but upon a right. He is as longwinded as a Ventiduct,[1] that fills as fast as it empties, or a Trade-Wind, that blows one Way for half a Year together, and another as long, as if it drew in its Breath for six Months, and blew it out again for six more. He has no Mercy on any Mans Ears or Patience, that he can get within his Sphere of Activity, but tortures him, as they correct Boys in *Scotland*, by stretching their Lugs without Remorse. He is like an Earwig,[2] when he gets within a Man's Ear he is not easily to be got out again. He will stretch a Story as unmercifully as he does the Ears of those he tells it to, and draw it out in length like a Breast of Mutton at the *Hercules* Pillars, or a Piece of Cloth set on the Tenters, till it is quite spoiled and good for nothing. If he be an Orator, that speaks *distincté et ornaté*, though not *apté*,[3] he delivers his Circumstances

---

[1] A ventilator.

[2] A small, harmless insect having many-jointed antennae; the name derives from the mistaken belief that they crept into the human ear. *Earwig* was a common metaphor for a whisperer or parasite.

[3] *Distincté*: marked or set off by distinctive ornament, coloring, etc.
Ornaté: elegantly, splendidly; with embellishment.
Apté: suitably, appropriately, fitly.

with the same mature Deliberation, that one that drinks with a Gusto swallows his Wine, as if he were loth to part with it sooner than he must of Necessity; or a Gamester, that pulls the Cards that are dealt him one by one, to enjoy the Pleasure more distinctly of seeing what Game he has in his Hand. He takes so much Pleasure to hear himself speak, that he does not perceive with what Uneasiness other Men endure him, though they express it ever so plainly; for he is so diverted with his own Entertainment of himself, that he is not at Leisure to take Notice of any else. He is a *Siren*[4] to himself, and has no Way to escape Shipwreck but by having his Mouth stoped, instead of his Ears. He plays with his Tongue as a Cat does with her Tail, and is transported with the Delight he gives himself of his own making. He understands no Happiness like that of having an Opportunity to shew his Abilities in public, and will venture to break his Neck to shew the Activity of his Eloquence, for *the Tongue is* not only *the worst Part of a bad Servant*, but of an ill Master, that does not know how to govern it; for then it is like *Gusman*'s Wife,[5] very *headstrong and not sure of Foot*.

AN HERMETIC PHILOSOPHER[a]/[1]

He is a Kind of Hector[2] in Learning, that thinks to maintain himself in Reputation by picking Quarrels with his gentle Readers, and compounding them to his own Advantage; as if he meant to baffle their Understandings, and fright them into a reverend Opinion

---

4 See the *Odyssey*, Bk. XII.

5 Cf. *Guzman de Alfarache*, Spanish picaresque romance by Mateo Aleman (1547–1610), English trans. *The Rogue* (1622). Guzman, after his life as a picaro, is unprepared for his first wife, who cannot be subdued because of her powerful will.

a "In Justice to the author I must declare, that this Character, though fairly copied out for the Press, is left by him without a Title; and that that, which it now bears, is only added for the Sake of Uniformity. . . ." [Thyer's note.]

1 "The Reader will from several Circumstances quickly perceive that the first Part of [the Character] is personal; and from the same one may with a good deal of Certainty pronounce, that it was intended for the Author of a Book entituled—MAGIA ADAMICA; or *the Antiquity of Magic, and its descent from ADAM*. . . ." [Thyer's note.]

The author of *Magia Adamica* and other works on alchemical learning is Thomas Vaughan (1622–66), twin brother of Henry Vaughan, the poet.

2 See p. 106, n. 2.

of his great Abilities. He comes forth in public with *his concealed Truths*,[3] as he calls them, like one that had stolen something under his Cloak; and being afraid to be stopped falls foul on any Man, that has the ill Hap to be in his Way: for if you dislike him it is at your own Peril, he is sure to put in a Caveat beforehand against your Understanding; and, like a Malefactor in Wit, is always furnished with Exceptions against his Judges. This puts him upon perpetual Apologies, Excuses, and Defences, but still by Way of Defiance, in a Kind of whiffling Strain, without Regard of any Man, that he thinks will stand in the Way of his Pageant. He shews as little Respect to Things as Persons; for his constant Method is to shuffle Things of different Kinds together, like a Pack of Cards, and then deal them out as they happen. He pretends to contemn the present Age, and address his Writings to Posterity, to shew, that he has a better Opinion of his own Prophesy, than the Knowledge of any Man now living; and that he understands more of the Ages to come, than this does of him. Next to Posterity he is in love with Antiquity, of which he seems to be so fond, that he contemns *Seth*'s Pillars[4] as modern, and derives

---

[3] As a rule, Rosicrucians kept their alchemical formulae and universal knowledge purposely obscure. Cf. John Heydon, "An Apologue for an Epilogue" in *The Wise-Man's Crown* (London, 1664):

Divine *Plato* commanded that holy and secret misteries should not be made publique to the people, *Pythagoras* and *Porphiry* consecrated their followers to a religious Silence, The *Rosie Crucians* with a certain terrible authority of religion, do exact an oath of silence from those they initiate to the Arts of Astronomy, Geomancy and Telesmaticall Images, because by them the dead are raised to life, by them they alter change and amend bodies, cure the diseased, prolong Life . . . renew youth in old folks, make dwarfs great men, make fools and Madmen wise and vertuous . . . by these Arts they know all things and resolve all manner of questions present or to come, as faith *Beata*.

[4] Seth, the son of Adam, left children who were the discoverers of the wisdom that relates to the heavenly bodies and their order, and that their discoveries not be lost they made two pillars, one of brick and the other of stone and worked their findings on both of them to be available for their posterity. [Josephus, *Antiquities of the Jews*, Bk. I, Chap. 2.]

See Guillaume Du Bartas, "The Fourth Part of the Second Day of the II Week," *Divine Weekes and Workes*, trans. Joshuah Sylvester in *The Complete Works of Joshuah Sylvester*, ed. Alexander Grosart (Edinburgh, 1880), I, 51–57 and 62–71:

Old Seth . . . *Adam*'s Scholler yerst
(Who was the Scholler of his Maker first)
Having attain'd to know the course and sites,
Th' aspect and greatness of Heav'n's glistering lights;

the Pedigree of Magic from *Adam*'s first green Britches;[5] because
Fig-leaves being the first Cloaths, that Mankind wore, were only used
for Covering, and therefore are the most ancient Monuments of concealed Mysteries.

He controuls his fellow Labourers in the Fire with as much Empire
and Authority, as if he were sole Overseer of the *great Work*,[6] to
which he lights his Reader like an *ignis fatuus*,[7] which uses to mislead
Men into Sloughs and Ditches; for when he has mired him in the
Chaos,[8] and told him, that the *Philosophers Stone* is Water, or a
Powder, he leaves him in the Dark. With this Chaos he makes more
Work, than the Fellow that interprets to the show of it, and with no
less Astonishment to the ignorant. Such of his learned Discoveries,
that signify any Thing, though it be vulgar and common, he calls

---

> He taught his Children, whose industrious wit
> Through diligence grew excellent in it . . .
> They, living lusty, trice the age of Rav'ns
> Observ'd the Twinkling Wonders of the Heav'ns:
> And on their Grand-sire's firm and goodly ground
> A sumptuous building they in time do found.
> But (by tradition *Cabalistik*) taught,
> That God would twice reduce this world to nought,
> By *Floud* and *Flame*; they reared cunningly
> This stately pair of *Pillars* which you see;
> Long-time safe-keeping, for their after Kin,
> A hundred learnéd Mysteries therein.

[5] The author of *Magia Adamica* (Thomas Vaughan) sets out to prove that
the early Magi learned wisdom from the very knowledge delivered by God
to Adam in Paradise. Perhaps also here is a burlesque of the Geneva translation
of the Bible (1599) which says of Adam and Eve, "they sewed fig leaves together, and made themselves *breeches*." [Nash, ed., *Hudibras*, I. i. 532 n.]

Butler's note to *Hudibras* confirms the first of these points, as do the lines in
Hudibras, I. i. 529–32, on Ralph:

> For mystic Learning, wondrous able
> In Magick *Talisman*, and *Cabal*,
> Whose Primitive Tradition reaches
> As far as Adam's first green Breeches. . . .

[6] The great work or *magnum opus*: the great work of alchemical reconstruc-
tion; the technical term for the conversion of baser metals into gold.

[7] Will-o'-the-wisp.

[8] The *prima materia*, expounded by Thomas Vaughan in *Anthroposophia
Theomagica* and *Magica Abscondita* and later works. He believed that the
prima materia was the main ingredient of the philosopher's stone and magic
elixir. [Miriam K. Starkman, *Swift's Satire on Learning in "A Tale of a Tub"*
(Princeton, 1950), p. 50.]

experimental truths, and those that mean nothing *Mysteries*, which with him is but another Word for Nonsense, though it be supported, like Heraldry, with Eagles, Dragons, and Lions; but as the Poet observes

> ——*Canibus pigris, scabieque vetusta*
> *Nomen erit Tigris, Leo, Pardus, siquid adhuc sit*
> *Quod fremit in Terris violentius*——[9]

so the Sense of these terrible Terms is equally contemptible; for a Maggot is of a higher Form in Nature than any Production of Metals. His War with the Schoolmen[10] is not amiss, but he persecutes it unmercifully, without giving Quarter; though being a Writer of Fortune he might consider his own Interest, and remember that they keep him in constant Employment: for whensoever he has Occasion to digress, that is to write more than six Lines, if the Schoolmen, or the Chaos, or *the great Work* did not supply him, according as he is disposed either to rail or cant, I know not what would become of him. To this Canting[11] he is so constantly inclined, that he bestows no small Pains in devising Nick-names for himself and his Patron, to whom he writes like one that whispers aloud, and says that in his Ear, that is meant for the hearing of others. The Judgment of this Gentleman is his Privilege, and his Epistles to him are like counterfeit Passes, which he makes for himself, and believes they will carry him through, though the Person be so unknown, that nobody can guess by his Account, whether he be his Tutor or his Pupil.

---

[9] Juvenal, *Satires*, VIII. 34–37.
> Canibus pigris scabieque vestusa
> levibus et siccae lambentibus ora lucernae
> nomen erit pardus tigris leo, si quid adhunc est
> quod fremat in terris violentius. . . .

("Lazy hounds that are bald with chronic mange, and who lick the edges of a dry lamp, will bear the name of 'Pard,' 'Tiger,' 'Lion,' or of any other animal in the world that roars more fiercely.") [In *Juvenal and Persius,* trans. Ramsay.]

[10] Cornelius Agrippa, for one, in *The Vanity of Arts and Sciences* attacks the reactionary schoolmen of his time. Agrippa was quite aware of that undiscovered world beyond the restricted areas of knowledge considered legitimate for study by the scholastic thinkers (i.e., matters found in the writings of the ancients). [See Lewis Spence, *Cornelius Agrippa: Occult Philosopher* (London, 1921), pp. 45–46.]

[11] Gabriel Naude, Franco-Rosicrucian critic, says " 'they have discovered a new language to give expression to the nature of all things.' " [Quoted by A. E. Waite, *The Real History of the Rosicrucians* (London, 1887), pp. 398–399.]

He adores *Cornelius Agrippa*[12] as an Oracle, yet believes he understands more of his Writings than he did himself; for he will not take his own Testimony concerning his three Books of occult Philosophy, which he confesses to have written without Wit or Judgment.[13] Yet it cannot be denied but he is very impartial to himself; for in forbidding his Disciples to read any modern Books, but only *Sandivogius*[14] and *Enchiridion physicæ restitutæ*,[15] he does Justice on his own Works, and very ingenuously shews us how they are best to be understood. This *Physica restituta* is his *great Magistery*, two Lines of which he uses to project[16] upon his baser Metal, and make it multiply to twice as many Pages. These are commonly set forth like a Shopkeeper's Stall, with so much of his coarser Wares, as will only serve to shew what he deals in—The best you may suppose is laid up carefully; for he always tells you what he could tell you, whereby it appears the Purpose of his Writing is but to let you know, that he knows, which if you can but attain to you are sufficiently learned, and may pass for *verè adeptus*,[17] though otherwise he will not allow any Man to be free of the *Philosophers*, that has not only served out

---

[12] Cornelius Heinrich Agrippa Von Nettelsheim (1486–1535), scholar and writer on the occult sciences; author of *De Occulta Philosophia* and *De Vanitate Scientiarum*. His learning was uncanny, and he was regarded as acquainted not only with the esoteric knowledge of the Theosophists, Cabalists, and Neoplatonists, but also with black magic.

[13] In his work *The Vanity of Arts and Sciences* (*De Vanitate Scientiarum*, 1531) Agrippa penned, " 'It is true . . . that being young, I wrote three books of magic myself in a considerable volume which I entitled *Occult Philosophy*, in which such errors as I then committed through the curiosity of youth, now grown weary, I do publicly recant, for I vainly wasted much of my time and means upon these vanities. This advantage I got that I know now by what arguments to exhort others against following the same way to ruin.' " [Quoted in Lewis Spence, *Cornelius Agrippa: Occult Philosopher* (London, 1921), p. 49.]

[14] Michael Sendivogius (1566–1646), chemist and hermetic philosopher. He is credited with a work done in part by his teacher Alexander Sethon, *A New Light of Chemistry*.

[15] The author is Jean D' Espagnet, Hermetic philosopher, and the work (1601) deals with the physical theory on which the possibility of transmutation is founded.

[16] A technical term in alchemy: to throw or cast (a substance) *in, into, on, upon* something (especially in the transmutation of metals).

[17] The technical name for one who has succeeded in converting one of the baser metals into gold and thus *has attained* the great secret.

his Time to a Furnace, but can cant and spit Fire like a Jugler. He is so full of the *great Secret*, that he cannot possibly hold, but is fain, when he is treating of other Matters, to withdraw very abruptly, and vent himself, *sed clam et cum scrobe*,[18] like him that digged a Hole in the Ground to whisper in, for nobody must expect to be the wiser for it; but though he bury his Talent, he never fails to write an Epitaph upon it, that shall improve it more among the credulous, than if he had put it forth. Yet no Man must say so, that will not either own, or contemn the Title of *barbarous* and *ignorant*; for with such Language he uses to fortify the weaker Parts of his Works, like a Ditch, against those, that shall venture to attempt them. He believes a Scholar can no more live in the University, than a Serpent in *Ireland*:[19] but those weak and feeble Wits, that will not carry Point-Blank, must be fain to aim above the Mark, or else they will shoot too low. He hath taken much Pains to prove, that Magic is not conjuring; and that Sir *Henry Cornelius* was no Conjurer, nor his Dog a Devil, but a mere natural Dog,[20] though he confesses, he could not chuse but have more in him than another Dog, having served such a Master, who in his Preface to *Lully*'s *Ars brevis*[21] professes in a few Weeks to have made ignorant old Men and young Children, with a mere Trick, able to dispute in all Sorts of Learning with the most profound Doctors in *Europe*.

He adores the *Brethren of the Rosy-Cross*[22] as the only Owls of

---

[18] "Indeed in secret and in a ditch (or grave)."

[19] Reference to the freedom from snakes enjoyed by Ireland, which is, in legend, credited to Saint Patrick.

[20] Butler's note to *Hudibras*, II. iii. 635: "*Cornelius Agrippa* had a Dog, that was suspected to be a Spirit, for some tricks he was wont to do, beyond the capacity of a Dog, as it was thought; but the Author of *Magia Adamica* [Thomas Vaughan] has taken a great deal of pains to vindicate both the doctor and the Dog, from that aspersion, in which he has shown a very great respect and kindness for them both."

Wierus, Agrippa's pupil and domestic, also cleared him from this charge. [Grey, ed., *Hudibras*, II. iii. 644 n.]

[21] Raymond Lully (1235–1315), Spanish scholastic and alchemist, *In Artem Brevem Raymondi Lulli*, Opera, Tom. ii. 331–436 (Cologne, 1533). The commentary, which I have not seen, presents at some length a sketch of this work of Lully's, which sets forth a technical system for the fitting of knowledge in the memory—the application of short and logical processes to the art of study. [See Henry Morley, *The Life of Henry Cornelius Agrippa* (London, 1856), II, 310.]

[22] "The Character, which has so far been personal, is now extended to a

Athens[23] that can see in the Dark; and wonders at them, like one of the Rabble of Birds—These are a Kind of *Philosophers Errant*, that wander up and down upon Adventures, and have an enchanted Castle, invisible to all but themselves, to which they are bound by their Order to repair at certain Seasons.[24] In this Tabernacle rests the Body of their Prophet or Founder, who dying, as they affirm, hid himself in a Kind of invisible Oven, where after an hundred Years he was discovered by a Kind of Prophesying Door, not overbaked nor cold, but warm, and looking (like a Woodcock's Head stuck in the Lid of a Pye) as if he were alive.[25] With him they found a World of most precious Secrets and Mysteries, with a deal of Treasure, and a Dictionary of all those Names, that *Adam* gave the Creatures;[26] and these they have since given one another: for they profess to understand the

---

general one of the *Rosicrucians*. . . ." [Thyer's note.]

Brethren of the Rosy-Cross: usually called Rosicrucians, members of a society devoted to occult lore and magic. By tradition the society owed its founding in the fourteenth or fifteenth century to a German named Christian Rosencruz. The Society is first mentioned in the early seventeenth century in the *Fama et confessione fraternitatis* (1614), published by Andreas Valentin, giving a history of a group of philosophical adepts. Whether such a society ever existed in the seventeenth century or earlier is open to doubt.

[23] Owls abounded in Athens, and thus to bring owls to Athens is equivalent to bringing coals to Newcastle. The owl was the emblem of Athena and proverbially associated with the city of Athens.

[24] In the preface to his translation of *The Fame and Confession of the Fraternity of R. C.* (1652) Thomas Vaughan affirms his belief in " 'the essence and existence of that admired chimaera, the Fraternitie of R. C.' " Further he states that " 'some of you may advise me to an assertion of the Capreols of del Phaebo, or a review of the library of that discreet gentleman of La Mancha, for in your opinions those knights and these brothers are equally invisible. . . .' " [Quoted by Waite, *Real History*, p. 311.]

In *The Holy Guide* (1662) John Heydon reports from a Dr. F. that "there is a castle in the West of England, in the earth and not on the earth, and there the Rosie Crucians dwell. . . ." [Waite, *Real History*, p. 337.]

[25] In the *Fama et confessione fraternitatis* (see p. 144, n. 22) there was a report that recently the burial vaults of the founder had been discovered. There was a heptagonal vault, illuminated by an artificial sun. The uncorrupted body of Christian Rosy Cross was found beneath the altar in the middle. [J. B. Craven, *Doctor Robert Fludd: the English Rosicrucian* (Kirkwall, 1902), p. 36. See also, on Rosicrucius's sepulchre, *Spectator* Paper 379.]

[26] Milton and Bacon believed that before the Fall Adam possessed a pure light of natural knowledge, which extended to all sciences, although its only recorded manifestation came in Adam's naming of the animals. [See Milton, *Paradise Lost*, VIII. 345–54, and Bacon, *The Advancement of Learning*, I. vi. 6.]

Language of Beasts and Birds, as they say *Solomon* did,[27] else he would never have said—*The Fowls of the Air can discover Treason against Princes*. This Knowledge, they affirm, may be attained by Eating, in a planetary Moment, a Rasher made of the Liver of a Camelion, the only broiled Lexicon in the World. For they will undertake to teach any Kind of mysterious Learning in the World by Way of Diet; and therefore have admirable Receipts,[28] to make several Dishes for *Talisman*, *Magic*, and *Cabal*,[29] in which Sciences a Man of an ingenious Stomach may eat himself into more Knowledge at a Meal, than he could possibly arrive at by seven Years Study.

They are better acquainted with the intelligible World,[30] than they are with this; and understand more of Ideas, than they do of Things. This intelligible World is a Kind of *Terra incognita*, a *Psittacorum Regio*,[31] of which Men talk what they do not understand. They would

---

[27] In Hebrew legend Solomon is said to have understood the languages of the beasts and birds. [*Jewish Encyclopedia*.]

In stories in the Talmud Solomon is given credit for ruling over wild beasts, the birds, and "creeping beasts" of earth. "He understood the languages of them all, and they understood him." [James Grant, *The Mysteries of All Nations* (London, 1880), p. 261.]

[28] The term "recipe" was used to mean "symbolic hermetic formula." For example, Thomas Vaughan gives a recipe for the universal medicine in *Anthroposophia Theomagica*. [See Jonathan Swift, *"A Tale of a Tub,"* to which is Added *"The Battle of the Books"* and the *"Mechanical Operation of the Spirit,"* ed. A. C. Guthkelch and D. Nichol Smith, 2d edition (Oxford, 1958), p. 350, note to p. 127.]

Miriam Starkman [*Swift's Satire on Learning*, p. 53] says, the "Rosicrucians were *adepti* at alchemical formulae and universal knowledge, and . . . they kept their recipes purposely obscure."

[29] Talisman: a magical inscription or figure, engraved or cast, by the direction of astrologers, under certain positions of the heavenly bodies. It was believed that talismans were especially useful for prevention of disease and all types of evil. For example, the image of any vermin cast in the right moment, under a particular position of the stars, would get rid of the vermin.

Cabal or Cabala: the secret or mysterious knowledge in Hebrew tradition believed to have been received by rabbis from Moses, or from Adam, and handed down from age to age orally.

[30] The Hermetic philosophers drew much from Platonic and Neoplatonic tradition. Their examination of the "elementary world" had as its end knowledge of the intelligible world, and they based their procedure on the concept of correspondences and the correlation between man and the universe (a widely held philosophical belief) but carried it to an extreme. [See Starkman, *Swift's Satire on Learning*, p. 46.]

[31] "Region of the Parrot"? "The Intelligible world, is a kind of *Terra del*

have us believe, that it is but the Counterpart of the elementary World; and that there is not so much as an individual Beard upon the Face of the Earth, that has not another there perfectly of the same Colour and Cut to match it.[32] Next to this, as they tell us, lies the celestial World, in which they are at Home—All the Dukes, Earls, and Barons in the Planets are their Godsons, if not their Bastards. These Lords spiritual hold so perfect a Conformance in all their Manners, Customs, and Usages with ours upon Earth, that a learned Antiquary would certainly conclude, they were at first some Colony transplanted hence. With these they are so familiar, that they have a Particular of every one's Estate, and can tell how many Tenants he has, that hold their Lands of him. These Spirits they use to catch by the Noses with Fumigations, as St. *Dunstan* did the Devil with a Pair of Tongs,[33] and make them compound for their Liberty by discovering[34] Secrets. By this Means they have found out the Way to make planetary Mousetraps, in which Rats and Mice shall take themselves without the Expence of toasted Cheese and Bacon.[35] They have fine Devices[36] to make counterfeit Maggots of Lute-Strings, translate Agues into Dogs, or fright them away with Spiders; to cure the Tooth-ach or sore Eyes with Medicines laid to the Imagination; kill

Fuego, or *Psittacorum Regio*, discovered only by the Philosophers, of which they talk, like Parrots, what they do not understand." [Butler's note to *Hudibras*, I. i. 535–36.]

[32] Cf. *Hudibras*, II. iii. 225–34, on Sidrophel:

> Th' *Intelligible world* he knew,
> And all, men dream on't, to be true:
> That in this *World*, there's not a *Wart*,
> That has not there a Counterpart;
> Nor can there on the *face* of Ground,
> An Individual *Beard* be found,
> That has not, in that foreign *Nation*,
> A fellow of that self-same fashion;
> So *cut*, so *color'd*, and so *curl'd*,
> As those are, in th' *Inferior* World.

[33] An allusion to the famous story that the Devil appeared in the form of a woman to tempt Dunstan (925–88; he became Archbishop of Canterbury in 961), who seized the apparition by the nose with red-hot blacksmith's tongs.

[34] Disclosing; revealing.

[35] Cf. p. 146, n. 29.

[36] For purposes of satire Butler, Shadwell, and Swift related actual experiments that sounded absurd to laymen or combined more than one into an absurdity.

Rats and Warts with Rhimes; quote Moles on any Part of the Body by an Index in the Face;[37] discover lost Maidenheads;[38] pimp with Figures, Charms, and Characters; cut Noses out of Buttocks with *Taliacotius*;[39] blow the Philosophers Fire with Words of pure Wind, and draw the glorify'd Spirit of the Elixir not out of gross Matter, but the pure incorporeal Hope and Faith of the Credulous, which is the best and the most rational Way of Multiplication; for a small Dose so prepared and projected upon the dullest Metal, converts it present-ly into Gold ready coined. They have found out a Way to make in-visible Hour-glasses for gifted Brethren to preach by,[40] who would give Offence to tender Consciences,[41] if it should seem, as if the Spirit could enable them to understand what to say, but not how much, without the Help of a carnal Hour-glass. They are now carry-ing on a *thorough*[42]-*Reformation* in the celestial World—They have repaired the old Spheres, that were worn as thin as a Cob-web, and fastened the Stars in them with a Screw, by which means they may be taken off, and put on again at Pleasure. They have pulled down all the ancient Houses[43] of the Planets, and set up Tents in their Places, as being more convenient in regard of their Easiness to be re-moved upon all Occasions. They have lately fallen on *DuBartas*'s De-sign to new-christen all the Constellations, and give them Scripture

---

[37] Cf. William Lilly, *Account of My Life*, where he tells of teaching one Humphries, a Pretender to Astrology, how to "discover the moles or marks of his Client" by setting an astrological figure, which he did successfully for his client. [2d edition (London, 1715), p. 36.]

[38] Diogenes Laertius tells that Democritus was "so nice in his observations," that he could determine whether a young woman was a virgin by her looks and could detect it even though she had been "corrupted" the preceding day. [Wil-liam Wotton, *Reflections Upon Ancient and Modern Learning*, 3d edition cor-rected (London, 1705), p. 97.] William Lilly also claimed to have this talent [Nash, ed., *Hudibras*, II, iii. 285 n.]

[39] Gasper Taliacotius (1553–99), a surgeon at Bologna and author of a treatise on the art of engrafting noses, ears, lips, etc.

[40] An hour-glass was part of the pulpit furniture and visible to the congrega-tion. It was said that if the minister did not preach until the glass was out that he was called lazy, and that if he went much beyond the time the congregation would yawn and stretch to make their impatience known. [Grey, ed., *Hudibras*, I. iii. 1061–62 n.]

[41] See p. 47, n. 9.

[42] See p. 87, n. 21.

[43] House: one of the twelve divisions of the circle representing the zodiac. Also *house* as a building.

Names,[44] a Work no doubt of singular Piety, and like in Time to convert the Astrologers, when they shall derive the Principles and Rudiments of their Science from divine Authority, which now they are fain to borrow of the old heathen Poets. This in Process of Time may enable them (as well as other Trades) to preach for themselves, and save the Charge of hiring old Mungrel Rabines, that are three Quarters *Jews*,[45] to make their Art as lawful as they can, with mighty Arguments drawn from Etymologies and Anagrams.[46] But their Intelligence in the upper World is nothing to what they have in the infernal; for they hold exact Correspondence with the Devils,[47] and can give a perfect Account of their ecclesiastical, civil, and military Discipline. By their Advice the Fiends lately attempted a *Reformation* of their Government, that is, to bring all Things into Confusion, which among them is the greatest Order. They have placed *Minos, Æacus,* and *Rhadamant*[48] on the Bench again since they received a Writ of Ease, and have given the Pettifogging[49] Devils, that were thrown over the Bar for their Honesty, leave to practise again, having first taken an *Engagement* to be true and faithful to the Government. They have entertained the *Furies* again, that were turned out of Service by the later Poets, and given *Charon* a new Coat and Badge. Indeed for their Militia, being out of the Way of Philosophers, they are not so exactly versed in it, and therefore are

---

[44] See lines 596–601 of Du Bartas, "The Fourth Part of the Second Day of the II Weeke," *Divine Weekes and Workes*, trans. Sylvester, in *Complete Works of Joshuah Sylvester*. These lines follow a description of the heavens:

> Yet (curteous Readers) who is it can say
> Whether our Nephews yet another-day
> (More zealous than ourselves in things Divine)
> This curious *Art* shall Christianly refine;
> And give to all these glistering *Figures* then
> Not *Heathen* names, but names of *Holy* men?

[45] A cabalist traditionally was a Jewish doctor who professed the study of the ancient oral tradition (see p. 146, n. 29).

[46] The tradition of the cabala had in some quarters degenerated into juggling with letters and formulas and had been the basis of some medieval magic.

[47] In their concern with the dark powers of the Universe, Hermetic philosophers were, in a sense, Satanists. Certainly they were accused of dealings with the Devil. Cf. the reference by Waite, for example, to a pamphlet published in France, called "Frightful Compacts between the Devil and the so-called Invisibles." [*Real History*, pp. 391–92.]

[48] Judges of the dead in the lower world. The *Furies; Charon,* the ferryman; and *Cerberus,* the three-headed dog, are other creatures of that world.

[49] See p. 111, n. 1.

forced to raise old Poetical Spirits only for Shew, and to make up their Number (like a Captain, that makes a false Number) in which *Cerberus* passes and receives Pay for three. All this they perform by Virtue and Dint of Numbers, which they will have to run through the three Worlds[50] like a Ladder of Ropes, holding the same Proportion in them all, and the universal Privilege of *the great Secret*, which they can prove to be the golden Bough, that served *Æneas* for a Pass to go to Hell with.[51] These Numbers they believe to be the better Sort of Spirits, by the Largeness of their Dominion, which extends from beyond the intelligible World, through all the inferior Worlds, to the Center, which is the uttermost bound of their Empire that Way. They had like to have been chosen Principles in the elementary World, in the Room of old doating *Privation*, but that *Darkness* carried it with the *Brotherhood*[52] in an indirect Way, having cast a Mist before their learned Eyes. They have agreed upon a Truce and Cessation of Hostility between the Elements, and are like to conclude a Peace, by declaring the old Quarrel to arise from the *Intension*, and not from the *Element*,[53] which is a clear Confutation of that old Maxim—*ex nihilo nihil fit*.[54] They believe, that Spirits have a strange natural Allegiance to hard Words, though they mean nothing; by which it should seem, that a well-taught Jackdaw, or one of *James Howel's Trees*[55] may be as able a Conjurer as *Friar Bacon*[56] himself.

---

[50] The Hermeticists speak of a threefold world (set forth by Agrippa in *De Occulta Philosophia*): the terrestrial, the celestial, and the intellectual [domains], which are linked in one by a series of correspondences. [Evelyn Holmes, *Henry Vaughan and the Hermetic Philosophy* (Oxford, 1932), p. 38.]

[51] Cf. *Aeneid*, VI. 136.

[52] I.e., the Brotherhood of the Rosy Cross.

[53] The reference may be to the sensations aroused in the perceiver rather than the properties in a body (element) itself.

[54] "From nothing, nothing is made." I.e., every effect must have a cause. This was the dictum by which Xenophanes, the founder of the Eleatic School, set forth the theory of the eternity of matter, the unity and unchangeableness of the Divine. [*Brewer's Dictionary of Phrase and Fable*; see also Persius, *Satires*, III. 84.]

[55] See James Howell, *Dodona's Grove, or the Vocall Forrest* (1640), a political allegory, where figures under the names of trees (or names derived from them) express various political views.

[56] Roger Bacon (1214?–94), philosopher and author of works in chemistry and alchemy as well as treatises on science. By his contemporaries and in legend he was regarded as a necromancer, and the creator of a brazen head that could speak. See *Friar Bacon and Friar Bungay* (1594) by Robert Greene.

Next to Words they are catched with Characters, which are nothing else but Marks, that Spirits make for their Names, because they cannot write—These the *Brethren* have always in Blanks, to which they can write what they please, and then arrest them upon it, and keep them safe, until they put in Bail to answer *whatsoever they shall be demanded.* By this means they have found out, who is the true Owner of the *Beast* in the *Apocalyps,* which has long passed for a Stray among the Learned; what is the true Product of 666, that has rung like *Whittington's* Bells[57] in the Ears of Expositors; how long it is to the Day of Judgment, and, which is more wonderful, whether it shall be in Winter or Summer.[58] They can tell the Age of *Time* without looking into his Mouth, like a Horse's, as the Chronologers do, or searching the Church-Book: for they have certain historical Spirits, that will give them as able an Account of the general History of the World, as *Rosse*[59] himself. By the Help of these they can immediately tell, who was the first Christian Cobler, without diving into *Arabic* Short-Hand, or travelling far into the *East*[60] (as some have done) to fetch that, which they might have had at home in the Legend—A very learned Oversight.

They have found out an admirable Way to decide all Controversies, and resolve Doubts of the greatest Difficulty by Way of *horary Questions;*[61] for as the learned Astrologers, observing the Impossibility of knowing the exact Moment of any Man's Birth, do use very prudently *to cast the Nativity of the Question*[62] (like him, that

---

[57] See p. 81, n. 11.

[58] Answers to such riddles were sought by cabalists.

[59] Alexander Ross or Rosse (1590–1654), a Scottish clergyman who wrote *A View of All Religions in the World, from the Creation, to his own Time* (1652). See also the reference to him in the opening lines of Part I, Canto II of *Hudibras.*

[60] "It is not an unusual device to account for obscure periods in the lives of Hermetic philosophers by extensive eastern travellings." [A. E. Waite, Preface to *Works of Paracelsus* (London, 1894), p. xi.]

The reputed founder of the Rosicrucians, Christian Rosencruz, is said to have traveled to the East, where he came into possession of much secret wisdom. [*Encyclopaedia Britannica.*]

[61] William Lilly, *Christian Astrology,* 2d edition (1659), p. 34, refers to "horary Questions" (or questions of the hour). For erecting or setting a figure, either of a Question or of a nativity, one must include in his consideration the year, month, day of the week, hour, or part of the hour of that day.

[62] When anyone came to an astrologer to have the nativity of his child cast and could not give the hour and minute of its birth, the astrologer took the

swallowed the Doctor's Bill instead of the Medicine)[63] and find the Answer as certain and infallible, as if they had known the very Instant, in which the Native, as they call him, crept into the World: so in Questions either so subtile and obscure, that Truth plays least in Sight, and Words and Terms go for no more than a Jugler's Canting; the only Way in the World is to consider the critical Minute of the Question, and from thence resolve it. This had been an excellent Course for the old Roundheaded *Stoics* to find out, whether *Bonum was Corpus, or Virtue an Animal,*[64] about which they had so many fierce Encounters in their *Stoa,* that about one thousand four hundred and forty lost their Lives upon the Place, and far many more their Beards, and Teeth, and Noses[65]—But this had never been, had the *Brethren* lived in those Days, who can not only part all the mad Frays of Controversy in Philosophy, but Religion also, and, like true canonical Constables, make those spiritual Swash-

---

position of the planets the minute the question itself was asked and by that means judged the future of the child, as if the child had been born at the time of the question. [Grey, ed., *Hudibras,* I. i. 605 n.]

[63] "This alludes to a well-known story told in Henry Stephen's apology for Herodotus. A physician having prescribed for a countryman, gave him the paper on which he had written, and told him, he must be sure to take that, meaning the potion he had therein ordered. The countryman, misunderstanding the doctor, wrapt up the paper like a bolus, swallowed it, and was cured." [Nash, ed., *Hudibras,* I. i. 604 n.]

[64] *Bonum was Corpus:* "The stoics allowed of no incorporeal substance, no medium between body and nothing. With them accidents and qualities, virtues and vices, the passions of the mind, and everything else, was body. . . ." [Ibid., II. ii. 18 n. See also Seneca, *Epistles,* CXIII.]

Virtue an Animal: "Philosophy, they [Stoics] say, is like an animal, Logic corresponding to the bones and sinews, Ethics to the fleshy parts, Physics to the soul." [Diogenes Laertius, "Zeno," trans. R. D. Hicks, in *Lives of Eminent Philosophers* (London and New York, 1925), VII. 40.]

[65] Butler here seems to depart from the account of Diogenes Laertius, who in "Zeno" (VII. 5) says that Zeno read his lectures in the stoa (portico), a place he [Diogenes] hopes will not be the site of more civil disturbances, for, he says, at the time when the thirty tyrants governed, 1400 citizens were killed there. He makes no mention of a brawl among philosophers, only of civil executions which took place at least a century before the stoical school was founded. [Nash, ed., *Hudibras,* II. ii. 22 n.]

But cf. Butler's note to *Hudibras,* III. ii. 15: "*In Porticu (Stoicorum Scholâ Athenis) Discipulorem seditionibus, mille Quadrigenti triginta Cives intersecti sunt. Diog. Laert. in vita Zenonis,* p. 383. Those old *Virtuoso's* were better Proficients in those Exercises, than the Modern, who seldom improve higher than Cuffing, and Kicking."

Bucklers deliver up their Weapons, and keep the Peace. Nor is their Power and Authority less in composing of civil Differences; for they have a Receipt to make two Armies, that are drawn up ready to fight, put up their Swords and face about. This is so easy, they say, that it has been done by Women: but their Way is to raise a Storm, which they can do at any Time with the Liver of a Wolf, and make it thunder and lighten, as easily as strike Fire in a Tinder-Box. This, they say, has been experimented between *Hanibal* and the *Romans*; and certainly it is more probable than that Course, which some modern Philosophers have taken to do it by Way of Argument, which is so preposterous, that they believe, they can prevent or compose all civil Wars by proving, that Mankind was born to nothing else;[66] and will undertake to persuade Men to Subjection and Obedience by making it appear, that Nature brought them forth all equal:[67] that pretend to secure the Titles of Princes by proving, that whosoever can get their Power from them has a Right to it; and persuade them and their Subjects to observe imaginary Contracts by arguing, that they are invalid as soon as made—But had these Men conversed with the *Brethren*, they would never have brought Contradictions so barefaced together, but have drest them up with some pretty Disguise, which they have always ready for such Occasions, that, though they had been never so subtile and senseless, should have made them pass at least for Mysteries. For though they very much contemn any Knowledge, that is either derived from Sense or reducible to it; and account Demonstration too gross and low an Aim for the sublime Speculations of the Intellect: Though they believe their own Senses base and unworthy of their Notice (like that delicate *Roman*, who being put in his Litter by his Servants, asked, whether he sat or no)[68] yet they never apply themselves to any Thing abstruse or subtile, but with much Caution; and commonly resolve all Questions of that Nature by Numbers—*Monades*, *Triades*, and *Decades*,[69] are with them a Kind of philosophical *Fulhams*,[70] with which, like cunning Gamesters, they can throw what they please, and be sure to win; for no Body can disprove them. And truly they are much to be commended, if for nothing else, yet for their ingenious

---

[66] Apparently a reference to Hobbes. See p. 29, n. 5.
[67] A reference to James Harrington. See p. 35, n. 20.
[68] I have found no identification of the Roman referred to here.
[69] Terms used in dicing.
[70] False dice.

Brevity: for they never entertain their Readers with tedious Circumstances, to the great Expence of their Time, but dispatch immediately, and make them understand as much of these Affairs in a few Minutes, as they can do in an Age; which is more than can be said of those, that use to tie Argument to Argument (as Monkies use to hang by one another's Tails in *India*) until they have made a Pair of learned Tarryers,[71] which neither they, nor any Body else knows how to undo. But the *Brethren*, if this will not do, have yet more curious Ways; for they have invented Optics, in which they will put Atoms and Ideas, and give the Eye as perfect an Account of their nicest Subtleties, as all the Philosophers in the World can with all their Disputations. In these you may see the Bone *Luz*,[72] and *Descartes*'s Die in the Brain[73] with every Spot in it, as exactly as the Eyes of a Flea in a magnifying Glass. They have made Spectacles to read *Jacob Boehmen*[74] and *Ben-Israel*[75] with, which, like those Glasses that revert the Object, will turn the wrong End of their Sentences upwards, and make them look like Sense. They have built a philosophical Hospital

---

[71] Loops or knots?

[72] "There is in man's body a certain little bone, which the Hebrews call LVZ, of the bigness of a pulse that is husked, which is subject to no corruption, neither is it overcome with fire, but is always preserved unhurt, out of which, as they say, as a plant out of a seed, or animal bodies shall in the resurrection of the dead spring up. And these Virtues are not cleared up by reason, but by experience." [C. Agrippa, *The Philosophy of Natural Magic*, ed. L. W. de Laurence (n.p., 1913), pp. 87–88.]

[73] " '. . . Descartes was the first who discovered a certain part of the brain, called by anatomists the Pineal Gland, to be the immediate receptacle of the soul, where she is affected with all sorts of perceptions, and exerts all her operations by the intercourse of the animal spirits which run through the nerves that are thence extended to all parts of the body.' " [*Guardian*, No. 35, April 21, 1713, in *British Essayists*, ed. Lionel T. Berguer (London, 1823), XVI, 164.]

See Descartes, *Les Passions de L'Ame* (*The Passions of the Soul*), Pt. I. xxxi.

[74] Jacob Boehme or Behmen (1575–1624): German mystic, known for writings which were unintelligible except to the initiated. The English translation of his works appeared 1645–62.

[75] Menasseh Ben-Israel (1604–59), a learned Jewish Rabbi born in Spain, who visited London first in 1655 to induce Cromwell to take steps for the readmission of Jews, who had been banished from England by Edward I. When a conference at Whitehall made up of representatives of the Church, the law, and trade could come to no conclusion, Cromwell acted on his own responsibility and announced to Parliament his intention to allow the Jews to settle in England, and in the following year immigration began.

Nash, ed., *Hudibras*, III. ii. 1616 n., refers the reader to information about the bone *Luz* (see n. 72 above) in Ben-Israel, *de Resurrectione*, II. 15.

for the Relief of those, that are blind, deaf, and dumb, by establishing a Community of the Senses, whereby any one may supply the Place of another in his Absence, and do his Business for him as well as that which is out of the Way. This is an Art to teach Men to see with their Ears, and hear with their Eyes and Noses, and it has been found true by Experience and Demonstration, if we may believe the History of the *Spaniard*,[76] that could see Words, and swallow Music by holding the Peg of a Fiddle between his Teeth; or him that could sing his Part backwards at first Sight, which those that were near him might hear with their Noses; or *Dubartas*'s Painter,[77] that could draw the Report of a Gun, as it is very faithfully rendered by Mr. *Silvester* thus—

> *There in a Wood behind a Box-Tree shrinking*
> *He draws a Fowler with his left Eye winking;*
> *Down falls the Cock, up from the touch-Pan flies*
> *A ruddy Flame, that in a Moment dies;*
> *Off goes the Gun, and through the Forest rings*
> *The thund'ring Bullet born on fiery Wings.*[78]

No doubt a very strange Landscape, and not unlike that, which *Anthroposophus*[79] has made of the *invisible Mountain of the Philos-*

---

[76] "This alludes to a Story told by Sir *Kenelme* Digby of a *Spanish* Nobleman, younger Brother to the Constable of *Castile*, who being born deaf, and consequently dumb, was taught to understand what was said to him by looking at the Person who spoke, and also to give proper and distinct Answers; from whence Sir *Kenelme* takes occasion to say—*that he could hear by his Eyes, and See Words.* See *Digby* of Body." [Thyer's note. The story referred to is in Chap. XXVIII.]

[77] On the Seventh Day of the First Week God in the similitude of a painter looks on what He has made.

[78] "The Seventh Day of the First Week," ll. 32–39, in Du Bartas, *Divine Weekes and Workes* [trans. Sylvester, in *Complete Works of Joshuah Sylvester*], reads as follows:

> There on his knee (behinde a Box-Tree shrinking)
> A skillfull Gunner, with his left eye winking,
> Levels directly at an Oak hard by;
> Whereon a hundred groaning Culvers cry;
> Down fals the Cock, up from the Touch-pan flies
> A ruddy flash that in a moment dyes.
> Off goes the Gun, and through the Forrest rings
> The thundring bullet, born on fiery wings.

[79] In the pamphlet war between Henry More, Cambridge Platonist, and Thomas Vaughan the name *Anthroposophus* was applied by More to Vaughan. See More, *Observations on "Anthroposophia Theomagica" and "Anima Magica*

ophers;[80] but nothing comparable to those Curiosities of Knowledge, which they have comprized in single Words, not inferior to the nine-Pins and a Bowl in a Cherry-Stone.[81] They will pick Mysteries out of Syllables and Letters, as Juglers do Money out of their Noses—This they learned of the Forefathers of Anagrams, the *Rabbins*.[82] Beside this they have admirable Methods to dispose and lay up Learning in, like those odd Contrivances in Cabinets, where nobody can tell how to find it but themselves. *Lully's* Ars Brevis[83] is one of these, wherein *Magnitudo, Bonitas,* and *Quomodo*[84] are several concealed Drawers, in which they, that have any Learning, may lay it up safe, and (if there be any Truth in his Commentator)[85] they that have none too, which is not altogether so strange—In these it will sprout and grow if it self, as Onions do in the Spring above Ground, and multiply no Man can imagine how, that does not very well understand the equivocal Generation[86] of Maggots.

They can grave the Signets of the Planets in precious Stones with their own Influences, as Diamonds are cut with their own Dust—These

---

Abscondita" (1650). *Anthroposophia Theomagica* (1650) is a book written to show the condition of men after death.

[80] Thomas Vaughan's *Lumen de lumine* contains a passage on the Invisible Mountain of the Magi.

A Rosicrucian Allegory describes a mountain in the center of the earth, which is both small and great; soft, but hard and strong; far off, but near; and it is invisible. Most valuable treasures are to be found there, and the way is open only to the courageous and the persistent. The greatest treasure to be gained is "a certain exalted tincture, with which the world, if it served God and were worthy of such gifts, might be tinged and turned into most pure gold." [Waite, *Real History*, pp. 443–44.]

[81] See the Character of A Curious Man for further examples.

[82] See p. 149, n. 45.

[83] Lully's *Ars Brevis* (see p. 144, n. 21) set forth his "technical system for the due fitting of knowledge to the memory, by a right use in reference either to simple or complex objects of study, of propositions, definitions, arguments, and exhaustive questions; the application, in fact, of a short and good logical process to the art of study. . . . Men who began their studies late, made, it was said, a surprising progress by its help. Cornelius Agrippa was among the learned men who used it." Agrippa, however, in *On the Vanity of Arts and Sciences* warned that it could be used to "display learning and wit, not . . . to increase it." [Morley, *The Life of Henry Cornelius Agrippa*, pp. 159–60.]

[84] Vague, general terms (greatness; goodness, excellence; in what manner, how).

[85] Henry Cornelius Agrippa. See p. 144.

[86] See p. 67, n. 2.

being made in a *right Minute*[87] have an admirable magnetic Virtue instilled, to draw Learning, Wit, Valour, Wealth, Honour, and Women after the Owner, just as the Loadstone does Iron. These were used much by the *Knights-errant*, which made them more valiant than Giants, and cunning than Conjurers; they were always furnished with Ladies and Damsels; and though we find little Mention made of their Wealth, yet they always lived at a high Rate, when the Value of a Knight's Estate in those Times was but a small Matter.

They have an admirable Way to distinguish the Influences of the Stars; for among so many Myriads of good and bad, that are confused and mixt together, they will presently separate those of virtuous Use from the Evil, like *Boccalini*'s Drum,[88] that would beat up all the Weeds in a Garden, and leave the Herbs standing—These they keep in Glasses, like the Powder made of the Sun-Beams, till they have Occasion to use them. They are commonly the better Half of *the great Magistery*; and serve them to innumerable Purposes in all their Professions of Philosophy, Magic, Divinity, Physics, Astrology, Alchimy, Bawdery, Witchcraft, &c. for, beside a rare Property they have to restore sinful old Age to Virtue, Youth, and Understanding, they are very sovereign to clear the Eyes of the Mind, and make a blear-ey'd Intellect see like a Cat in the Dark, though it be stark blind in the Light.

These Influences, they would make us believe, are a Kind of little invisible Midwives, which the Stars employ at the Nativities of Men, to swathe and bind up their Spirits, (just as Midwives do their Bodies) which being then most tender and flexible, they can mold into what Form they please: for mixing with the Air their first breath, they do not only infect the Soul and Body, and their Faculties, but the

---

[87] I.e., when the planets are in the correct positions.

[88] See Trajano Boccalini, *Irragguagli di Parnasso* or, *Advertisements from Parnassus*, trans. Henry, Earl of Monmouth, 3d edition corrected [London, 1674], pp. 18–19.

Ambassadors from all the Gardeners of the world came to the court of Apollo to obtain some instrument to better weed their gardens. They had been impressed by the benefits given to princes by the miraculous Instrument of Drum and Trumpet, that had purged the state from "evil weeds, and seditious plants." But Apollo said in refusing them that, if seditious men could be as easily discerned as weeds, he would have given garden instruments to the princes. Apollo sent the Ambassadors away, for he believed it was "impertinent and ridiculous to compare the purging of the world from seditious Spirits, with the weeding of noysom herbs out of a Garden."

Tempers, Disposition, Opinions, Actions (and their Events) of Men with a certain fatal Contagion; which, like a slow-working Poison lying still for many Years, shall afterwards, like Diseases and Sores, break out in the several Actions and Emergencies of their Lives. And yet it should seem, these Influences are but a Kind of Mock-*destinies*, whose Business it is to tamper with all Men, but compel none—This the Learned call *inclining* not *necessitating*.[89] They have a small precarious Empire, wholly at the Will of the Subject; they can raise no Men but only Volunteers, for their Power does not extend to press any. Their Jurisdiction is only to invite Men to the Gallows, or the Pillory in a civil Way, but force none so much as to a Whipping, unless, like *Catholic* Penitents, they have a mind to it, and will lay it on themselves. They are very like, if not the same, to the Temptations of the *Devil*—They can persuade a Man to break his Neck, or drown himself, present him with a Rope and a Dagger, and desire him to make Choice of which he pleases; but if they do not take him just in the Humour, they may as well go hang themselves. As little Good as Hurt can they do any Man against his Will—They cannot make a private Man a Prince, unless he have a very strong Desire to be so; nor make any Man happy in any Condition whatsoever, unless his own Liking concur. They could never put Fools in Authority, as they use to do, if they did not take Delight in it; nor make them great Philosophers and profound Scholars, unless they pleased themselves with Study. As for the Wise, the Learned tell us, they have nothing to do with them; and if they make any Attempt upon them; it is to no Purpose: for when they *incline* a Man to be a Knave, and prevail upon him, he must be a Fool (for they have no Power over the Wise) and so all their Labour is lost.

They use to make solemn Vows to Almighty God, never to discover[90] *the great Secret*[91] to any Person living (as *Lully* does)[92] and

---

[89] "There be those who think they are necessitated by Fate, their Stars have so decreed, and therefore they grumble at their hard fortune. . . . Yet let no man be troubled, or find himself grieved by such Predictions, as *Hier.* [Hieronymous] *Wolfius* well saith in his Astrological Dialogue [*Praefix. gen. Leovitii*], *non sunt praetoriana decreta*, they be but conjectures, the Stars incline, but not enforce. . . ." [Burton, *Anatomy of Melancholy*, ed. Shilleto, III, 279.]

[90] Reveal.

[91] See p. 140, n. 3.

[92] Raymond Lully (see p. 156, n. 83 and p. 144, n. 21) is said by Eliphas Levi to have been "a grand and sublime adept of Hermetic science" who left behind as "monuments of his unparalleled alchemical proficiency" treatises, testaments,

yet presently will undertake to teach it; but conjure every Scholar to keep it to himself, like Treason that dies if it take Air. Then they forbid them to converse with any, that have not Faith in the Art, that they may hear as little against it as they have to say for it; an excellent Preservative to keep an implicit Faith from taking cold—This is the high-Way of all Imposters, who can never do more than another believes. But after so many Precepts and Rules delivered with the greatest Confidence and Presumption of Certainty, they will tell you, that this Art is not to be attained but by divine Revelation, and only to be expected by holy and sanctified Persons, that have left behind them all the concernments of this World; whereby it seems, *this Shadow of Art follows those only that fly it, and flies from those that follow it.*

AN ALDERMAN

Has taken his Degree in Cheating, and the highest of his Faculty; or paid for refusing his *Mandamus*. He is a Peer of the City, and a Member of their upper House, who, as soon as he arrives at so many thousand Pounds, is bound by the Charter to serve the Public with so much Understanding, what shift soever he make to raise it, and wear a Chain[1] about his Neck like a Raindeer, or in Default to commute, and make Satisfaction in ready Money, the best Reason of the Place; for which he has the Name only, like a titular Prince, and is an *Alderman extraordinary*.[2] But if his Wife can prevail with him to stand, he becomes one of the City-supporters, and, like the Unicorn in the King's Arms, wears a Chain about his Neck very right-worshipfully. He wears Scarlet, as the Whore of *Babylon*[a]/[3] does, not for her honesty, but the Rank and Quality she is of among the Wicked. When he sits as a Judge in his Court he is absolute, and uses arbitrary Power; for he is not bound to understand what he

---

codicils. There is some question about the genuineness of some of the writings ascribed to Lully and about whether there were two men with the same name. [A. E. Waite, "Raymond Lully," in *Lives of the Alchemystical Philosophers* (London, 1888).]

  [1] See p. 105, n. 2.

  [2] Supernumerary.

  [a] Babylon] Balylon

  [3] Revelation, XVII.

does, nor render an Account why he gives Judgment on one Side rather than another; but his Will is sufficient to stand for his Reason, to all Intents and Purposes. He does no public Business without eating and drinking, and never meets about Matters of Importance, but the Cramming his Inside is the most weighty Part of the Work of the Day. He dispatches no public Affair until he has thoroughly dined upon it, and is fully satisfied with Quince-Pye and Custard: for Men are wiser, the *Italians* say, after their Bellies are full, than when they are fasting, and he is very cautious to omit no Occasion of improving his Parts that Way. He is so careful of the Interest of his Belly, and manages it so industriously, that in a little Space it grows great and takes Place of all the rest of his Members, and becomes so powerful, that they will never be in a Condition to rebel against it any more.[4] He is cloathed in Scarlet the Livery of his Sins, like the rich Glutton, to put him in Mind of what Means he came to his Wealth and Preferment by. He makes a Trade of his Eating, and, like a Cock, scrapes when he feeds; for the Public pays for all and more, which he and his Brethren share among themselves; for they never make a dry Reckoning. When he comes to be Lord-Mayor he does not keep a great House, but a very great House-warming for a whole Year; for though he invites all the *Companies* in the City he does not treat them, but they club to entertain him, and pay the Reckoning beforehand. His Fur-gown[5] makes him look a great deal bigger than he is, like the Feathers of an Owl, and when he pulls it off, he looks as if he were fallen away, or like a Rabbet, had his Skin pulled off.

A DISPUTANT

Is a Holder of Arguments, and Wagers too, when he cannot make them good. He takes naturally to Controversy, like Fishes in *India* that are said to have Worms in their Heads, and swim always against the Stream. The greatest Mastery of his Art consists in turning and winding the State of the Question, by which means he can easily defeat whatsoever has been said by his Adversary, though excellently to the Purpose, like a Bowler, that knocks away the Jack, when he

---

[4] The fable of the members rebelling against the belly was a Renaissance commonplace. Versions are found in Livy [II. xxxii], Plutarch, and Annaeus Florus [I. xxiii], but more familiarly in Shakespeare's *Coriolanus*, I. i.

[5] See p. 107, n. 1.

sees another Man's Bowl lye nearer to it than his own.[1] Another of his Faculties is with a Multitude of Words to render what he says so difficult to be recollected, that his Adversary may not easily know what he means, and consequently not understand what to answer, to which he secretly reserves an Advantage to reply by interpreting what he said before otherwise than he at first intended it, according as he finds it serve his Purpose to evade whatsoever shall be objected. Next to this, to pretend not to understand, or misinterprets what his Antagonist says, though plain enough, only to divert him from the Purpose, and to take Occasion from his Exposition of what he said to start new Cavils on the Bye, and run quite away from the Question: but when he finds himself prest Home and beaten from all his Guards, to amuse the Foe with some senseless Distinction, like a falsified Blow, that never hits where 'tis aimed, but while it is minded makes Way for some other Trick that may pass. But that which renders him invincible is Abundance of Confidence and Words, which are his offensive and defensive Arms; for a brazen Face is a natural Helmet or Beaver, and he that has Store of Words needs not surrender for Want of Ammunition—No Matter for Reason and Sense, that go for no more in Disputations than the Justice of a Cause does in War, which is understood but by few, and commonly regarded by none. For the Custom of Disputants is not so much to destroy one another's Reason, as to cavil at the Manner of expressing it, right or wrong; for they believe—*Dolus an Virtus*,[2] &c. ought to be allowed in Controversy as War, and he that gets the Victory on any Terms whatsoever deserves it, and gets it honourably. He and his Opponent are like two false Lute-strings, that will never stand in Tune to one another; or like two Tennis-players, whose greatest Skill consists in avoiding one another's Strokes.

A SOT

Has found out a Way to renew, not only his Youth, but his Childhood, by being stewed, like old *Æson*,[1] in Liquor; much better

---

[1] See p. 58, n. 16 on the game of bowls.

[2] "Deceit or Valour . . . ." See p. 30, n. 6.

[1] Jason's father, Aeson, was made young again when Medea took the blood from his veins and refilled them with the juice of certain herbs. See Ovid, *Metamorphoses*, Bk. VII.

than the *Virtuoso*'s Way of making old Dogs young again:[2] for he is a Child again at second hand, never the worse for the Wearing, but as purely fresh, simple, and weak, as he was at first. He has stupify'd his Senses by living in a moist Climate according to the Poet—*Bœotum in crasso jurares aëre natum*.[3] He measures his Time by Glasses of Wine, as the Ancients did by Water-Glasses; and as *Hermes Trismegistus*[4] is said to have kept the first Accompt of Hours by the pissing of a Beast dedicated to *Serapis*,[5] he revives that Custom in his own Practice, and observes it punctually in passing his Time. He is like a Statue placed in a moist Air; all the Lineaments of Humanity are mouldered away, and there is nothing left of him but a rude Lump of the Shape of a Man, and no one part entire. He has drowned himself in a But of Wine, as the Duke of *Clarence* was served by his Brother.[6] He has washed down his Soul and pist it out; and lives now only by the Spirit of Wine or Brandy, or by an Extract drawn off his Stomach. He has swallowed his Humanity, and drunk himself into a Beast, as if he had pledged *Madam Circe*,[7] and done her Right. He is drowned in a Glass like a Fly, beyond the Cure of Crums of Bread, or the Sun Beams. He is like a Spring-Tide; when he is drunk to his high-Water-Mark he swells and looks big, runs against the Stream, and overflows every Thing that stands in his Way; but when the Drink within him is at an Ebb, he shrinks within his Banks, and falls so low and shallow, that Cattle may pass over him. He governs all his Actions by the Drink within him, as a *Quaker* does by the Light within him;[8] has a different Humour for every Nick his Drink rises to, like the Degrees of

[2] See p. 124 and p. 124, n. 10.

[3] "You would swear he was born in the heavy air of Boetia." [Horace, *Epistles*, II. i. 244, in *Satires, Epistles and Ars Poetica*, trans. Fairclough.]

As the dense atmosphere of the moist lowlands of Boetia was contrasted with the clear atmosphere of Attica, so the contrast was made between the proverbial dullness of the Boetians and the sharp wit of the Athenians.

[4] The "thrice great Hermes" of Milton's "Il Penseroso." Hermes Trismegistus is the name given to the author of the so-called Hermetic writings on philosophy and religion, which combined Neoplatonic, Judaic, and Cabalistic theosophy (and probably were written about the fourth century). The name is applied also to the Egyptian god Thoth, who is more or less the same as the Greek Hermes, the author of all mystical doctrine.

[5] The sacred beast is the baboon, which is solary and, according to Hermes Trismegistus, suggested to man his divisions of time. [Agrippa, *The Philosophy of Natural Magic*, p. 98 and p. 98 n.]

[6] See Shakespeare, *Richard III*, I. iv.

[7] See the *Odyssey*, Bk. X.

[8] See the Character of A Quaker.

the Weatherglass,[9] and proceeds from Ribaldry and Bawdery to Politics, Religion, and Quarreling, until it is at the Top, and then it is the Dog-Days with him; from whence he falls down again, until his Liquor is at the Bottom, and then he lyes quiet, and is frozen up.

AN ATHEIST

Is a bold Disputant, that takes upon him to prove the hardest Negative in the whole World, and from the Impossibility of his Attempt may be justly concluded not to understand it: for he that does not understand so much as the Difficulty of his Undertaking, can know nothing else of it; and he, that will venture to comprehend that, which is not within his Reach, does not know so far as his own Latitude, much less the Extent of that which lies beyond it. He denies that to be, which he finds by undeniable Inference to be in all Things; and, *because it is every where, would have it to be no where*; as if that old Gingle were logically true in all Things, because it is so in nothing. If a blind Man should affirm, there is no such Thing as Light, and an Owl no such Thing as Darkness, it would be hard to say, which is the verier Owl of the two; and yet both would speak *true*, according to their own Apprehensions and Experience, but *false*, because it is of Things beyond the Reach of their Capacities. He draws a Map of Nature by his own Fancy, and bounds her how he pleases, without Regard to the Position of the Heavens, by which only her Latitude is to be understood, and without which all his Speculations are vain, idle, and confused. Nothing but Ignorance can produce a Confidence bold enough to determine of the first Cause; *for all the inferior Works of Nature are Objects more fit for our Wonder, than Curiosity; and she conceals the Truth of Things, that lye under our View, from us, to discourage us from attempting those, that are more remote.* He commits as great an Error in making *Nature* (which is nothing but the Order and Method, by which all Causes and Effects in the World are governed) to be the first Cause, as if he should suppose the Laws, by which a Prince governs, to be the Prince himself.

A JUGLER

Is an artificial Magician, that with his Fingers casts a Mist before the Eyes of the Rabble, and makes his Balls walk invisible

---

[9] See p. 137, n. 2.

which Way he pleases. He does his Feats behind a Table,[1] like a *Presbyterian* in a Conventicle, but with much more Dexterity and Cleanliness, and therefore all Sorts of People are better pleased with him. Most Professions and Mysteries derive the Practice of all their Faculties from him, but use them with less Ingenuity and Candour; for the more he deceives those he has to do with, the better he deals with them, while those that imitate him in a lawful Calling are far more dishonest; for the more they impose the more they abuse. All his Cheats are primitive, and therefore more innocent and of greater Purity than those that are by Tradition from Hand to Hand derived to them: for he conveys Money out of one Man's Pocket into another's with much more Sincerity and Ingenuity than those, that do it in a *legal* Way, and for a less considerable, though more conscientious, Reward. He will fetch Money out of his own Throat with a great deal more of Delight and Satisfaction to those that pay him for it, than any Haranguer whatsoever, and make it chuck in his Throat better than a Lawyer, that has talked himself hoarse, and swallowed so many Fees, that he is almost choaked. He will spit Fire, and blow Smoke out of his Mouth, with less Harm and Inconvenience to the Government, than a seditious Holder-forth;[2] and yet all these disown and scorn him, even as Men, that are grown great and rich, despise the Meanness of their Originals. He calls upon *Presto begone*, and the *Babylonian*'s *Tooth*,[3] to amuse and divert the Rabble from looking too narrowly into his Tricks; while a zealous Hypocrite, that calls Heaven and Earth to witness his, turns up the Eye, and shakes the Head at his Idolatry and Profanation. He goes the Circuit to all Country Fairs, where he meets with good strolling Practice, and comes up to *Bartholomew* Fair[4] as his *Michaelmas* Term;[5] after which he removes to some great Thorough-fare, where he hangs out himself in Effigie, like a *Dutch* Malefactor, that all those, that pass by, may for their Money have a Trial of his Skill. He endeavours to plant himself, as near as he can, to some Puppet-Play, Monster, or Mountebank, as the most convenient Situation, and, when Trading grows

---

[1] Puritans insisted that the Communion table be placed in the body of the church. Altars were to them Popish inventions.

[2] Preacher.

[3] Some kind of mumbo jumbo. A "Babylonian" is figuratively an "astrologer."

[4] See p. 117, n. 14.

[5] The term or session beginning September 29, the Feast of Saint Michael, for the Courts of Justice in England. (Note here the comparison of the juggler with a judge riding on quarterly circuit.)

scant, they join all their Forces together, and make up one grand Shew, and admit the Cut-Purse[6] and Ballad-Singer to trade under them, as Orange-Women[7] do at a Playhouse.

A SCEPTIC

Is a Critic, that deals in Wholesale; he never censures but in gross, as being the most thriving and easy Trade of Wit: for the Discovery of particular Errors in Knowledge requires deeper Insight, has more of difficult Subtlety, and less of Glory; as it is easier by much to cry down a Science than understand it, and more brave to appear above it, than skilful in it. He has a natural Inclination and Ambition to Knowledge; but being unfortunate in a Temper of Wit not capable of it, derives his Glory from the Remedy of his Defects (as Men do their Bravery from their Nakedness) and undervaluing that, which he cannot attain to, would make his Necessity appear a Virtue, and his Ignorance the Choice of his Judgment. Much of this proceeds from his Envy, which is so impatient of seeing any Man exceed him in that, which he would gladly pretend to, that with *Caesar* he had rather destroy the Commonwealth of Letters, than endure another to be greater than himself in it.[1] If it be his Misfortune to be engaged in an Argument, his constant Method is Catechism; for he will be sure to ask Questions only, and put others to answer, a Game at which the dullest Idiot may play with the wisest in the World, and be too hard for him; and when with his Pedigree of

---

[6] A pickpocket. In the day when men hung their purses by a strap to their belts on the outside, the term *cutpurse* was appropriate to the procedure.

[7] In the pit, where the poorer classes watched the entertainment, women selling oranges pushed through the spectators, adding to the tumult in the Restoration theater. Men often left their seats in the tiers to flirt with the "racy-tongued" orange girls. Fruit, ale, nuts, and tobacco were on sale also. [See Bryant, *The England of Charles II*, p. 36, and Christina Hole, *English Sports and Pastimes* (London and New York, 1949), pp. 141 and 138.]

[1] Perhaps pertinent are these words on the "envious and malicious," "insolent and cruel" Gaius Caligula: "He even thought of destroying the poems of Homer, asking why he should not have the same privilege as Plato, who excluded Homer from his ideal commonwealth. More than that he all but removed the writings and the busts of Vergil and of Titus Livius from all the libraries, railing at the former as a man of no talent and very little learning, and the latter as a verbose and careless historian." [Suetonius, "Gaius Caligula," in *Lives of the Caesars*, trans. Rolfe, IV. xxxiv. 2.]

Questions, that beget one another, he has driven you as far as the Wit of Man can reach, because you can go no further, he will conclude you have not moved at all. As if you should tell him of the Siege of *Troy*, and do not begin (as *Horace*'s Poetaster did) with the hatching of *Castor* and *Pollux*,[2] he will not believe you can say any Thing of *Hector* and *Ajax*. He is a worse Tyrant than *Caligula* wished himself; for in denying Reason, Sense, and Demonstration he cuts off all the best Heads of Mankind at a Blow.[3]

A PROJECTOR[1]

Is by Interpretation a Man of *Forecast*. He is an Artist of Plots, Designs, and Expedients to find out Money, as others hide it, where nobody would look for it. He is a great Rectifier of the Abuses of all Trades and Mysteries, yet has but one Remedy for all Diseases, that is, by getting a Patent to share with them, by Virtue of which they become authorised, and consequently cease to be Cheats. He is a great Promoter of the public Good, and makes it his Care and Study to contrive Expedients, that the Nation may not be ill served with false Rags, arbitrary Puppet-Plays, and insufficient Monsters, of all which he endeavours to get the Superintendency. He will undertake to render treasonable Pedlars, that carry Intelligence between *Rebels*

---

[2] Stasimus is credited with the authorship of *Cypria*, a poem in eleven books which forms an introduction to the *Iliad*. *Cypria* begins not *in medias res* (as does the *Iliad*) but rather at the beginning, with the story of the eggs of Leda. Cf. Horace, *Ars Poetica*: "Nor does he [the poet] begin . . . the war of Troy from the twin eggs. Ever he hastens to the issue, and hurries his hearer into the story's midst, as if already known. . . ." [In *Satires, Epistles, and Ars Poetica*, trans. Fairclough, pp. 146–49.]

Castor and Pollux, twin sons of Zeus also known as the Dioscuri, Homer says were sons of Leda and Tyndareus, King of Lacedaemon, and thus brothers of Helen. Jupiter is said to have visited Leda in the form of a swan. She produced two eggs: from one came Castor and Clytemnestra; from the other Pollux and Helen.

[3] Angered at the rabble for applauding a faction which he opposed, Caligula cried, " 'I wish the Roman people had but a single neck'. . . ." [Suetonius, "Gaius Caligula," in *Lives of the Caesars*, trans. Rolfe, IV. xxx; referred to by Seneca, *De Ira*, III. xix. 2.

[1] Literally, one who forms a project or designs some enterprise but at this period the term was usually used with an invidious connotation: a schemer, one who lives by his wits, a speculator, a cheat. [*O.E.D.*]

and *Fanatics*, true Subjects and well-affected to the Government for half a Crown a Quarter, which he takes for giving them Licence to do so securely and uncontrouled. He gets as much by those Projects that miscarry, as by those that hold (as Lawyers are paid as well for undoing as preserving of Men) for when he has drawn in Adventurers to purchase Shares of the Profit, the sooner it is stopped, the better it proves for him; for, his own Business being done, he is the sooner rid of theirs. He is very expert at gaging the Understandings of those he deals with, and has his Engines always ready with mere Air to blow all their Money out of their Pockets into his own, as Vintners do Wine out of one Vessel into another. He is very amorous of his Country, and prefers the public Good before his own Advantage, until he has joined them both together in some Monopoly, and then he thinks he has done his Part, and may be allowed to look after his own Affairs in the second Place. The chiefest and most useful Part of his Talent consists in Quacking and Lying, which he calls answering of Objections, and convincing the Ignorant: Without this he can do nothing; for as it is the common Practice of most Knaveries, so it is the surest and best fitted to the vulgar Capacities of the World; and though it render him more ridiculous to some few, it always prevails upon the greater Part.

A COMPLEMENTER

Is one that endeavours to make himself appear a very fine Man, in persuading another, that *He* is so; and by offering those Civilities, which he does not intend to part with, believes he adds to his own Reputation, and obliges another for nothing. He is very free in making Presents of his Services, because he is certain, he cannot possibly receive in return less than they are worth. He differs very much from all other Critics in Punctilios of Honour; for he esteems himself very uncivilly dealt with, if his Vows and Protestations pass for any Thing, but mere Lies and Vanities. When he gives his Word, he believes it is no longer his, and, therefore, holds it very unreasonable to give it, and keep it too. He divides his Services among so many, that there comes but little, or nothing to any one Man's Share; and, therefore, they are very willing to let him take it back again. He makes over himself *in trust* to every Man, but still it is to *his own Uses*, to secure his Title against all other Claims, and cheat his

Creditors. He is very generous of his Promises, but still it is without *lawful Consideration*, and so they go for nothing. He extols a Man to his Face, like those that write in Praise of an Author, to show his own Wit, not his, whom they undertake to commend. He has certain set Forms and Routines[1] of Speech, which he can say over, while he thinks on any Thing else, as a *Catholic* does his Prayers; and, therefore, never means what he says. His Words flow easily from him, but so shallow, that they will bear no Weight at all. All his Offers of Endearment are but like Terms of Course, that carry their own Answers along with them; and, therefore, pass for nothing between those that understand them, and deceive those only, that believe in them. He professes most Kindness commonly to those, he least cares for, like an Host, that bids a Man welcome, when he is going away. He had rather be every Man's menial Servant, than any one Man's Friend; for Servants gain by their Masters, and Men often lose by their Friends.

A CHURCHWARDEN

Is a public Officer, intrusted to rob the Church by Virtue of his Place, as long as he is in it. He has a very great Care to eat and drink well upon all public Occasions, that concern the Parish: for *a good Conscience being a perpetual Feast*,[1] he believes, the better he feeds, the more Conscience he uses in the Discharge of his Trust; and as long as there is no Dry[2]-money-cheat used, all others are allowed, according to the Tradition and Practice of the Church in the purest Times. When he lays a Tax upon the Parish[3] he commonly raises it a fourth Part above the Accompt, to supply the Default of Houses that may be burnt, or stand empty; or Men that may break and run away; and if none of these happen, his Fortune is the greater, and his Hazard never the less; and therefore he divides the overplus

---

[1] See p. 42, n. 41.

[1] A good conscience is a continual feast—a proverb, often quoted by Francis Bacon.

[2] Dry: of money, rent, etc., paid in hard cash.

[3] The parish was the local unit of civil administration, a unit of ecclesiastical organization in the territorial charge of a priest. For administrative work the priest was assisted by two churchwardens, who were elected by the parishioners and who by common law were sanctioned to levy taxes from the parishioners for repair of the church. [W. E. Lunt, *History of England*, 4th edition (New York, 1956), p. 383.]

between himself and his Colleagues, who were engaged to pay the whole, if all the Parish had run away, or hanged themselves. He over-reckons the Parish in his Accompts, as the Taverns do him, and keeps the odd Money himself, instead of giving it to the Drawers. He eats up the Bell-Ropes like the Ass in the Emblem,[4] and converts the broken Glass-Windows into whole Beer-Glasses of Sack; and before his Year is out, if he be but as good a Fellow as the drinking Bishop was, pledges a whole Pulpit-full. If the Church happen to fall to decay in his Time, it proves a Deodand[5] to him; for he is Lord of the Manor, and does not only make what he pleases of it, but has his Name recorded on the Walls among Texts of Scripture and leathern Buckets, with the Year of his Office, that the Memory of the Unjust, as well as the Just, may last as long as so transitory a Thing may. He interprets his Oath, as *Catholics* do the Scripture, not according to the Sense and Meaning of the Words, but the Tradition and Practice of his Predecessors; who have always been observed to swear what others please, and do what they please themselves.

A ROMANCE WRITER

Pulls down old Histories to build them up finer again, after a new Model of his own designing. He takes away all the Lights of Truth in History to make it the fitter Tutoress of Life; for *Truth* herself has little or nothing to do in the Affairs of the World, although all Matters of the greatest Weight and Moment are pretended and done in her Name; like a weak Princess, that has only the Title, and *Falshood* all the Power. He observes one very fit Decorum in dating his Histories in the Days of old, and putting all his own Inventions upon ancient Times; for when the World was younger, it might, perhaps, love, and fight, and do generous Things at the Rate he describes them; but since it is grown old, all these heroic Feats are laid by and utterly given over, nor ever like to come in Fashion again; and therefore all his Images of those Virtues signify no more than

---

[4] Such an emblem may be found reproduced in *Whitney's "Choice of Emblemes,"* A Fac-simile Reprint, ed. Henry Green (London, 1866), p. 48. The act of giving a rope (made of rushes and grass), the product of long work, to the ass is cited as an example of wastefulness in the lines accompanying the emblem.

[5] A thing which, because it had been the immediate cause of the death of a person, was given to God—that is, forfeited to the crown for pious uses.

the Statues upon dead Men's Tombs, that will never make them live again. He is like one of *Homer*'s Gods, that sets Men together by the Ears,[1] and fetches them off again how he pleases; brings Armies into the Field like *Janello*'s leaden Soldiers;[2] leads up both Sides himself, and gives the Victory to which he pleases, according as he finds it fit the Design of his Story; makes Love and Lovers too, brings them acquainted, and appoints Meetings when and where he pleases, and at the same Time betrays them in the Height of all their Felicity to miserable Captivity, or some other horrid Calamity; for which he makes them rail at the Gods, and curse their own innocent Stars, when he only has done them all the Injury—Makes Men Villains, compells them to act all barbarous Inhumanities by his own Directions, and after inflicts the cruellest Punishments upon them for it. He makes all his Knights fight in Fortifications, and storm one another's Armour, before they can come to encounter Body for Body; and always matches them so equally one with another, that it is a whole Page before they can guess which is likely to have the better; and he that has it is so mangled, that it had been better for them both to have parted fair at first; but when they encounter with those, that are no Knights, though ever so well armed and mounted, ten to one goes for nothing—As for the Ladies, they are every one the most beautiful in the whole World, and that's the Reason why no one of them, nor all together with all their Charms have Power to tempt away any Knight from another. He differs from a just Historian as a Joyner does from a Carpenter, the one does Things plainly and substantially for Use, and the other carves and polishes merely for Show and Ornament.

A CHEAT

Is a Freeman of all Trades, and all Trades of his. Fraud and Treachery, are his *Calling*, though his *Profession* be the strictest Integ-

---

[1] A common expression for the creation of ill will or dissension. See, for example, *Gulliver's Travels*, Pt. IV, Chap. VII: ". . . if . . . you throw among five yahoos as much food as would be sufficient for fifty, they will, instead of eating peaceably, fall together by the ears, each single one impatient to have all to himself. . . ."

[2] "This alludes to some Kind of Puppet-Performance in those Times, as I find the Name *Janello*, in another imperfect Piece of Butler's, introduced as belonging to a famous Operator in that Art." [Thyer's note.]

rity and Truth. He spins Nets, like a Spider, out of his own Entrails, to entrap the Simple and Unwary that light in his Way, whom he devours and feeds upon. All the greater Sort of Cheats, being allowed by Authority, have lost their Names (as *Judges*, when they are called to the Bench, are no more stiled *Lawyers*) and left the Title to the meaner only, and the unallowed. The common Ignorance of Mankind is his Province, which he orders to the best Advantage. He is but a tame Highwayman, that does the same Things by Stratagem and Design, which the other does by Force, makes Men deliver their Understandings first, and after their Purses. Oaths and Lies are his Tools that he works with, and he gets his Living by the Drudgery of his Conscience. He endeavours to cheat the Devil by mortgaging his Soul so many Times over and over to him, forgetting that he has Damnations, as Priests have Absolutions, of all Prices. He is a Kind of a just Judgment, sent into this World to punish the Confidence and Curiosity of Ignorance, that out of a natural Inclination to Error will tempt its own Punishment, and help to abuse itself. He can put on as many Shapes, as the Devil that set him on Work, is one that fishes in muddy Understandings, and will tickle a Trout[1] in his own Element, till he has him in his Clutches, and after in his Dish, or the Market. He runs down none but those, which he is certain are *fera Natura*, mere natural Animals, that belong to him that can catch them. He can do no Feats without the cooperating Assistance of the Chowse,[2] whose Credulity commonly meets the Impostor half Way, otherwise nothing is done; for all the Craft is not in the Catching (as the Proverb says) but the better half at least in being catched. He is one that, like a Bond *without Fraud, Covin,*[3] *and further Delay, is void and of none Effect, otherwise does stand and remain in full Power, Force, and Virtue.* He trusts the Credulous with what Hopes they please at a very easy Rate, upon their own Security, until he has drawn them far enough in, and then makes them pay for all at once. The first Thing he gets from him is a good Opinion, and afterwards any Thing he pleases; for after he has drawn him from his

---

[1] A rather unique way to fish was "tickling," whereby a fisherman would carefully feel under a bank until he came upon a trout with his hand. Then slowly he tickled it until he could actually grasp it. [Lilly C. Stone, "English Sports and Recreations," in *Life and Letters,* ed. Wright and LaMar, p. 447.]

[2] Gull, dupe.

[3] Deceit.

Guards, he deals with him like a Surgeon, and tyes his Arm before he lets him[4] Blood.

A LIBELLER

Is a certain Classic Author, that handles his Subject Matter very ruggedly, and endeavours with his own evil Words to corrupt another Man's good Manners. All his Works treat but of two Things, his own Malice, and another Man's Faults; both which he describes in very proper and pertinent Language. He is not much concerned whether what he writes be *true* or *false*, that's nothing to his Purpose, which aims only at *filthy* and *bitter*; and therefore his Language is, like Pictures of the Devil, the fouler the better. He robs a Man of his good Name, not for any good it will do him (for he dares not own it) but merely as a Jackdaw[1] steals Money, for his Pleasure. His Malice has the same Success with other Man's Charity, to be rewarded in private; for all he gets is but his own private Satisfaction, and the Testimony of an evil Conscience; for which, if it be discovered, he suffers the worst Kind of Martyrdom, and is paid with condign Punishment, so that at the best he has but his *Labour* for his *Pains*. He deals with a Man as the *Spanish* Inquisition does with Heretics, cloaths him in a Coat painted with hellish Shapes of Fiends, and so shews him to the Rabble, to render him the more odious. He exposes his Wit like a Bastard, for the next Comer to take up and put out to Nurse, which it seldom fails of, so ready is every Man to contribute to the Infamy of another. He is like the Devil, that sows Tares in the Dark, and while a Man sleeps plants Weeds among his corn. When he ventures to fall foul on the Government or any great Persons, if he has not a special Care to keep himself, like a Conjurer, safe in his Circle, he raises a Spirit that falls foul on himself, and carries him to *Limbo*;[2] where his neck is clapped up in the Hole, out of which it is never released, until he has paid his Ears down on the Nail[3] for Fees. He is in a worse Condition than a School-boy; for when he is discovered, he is whipped for his Exercise, whether it be well or ill done; so that he takes a wrong Course to shew his Wit, when

---

[4] His.

[1] The daw or jackdaw, a frequenter of church towers, old buildings, etc., is noted for its loquacity and thievish propensities.

[2] Here, a place of confinement.

[3] A common punishment for victims in the pillory.

his best Way to do so is to conceal it; otherwise he shews his Folly instead of his Wit, and pays dear for the Mistake.

A TEDIOUS MAN

Talks to *no End*, as well as to no Purpose; for he would never come at it willingly. His Discourse is like the Road-Miles in the *North*,[1] the filthier and dirtier the longer; and he delights to dwell the longer upon them to make good the old Proverb that says— *they are good for the Dweller, but ill for the Traveller.* He sets a Tale upon the Rack, and stretches until it becomes lame and out of Joint. *Hippocrates* says— *Art is long*;[2] but he is so for Want of Art. He has a Vein of Dullness, that runs through all he says or does; for nothing can be tedious, that is not dull and insipid. Digressions and Repetitions, like Bag and Baggage, retard his March, and put him to perpetual Halts. He makes his Approaches to a Business by oblique Lines, as if he meant to besiege it, and fetches a wide Compass about to keep others from discovering what his Design is. He is like one that travels in a dirty deep Road, that moves slowly; and, when he is at a Stop, goes back again, and loses more Time in picking of his Way, than in going it. How troublesome and uneasy soever he is to others, he pleases himself so well, that he does not at all perceive it; for though *home be homely*, it is more delightful than finer Things abroad; and he, that is used to a Thing and knows no better, believes that other Men, to whom it appears otherwise, have the same Sense of it that he has; as melancholy Persons, that fancy themselves to be Glass, believe that all others think them so too; and therefore that, which is tedious to others, is not so to him, otherwise he would avoid it; for it does not so often proceed from a natural Defect, as Affectation, and Desire to give others that Pleasure which they find themselves, though it always falls out quite contrary. He that converses with him is like one that travels with a Companion, that rides a lame Jade; he must either endure to go his Pace, or stay for him; for though he understands long before what he would be at better than he does himself, he must have Patience and stay for him, until with much ado to little Purpose, he at length comes to him; for he believes himself injured, if he should bate a Jot of his own Diversion.

---

[1] See p. 181, n. 1. Roads in the North were especially bad.

[2] "Art is long, life is short"—the first of Hippocrates' Aphorisms.

A TAYLOR

Came in with the Curse; and is younger Brother unto Thorns, and Thistles, and Death; for if *Adam* had not fallen, he had never sat cross-leg'd.[1] Sin and he are Partners; for as Sin first brought him into Employment, so he by cheating and contributing to Pride and Vanity works to Sin, and the old Trade is still kept up between both. Our *Saviour* wore his Coat without Seam, rather than he would have any Thing to do with him; and *Elias*,[2] when he went to Heaven, left his Mantle behind, because it had been polluted by his Fingers. The *Jews* in all great Calamities were wont to rent their Garments, only to testify, that they defy'd him and all his Works. All Men love and admire Cloaths, but scorn and despise him that made them, as Princes approve of Treason, but hate Traitors. He sits cross-leged to shew that he is originally a *Turk*, and calls himself *Merchant-Taylor* upon no other Account, but only as he descended from *Mahomet*, who was a Merchant's Prentice himself in his Youth. And his constant Custom of making the Calves of his Legs a Stool to sit upon, has rendered him so stiff in the Hams, that he walks as if he was newly circumcised, to distinguish himself from a *Christian*. He lives much more by his Faith than good Works; for he gains more by trusting and believing in one that pays him at long Running, than six that he works for, upon an even Accompt, for ready Money. He never cuts his Coat according to his Cloth; but always the more he is allowed the less he puts in a Garment; and he believes he has Reason for it; for he is fain to take double Pains in contriving how to dispose both what he steals, and what he uses, to the best Advantage, which costs him twice as much Labour as that which he gets nothing by. He never cuts a Man's Cloaths but he cuts his Purse into the Bargain; and when he makes a Pocket takes Handsel[3] of it, and picks it first himself. He calls Stealing *damning*, by a Figure in Rhetoric called the Effect for the Efficient,[4] and the Place where he lodges all his Thieveries *Hell*,[5] to put him in mind of his latter End; and what he

---

[1] Butler's play on two senses of *fallen* culminates in a description of the tailor's traditional position, cross-legged.

[2] Also called Elijah. For an account of his going to heaven see II Kings, III. 11.

[3] A first gift on any occasion.

[4] The cause which makes effects to be what they are. [*O.E.D.*]

[5] A place where a tailor throws his shreds.

steals by Retail the Broker takes off his Hands by Wholesale. He keeps his Wife in Taffety to save Charges; for when her Petticoats are worn out, they serve him to line Vests with, as well as if they were new, and when he is unfurnished of these, old Satten and Taffety Men supply him for Ends of Gold and Silver. He gets more by the Trimming and Garniture of Cloaths than all the rest; for he can swallow Ribbands like a Jugler, and put whole Pieces more in his Bill than ever he made use of, and stretch Lace, as a Shoe-maker does Leather with his Teeth, when he sets it on. The Mercers are in Fee with him to revive old rotten Stuffs by giving them new fantastic Names; and he brings them into the Mode by swearing they are new come up; in Consideration of which he is allowed to buy cheap and sell dear; for he is loth to undervalue his Conscience, and put it off at a mean Rate, as long as he sees his Neighbours can make more of theirs—He scorns that.

A FACTIOUS MEMBER

Is sent out laden with the Wisdom and Politicks of the Place he serves for, and has his own Freight and Custom free. He is trusted like a Factor to trade for a Society, but endeavours to turn all the public to his own private Advantages. He has no Instructions but his Pleasure, and therefore strives to have his Privileges as large. He is very wise in his politic Capacity as having a full Share in the House, and an implicit Right to every Man's Reason, though he has none of his own, which makes him appear so simple out of it. He believes all Reason of State consists in Faction, as all Wisdom in Haranguing, of which he is so fond, that he had rather the Nation should perish than continue ignorant of his great Abilities that Way; though he that observes his Gestures, Words, and Delivery, will find them so perfectly agreeable to the Rules of the House, that he cannot but conclude he learnt his Oratory the very same Way that Jackdaws and Parrots practise by. For he coughs, and spits, and blows his Nose with that discreet and prudent Caution, that you would think he had buried his Talent in a Handkerchief, and were now pulling it out to dispose of it to a better Advantage. He stands and presumes so much upon *the Privileges of the House*, as if every Member were a *Tribune* of the People, and had as absolute Power as they had in *Rome*, according to the lately established fundamental Custom and Practice of their quarter'd Predecessors of unhappy Memory. He endeavours to shew his

Wisdom in nothing more than in appearing very much unsatisfy'd with the present Manage of State-Affairs, although he knows nothing of the Reasons; so much the better; for the Thing is the more difficult, and argues his Judgment and Insight the greater; for any Man can judge that understands the Reasons of what he does, but very few know how to judge mechanically without understanding why or wherefore. It is sufficient to assure him, that the public Money has been diverted from the proper Uses it was raised for, because he has had no Share of it himself; and the Government ill-managed, because he has no hand in it, which, truly, is a very great Grievance to the People, that understand, by himself and his Party, that are their Representatives, and ought to understand for them, how able he is for it. He fathers all his own Passions and Concerns, like Bastards, on the People, because being entrusted by them without Articles or Conditions, they are bound to acknowledge whatsoever he does as their own Act and Deed.

A PRETENDER

Is easily acquainted with all Knowledges, but never intimate with any; he remembers he has seen them somewhere before, but cannot possibly call to mind where. He will call an Art by its Name, and claim Acquaintance with it at first Sight. He knew it perfectly, as the *Platonics* say, in the other World,[1] but has had the Unhappiness to discontinue his Acquaintance ever since his Occasions called him into this. He claps on all the Sail he can possibly make, though his Vessel be empty and apt to overset. He is of a true philosophical Temper contented with a little, desires no more Knowledge than will satisfy Nature, and cares not what his Wants are, so he can but keep them from the Eyes of the World. His Parts are unlimited; for as no Man knows his Abilities, so he does his Endeavour, that as few should his Defects. He wears himself in Opposition to the Mode, for his Lining is much coarser than his Outside; and as others line their Serge with Silk, he lines his Silk with Serge. All his Care is employed to appear, not to be; for things that are not, and Things that appear not, are not only the same in Law, but in all other Affairs of the World.

---

[1] Reference to the Neoplatonic concept of the *nous* (or Spirit or Divine Mind), whence emanates the soul and is its true home and to which the soul seeks to return.

It should seem that the most impudent Face is the best; for he that does the shamefullest Thing most unconcerned is said *to set a good Face upon it*: For the Truth is, the Face is but the Outside of the Mind, but all the Craft is to know how 'tis lined.[2] Howsome'er he fancies himself as able as any Man, but not being in a Capacity to try the Experiment, the Hint[3]-Keeper of *Gresham* College is the only competent Judge to decide the Controversy.[4] He may, for any Thing he knows, have as good a Title to his Pretences as another Man; for Judgment being not past in the Case (which shall never be by his Means) his Title still stands fair. All he can possibly attain to is but to be another Thing than Nature meant him, though a much worse. He makes that good that Pliny says of Children *qui celerius fari cepere, tardius ingredi incipiunt*.[5] The apter he is to smatter, the slower he is in making any Advance in his Pretences. He trusts Words before he is thoroughly acquainted with them, and they commonly shew him a Trick before he is aware; and he shews at the same Time his Ignorance to the Learned, and his Learning to the Ignorant.

A NEWS-MONGER

Is a Retailer of Rumour, that takes up upon Trust, and sells as cheap as he buys. He deals in a perishable Commodity, that will not keep: for if it be not fresh it lies upon his Hands, and will yield nothing. True or false is all one to him; for Novelty being the Grace of both, a Truth grows stale as soon as a Lye; and as a slight Suit will last as well as a better while the Fashion holds, a Lye serves as well as Truth till new ones come up. He is little concerned whether it be good or bad, for that does not make it more or less News; and, if there be any Difference, he loves the bad best, because it is said to come soonest; for he would willingly bear his Share in any public Calamity, to have the Pleasure of hearing and telling it. He is deeply read in

---

[2] See p. 38, n. 29.

[3] A nonce-word as used here. A hint-keeper seems to be one who keeps account of the suggestions that the Society has gathered. Cf. Glanvill: "Put these passages into your Hint-box, or into your Snuff-box, if you think fit." [*O.E.D.*]

[4] *O.E.D.* cites this passage under "hint-keeper."

[5] "Those who began to speak quicker are slower in starting to walk." [*Natural History*, trans. Rackham, XI. cxii. 270.]

Diurnals,[1] and can give as good an Account of *Rowland Pepin*,[2] if need be, as another Man. He tells[3] News, as Men do Money, with his Fingers; for he assures them it comes from very good Hands. The whole Business of his Life is like that of a Spaniel; to fetch and carry News, and when he does it well he is clapt on the Back, and fed for it; for he does not take to it altogether like a Gentleman for his Pleasure, but when he lights on a considerable Parcel of News, he knows where to put it off for a Dinner, and quarter himself upon it, until he has eaten it out; and by this Means he drives a Trade, by retrieving the first News to truck it for the first Meat in Season; and like the old *Roman* Luxury ransacks all Seas and Lands to please his Palate; for he imports his Narratives from all Parts within the Geography of a Diurnal, and eats as well upon the *Russ* and *Polander*, as the *English* and *Dutch*. By this means his Belly is provided for, and nothing lyes upon his Hands but his Back, which takes other Courses to maintain itself by weft and stray Silver Spoons, stragling Hoods and Scarfs, pimping, and Setts at *L'Ombre*.[4]

AN EMBASSADOR

Is accountable to Honour in his private Capacity, but not at all in his public; for as he represents his Prince, that has the Disposing of Honour, he is above it, and cannot be disposed by it. The greatest Part of his Qualification consists in the Bravery[1] of his Followers, and he carries his Abilities on his Servant's Backs. He is obliged to be witty by his Place, and bound to make smart Repartees, what Shift soever he makes to come by them. He represents his Prince's Person, when he comes near to the Person of the Prince that gives him Audience, but not before, as appears by the profound Reverence he observes, and the Legs he makes. His Instructions are his Part, which he learns by Art; and there is nothing left to him but the Action and Delivery. He carries Letters of Credence with him, to enable him better to manage

---

[1] Newspapers published daily or at short periodical intervals. Cf. John Cleveland, "The Character of a Diurnal-Maker."

[2] The context suggests that this is an allusion to a figure of some contemporary fame.

[3] A play on *tells*, meaning *counts*.

[4] See p. 109, n. 3.

[1] Fine clothes.

that great *Arcanum Imperii*,[2] or politic Art of Government, Dissembling and Lying, which he is entrusted withal, and engaged in Honour to enforce, as far as solemn Vows and Protestations, and if need be, pawning his Salvation to the Devil, can enable him. He brings Materials with him from Home, to serve for all politic Occasions that can fall out, and is bound only to make Speeches and Legs to them; and, the slighter they are, to afford the more Gravity and solemn Formality for Allowance: For he is intrusted with the Wisdom of the Nation which he comes from, and ought to use it to the best Advantage, and preserve it so safe, that no Man living may know where to find it out. He is very tender conscienced[3] in his politic Capacity, will not endure that any Man should excel him in going or sitting; and will rather give his Soul, than so much Place as it would take up on the Point of a Needle. When he puts on the Person of his Prince, he makes all other Reasons of State march behind, like a Retinue to attend and wait upon it. He travels like a *Lapland* Witch, and leaves his own Person behind him in a Trance, till he returns Home, and then takes it up again, and comes to himself.[4] He goes a Wooing with Letters of Commendation from his Master in his own Behalf, makes passionate Love to some foreign Interest, and when he meets with an equal Return of Affection, and has won the tender Heart of the State, he puts all his politic Capacities into one Leg, and espouses his Queen with it, as if he sat in the Stocks. He has more Tricks to avoid rencounters with other Embassadors and Disputes of Precedence, than a Coward has to meet his Enemy in the Field; and when he is engaged by Accident, has as many Expedients to save his Honour harmless, as the learned Critics of the Sword have with curious and subtle Contemplation found out.

A PLAY-WRITER

Of our Times is like a *Fanatic*,[1] that has no Wit in ordinary easy Things, and yet attempts the hardest Task of Brains in the whole

---

[2] State secrets.

[3] See p. 47, n. 9.

[4] Lapland was the fabled home of witches and magicians. Richard Boulton reports on the practice of witchcraft, including witches' "transportation through the Air; their travelling in Spirit, whilst their Body is cast into a Trance." [*A Compleat History of Magick, Sorcery, and Witchcraft* (1716), II, 37.]

[1] See p. 55, n. 2.

World, only because, whether his Play or Work please or displease, he is certain to come off better than he deserves, and find some of his own Latitude[2] to applaud him, which he could never expect any other Way; and is as sure to lose no Reputation, because he has none to venture.

> Like gaming Rooks, that never stick
> To play for hundreds upon Tick,
> 'Cause, if they chance to lose at Play,
> Th'ave not one halfpenny to pay;
> And, if they win a hundred Pound,
> Gain, if for Sixpence they compound.

Nothing encourages him more in his Undertaking than his Ignorance, for he has not Wit enough to understand so much as the Difficulty of what he attempts; therefore he runs on boldly like a foolhardy Wit, and *Fortune*, that favours Fools and the Bold, sometimes takes Notice of him for his double Capacity, and receives him into her good Graces. He has one Motive more, and that is the concurrent ignorant Judgment of the present Age, in which his sottish Fopperies pass with Applause, like *Oliver Cromwel*'s Oratory among *Fanatics* of his own canting Inclination.[3] He finds it easier to write in Rhime than Prose; for the World being overcharged with Romances, he finds his Plots, Passions, and Repartees ready made to his Hand; and if he can but turn them into Rhime, the Thievery is disguised, and they pass for his own Wit and Invention without Question; like a stolen Cloke made into a Coat, or dyed into another Colour. Besides this he makes no Conscience of stealing any Thing that lights in his Way, and borrows the Advice of so many to correct, enlarge, and amend what he has ill-favouredly patcht together, that it becomes like a Thing drawn by Council, and none of his own Performance, or the Son of a Whore that has no one certain Father. He has very great Reason to prefer Verse before Prose in his Compositions; for Rhime is like Lace, that

---

[2] Breadth, scope.

[3] Cromwell's "public speeches in general are long-winded, obscure, flat and ambiguous." [William Harris, *An Historical and Critical Account of the Life of Oliver Cromwell*, 2d edition (London, 1772), pp. 33–34.] ". . . the reason of these defects seem [sic] to be sometimes the enthusiasm of his temper, which produc'd a kind of expression savoring of cant. . . ." [Ibid., p. 36 n.] Norman Sykes says that the speeches must be viewed with recognition of the belief in the promptings of the Spirit and the idiom of the Authorized Version of the Bible. ["Religion," in *Life Under the Stuarts*, ed. J. E. Morpurgo (London, 1950), p. 48.]

serves excellently well to hide the Piecing and Coarsness of a bad
Stuff, contributes mightily to the Bulk, and makes the less serve by
the many Impertinencies it commonly requires to make Way for it;
for very few are endowed with Abilities to bring it in on its own
Accompt. This he finds to be good Husbandry, and a Kind of necessary Thrift; for they that have but a little ought to make as much of
it as they can. His Prologue, which is commonly none of his own, is
always better than his Play, like a Piece of Cloth that's fine in the
Beginning and coarse afterwards, though it has but one Topic, and
that's the same that is used by Malefactors, when they are to be tried,
to except against as many of the Jury as they can.

A MOUNTEBANK

Is an epidemic Physician, a Doctor-Errant, that keeps himself up by being, like a Top, in Motion; for if he should settle, he
would fall to nothing immediately. He is a Pedlar of Medicines, a
petty Chapman of Cures, and Tinker empirical to the Body of Man.
He stroles about to Markets and Fairs; where he mounts on the Top
of his Shop, that is his Bank, and publishes his Medicines as universal
as himself; for every Thing is for all Diseases, as himself is of all
Places, that is to say, of none. His Business is to shew Tricks and Impudence: as for the Cure of Diseases it concerns those that have them,
not him, farther than to get their Money. His *Pudding*[1] is his Setter,
that lodges the Rabble for him, and then slips him, who opens with a
deep Mouth, and has an ill Day, if he does not run down some. He
baits his Patient's Body with his Medicines, as a Rat-catcher does a
Room, and either poisons the Disease, or him. As soon as he has got
all the Money, and spent all the Credit the Rabble could spare him,
he then removes to fresh Quarters, where he is less known, and better
trusted. If but one in twenty of his Medicines hit by Chance, when
Nature works the Cure, it saves the Credit of all the rest, that either
do no Good or Hurt; for whosoever recovers in his Hands, he does
the Work *under God*; but if he die, God does it *under him*; his Time
was come, and there's an End. A Velvet Jerkin is his prime Qualification, by which he is distinguished from his *Pudding*, as *He* is with his
Cap from him. This is the Usher of his School, that draws the Rabble
together, and then He draws their Teeth. He administers Physic with
a Farce, and gives his Patients a Preparative of Dancing on the Rope,

[1] See p. 44, n. 44.

to stir the Humours, and prepare them for Evacuation. His Fool serves for his Foil, and sets him off, as well as his Bragging and Lying. The first Thing he vents is his own Praise, and then his Medicines wrapt up in several Papers and Lies. He mounts his Bank as a Vaulter does his wooden Horse, and then shews Tricks for his Patients, as Apes do for the King of *Spain*.[2] He casts the Nativity[3] of Urinals, and tries Diseases, like a Witch, by Water. He bails the Place with a Jigg, draws the Rabble together, and then throws his Hook among them. He pretends to universal Medicines, that is such, as, when all Men are sick together, will cure them all, but till then no one in particular.

A MODERN CRITIC

Is a Corrector of the Press gratis; and as he does it for nothing, so it is to no Purpose. He fancies himself Clerk of *Stationers-Hall*,[1] and nothing must pass Current, that is not entered by him. He is very severe in his supposed Office, and crys, *Woe to ye Scribes*, right or wrong. He supposes all Writers to be Malefactors without *Clergy*,[2] that claim the Privilege of their Books, and will not allow it, where the Law of the Land and common Justice does. He censures in gross, and condemns all without examining Particulars—If they will not confess and accuse themselves, he will rack them until they do. He is a *Committee-Man*[3] in the Commonwealth of Letters, and as great a

---

[2] Cf. The Introduction to Ben Jonson, *Bartholomew Fair*. The Stage-Keeper who spells out what will not be shown continues: "Nor a Jugler with a well-educated Ape to come over the chaine, for the *King of England*, and backe againe for the *Prince*, and sit still on his arse for the Pope, and the *King of Spaine!*" [Ben Jonson, ed. C. H. Herford and Percy Simpson (Oxford, 1925–52), VI, 13.]

See also John Donne, *Satyres*, I. 79–82:

> . . . he doth move no more
> Then the wise, politique horse would heretofore,
> Or thou O Elephant or Ape wilt doe,
> When any names the King of Spaine to you.

[3] See p. 110, n. 4.

[1] The Stationers' Company: incorporated by royal charter in 1557. Every member was required to enter on the register of the Company the name of any book he desired to print.

[2] This variation on "benefit of clergy" would seem to suggest that these writers are ineligible because they are illiterate.

[3] Reference to the committees that pursued the Civil Wars. The Committee

Tyrant; so is not bound to proceed but by his own Rules, which he will not endure to be disputed. He has been an Apocryphal Scribler himself; but his Writings wanting Authority he grew discontent, and turned Apostate, and thence becomes so severe to those of his own Profession. He never commends any Things but in Opposition to something else, that he would undervalue, and commonly sides with the weakest, which is generous any where but in Judging. He is worse than an *Index expurgatorius*;[4] for he blots out all, and, when he cannot find a Fault, makes one. He *demurrs* to all Writers, and when he is *over-ruled*, will run into *Contempt*. He is always bringing *Writs of Errour*, like a Pettifogger,[5] and *reversing of Judgments*, tho' the Case be never so plain. He is a Mountebank, that is always quacking of the infirm and diseased Parts of Books, to shew his Skill; but has nothing at all to do with the Sound. He is a very ungentle Reader, for he reads Sentence on all Authors, that have the Unhappiness to come before him; and therefore Pedants, that stand in Fear of him, always appeal from him beforehand, by the Name of *Momus* and *Zoilus*,[6] complain sorely of his extrajudicial Proceedings, and protest against him as corrupt, and his Judgment *void and of none Effect*; and put themselves into the Protection of some powerful Patron, who, like a Knight-Errant, is to encounter with the Magician, and free them from his Enchantments.

A WITTAL[1]

Is a Person of great Complaisance, and very civil to all that have Occasion to make Use of his Wife. He married a Wife as a common Proxy for the Service of all those, that are willing to come in for

---

of Both Kingdoms was established by Parliament to perform executive functions and given power to "order and direct" the war. It was composed of Scots and twenty-one members of the Long Parliament. The Derby House Committee, without Scots Commissioners, served during the Second Civil War. [Lunt, *History of England*, p. 428, and Trevelyan, *England Under the Stuarts*, p. 236 n.]

[4] An authoritative specification of the passages to be expunged or altered in works otherwise permitted. [*O.E.D.*]

[5] See p. 111, n. 1.

[6] Momus: mythological god of mockery and censure.

Zoilus: rhetorician and critic of the fourth century B.C. who gained a reputation by his critical assaults on Homer and Plato; his name became proverbial for a carping critic.

[1] A man who knows of his wife's infidelity and submits to it.

their Shares—He ingrossed her first by Wholesale, and since puts her off by Retail—He professes a Form of Matrimony, but utterly denies the Power thereof. They that tell Tales are very unjust; for having not put in their Claims before Marriage, they are bound for ever after to hold their Tongues. The Reason why Citizens are commonly Wittals is, because Men that drive a Trade and are Dealers in the World, seldom provide any Thing for their own Uses, which they will not very willingly put off again for considerable Profit. He believes it to be but a vulgar[2] Error, and no such Disparagement as the World commonly imagines, to be a Cuckold; for Man being the Epitomy and Representation of all Creatures, cannot be said to be perfect, while he wants that Badge and Character, which so many several Species wear both for their Defence and Ornament. He takes the only wise and sure Course that his Wife should do him no Injury; for having his own free Consent it is not in her Power that Way to do him any Wrong at all. His Wife is, like *Eve* in Paradise, married to all Mankind, and yet is unsatisfied that there are no more Worlds, as *Alexander the Great* was. She is a Person of public Capacity, and rather than not serve her Country would suffer an Army to march over her Belly, as *Sir Rice ap Thomas*[3] did. Her Husband and she give and take equal Liberty, which preserves a perfect Peace and good Understanding between both; while those, that are concerned in one another's Love and Honour, are never quiet, but always catter-walling. He differs from a jealous Man, as a valiant Man does from a Coward, that trembles at a Danger, which the other scorns and despises. He is of a true philosophical Temper, and suffers what he knows not how to avoid with a more than *Stoical* Resolution—He is one of those the Poet speaks of.

> ———*Qui ferre incommoda Vitæ,*
> *Nec jactare jugum, vita didicere Magistra.*[4]

---

[2] Common; widespread.

[3] In Henry VIII's expedition to France in 1513 Sir Rice ap Thomas was captain of the light-horse. See Lord Herbert's *Henry VIII* (1870), p. 143 and passim. This is all I have found about him.

[4] Juvenal, *Satires*, XIII. 20–22.
> ". . . ducimus autem
> hos quoque felices, qui ferre incommoda vitae
> nec iactare iugum vita didicere magistra."

("But they too are to be deemed happy who have learnt under the schooling of life to endure its ills without fretting against the yoke.") [In *Juvenal and Persius*, trans. Ramsay.]

He is as much pleased to see many Men approve his Choice of his Wife; and has as great a Kindness for them, as Opiniasters have for all those whom they find to agree with themselves in Judgment, and approve the Abilities of their Understandings.

A BUSY MAN

Is one, that seems to labour in every Man's Calling, but his own; and like *Robin-Good-Fellow* does any Man's Drudgery, that will let him. He is like an Ape, that loves to do whatsoever he sees others do; and is always as busy as a Child at Play. He is a great Undertaker,[1] and commonly as great an Under-Performer. His Face is like a Lawyer's Buckram Bag, that has always Business in it; and as he trots about, his Head travels as fast as his Feet. He *covets* his Neighbour's Business, and his own is to meddle, not do. He is very lavish of his Advice, and gives it freely, because it is worth nothing, and he knows not what to do with it himself. He is a *common-Barreter*[2] for his Pleasure, that takes no Money, but pettifogs[3] gratis. He is very inquisitive after every Man's Occasions, and charges himself with them like a public Notary. He is a great Overseer of State-Affairs; and can judge as well of them before he understands the Reasons, as afterwards. He is excellent at preventing Inconveniencies, and finding out Remedies, when 'tis too late; for like Prophesies, they are never heard of till it is to no Purpose. He is a great Reformer, always contriving of Expedients, and will press them with as much Earnestness, as if himself and every Man he meets had Power to impose them on the Nation. He is always giving Aim to State Affairs, and believes by screwing of his Body he can make them shoot which Way he pleases.[4] He enquires into every Man's History, and makes his own Commentaries upon it, as he pleases to fancy it. He wonderfully affects to seem full of Employments, and borrows Men's Business only to put on and appear in; and then returns it back again, only a little worse. He frequents all public Places, and like a Pillar in the *old Exchange*[5] is hung

---

[1] In the general sense of one who undertakes any task or enterprise.

[2] See p. 111, n. 2.

[3] See p. 111, n. 1 ["pettyfog"].

[4] The image is that of a player in the game of bowls.

[5] The Royal Exchange, founded in 1566 and opened by Queen Elizabeth, was destroyed by the Great Fire of 1666.

with all Men's Business both public and private; and his own is only
to expose them. He dreads nothing so much as to be thought at
Leisure, though he is never otherways,[6] for though he be always doing, he never does any Thing.

A LITIGIOUS MAN

Goes to Law, as Men do to Bawdy-Houses, to spend his
Money, and satisfy his Concupiscence of Wrangling. He is a constant
Customer to the old reverend Gentlewoman *Law*, and believes her
to be very honest, though she picks his Pockets, and puts a thousand
Tricks and Gulleries upon him. He has a strange Kindness for *an Action of the Case*, but a most passionate Loyalty for the *King's Writ*.[1]
A well drawn Bill and Answer will draw him all the World over, and
a Breviate as far as the Line.[2] He enters the Lists at *Westminster*,[3]
like an old Tilter, runs his Course in Law, and breaks an Oath or two
instead of a Lance; and if he can but unhorse the Defendant, and get
the Sentence of the Judges on his Side, he marches off in Triumph.
He prefers a Cry of Lawyers at the Bar before any Pack of the best
mouthed Dogs in all the North. He has commonly once a Term a
Tryal of Skill with some other Professor of the noble Science of Contention at the several Weapons of *Bill and Answer*, *Forgery*, *Perjury*,
Subornation, *Champarty*, *Affidavit*, *Common Barretry*, *Maintenance*,
&c. and, though he come off with the worst, he does not greatly care,
so he can but have another Bout for it. He fights with Bags of Money,
as they did heretofore with Sand-Bags, and he that has the heaviest
has the Advantage, and knocks down the other right or wrong; and
he suffers the Penalties of the Law for having no more Money to show
in the Case. He is a Client by his Order, and Votary of the long Robe;[4]
and though he were sure the *Devil* invented it to hide his cloven Feet,
he has the greater Reverence for it; for as evil Manners produce good
Laws, the worse the Inventor was, the better the Thing may be. He
keeps as many Knights of the Post[5] to swear for him, as the King does

---

[6] Otherwise.

[1] A written order issued by a court in the name of the sovereign. Here, probably the legal document necessary to introduce a court action.

[2] Border.

[3] See p. 71, n. 5.

[4] Legal profession.

[5] Persons who hired themselves out as false witnesses in the courts of justice;

poor Knights at *Windsor* to pray for him. When he is Defendant and like to be worsted in a Suit, he puts in a Cross Bill, and becomes Plaintiff, for the Plainant is eldest Hand, and has not only that Advantage, but is understood to be the better Friend to the Court, and is considered for it accordingly.

A PEDANT

Is a dwarf Scholar, that never outgrows the Mode and Fashion of the School, where he should have been taught. He wears his little Learning, unmade-up, puts it on, before it was half finished, without pressing or smoothing. He studies and uses Words with the greatest Respect possible, merely for their own Sakes, like an honest Man, without any Regard of Interest, as they are useful and serviceable to Things, and among those he is kindest to Strangers (like a civil Gentleman) that are far from their own Country and most unknown. He collects old Sayings and Ends of Verses, as Antiquaries do old Coins, and is as glad to produce them upon all Occasions. He has Sentences ready lying by him for *all* Purposes, though to *no one*, and talks of Authors as familiarly as his Fellow-Collegiates. He will challenge Acquaintance with those, he never saw before, and pretend to intimate Knowledge of those, he has only heard of. He is well stored with Terms of Art, but does not know how to use them, like a Country-Fellow, that carries his Gloves in his Hands, not his Hands in his Gloves. He handles Arts and Sciences like those, that can play a little upon an Instrument, but do not know, whether it be in Tune or not. He converses by the Book; and does not talk, but quote. If he can but screw in something, that an ancient Writer said, he believes it to be much better than if he had something of himself to the Purpose. His Brain is not able to concoct what it takes in, and therefore brings things up as they were swallowed, that is, crude and undigested, in whole Sentences,[1] not assimilated Sense, which he rather affects; for his Want of Judgment, like Want of Health, renders his Appetite preposterous. He pumps for affected and far-fet[2] Expressions, and they always prove as far from the Purpose. He admires Canting above

so called because they were to be found at the posts on which sheriffs put up proclamations. See the Character of A Knight of the Post.

[1] A play on two meanings: (1) a grammatical unit; (2) a pithy, aphoristic statement (*sententia*).

[2] Far-fetched.

Sense. He is worse than one, that is utterly ignorant, as a Cock that sees a little, fights worse than one, that is stark-blind. He speaks in a different Dialect from other Men, and much affects forced Expressions, forgetting that *hard Words*, as well as *evil ones*, *corrupt good Manners*. He can do nothing, like a Conjurer, out of the Circle of his Arts, nor in it without canting and[a] . . . . If he professes Physic, he gives his Patients sound hard Words for their Money, as cheap as he can afford; for they cost him Money and Study too, before he came by them, and he has Reason to make as much of them as he can.

A HUNTER

Is an auxiliary Hound, that assists one Nation of Beasts to subdue and over-run another. He makes mortal War with the Fox for committing Acts of Hostility against his Poultry. He is very solicitous to have his Dogs well descended of worshipful Families, and understands their Pedigree as learnedly as if he were a Herald;[1] and is as careful to match them according to their Rank and Qualities, as High-Germans are of their own Progenies. He is both Cook and Physician to his Hounds, understands the Constitutions of their Bodies, and what to administer in any Infirmity or Disease, acute or chronic, that can befal them. Nor is he less skilful in Physiognomy, and from the Aspects of their Faces, Shape of their Snouts, falling of their Ears and Lips, and Make of their Barrels will give a shrewd Guess at their Inclinations, Parts, and Abilities, and what Parents they are lineally descended from; and by the Tones of their Voices and Statures of their Persons easily discover, what Country they are Natives of. He believes no Music in the World is comparable to a Chorus of their Voices, and that when they are well matched they will hunt their Parts as true at first Scent, as the best Singers of Catches, that ever opened in a Tavern, that they understand the Scale as well as the best Scholar, that ever learned to compose by the Mathematics; and that when he winds his Horn to them, 'tis the very same Thing with a Cornet in a Quire; that they will run down the Hare with a Fuge, and a double D-fol-re-Dog hunt a thorough-base[2] to them all the while;

---

[a] Ellipses appear here in Thyer's edition.

[1] See p. 60, n. 27.

[2] A bass part extending through a piece of music but separated from other parts, with figures indicating the chords or harmonies to be played with it. [*O.E.D.*]

that when they are at a loss they do but rest, and then they know by turns who are to continue a Dialogue between two or three of them, of which he is commonly one himself. He takes very great Pains in his Way, but calls it Game and Sport, because it is to no Purpose; and he is willing to make as much of it as he can; and not be thought to bestow so much Labour and Pains about nothing. Let the Hare take which Way she will, she seldom fails to lead him at long-running to the Alehouse, where he meets with an Aftergame of Delight, in making up a Narrative, how every Dog behaved himself; which is never done without long Dispute, every Man inclining to favour his Friend as far as he can; and if there be any Thing remarkable, to his Thinking, in it, he preserves it to please himself; and, as he believes, all People else with, during his natural Life, and after leaves it to his Heirs Male entailed upon the Family, with his Bugle-Horn and Seal-Ring.

A HUMORIST

Is a peculiar Fantastic, that has a wonderful natural Affection to some particular Kind of Folly, to which he applies himself, and in Time becomes eminent. 'Tis commonly some outlying Whimsie of *Bedlam*, that being tame and unhurtful is suffered to go at Liberty. The more serious he is, the more ridiculous he becomes, and at the same Time pleases himself in Earnest, and others in Jest. He knows no mean; for that is inconsistent with all Humour, which is never found but in some Extreme or other. Whatsoever he takes to, he is very full of, and believes every Man else to be so too; as if his own Taste were the same in every Man's Palate. If he be a *Virtuoso*,[1] he applies himself with so much Earnestness to what he undertakes, that he puts his Reason out of Joint, and strains his Judgment: And there is hardly any Thing in the World so slight or serious, that some one or other has not squandered away his Brains, and Time, and Fortune upon, to no other Purpose, but to be ridiculous. He is exempted from a dark Room and a Doctor, because there is no Danger in his Frenzy; otherwise he has as good a Title to fresh Straw as another. Humour is but a Crookedness of the Mind,[2] a disproportioned Swelling of the Brain,

---

[1] Cf. the Character of a Virtuoso.
[2] Cf. Thomas Shadwell's Epilogue to *The Humorists* (1670):
    A Humor is the Byas of the Mind
    By which with violence 'tis one way inclined:
    It makes our Actions lean on one side still,
    And in all Changes that way bends the will.

that draws the Nourishment from the other Parts, to stuff an ugly and deformed Crup³-Shoulder. If it have the Luck to meet with many of its own Temper, instead of being ridiculous, it becomes a Church, and from Jest grows to Earnest.

A LEADER OF A FACTION

Sets the Psalm, and all his Party sing after him. He is like a Figure in Arithmetic, the more Ciphers he stands before, the more his Value amounts to. He is a great Haranguer, talks himself into Authority, and, like a Parrot, climbs with his Beak. He appears brave in the Head of his Party, but braver in his own; for Vain-Glory leads him, as he does them, and both many Times out of the King's Highway, over Hedges and Ditches, to find out Bye-ways and shorter Cuts, which generally prove the furthest about, but never the nearest Home again. He is so passionate a Lover of the Liberty of the People, that his Fondness turns to Jealousy—He interprets every Trifle in the worst Sense to the Prejudice of her Honesty, and is so full of Caprices and Scruples, that, if he had his Will, he would have her shut up, and never suffered to go abroad again, if not made away, for her Incontinence. All his Politics are speculative, and for the most part impracticable, full of curious Niceties, that tend only to prevent future imaginary Inconveniencies with greater real and present. He is very superstitious of having the Formalities and Punctilios of Law held sacred, that, while they are performing, those, that would destroy the very Being of it, may have Time to do their Business, or escape. He bends all his Forces against those that are above him, and like a freeborn *English* Mastiff, plays always at the Head. He gathers his Party as *Fanatics* do a Church, and admits all his Admirers how weak and slight soever; for he believes it is Argument of Wisdom enough in them to admire, or, as he has it, to understand him. When he has led his Faction into any Inconvenience, they all run into his Mouth, as young Snakes do into the old ones,¹ and he defends them with his Oratory as well as he is able; for all his Confidence depends upon his Tongue more than his

---

³ Brittle.

¹ "The young one [viper] supposed to break through the belly of the Dam, will upon any fright for protection run into it; for then the old one receives them in at her mouth. . . ." [Browne, *Pseudodoxia Epidemica*, III. 16, in *Works*, ed. Keynes, II, 238.]

Brain or Heart, and if that fail the others surrender immediately; for though *David* says *it is a two-edged Sword*,[2] a wooden Dagger is a better Weapon to fight with. His Judgment is like a nice Ballance, that will turn with the twentieth Part of a Grain, but a little using renders it false, and it is not so good for use as one, that will not stir without a greater Weight.

A DEBAUCHED MAN

Saves the Devil a Labour, and leads himself into Temptation, being loath to lose his good Favour in giving him any Trouble, where he can do the Business himself without his Assistance, which he very prudently reserves for Matters of greater Concernment. He governs himself in an arbitrary Way, and is absolute, without being confined to any Thing but his own Will and Pleasure, which he makes his Law. His Life is all Recreation, and his Diversions nothing but turning from one Vice, that he is weary of, to entertain himself with another that is fresh. He lives above the State of his Body as well as his Fortune, and runs out of his Health and Money, as if he had made a Match and betted on the Race, or bid the Devil take the Hindmost. He is an amphibious Animal, that lives in two Elements wet and dry; and never comes out of the first, but, like a Sea-Calf, to sleep on the Shore. His Language is very suitable to his Conversation, and he talks as loosely as he lives. Ribaldry and Profanation are his Doctrine and Use; and what he professes publicly he practises very carefully in his Life and Conversation, not like those Clergymen, that to save the Souls of other Men condemn themselves out of their own Mouths. His whole Life is nothing but a perpetual Lordship of Misrule,[1] and a constant Ramble Day and Night as long as it lasts, which is not according to the Course of Nature, but its own Course; for he cuts off the latter End of it, like a pruned Vine, that it may bear the more Wine, although it be the shorter. As for that which is left, he is as lavish of it as he is of every Thing else; for he sleeps all Day, and sits up all Night, that he may not see how it passes, until, like one that travels in a Litter and sleeps, he is

---

[2] Psalms, LVII. 4; LXIV. 3.

[1] Lord of Misrule: an officer appointed at court, at some university colleges, at inns of court, and in houses of great men to preside over Christmas games and revels.

at his Journey's End before he is aware;[a] for he is spirited away by
his Vices, and clapped under Hatches, where he never knows whither
he is going, until he is at the End of his Voyage.

THE SEDITIOUS MAN

Is a civil Mutineer, and as all Mutinies for the most Part are
for Pay, if it were not for that he would never trouble himself with
it. His Business is to kindle and blow up Discontents against the Government, that, when they are inflamed, he may have the fairer Opportunity to rob and plunder, while those, that are concerned, are employed in quenching it. He endeavours to raise Tumults, and, if he
can, civil War, a Remedy which no Man, that means well to his Country, can endure to think on, though the Disease were never so desperate. He is a State-Mountebank, whose Business is to persuade the
People that they are not well in Health, that he may get their Money
to make them worse. If he be a Preacher, he has the Advantage of all
others of his Tribe; for he has a Way to vent Sedition by Wholesale;
and as the foulest Purposes have most need of the fairest Pretences;
so when Sedition is masked under the Veil of Piety, Religion, Conscience, and holy Duty, it propagates wonderfully among the Rabble,
and he vents more in an Hour from the Pulpit, than others by News
and Politics can do in a Week. Next him Writers and Libellers are
most pernicious; for though the Contagion they disperse spreads
slower and with less Force than preaching, yet it lasts longer, and in
Time extends to more, and with less Danger to the Author, who is not
easily discovered, if he use any Care to conceal himself. And therefore
as we see stinging Flies vex and provoke Cattle most immediately before Storms: so Multitudes of those Kinds of Vermin do always appear to stir up the People, before the Beginning of all troublesome
Times; and nobody knows who they are, or from whence they came,
but only that they were printed the present Year, that they may not
lose the Advantage of being known to be new. Some do it only out of
Humour and Envy, or desire to see those that are above them pulled
down, and others raised in their Places; as if they held it a Kind of
Freedom to change their Governours, though they continue in the
same Condition themselves still, only they are a little better pleased

---

[a] he is aware] he aware

with it, in observing the Dangers Greatness is exposed to. He delights in nothing so much as civil Commotions, and like a Porpoise always plays before a Storm. Paper and Tinder are both made of the same material Rags; but he converts them both into the same again, and makes his Paper Tinder.

AN AFFECTED MAN

Carries himself like his Dish (as the Proverb says) very uprightly, without spilling one Drop of his Humour. He is an Orator and Rhetorician, that delights in Flowers and Ornaments of his own devising to please himself, and others that laugh at him. He is of a leaden dull Temper, that stands stiff, as it is bent, to all crooked Lines, but never to the Right. When he thinks to appear most graceful, he adorns himself most ill favouredly, like an *Indian* that wears Jewels in his Lips and Nostrils. His Words and Gestures are all as stiff as Buckram, and he talks as if his Lips were turned up as well as his Beard. All his Motions are regular as if he went by Clockwork, and he goes very true to the Nick as he is set. He has certain favourite Words and Expressions, which he makes very much of, as he has Reason to do, for they serve him upon all Occasions, and are never out of the Way when he has use of them, as they have Leisure enough to do; for nobody else has any Occasion for them but himself. All his Affectations are forced and stolen from others, and though they become some particular Persons where they grow naturally, as a Flower does on its Stalk, he thinks they will do so by him, when they are pulled and dead. He puts Words and Language out of its ordinary Pace, and breaks it to his own Fancy, which makes it go so uneasy in a Shuffle, which it has not been used to. He delivers himself in a forced Way like one that sings with a feigned Voice beyond his natural Compass. He loves the Sound of Words better than the Sense, and will rather venture to incur Nonsense than leave out a Word, that he has a Kindness for. If he be a Statesman, the slighter and meaner his Employments are, the bigger he looks, as an Ounce of Tin swells and looks bigger than an Ounce of Gold; and his Affectations of Gravity are the most desperate of all, as the Aphorism says—Madness of Study and Consideration are harder to be cured than those of lighter and more fantastic Humour.

A MEDICINE-TAKER

Has a sickly Mind, and believes the Infirmity is in his Body; like one, that draws the wrong Tooth, and fancies his Pain in the wrong Place. The less he understands the Reason of Physic, the stronger Faith he has in it, as it commonly fares in all other Affairs of the World. His Disease is only in his Judgment, which makes him believe a Doctor can fetch it out of his Stomach, or his Belly; and fright those Worms out of his Guts, that are bred in his Brain. He believes a Doctor is a Kind of Conjurer, that can do strange Things, and he is as willing to have him think so; for by that means he does not only get his Money, but finds himself in some Possibility, by complying with that Fancy, to do him good for it, which he could never expect to do any other Way; for like those that have been cured by drinking their own Water, his own Imagination is a better Medicine than any the Doctor knows how to prescribe, even as the Weapon-Salve[1] cures a Wound by being applied to that which made it. He is no sooner well, but any Story or Lye of a new famous Doctor, or strange Cure puts him into a Relapse, and he falls sick of a Medicine instead of a Disease, and catches Physic, like him that fell into a Looseness at the Sight of a Purge. He never knows when he is well, nor sick, but is always tampering with his Health till he has spoiled it, like a foolish Musician, that breaks his Strings with striving to put them in Tune; for *Nature*, which is *Physic*, understands better how to do her own Work than those that take it from her at second hand. *Hippocrates* says—*Ars longa, Vita brevis*,[2] and it is the truest of all his Aphorisms,

> *For he that's giv'n much to the long Art,*
> *Does not prolong his Life, but cut it short.*

THE RUDE MAN

Is an *Ostro-Goth*, or northern *Hun*, that wheresoever he comes, invades and all the World does overrun, without Distinction

---

[1] An ointment or powder, also called the "sympathetic powder," believed to heal a wound by "sympathy" or affinity after being applied to either the weapon by which the wound was made or blood from the wound. See Sir Kenelm Digby, *A Late Discourse Touching the Cure of Wounds by the Powder of Sympathy*, trans. R. White, 2d edition (London, 1658).

[2] See p. 173, n. 2.

of Age, Sex, or Quality. He has no Regard to any Thing but his own Humour, and that he expects should pass every where without asking Leave, or being asked wherefore, as if he had a Safe-conduct for his Rudeness. He rolls up himself, like a Hedgehog, in his Prickles, and is as untractable to all that come near him. He is an ill-designed Piece, built after the rustic Order; and all his Parts look too big for their Height. He is so ill contrived, that that which should be the Top in all regular Structures, i.e. Confidence, is his Foundation. He has neither Doctrine nor Discipline in him, like a fanatic Church, but is guided by the very same Spirit, that dipped the Herd of Swine in the Sea.[1] He was not bred but reared, not brought up to Hand, but suffered to run wild, and take after his Kind, as other People of the Pasture do. He takes that Freedom in all Places, as if he were not at Liberty, but had broken loose, and expected to be tied up again. He does not eat but feed, and when he drinks goes to Water. The old *Romans* beat the barbarous Part of the World into Civility; but if he had lived in those Times he had been invincible to all Attempts of that Nature, and harder to be subdued and governed than a Province. He eats his Bread, according to the Curse, with the Sweat of his Brows, and takes as much Pains at a Meal as if he earn'd it; puffs and blows like a Horse that eats Provender, and crams his Throat like a screwed Gun[2] with a Bullet bigger than the Bore. His Tongue runs perpetually over every Thing that comes in its Way, without Regard of what, where, or to whom; and nothing but a greater Rudeness than his own can stand before it; and he uses it to as slovenly Purposes as a Dog does, that licks his Sores and the Dirt off his Feet. He is the best Instance of the Truth of *Pythagoras*'s Doctrine,[3] for his Soul past through all Sorts of brute Beasts before it came to him, and still retains something of the Nature of every one.

THE MISER

Is like the Sea, that is said to be richer than the Land, but is not able to make any Use of it at all, and only keeps it from those that

---

[1] Matthew, VIII. 32; Mark, V. 13.

[2] Furnished with a screwed barrel; having a helically grooved bore. *O.E.D.*'s first entry: 1646 Evelyn, *Diary*—excellent screwed guns.

[3] The Pythagoreans believed in the immortality of the soul, and they believed that it passed through a cycle of births, appearing in various guises on earth, depending on the life it led in its preceding existence. [W. T. Jones, *A History of Western Philosophy* (New York, 1952), p. 52.]

know how to enjoy it if they had it. The Devil understood his Business very well, when he made Choice of *Judas*'s Avarice to betray *Christ*; for no other Vice would have undertaken it; and it is to be feared, that his Vicars now on Earth, by the Tenderness they have to the Bag, do not use him much better than his Steward did then. He gathers Wealth to no Purpose but to satisfy his Avarice, that has no End; and afflicts himself to possess that, which he is of all Men the most incapable of ever obtaining. His Treasure is in his Hands in the same Condition as if it were buried under Ground, and watched by an evil Spirit. His Desires are like the bottomless Pit which he is destined to; for the one is as soon filled as the other. He shuts up his Money in close Custody; and that, which has Power to open all Locks, is not able to set itself at Liberty. If he ever lets it out, it is upon good Bail and Mainprize,[1] to render itself Prisoner again, whensoever it shall be summoned. He loves Wealth as an Eunuch does Women, whom he has no Possibility of enjoying, or one that is bewitched with an Impotency, or taken with the Falling-Sickness. His greedy Appetite to Riches is but a Kind of Dog-Hunger, that never digests what it devours; but still the greedier and more eager it crams itself becomes more meager. He finds that Ink and Parchment preserves Money better than an iron Chest and Parsimony, like the Memories of Men that lye dead and buried when they are committed to Brass and Marble, but revive and flourish when they are trusted to authentic Writings, and encrease by being used. If he had lived among the *Jews* in the Wilderness, he would have been one of their chief *Reformers*, and have worshipped any Thing that is cast in Gold, though a sillier Creature than a Calf. *St. John* in the Revelations describes the new *Jerusalem* to be built all of Gold and Silver and precious Stones; for the Saints commonly take so much Delight in those Creatures, that nothing else could prevail with them ever to come thither: and as those Times are called the golden Age,[2] in which there was no Gold at all in use; so Men are reputed godly and rich, that make no Use at all of their Religion or Wealth. All that he has gotten together with perpetual Pains and Industry is not Wealth, but a Collection, which he intends to keep by him more for his own Diversion than any other Use; and he that made Ducks and Drakes with his Money enjoyed it every Way as much. He makes no Conscience of any Thing but part-

---

[1] The action of procuring the release of a prisoner by becoming surety ("Mainpernor") for his appearance in court at a specified time. [*O.E.D.*]

[2] See p. 86, n. 16.

ing with his Money, which is no better than a Separation of Soul and Body to him, and he believes it to be as bad as self-Murther if he should do it willfully; for the Price of the Weapon, with which a Man is killed, is always esteemed a very considerable Circumstance, and next to *not having the Fear of God before his Eyes*. He loves the Bowels of the Earth broiled on the Coals above any other Cookery in the World. He is a Slave condemned to the Mines. He laughs at the golden Mean[3] as ridiculous, and believes there is no such Thing in the World; for how can there be a Mean of that, of which no Man ever had enough? He loves the World so well, that he would willingly lose himself to save any Thing by it. His Riches are like a Dunghil, that renders the Ground unprofitable that it lies upon, and is good for nothing, until it be spread and scattered abroad.

A RABBLE

Is a Congregation, or Assembly of the States-General sent from their several and respective Shops, Stalls, and Garrets. They are full of Controversy, and every one of a several Judgment concerning the Business under present Consideration, whether it be Mountebank, Show, Hanging, or Ballad-Singer. They meet, like *Democritus*'s Atoms[1] *in vacuo*, and by a fortuitous Justling together produce the greatest and most savage Beast in the whole World: For, tho' the Members of it may have something of human Nature, while they are asunder, when they are put together, they have none at all; as a Multitude of several Sounds make one great Noise unlike all the rest, in which no one Particular is distinguished. They are a great Dunghill, where all Sorts of dirty and nasty Humours[2] meet, stink, and ferment; for all the Parts are in a perpetual Tumult. 'Tis no wonder, they make strange Churches, for they take naturally to any Imposture, and have a great Antipathy to Truth and Order, as being contrary to their original Confusion. They are a Herd of Swine possest with a dry Devil,[3] that run after Hanging, instead of Drowning. Once a Month

---

[3] See Aristotle, *Nicomachean Ethics*, IV. vi.

[1] Democritus (c. 460–c. 370 B.C.): Greek philosopher who developed the theory (founded by Leucippus) that the world was formed by the gathering of atoms. This theory was later expounded by Lucretius.

[2] Vapors. Perhaps suggesting also the *bents* or *dispositions* of the persons in the rabble.

[3] See p. 195, n. 1.

they go on Pilgrimage to the Gallows, to visit the Sepulchres of their Ancestors, as the *Turks* do once a Week. When they come there they sing Psalms, quarrel, and return full of Satisfaction and Narrative. When they break loose they are like a public Ruin, in which the highest Parts lye undermost, and make the noblest Fabrics heaps of Rubbish. They are like the Sea, that's stirred into a Tumult with every Blast of Wind, that blows upon it, till it become a watry *Appenine*, and heap Mountain Billows upon one another, as once the Giants did in the War with Heaven.[4] A Crowd is their proper Element, in which they make their Way with their Shoulders, as Pigs creep through Hedges. Nothing in the World delights them so much as the Ruin of great Persons, or any Calamity, in which they have no Share, though they get nothing by it. They love nothing but themselves in the Likeness of one another, and, like Sheep, run all that Way, the first goes, especially if it be against their Governors, whom they have a natural Disaffection to.

A SHOPKEEPER

Lives by the Labour of his own Tongue and other Men's Hands; and gains more by his flat downright Lying, than the Artificer does by all his Industry, Pains and Ingenuity: for his Tongue is a Kind of Taylor's Goose[1] or hot Press, with which he sets the last Gloss upon his coarse decayed Wares. His chief Qualification consists in a confident Outfacing of Truth, and persuading his Customers to believe him rather than their own Senses, which they have little Reason to do; for he, that will use false Lights, false Weights, and false Measures, will never stick at false Words: and as the more he stretches his Stuffs in the Measure the scantier it always proves; so the more he commends it the worse it afterwards appears upon Trial. The greatest Hazard he runs is Trusting, which yet he knows how to insure; for as when he takes a Thief he makes him pay for all and more than he has lost by other Thieves: so when he trusts, it is at such a Rate, that he that pays him pays for all those that do not. He walks in his Shop with a Yard always in his Hand instead of a

---

[4] Reference to the overthrow of Cronus (lord of the universe, who was aided by his brother Titans) by Zeus (son of Cronus, aided by his five brothers), a war that nearly destroyed the world, for Zeus released from prison the hundred-headed monsters who used weapons of thunder, lightning, and earthquakes.

[1] Smoothing iron.

Staff, that it may wear shorter and save his Conscience harmless, if
he should have Occasion to swear it was never cut since he had it.
His Custom of Lying, and the Profit he receives by it produces a Kind
of natural Inclination in him to all Sorts of Impostors, and therefore
he is as easily cheated out of his Way, as he cheats others in it,
takes naturally to all *Fanatic* Whimsies in Religion, and is as easily
misled by a seditious Teacher, as a Child is by a *Jamaica* Spirit; as
for Truth he gains nothing by it, and therefore will have nothing to
do with it. He never troubles his Head with Speculations but only
in Divinity and Politics, in which his Ignorance is so prevailing, that
he believes himself a great deal abler than his Governors. He sets a
value on his Commodities, not according to their true Worth, but
the Ignorance of the Buyers; and always sells cheapest to those whom
he finds to understand most of his Trade; but he that leaves it to
him is sure to be cheated; for he that lives by Lying will never be
scrupulous in taking Money for his Reputation. He calls his profession a *Mystery*, which being rightly interpreted by his Practice signifies only this—That as all *Turks* are Tradesmen, even so all Tradesmen are *Turks*.[2] His false Lights are a Kind of *Deceptio visus*,[3] with
which he casts a Mist, like a Conjurer, before the Eyes of his Customers, that they may take no Notice of the Imperfections and Infirmities
of his spotted and stained Stuffs, until it is too late. The more Trust
Men repose in him, the more he is sure to cheat them, as Taylors all
ways make the Cloaths of those scantiest, who allow them the largest
Measure—Those of the same Trade commonly set up together in a
Street, as Rooks build together in a Tuft of Trees. Country Gentlemen always design the least hopeful of their Children to Trades, and
out of that Stock the City is supplied with that sottish Ignorance,
which we see it perpetually abound with.

A QUAKER[1]

Is a Scoundrel Saint, of an Order without Founder, Vow,
or Rule; for he will not swear, nor be tyed to any Thing, but his

[2] See p. 42, n. 40.
[3] Optical illusion.
[1] A member of the sect that began in the 1640's and got the name of Quakers
about 1650. It is said that a Derbershire Justice of the Peace assigned the name
because they seemed fond of the text from Jeremiah, V. 22, which they addressed to him and a fellow magistrate: "Fear ye not me? saith the Lord; will

own Humour. He is the Link-Boy[2] of the Sectaries, and talks much
of his Light, but puts it under a Bushel, for nobody can see it but
himself. His Religion is but the cold Fit of an Ague, and his Zeal
of a contrary Temper to that of all others, yet produces the same
Effects; as cold Iron in *Greenland*, they say, burns as well as hot;
which makes him delight, like a Salamander, to live in the Fire[3] of
Persecution. He works out his Salvation, not with *Fear*, but *Confidence and Trembling*. His Profession is but a Kind of Winter-
Religion; and the Original of it as uncertain as the hatching of
Woodcocks, for no Man can tell from whence it came. He Vapours
much of the Light within him, but no such Thing appears, unless he
means as he is light-headed. He believes he takes up the Cross in being
cross to all Mankind. He delights in Persecution, as some old extravagant Fornicators find a Lechery in being whipt; and has no Ambition but to go to Heaven in what he calls a fiery Chariot, that is, a
Wood-monger's Faggot Cart. You may perceive he has a Crack in
his Skull by the flat Twang of his Nose[4] and the great Care he takes
to keep his Hat on,[5] lest his sickly Brains, if he have any, should take

ye not tremble at my presence?" Another version of the origin of the name
comes from Robert Barclay's *Apology for Quakers* (1675): in the early meetings of "The Children of Light," as they first called themselves, there were
frequent agitations, often signaling conversions.

In theology the Quakers differed little from the other fervid Evangelical
sects. Especially strong is their belief in the gift of the Spirit in the soul of the
individual believer, a constant inner light, and the motion and teaching of the
Spirit in the soul of the believer. [Masson, *Life of Milton*, V, 22–23.]

[2] A boy who carried a torch to light the way for people along the streets.
Butler plays, of course, on the idea of *inner* light.

[3] "That a Salamander is able to live in flames, to endure and put out fire, is
an assertion, not only of great antiquity, but confirmed by frequent, and not
contemptible testimony. The Egyptians have drawn it into their Hieroglyphicks,
Aristotle seemeth to embrace it; more plainly Nicander, Serenus Sammonicus,
Ælian and Pliny, who assigns the cause of this effect: An Animal (saith he) so
cold that it extinguisheth the fire like Ice." [Browne, *Pseudodoxia Epidemica*,
III. 14, in *Works*, ed. Keynes, II, 231.]

[4] Macaulay writes that the signs of godliness in the days of the Barebones
Parliament were "the sad-coloured dress, the sour look, the straight hair, the
nasal whine, the speech interspersed with quaint texts." [*History of England*, I,
182. See also Swift, *The Mechanical Operation of the Spirit*, in "*A Tale of a
Tub*," to which is Added "*The Battle of the Books*" and the "*Mechanical Operation of the Spirit*," ed. Guthkelch and Smith, pp. 282 and 284.]

[5] In their simplification of life and worship the Quakers prohibited ceremonies of honor or courtesy-titles among men; the hat was to be taken off to
no one. [Masson, *Life of Milton*, V, 25.]

Cold at it. He believes his Doctrine to be heavenly, because it agrees perfectly with the *Motus Trepidationis*.⁶ All his Hopes are in the *Turks* overrunning of Christendom, because he has heard they count Fools and Madmen Saints, and doubts not to pass muster with them for great Abilities that Way. This makes him believe he can convert the *Turk*, tho' he could do no good on the *Pope*,⁷ or the *Presbyterian*. Nothing comes so near his quaking Liturgy, as the Papistical Possessions of the *Devil*, with which it conforms in Discipline exact. His Church, or rather Chapel,⁸ is built upon a flat Sand, without superior or inferior in it, and not upon a Rock, which is never found without great Inequalities. Next Demoniacs he most resembles the Reprobate, who are said to be condemned to Weeping and Gnashing of Teeth. There was a Botcher of their Church, that renounced his Trade and turned Preacher, because he held it superstitious to sit *cross-legged*.⁹ His Devotion is but a Kind of spiritual Palsy, that proceeds from a Distemper in the Brain, where the Nerves are rooted. They abhor the Church of *England*, but conform exactly with those primitive Fathers of their Church, that heretofore gave Answers at the *Devil's* Oracles, in which they observed the very same Ceremony of quaking and gaping now practised by our modern Enthusiasts at their Exorcisms, rather than Exercises of Devotion. He sucks in the Air like a Pair of Bellows,¹⁰ and blows his inward Light with it, till he dung Fire, as Cattle do in *Lincolnshire*.¹¹ The general Ignorance of their whole Party make it appear, that whatsoever their Zeal may be, it is not *according to Knowledge*.

⁶ Agitated or restless movement.

⁷ Papist.

⁸ The Quaker meeting was held in a "chapel" for mutual edification and worship with unrestricted participation by members as the spirit moved them. A "church" in the Quakers' view, which they called a steeple-house, was presided over by a hired performer, the parson. [See Masson, *Life of Milton*, III, 25.]

⁹ See p. 174.

¹⁰ To the enthusiast awaiting divine communication a painful agony was apparent as the light tried to break into the darkness of the soul, an agony accompanied by shaking, groans, sighs, and tears. [Masson, *Life of Milton*, III, 22–23.]

¹¹ "Lincolnshire, *where hogs shite sope and cows shite fire*. The inhabitants of the poorer sort washing their clothes with hogs dung, and burning dried cowdung for want of better fuel." [*The Oxford Dictionary of English Proverbs*, comp. William George Smith, with Introduction and Index by Janet E. Heseltine (Oxford, 1935).]

A SWEARER

Is one, that sells the *Devil* the best Pennyworth that he meets with any where; and like the *Indians*, that Part with Gold for Glass-Beads, he damns his Soul for the slightest Trifles imaginable. He betroths himself oftner to the Devil in one Day, than *Mecænas* did in a Week to his Wife, that he was married a thousand times to.[1] His Discourse is inlaid with Oaths, as the Gallows is with Nails, to fortify it against the Assaults of those, whose Friends have made it their Death-bed. He takes a preposterous Course to be believed, and persuade you to credit what he says, by saying that, which at the best he does not mean; for all the Excuse he has for his voluntary damning of himself is, that he means nothing by it. He is as much mistaken in what he does intend really; for that which he takes for the Ornament of his Language renders it the most odious and abominable. His Custom of Swearing takes away the Sense of his Saying. His Oaths are but a dissolute Formality of Speech, and the worst Kind of Affectation. He is a *Knight-Baronet of the Post*,[2] or Gentleman Blasphemer, that swears for his Pleasure only, a *Lay-affidavit Man, in Voto*[3] only, and not *in Orders*. He learned to swear, as Magpies do to speak, by hearing others. He talks nothing but *Bell, Book*, and *Candle*,[4] and delivers himself over to *Satan* oftner than a *Presbyterian Classis*[5] would do. He plays with the Devil for sport only, and stakes his Soul to nothing. He overcharges his Oaths till they break, and hurt himself only. He discharges them as fast as a Gun, that will shoot nine times with one loading. He is the Devil's Votary, and fails not to commend himself into his Tuition upon all Occasions. He out-

---

[1] Mecaenas: the patron of Virgil and Horace. See Seneca, *Epistles*, trans. Gummere, CXIV. 6: "Hunc esse, qui uxorem milliens duxit, cum unam habnerit?" ("This was the man [Mecaenas] who had but one wife, and yet was married countless times?" [i.e., often repulsed by his wife Terentia, and then restored to grace]).

[2] See p. 186, n. 5, on the Knight of the Post and the Character itself.

Baronet: the lowest degree of honour hereditary, founded by King James I in 1611. [Bailey, *Universal Etymological Dictionary*.]

[3] *In voto*: evidently the state of a religious novice.

[4] Articles used in the office of excommunication. After the reading of the sentence a *bell* is rung, a *book* closed, and a *candle* extinguished.

[5] An inferior judicatory consisting of the elders or pastors of the parishes or churches of a district; a presbytery. [*O.E.D.*]

swears an Exorcist, and outlies the Legend. His Oaths are of a wider Bore and louder Report than those of an ordinary Perjurer, but yet they do not half the Execution. Sometimes he resolves to leave it, but not too suddenly, lest it should prove unwholesome, and injurious to his Health, but by Degrees as he took it up. Swearing should appear to be the greatest of Sins; for tho' the Scripture says, *God sees no Sin in his Children,*[6] it does not say he hears none.

THE LUXURIOUS

Places all Enjoyment in spending, as a covetous Man does in getting, and both are treated at a Witch's Feast, where nothing feeds but only the Imagination: and like two Madmen, that believe themselves to be the same Prince, laugh at one another. He values his Pleasures as they do honour, by the Difficulty and Dearness of the Purchase, not the Worth of the Thing; and the more he pays the better he believes he ought to be pleased, as Women are fondest of those Children, which they have groaned most for. His Tongue is like a great Practiser's in Law; for as the one will not stir, so the other will not taste without a great Fee. He never reckons what a Thing costs by what it is worth, but what it is worth by what it costs. All his Senses are like corrupt Judges, that will understand nothing, until they are thoroughly informed and satisfied with a convincing Bribe. He relishes no Meat but by the Rate; and a high Price is like Sauce to it, that gives it a high Taste, and renders it savoury to his Palate. He believes there is nothing dear, nor ought to be so, that does not cost much, and that the dearest bought is always the cheapest. He tastes all Wines by the Smallness of the Bottles, and the Greatness of the Price; and when he is over-reckoned takes it as an extraordinary Value set upon him, as *Dutchmen* always reckon by the Dignity of the Person, not the Charge of the Entertainment he receives, put his Quality and Titles into the Bill of Fare, and make him pay for feeding upon his own Honour and Right-Worship, which he brought along with him. He debauches his Gluttony with an unnatural Appetite to Things never intended for Food, like preposterous Venery, or the unnatural Mixtures of Beasts of several Kinds. He is as curious of his Pleasures as an Antiquary of his Rarities, and cares

---

[6] I John, III. 9.

for none but such as are very choice and difficult to be gotten, disdains any Thing that is common, unless it be his Women, which he esteems a common Good, and therefore the more communicative the better. All his Vices are like Children[a] that have been nicely bred, a great Charge to him, and it costs him dear to maintain them like themselves, according to their Birth and Breeding; but he, like a tender Parent, had rather suffer Want himself than they should: for he considers, a Man's Vices are his own Flesh and Blood, and though they are but By-blows he is bound to provide for them, out of natural Affection, as well as if they were lawfully begotten.

AN UNGRATEFUL MAN

Is like Dust in the Highway, that flies in the Face of those that raise it. He that is ungrateful is all Things that are amiss—He is like the *Devil*, that seeks the Destruction if those most of all, that do him the best Service; or an unhealthful Sinner, that receives Pleasure, and returns nothing but Pox and Diseases. He receives *Obligations* from all that he can, but they presently *become void and of none Effect*; for good Offices fare with him like Death, from which there is no Return. His ill-nature is like an ill Stomach, that turns its Nourishment into bad Humours. He should be a Man of very great Civilities; for he receives all that he can, but never parts with any. He is like a barren Soil, plant what you will on him, it will never grow; nor any Thing but Thorns and Thistles, that came in with the Curse. His Mother died in Childbed of him; for he is descended of the Generation of Vipers,[1] in which the Dam always eats off the Sire's Head,[2] and the young ones their Way through *her* Belly.[3] He is like a Horse in a Pasture, that eats up the Grass, and dungs it in Requital. He puts the Benefits he receives from others and his own Faults together in that End of the Sack, which he carries behind his Back. His ill-Nature, like a contagious Disease, infects others that are

---

[a] like Children] like, Children

[1] Used several times in the Bible; see Matthew, III. 7, XII. 34, XXIII. 33; and Luke, III. 7.

[2] "Snakes mate by embracing, intertwining so closely that they could be taken to be a single animal with two heads. The male viper inserts its head into the female viper's mouth, and the female is so enraptured with pleasure that she gnaws it off." [Pliny, *Natural History*, trans. Rackham, X. lxxxii. 169.]

[3] Cf. ibid., 170.

of themselves good, who observing his Ingratitude become less inclined to do good, than otherwise they would be: And as the sweetest Wine, if ill preserved, becomes the sourest Vinegar; so the greatest Endearments with him turn to the bitterest Injuries. He has an admirable Art of Forgetfulness, and no sooner receives a Kindness, but he owns it by Prescription, and claims *from Time out of Mind.* All his Acknowledgments appear before his Ends are served, but never after, and, like *Occasion,* grow very thick before, but bare behind.[4] He is like a River, that runs away from the Spring that feeds it, and undermines the Banks that support it; or like Vice and Sin, that destroy those that are most addicted to it; or the Hangman, that breaks the Necks of those whom he gets his Living by, and whips those that find him Employment, and brands his Masters that set him on Work. He pleads the *Act of Oblivion*[5] for all the good Deeds that are done him, and *pardons* himself for the evil Returns he makes. He never looks backward (like a right Statesman) and Things that are past are all one with him, as if they had never been: And as Witches, they say, hurt those only from whom they can get something and have a Hank upon;[6] he no sooner receives a Benefit, but he converts it to the Injury of that Person, who conferred it on him—It fares with Persons as with Families, that think better of themselves, the further they are off their first Raisers.

A KNIGHT OF THE POST[1]

Is a Retailer of Oaths, a Deposition-Monger, an Evidence-Maker that lives by the Labour of his Conscience. He takes Money to kiss the Gospel, as *Judas* did *Christ,* when he betrayed him. As *a*

---

[4] Among the moral precepts (II. 26) in the famous collection of the fourth century known as *Dionysii Catonis disticha de moribus ad filium,* which was much admired and widely used in the schools during the middle ages. The reputed author or collector was Dionysus Cato.

[5] See p. 32, n. 14.

[6] Hank: a hold on, or power, over [someone]. Witches were believed to use such tangible physical means as were associated with magic and sorcery—ointments, dust, herbs, or potions, knotted cords or ligatures, waxen images, etc. Or they might try to get hold of some personal belonging of the victim, such as a tooth, nail clippings, hair, or bits of clothing, to use in working their evil. [Robbins, *The Encyclopedia of Witchcraft and Demonology,* pp. 332–33.]

[1] See p. 186, n. 5.

good Conscience is a continual Feast;[2] so an ill one is with him his daily Food. He plys at a Court of Justice, as Porters do at a Market; and his Business is to bear Witness, as they do Burthens, for any Man that will pay them for it. He will swear his Ears through an Inch-Board,[3] and wear them merely by Favour of the Court; for being *Amicus curiæ*,[4] they are willing to let him keep the Pillory out of Possession, though he has forfeited his Right never so often: For when he is once outed of his Ears, he is past his Labour, and can do the Commonwealth of Practisers no more Service. He is a false Weight in the Ballance of Justice; and as a Lawyer's Tongue is the Tongue of the Ballance, that inclines either Way, according as the Weight of the Bribe inclines it, so does his. He lays one Hand on the Book, and the other is in the Plaintiff's or Defendant's Pocket. He feeds upon his Conscience, as a Monkey eats his Tail. He kisses the Book to show he renounces, and takes his leave of it—Many a parting Kiss has he given the Gospel. He pollutes it with his Lips oftner than a Hypocrite. He is a sworn Officer of every Court, and a great Practiser; is admitted within the Bar, and makes good what the rest of the Council say. The Attorney and Sollicitor see and instruct him in the Case; and he ventures as far for his Client, as any Man, to be laid by the Ears: He speaks more to the Point than any other, yet gives false Ground to his Brethren of the Jury, that they seldom come near the Jack.[5] His Oaths are so brittle, that not one in twenty of them will hold the Taking, but fly as soon as they are out. He is worse than an ill Conscience; for that bears true Witness, but his is always false; and though his own Conscience be said to be a thousand Witnesses, he will out-swear and out-face them all. He believes it no Sin to bear false Witness for his Neighbour, that pays him for it, because it is not forbidden, but only to bear false Witness against his Neighbour.

AN UNDESERVING FAVOURITE

Is a Piece of base Metal with the King's Stamp upon it, a Fog raised by the Sun, to obscure his own Brightness. He came to

---

[2] See p. 168, n. 1.

[3] A common punishment for forgery, cheating, or libeling, etc. was placement in a pillory, a whipping, and sometimes the nailing of one or both ears to the pillory, or cutting off the ears.

[4] A friend of the court; technically, a disinterested adviser.

[5] In the game of bowls (see p. 58, n. 16) the mark at which the players aim.

Preferment by unworthy Offices, like one that rises with his Bum forwards, which the Rabble hold to be fortunate. He got up to Preferment on the wrong Side, and sits as untoward in it. He is raised rather above himself than others; or as base Metals are by the Test of Lead, while Gold and Silver continue still unmoved. He is raised and swells, like a Pimple, to be an Eye-sore, and deform the Place he holds. He is born like a Cloud on the Air of the Prince's Favour, and keeps his Light from the rest of his People. He rises, like the light End of a Ballance, for Want of Weight; or as Dust and Feathers do for being light. He gets into the Prince's Favour by wounding it. He is a true *Person* of Honour; for he does but act it at the best, a Lord made only to justify all the Lords of Maypoles, Morrice-Dances, and Misrule,[1] a Thing that does not live, but lye in State, before he's dead, such as the Heralds dight at Funerals.[2] His Prince gives him Honour out of his own Stock, and Estate out of his Revenue, and lessens himself in both.

> *He is like Fern, that vile unuseful Weed,*
> *That springs equivocally, without Seed.*

He was not made for Honour, nor it for him, which makes it sit so unfavouredly upon him. The Forepart of himself, and the hinder Part of his Coach publish his Distinction;[3] as *French* Lords, that have *haute Justice*, that is, may hang and draw, distinguish their Qualities by the Pillars of their Gallowses.[4] He got his Honour easily, by Chance, without the hard laborious Way of Merit, which makes him so prodigally lavish of it. He brings down the Price of Honour, as the Value of any Thing falls in mean Hands. He looks upon all Men in the State of Knighthood and plain Gentility as most deplorable; and wonders how he could endure himself, when he was but of that Rank. The greatest Part of his Honour consists in his well-sounding Title, which he therefore makes Choice of, tho' he has none to the Place, but only a Patent to go by the Name of it. This appears at the End of his Coach in the Shape of a Coronet, which his Footmen set their Bums against, to the great Disparagement of the wooden Repre-

---

[1] See p. 191, n. 1 on Lord of Misrule.

[2] One function of heralds was the supervision of funerals.

[3] I.e., by the emblem mentioned below, a coronet.

[4] "The distinguishing their Qualities by the Pillars of their Gallowses may probably allude to a Cross in Coats of Arms, which, from its Resemblance to the Letter T or a double Gibbet, is called *Crux patibulata*, or *la Croix Potencée*." [Thyer's note.]

sentative. The People take him for a general Grievance, a Kind of public Pressure, or Innovation, and would willingly give a Subsidy to be redressed of him. He is a strict Observer of Men's Addresses to him, and takes a mathematical Account, whether they stoop and bow in just Proportion to the Weight of his Greatness, and allow full Measure to their Legs and Cringes accordingly. He never uses Courtship, but in his own Defence, that others may use the same to him, and, like a true Christian, does as he would be done unto. He is intimate with no Man but his Pimp and his Surgeon, with whom he keeps no State, but communicates all the States of his Body. He is raised like the Market, or a Tax, to the Grievance and Curse of the People. He that knew the Inventory of him would wonder what slight Ingredients go to the making up of a great Person; howsoever he is turned up Trump, and so commands better Cards than himself, while the Game lasts. He has much of Honour according to the original Sense of it, which among the Ancients (*Gellius* says) signified *Injury*.[5] His Prosperity was greater than his Brain could bear, and he is drunk with it; and if he should take a Nap as long as *Epimenides*[6] or the seven Sleepers,[7] he would never be sober again. He took his Degree, and went forth Lord by *mandamus*,[8] without performing Exercises of Merit. His Honour's but an Immunity from Worth, and his Nobility a Dispensation for doing Things ignoble. He expects that Men's Hats should fly off before him like a Storm, and not presume to stand in the Way of his Prospect, which is always over their Heads. All the Advantage he has is but to go before, or sit before, in which his nether Parts take place of his upper, that continue

---

[5] Gellius says, in writing about ambiguous words (ones that can be used in a good sense or a bad one): "Sed 'honorem' quoque mediam vocem fuisse et ita appellatum, ut etian 'malus honos' diceretur et significaret iniuriam, id profecto rarissimum." ("But the use of *honor* as an indifferent word, so that people ever spoke of 'bad honour' signifying 'wrong' or 'injury' is indeed very rare.") [Aulus Gellius, *The Attic Nights of Aulus Gellius*, trans. John C. Rolfe (London and New York, 1927–28), XII. ix. 3.]

[6] Epimenides was a semi-mythical Cretan poet and soothsayer and is said to have visited Athens in the sixth century B.C. to purify the city from the taint of a sacrilege. It is also said that, while he tended the flocks of his father in his childhood, one day he entered a cave and fell asleep and did not awaken for fifty-seven years.

[7] The noble Christian youths of Ephesus, who fleeing from the Decian persecution (A.D. 250) took refuge in a cave and, ordered to be walled up therein by the emperor, slept there for 187 years. Cf. Donne, "The Good Morrow."

[8] A prerogative writ.

still, in Comparison, but *Commoners*. He is like an open Summer-House, that has no Furniture but bare Seats. All he has to show for his Honour is his Patent, which will not be in Season until the third or fourth Generation, if it lasts so long. His very *Creation* supposes him nothing before; and as Taylors rose by the Fall of *Adam*,[9] and came in, like Thorns and Thistles, with the Curse, so did he by the Frailty of his Master. His very Face is his Gentleman-Usher, that walks before him in State, and cries, *give Way*. He is as stiff, as if he had been dipt in petrifying Water, and turned into his own Statue. He is always taking the Name of his Honour in vain, and will rather damn it like a Knighthood of the Post, than want Occasion to pawn it for every idle Trifle, perhaps for more than it is worth, or any Man will give to redeem it; and in this he deals uprightly, tho' perhaps in nothing else.

A CUCKOLD

Is his Wife's Bastard Issue, begotten upon her Body by her Gallant. He is like a Pack-saddle, and his Wife carries him to carry somebody else upon. He is a Creature, that *Adam* never gave Name to, for there was none of his Kind in Paradise. He is no natural Production, but made by his Wife's Mechanics—A Stock, that another grafts upon, and leaves him to maintain the Fruit. His own Branches his Horns are as mystical as the Whore of *Babylon*'s Palfreys,[1] not to be seen but in a Vision, and his Wife rides him as that great Lady does her Gelding. There are two Orders of them, the Wittol,[2] that's a Volunteer, and the Cuckold, that's imprest. They talk of Asses in *India*, that have Horns on their Rumps; and for certain his grow out of his Wives Haunches. He is but an Undertaker in his Spouse, and his Partners go Shares with him. Her Faults are written in his Forehead, and he wears her Phylactery.[3] His Horns,[4] like

---

[9] I.e., because human beings began to wear clothes. Cf. p. 174.

[1] Revelation, XVII. 3.

[2] See the Character of A Wittal.

[3] A little box containing quotations from the Mosaic law which was worn on the forehead by pious Jews, especially during morning prayers, as a reminder of the obligation to keep the law.

[4] A reference to the invisible horns which the cuckold was supposed to have as a sign of his condition. References to those horns abound in writings of the Elizabethan period and some years following.

those in a Country Gentleman's Hall, serve his Wife to hang Cloaths upon, with which she covers all her Faults, which he is fain to father, as well as her Children. He is a Man of great Hospitality; for he does not only keep open House, but open Wife for all Comers. He went about to enclose the Common, but his Neighbours threw it up again. He is but one Ingredient of a Husband, and there goes as many to the making of him up, as there do Taylors to a Man.[5] If he be notorious he is like a Belweather, and has a Larum tied to his Horns, which every body knows him by. If he be a Wittol or contented Cuckold, he is like a Gentleman, that wears a Horn for his Pleasure; but he, that makes it his Calling, is a Sowgelder, that blows a Horn to get Money. But if he be jealous, his Head is troubled with a forked Distinction *discrimine facta Bicorni*,[6] like *Pythagoras* his Letter,[7] and he knows not which to take to, his Wife's Virtue, or Vice; and, whatsoever she proves, he remains a speculative Cuckold, well studied in the Theory of Horns, but in vain, for *Naturam expellat furca licet, usque recurret*.[8] He fears his Park lies too convenient for Deer-stealers, and his Thoughts walk the Round perpetually with a dark Lanthorn to surprize them, but neither meets with them, nor Satisfaction. The Poets say, the Gate of Sleep is made of Horn,[9] and certainly his is so; for he dreams of nothing else sleeping or waking. Thus he apprehends himself, upon Suspicion, for a Cuckold, is cast by his own Confession; and, as he that believed he had pist a Mouse, because he found one drowned in his Chamber-Pot,[10] he interprets every Thing in favour of his Horns, until he becomes really a Cuckold in his Heart.

---

[5] "Nine tailors make a man." [Proverbial.]

[6] "A distinction wrought in a double horn."

[7] The Greek upsilon (Υ) said to have been used by Pythagoras of Samos to represent the divergent paths of virtue and vice. Alluded to by Rabelais (*Pantagruel*, IV. 33), John Donne (A Lent-Sermon, pp. 173–88 in Vol. IX of Evelyn N. Simpson and George R. Potter, eds., *Sermons*, 10 vols.[Berkeley, 1953–62], and Sir Thomas Browne (*Pseudodoxia Epidemica*, V. 19, in *Works*, ed. Keynes, III, 135).

[8] Horace, *Epistles*, I. x. 24–25:
Naturam expellas furca, tamen usque recurret,
    et mala perrumpet furtim fastidia victrix.
"You may drive out Nature with a pitchfork, yet she will ever hurry back, and, ere you know it, will burst through your foolish contempt in triumph." [In *Satires, Epistles and Ars Poetica*, trans. Fairclough.]

[9] *Odyssey*, XIX. 562; *Aeneid*, VI. 893.

[10] I have found no source for this story.

A MALICIOUS MAN

Has a strange natural Inclination to all ill Intents and Purposes. He bears nothing so resolutely as Ill-will, which he takes naturally to, as some do to Gaming, and will rather hate for nothing than sit out. He believes the *Devil* is not so bad as he should be, and therefore endeavours to make him worse by drawing him into his own Party offensive and defensive; and if he would but be ruled by him does not doubt but to make him understand his Business much better than he does. He lays nothing to Heart but Malice, which is so far from doing him hurt, that it is the only Cordial that preserves him. Let him use a Man never so civilly to his Face, he is sure to hate him behind his Back. He has no Memory for any good that is done him; but Evil, whether it be done him or not, never leaves him, as Things of the same Kind always keep together. Love and Hatred, though contrary Passions, meet in him as a third, and unite; for he loves nothing but to hate, and hates nothing but to love. All the Truths in the World are not able to produce so much Hatred, as he is able to supply. He is a common Enemy to the World; for being born to the Hatred of it, Nature that provides for every Thing she brings forth, has furnished him with a Competence suitable to his Occasions; for all Men together cannot hate him so much, as he does them one by one. He loses no Occasion of Offence, but very thriftily lays it up, and endeavours to improve it to the best Advantage. He makes Issues in his Skin, to vent his ill Humours, and is sensible of no Pleasure so much as the Itching of his Sores. He hates Death for nothing so much, as because he fears it will take him away, before he has paid all the Ill-will he owes, and deprive him of all those precious Feuds, he has been scraping together all his Life-time. He is troubled to think what a Disparagement it will be to him to die before those, that will be glad to hear he is gone; and desires very charitably, they might come to an Agreement like good Friends, and go Hand in Hand out of the World together. He loves his Neighbour as well as he does himself, and is willing to endure any Misery, so they may but take Part with him, and undergo any Mischief rather than they should want it. He is ready to spend his Blood, and lay down his Life for theirs, that would not do half so much for him; and rather than fail would give the *Devil* suck, and his Soul into the Bargain, if he would but make him his Plenipotentiary, to determine all Differences between himself and others. He contracts Enmities as others do Friendships, out of Likenesses, Sympathies, and Instincts; and when he lights upon one of his own Temper, as Contraries produce the same Effects, they perform all the Offices of Friendship, have the same Thoughts, Affections, and Desires of one another's Destruction, and please themselves as heartily, and perhaps as securely, in hating one another, as others do in loving. He seeks out Enemies to avoid falling out with himself; for his Temper is like that of a flourishing Kingdom, if it have not a foreign Enemy it will fall into a civil War, and turn its Arms upon it self, and so does but hate in his own Defence. His Malice is all Sorts of Gain to him; for as Men take Pleasure in pursuing, entrapping, and destroying all Sorts of Beasts and Fowl, and call it Sports, so would he do Men, and if he had equal Power would never be at a Loss, nor give over his Game without his Prey, and in this he does nothing but Justice; for as Men take Delight to destroy Beasts, he being a Beast does but do as he is done by in endeavouring to destroy Men. The Philosopher said—*Man to Man is a God and a Wolf*;[1] but he being incapable of the first does his Endeavour to make as much of the last as he can, and shews himself as excellent in his Kind, as it is in his Power to do.

A SQUIRE OF DAMES

Deals with his Mistress as the Devil does with a Witch, is content to be her Servant for a Time, that she may be his Slave for ever. He is Esquire to a Knight-Errant, Donzel to the Damzels, and Gentleman Usher daily waiter on the Ladies, that rubs out his Time in making Legs and Love to them. He is a Gamester, that throws at all Ladies that are set him, but is always out, and never wins but when he throws at the Candlestick, that is for nothing;[1] a general Lover, that addresses unto all but never gains any, as Universals produce nothing. He never appears so gallant a Man as when he is in the Head of a Body of Ladies, and leads them up with admirable Skill and Conduct. He is an *Eunuch-Bashaw*,[2] that has Charge of the Women, and governs all their public Affairs, because he is not able to do them any considerable private Services. One of his prime Qualifications is to convey their Persons in and out of Coaches, as tenderly

---

[1] "Homo homini aut deus aut lupus." ("Man is to man either god or wolf.") [Proverbial.]

[1] For a similar expression of the lover in the image of an unsuccessful gambler who wins in worthless pursuits only see p. 91.

[2] *Bashaw*: Turkish title of honor, now written *pasha*; thus, a magnate or grandee.

as a Cook sets his Custards in an Oven and draws them out again, without the least Discomposure or Offence to their inward or outward Woman, that is, their Persons and Dresses. The greatest Care he uses in his Conversation with Ladies is, to order his Peruque methodically, and keep off his Hat with equal Respect both to *it*, and their Ladyships, that neither may have Cause to take any just Offence, but continue him in their good Graces. When he squires a Lady, he takes her by the Handle of her Person the Elbow, and steers it with all possible Caution, lest his own Foot should, upon a Tack, for want of due Circumspection, unhappily fall foul on the long Train she carries at her Stern. This makes him walk upon his Toes, and tread as lightly as if he were leading her a Dance. He never tries any Experiment solitary with her, but always in Consort, and then he acts the Woman's Part, and she the Man's, talks loud and laughs, while he sits demurely silent, and simpers or bows, and cries *anon Madam, excellently good!* &c. &c. He is a Kind of Hermaphrodite; for his Body is of one Sex, and his Mind of another, which makes him take no Delight in the Conversation or Actions of Men, because they do so by his, but apply himself to Women, to whom the Sympathy and Likeness of his own Temper and Wit naturally inclines him, where he finds an agreeable Reception for want of a better; for they, like our *Indian* Planters, value their Wealth by the Number of their Slaves.[3] All his Business in the Morning is to dress himself, and in the Afternoon to shew his Workmanship to the Ladies; who after serious Consideration approve or disallow of his Judgment and Abilities accordingly, and he as freely delivers his Opinion of theirs. The Glass is the only Author he studies, by which his Actions and Gestures are all put on like his Cloaths, and by that he practises how to deliver what he has prepared to say to the Dames, after he has laid a Train to bring it in.

A KNAVE

Is like a Tooth-drawer, that maintains his own Teeth in constant eating by pulling out those of other Men. He is an ill moral Philosopher, of villainous Principles, and as bad Practice. His Tenets are to hold what he can get, right or wrong. His Tongue and his

---

[3] The planters in the West Indies were the chief slave-owners in the Empire. Development of the West Indies by England was begun largely through the efforts of Cromwell, who procured emigrants for Jamaica after it was seized by his men who had recently been repulsed in their attack on Santo Domingo. [Lunt, *History of England*, p. 646.]

Heart are always at Variance, and fall out, like Rogues in the Street, to pick somebody's Pocket. They never agree but, like *Herod* and *Pilate*, to do Mischief. His Conscience never stands in his Light, when the *Devil* holds a Candle to him; for he has stretched it so thin, that it is transparent. He is an Engineer of Treachery, Fraud, and Perfidiousness, and knows how to manage Matters of great Weight with very little Force, by the Advantage of his trepanning Screws.[1] He is very skilful in all the Mechanics of Cheat, the mathematical Magic of Imposture; and will outdo the Expectation of the most Credulous, to their own Admiration and Undoing. He is an excellent Founder, and will melt down a leaden Fool, and cast him into what Form he pleases. He is like a Pike in a Pond, that lives by Rapine, and will sometimes venture on one of his own Kind, and devour a Knave as big as himself—He will swallow a Fool a great deal bigger than himself; and if he can but get his Head within his Jaws, will carry the rest of him hanging out at his Mouth, until by Degrees he has digested him all. He has a hundred Tricks, to slip his Neck out of the Pillory, without leaving his Ears behind.[2] As for the Gallows, he never ventures to show his Tricks upon the high-Rope, for fear of breaking his Neck. He seldom commits any Villany, but in a legal Way, and makes the Law bear him out in that, for which it hangs others. He always robs under the Vizard of Law, and picks Pockets with Tricks in Equity. By his Means the Law makes more Knaves than it hangs, and, like the *Inns-of-Court*[3] protects Offenders against itself. He gets within the Law, and disarms it. His hardest Labour is to wriggle himself into Trust, which if he can but compass, his Business is done; for Fraud and Treachery follow as easily, as a Thread does a Needle. He grows rich by the Ruin of his Neighbours, like Grass in the Streets in a great Sickness. He shelters himself under the Covert of the Law, like a Thief in a Hemp-Plot, and makes that secure him, which was intended for his Destruction.

AN ANABAPTIST[1]

Is a Water-Saint, that, like a Crocodile, sees clearly in the Water, but dully on Land. He does not only live in two Elements,

---

[1] Trepan: (1) A tool used in boring shafts. (2) A person who traps or decoys others; also a stratagem or trick.

[2] See p. 206, n. 3.

[3] See p. 102, n. 2.

[1] The Anabaptists (or Baptists) formed the most numerous of dissenting

like a Goose, but two Worlds at once, this, and one of the next. He is contrary to a Fisher of Men; for, instead of pulling them out of the Water, he dips them in it. He keeps Souls in Minority, and will not admit them to inherit the Kingdom of Heaven, till they come to Age, fit to be trusted with their own Belief. He defies Magistracy and Ministry as the Horns of *Antichrist*; but would fain get them both into his own Hands. His Babes of Grace are all *Pagan*, and he breeds them up as they do young Trees in a Nursery, lets them grow up, and then transplants them into the new Soil of his own Church. He lets them run wild, as they do young Colts on a Common, until th'are old enough to be taken up and backed, and then he breaks and paces them with his own *Church-walkings*.[2] He is a Landerer of Souls, and tries them, as Men do Witches, by Water. He dips them all under Water, but their Hands, which he holds them up by—those do still continue *Pagan*; and that's the Reason, why they make no Conscience of their Works, when they can get Power in their Hands, but act the most barbarous Inhumanities in the World. His dipping makes him more obstinate and stiff in his Opinions, like a Piece of hot Iron, that grows hard by being quenched in cold Water. He does not like the use of Water in his Baptism, as it falls from Heaven in Drops, but as it runs out of the Bowels of the Earth, or stands putrefying in a dirty Pond. He chuses the coldest Time in the Year to be dipped in, to shew the Heat of his Zeal, and this renders him the more obstinate. Law and Government are great Grievances to him, and he believes Men may live very well without them, if they would be ruled by him; and then he would have nothing of Authority but his own Revelations. He is a *Saint-Errant*; for he calls his Religion *Walking*,[3]

---

groups. Though their enemies connected them with the anarchical German Anabaptists of the Reformation, the Anabaptists claimed their origin lay in the practice of the primitive or Apostolic Church, where only adult believers were baptized, only by being fully immersed in the water.

Except on the subject of Baptism the Anabaptists resembled the Congregationalists or Independents. [Masson, *Life of Milton*, III, 146 and 148.]

[2] A cant phrase used by Presbyterians and other sectaries to suggest walking the path of righteousness.

Cf. J. R. Green's remarks: A group of Separatists rejected ceremonies and the rule of Bishops, joined in " 'a Church estate on the fellowship of the Gospel.' " Feeling their way forward to the great principle of liberty of conscience, they asserted their Christian right " 'to walk in all the ways which God had made known or should make known to them.' " [*A Short History of the English People* (New York and London, 1912), II, 597–98.]

[3] See n. 2 above.

which he opposes to the Pope's *Sitting* as the more orthodox and infallible. His Church is a Kind of *round Table* without upper End, or lower End; for they observe no Order, nor admit of Degrees.[4] It is like the Serpent *Amphisbæna*,[5] that has a Head at either End of it: for such is their spiritual Envy and Ambition, that they can endure no superior, but high and low are tied together, like long and short Sticks in a Faggot.

He defies the World in his own Defence, because it slighted him first, and is rather a Renegado to *it*, than a Convert to the *other*. He renounced it, because it was not for his Turn, and gave it over because he knew not how to enjoy it. His Ambition, like a Weed, grows highest on the lowest Grounds; and he fancies himself above the World by despising what he would, but could not aspire to. His Charity extends no further than his own Diocese, and is nothing else but Self-Love, and natural Affection to his own Opinions in other Men. He cries down Learning, as he does the World, because it is not within his Reach, and gives unjust Judgment upon that, which he understands nothing of. He leaves the Road of the Church, and crosses over Bye-ways, as Thieves do, when they have committed a Robbery. All the spiritual Knowledge, he brags so much of, is but his at the second Hand, and borrowed from Translations; and, if those err, his Spirit (tho' infallible as the *Pope's*) must do so too. The prodigious Height of Confidence, he has arrived to, is not possible to be attained without an equally impregnable Ignorance. His Church is under the watry Government of the Moon, when she was in *Aquarius*. He places himself on a Pinnacle of the Temple,[6] to see if the *Devil* dare cap Texts with him. He had a Mind to dispose of his Religion, how he pleased, and so *suffered a Recovery*, to cut it

---

[4] As in the Congregational or Independent sects the Anabaptists had no hierarchy in the church. Some of the preachers were laymen who assumed the office of preacher or were "called" because of "natural gifts" but had little or no formal education. All the powers of the church were in the hands of the people; the powers of preaching and celebrating sacraments were given to any of the gifted members. They even had women preachers. [Masson, *Life of Milton*, III, 148–149.]

[5] "That the Amphisbæna, that is, a smaller kind of Serpent, which moveth forward and backward, hath two heads, or one at either extream, was affirmed first by Nicander, and after by many others, by the author of the Book *De Theriaca ad Pisonem*, ascribed unto Galen; more plainly Pliny. . . ." [Browne, *Pseudodoxia Epidemica*, III. 15, in *Works*, ed. Keynes, II, 233.]

[6] See p. 80, n. 6.

off from his right Heirs, and settle it to such Uses, as he pleased. He broaches false Doctrines out of his Tub. He sees Visions when he is fast asleep, and dreams Dreams when he is broad awake. They stick to one another, like Loaves of Bread in the Oven of Persecution. He canonises himself a Saint in his own Life-time, as *Domitian* made himself a God;[7] and enters his Name in the Rubric[8] of his Church by Virtue of a Picklock, which he has invented, and believes will serve his Turn, as well as St. *Peter*'s Keys. He finds out Sloughs and Ditches, that are aptest for launching of an Anabaptist; for he does not christen, but launch his Vessel. He believes, because Obedience is better than Sacrifice,[9] the less of it will serve. He uses Scripture in the same Manner as false Witnesses do, who never lay their Hands on it, but to give Testimony against the Truth.

A VINTNER

Hangs out his Bush to shew he has not good Wine; for that, the Proverb says, needs it not.[1] If Wine were as necessary as Bread, he would stand in the Pillory for selling false Measure, as well as Bakers do for false Weight; but since it is at every Man's Choice to come to his House or not, those that do, are guilty of half the Injuries he does them, and he believes the rest to be none at all, because no Injury can be done to him, that is willing to take it. He had rather sell bad Wine, than good that stands him in no more, for it makes Men sooner drunk, and then they are the easier over-reckoned. By the Knaveries he acts above-board, which every Man sees, one may easily take a Measure of those he does under Ground in his Cellar; for he that will pick a Man's Pocket to his Face, will not stick to use him

---

7 The Emperor Domitian (reigned A.D. 81–96) was famous as an aristocratic ruler who buoyed up his position by ostentation of power. Suetonius and Dio Chrysostomus assert that he styled himself "Master and God" and liked to be so addressed. [Suetonius, "Domitian," in *Lives of the Caesars*, trans. Rolfe, VIII. xiii. 2; Dio Chrysostom, "Discourses," in *Dio Chrysostom*, trans. H. Lamar Crosby (Cambridge, Mass., 1946), XLVI. 1.]

8 The red-letter entry (of a saint's name) in the church calendar.

9 See p. 48, n. 12.

1 "Good wine needs no bush"—i.e., needs nothing to advertise where it is sold. The tavern-keeper once displayed both a bush and a sign. Several references indicate that a bush at the end of a pole signified a country alehouse. [John Brand, *Popular Antiquities of Great Britain* (London, 1905).]

worse in private when he knows nothing of it. When he has poisoned his Wines he raises his Price, and to make amends for that abates his Measure, for he thinks it a greater Sin to commit Murder for small Gains, than a valuable Consideration. He does not only spoil and destroy his Wines, but an ancient reverend Proverb, with brewing and racking, that says, *In vino veritas*,[2] for there is no Truth in his, but all false and sophisticated; for he can counterfeit Wine as cunningly as *Apelles* did Grapes, and cheat Men with it, as *he* did Birds.[3] He brings every Bottle of Wine he draws to the *Bar*, to confess it to be a Cheat, and afterwards puts himself upon the Mercy of the Company. He is an *Antichristian* Cheat; for Christ turned Water into Wine, and he turns Wine into Water. He scores all his Reckonings upon two Tables made like those of the ten Commandments, that he may be put in Mind to break them as oft as possibly he can; especially that of stealing and bearing false Witness against his Neighbour, when he draws him bad Wine and swears it is good, and that he can take more for the Pipe than the Wine will yield him by the Bottle, a Trick that a *Jesuit* taught him to cheat his own Conscience with. When he is found to over-reckon notoriously, he has one common Evasion for all, and that is, to say it was a Mistake, by which he means, that he thought they had not been sober enough to discover it; for if it had past, there had been no Error at all in the Case.

AN HYPOCRITE

Is a Saint that goes by Clockwork, a Machine made by the *Devil's* Geometry, which he winds and nicks to go as he pleases. He is the *Devil's* Finger-Watch,[1] that never goes true, but too fast, or too slow, as he sets him. His Religion goes with Wires, and he serves the *Devil* for an Idol to seduce the Simple to worship and believe

---

[2] "Truth comes out in wine." [Proverbial from Pliny; cf. *Natural History*, XIV. xxviii. 141.]

[3] The story of birds who flew down to peck at a bunch of painted grapes is also applied to Zeuxis, a famous painter in Greece of the 5th century B.C. However, Appelles, born in Ionia in the 4th century B.C., was considered the greatest painter of antiquity, and was the favorite painter of Alexander the Great, who sat for several portraits.

For a reference to birds "fatted by painted grapes in winter" see John Lyly, *Alexander and Campaspe*, I. i.

[1] A watch that can be set forward or backward by the finger.

in him. He puts down the true Saint with his Copper-Lace[2] Devotion, as Ladies, that use Art, paint fairer than the Life. He is a great Bustler in Reformation, which is always most proper to his Talent, especially if it be tumultuous; for Pockets are no where so easily and safely picked as in justling Crouds: And as Change and Alterations are most agreeable to those, who are tied to nothing, he appears more zealous and violent for the *Cause*;[3] than such as are retarded by Conscience or Consideration. His Religion is a Mummery, and his *Gospel-walkings*[4] nothing but dancing a Masquerade. He never wears his own Person, but assumes a Shape, as his Master the *Devil* does, when he appears. He wears counterfeit Hands (as the *Italian* Pickpocket did)[5] which are fastened to his Breast, as if he held them up to Heaven, while his natural Fingers are in his Neighbour's Pocket. The whole Scope of all his Actions appears to be directed, like an Archer's Arrow, at Heaven, while the Clout he aims at sticks in the Earth. The *Devil* baits his Hook with him, when he fishes in troubled Waters. He turns up his Eyes to Heaven like Bird's that have no upper Lid. He is a Weathercock upon the Steeple of the Church, that turns with every Wind, that blows from any Point of the Compass. He sets his Words and Actions like a Printer's Letters,[6] and he that will understand him must read him backwards. He is much more to be suspected than one that is no Professor; as a Stone of any Colour is easier counterfeited, than a Diamond that is of none. The Inside of him tends quite cross to the Outside, like a Spring that runs upward within the Earth, and down without. He is an Operator for the Soul, and corrects other Men's Sins with greater of his own, as the *Jews* were punished for their Idolatry by greater Idolaters

---

[2] Perhaps an analogy to hypocrisy that this is "copper" lace and not "gold" lace but also suggestive of the "false face" provided by cosmetics, "copper lace" being a variegated or streaked copper coloring in makeup. A contemporary poem reads:

> Here's black Bags, Ribbons, Copper Laces,
> Paintings, and beauty spots for faces?

[Laurence Price, "Here's Jack in a Box . . . or a new list of the New Fashions now used in *London*," London, 1656. Reprinted in John Ashton, *Humour, Wit, and Satire of the Seventeenth Century* (London, 1883), p. 199.]

[3] See p. 45, n. 2.

[4] See p. 215, n. 2.

[5] The ingenuity of clever Italians was assumed in this day.

[6] Reference to placement of type in a composing stick, in which the letters are placed upside-down and right to left.

than themselves. He is a spiritual Highwayman, that robs on the Road to Heaven—His Professions and his Actions agree like a sweet Voice and a stinking Breath.

AN OPINIATER

Is his own Confident, that maintains more Opinions than he is able to support. They are all Bastards commonly and unlawfully begotten; but being his own, he had rather, out of natural Affection, take any Pains, or beg, than they should want a Subsistence. The Eagerness and Violence he uses to defend them argues they are weak, for if they were true, they would not need it. How false soever they are to him he is true to them; and as all extraordinary Affections of Love or Friendship are usually upon the meanest Accounts, he is resolved never to forsake them, how ridiculous soever they render themselves and him to the World. He is a Kind of a Knight-Errant, that is bound by his Order to defend the weak and distressed, and deliver enchanted Paradoxes, that are bewitched, and held by Magicians and Conjurers in invisible Castles. He affects to have his Opinions as unlike other Men's as he can, no Matter whether better or worse, like those that wear fantastic Cloaths of their own devising. No Force of Argument can prevail upon him; for, like a Madman, the Strength of two Men in their Wits is not able to hold him down. His Obstinacy grows out of his Ignorance; for Probability has so many Ways, that whosoever understands them will not be confident of any one. He holds his Opinions as Men do their Lands, and, though his Tenure be litigious, he will spend all he has to maintain it. He does not so much as know what Opinion means, which always supposing Uncertainty, is not capable of Confidence. The more implicit his Obstinacy is, the more stubborn it renders him; for implicit Faith is always more pertinacious than that, which can give an Account of it self; and as Cowards, that are well backed, will appear boldest, he that believes as the Church believes is more violent, though he knows not what it is, than he that can give a Reason for his Faith—And as Men in the dark endeavour to tread firmer than when they are in the Light, the Darkness of his Understanding makes him careful to stand fast wheresoever he happens, though it be out of his Way.

A CHOLERIC MAN

Is one that stands for Madman, and has as many Voices as another—If he miss he has very hard Dealing; for if he can but come to a fair polling of his Fits against his Intervals, he is sure to carry it. No doubt it would be a singular Advantage to him; for as his present Condition stands, he has more full Moons in a Week than a Lunatic has in a Year.[1] His Passion is like Tinder, soon set on Fire, and as soon out again. The smallest Occasion imaginable puts him in his Fit, and then he has no Respect of Persons, strikes up the Heels of Stools and Chairs, tears Cards Limbmeal[2] without Regard of Age, Sex, or Quality, and breaks the Bones of Dice, and makes them a dreadful Example to deter others from daring to take Part against him. He is guilty but of Misprision of Madness, and if the worst come to the worst, can but forfeit Estate, and suffer perpetual Liberty to say what he pleases. 'Tis true he is but a Candidate of *Bedlam*, and is not yet admitted Fellow, but has the License of the College to practise, and in Time will not fail to come in according to his Seniority. He has his Grace for Madman, and has done his Exercises,[3] and nothing but his good Manners can put him by his Degree. He is, like a foul Chimney, easily set on Fire, and then he vapours and flashes, as if he would burn the House, but is presently put out with a greater Huff, and the mere Noise of a Pistol reduces him to a quiet and peaceable Temper. His Temper is, like that of a Meteor, an imperfect Mixture, that sparkles and flashes until it has spent it self. All his Parts are irascible, and his Gall is too big for his Liver. His Spleen[4] makes others laugh at him, and as soon as his Anger is over with others he begins to be angry with himself and sorry. He is sick of a preposterous Ague, and has his hot Fit always before his cold. The more violent his Passion is the sooner it is out, like a running Knot, that strains hardest, but is easiest loosed. He is never very passionate but for Trifles, and is

---

[1] Lunatic: literally, one moon-struck. The Romans held that the moon affected the mind and that "lunatics" grew more and more mad as the moon grew to the full. [*Brewer's Dictionary of Phrase and Fable.*]

[2] Limb from limb. [*O.E.D.*]

[3] Following the analogy to procedures in the universities, Butler uses the terms *grace* (the permission obtained by a candidate for a degree from his College) and *exercises* (training).

[4] See p. 85, n. 11.

always most temperate where he has least Cause, like a Nettle, that stings worst when it is touched with soft and gentle Fingers, but when it is bruised with rugged hardned Hands returns no Harm at all.

A LOVER

Is a Kind of *Goth* and *Vandal*, that leaves his native Self to settle in another, or a Planter that forsakes his Country, where he was born, to labour and dig in *Virginia*.[1] His Heart is catched in a Net with a Pair of bright shining Eyes, as Larks are with Pieces of a looking-Glass.[2] He makes heavy Complaints against it for deserting of him, and desires to have another in Exchange for it, which is a very unreasonable Request; for if it betrayed its bosom Friend, what will it do to a Stranger, that should give it Trust and Entertainment? He binds himself, and cries out he is robbed of his Heart, and charges the Innocent with it, only to get a good Composition, or another for it, against all Conscience and Honesty. He talks much of his Flame, and pretends to be burnt by his Mistress's Eyes, for which he requires Satisfaction from her, like one that sets his House on Fire to get a Brief for charitable Contributions. He makes his Mistress all of Stars, and when she is unkind, rails at them, as if they did ill Offices between them, and being of her Kin set her against him. He falls in Love as Men fall sick when their Bodies are inclined to it, and imputes that to his Mistresses Charms, which is really in his own Temper; for when that is altered, the other vanishes of it self, and therefore one said not amiss,

——The Lilly and the Rose
Not in her Cheeks, but in thy Temper grows.

When his Desires are grown up, they swarm, and fly out to seek a new Habitation, and wheresoever they light they fix like Bees, among which some late Philosophers have observed that it is a Female that leads all the rest. Love is but a Clap of the Mind, a Kind of running of the Fancy, that breaks out, if it be not stopped in Time, into

---

[1] The development of agriculture, especially the cultivation of tobacco, prevented the failure of the venture of the Virginia Company (chartered by James I), founded especially for the discovery of gold and trade with the Indians, neither of which materialized. [Lunt, *History of England*, p. 402.]

[2] See p. 41, n. 36.

Botches of heroic Rime; for all Lovers are Poets for the Time being, and make their Ladies a Kind of mosaic Work of several coloured Stones joined together by a strong Fancy, but very stiff and unnatural; and though they steal Stars from Heaven, as *Prometheus* did Fire, to animate them, all will not make them alive, nor alives-liking.

A TRANSLATER

Dyes an Author, like an old Stuff, into a new Colour, but can never give it the Beauty and Lustre of the first Tincture; as Silks that are twice died lose their Glosses, and never receive a fair Colour. He is a small Factor, that imports Books of the Growth of one Language into another, but it seldom turns to Accompt; for the Commodity is perishable, and the finer it is the worse it endures Transportation; as the most delicate of *Indian* Fruits are by no Art to be brought over. Nevertheless he seldom fails of his Purpose, which is to please himself, and give the World notice that he understands one Language more than it was aware of; and that done he makes a saving Return. He is a *Truch-Man*,[1] that interprets between learned Writers and gentle Readers, and uses both how he pleases; for he commonly mistakes the one, and misinforms the other. If he does not perfectly understand the full Meaning of his Author as well as he did himself, he is but a Copier, and therefore never comes near the Mastery of the Original; and his Labours are like Dishes of Meat twice drest, that become insipid, and lose the pleasant Taste they had at first. He differs from an Author as a Fidler does from a Musician, that plays other Men's Compositions, but is not able to make any of his own. All his Studies tend to the Ruin of the Interests of Linguists; for by making those Books common, that were understood but by few in the Original, he endeavours to make the Rabble as wise as himself without taking Pains, and prevents others from studying Languages, to understand that which they may know as well without them. The Ancients, who never writ any Thing but what they stole and borrowed from others (and who was the first Inventor nobody knows) never used this Way; but what they found for their Purposes in other Authors they disguised, so that it past for their own: but to take whole Books and render them, as

---

[1] Truchman: an interpreter.

our Translators do, they always forbore, out of more or less Ingenuity is a Question; for they shewed more in making what they liked their own, and less in not acknowledging from whence they had it. And though the *Romans* by the Laws of War laid claim to all Things, both sacred and profane, of those Nations whom they conquered; yet they never extended that Privilege to their Wit, but made that their own by another Title of the same Kind, and over-came their Wit with Wit.

A REBEL

Is a voluntary Bandit, a civil Renegado, that renounces his Obedience to his Prince, to raise himself upon the public Ruin. He is of great Antiquity, perhaps before the Creation, at least a *Præadamite*;[1] for *Lucifer* was the first of his Family, and from him he derives himself in an indirect Line. He finds Fault with the Government, that he may get it the easier into his own Hands, as Men use to undervalue what they have a Desire to purchase. He is a Botcher of Politics, and a State-Tinker, that makes Flaws in the Government, only to mend them again. He goes for a public-spirited Man, and his Pretences are for the public Good, that is, for the Good of his own public Spirit. He pretends to be a great Lover of his Country, as if it had given him Love-powder, but it is merely out of natural Affection to himself. He has a great Itch to be handling of Authority, though he cut his Fingers with it; and is resolved to raise himself, though it be but upon the Gallows. He is all for Peace and Truth, but not without Lying and Fighting. He plays a Game with the Hangman for the Cloaths on his Back, and when he throws out,[2] he strips him to the Skin. He dies in hempen Sheets, and his Body is hanged, like his Ancestor *Mahomet*'s, in the Air.[3] He might have lived

---

[1] Pre-adamite: the name given by Isaac de la Peyrère in *Prae-adamitae* (1655) to a race of men (who were Gentiles) who lived before Adam, who he contends was only the first Jew, not the very first man.

[2] See p. 49, n. 17.

[3] Legend had it that Mahomet's coffin at Medina was suspended in mid-air without any support. Sir Thomas Browne stated that the idea of the tomb's hanging between two powerful loadstones above and below is false, for witnesses have said it is made of stone and lies on the ground. He attributed the legend to Mahometans. [*Pseudodoxia Epidemica*, II. 3, in *Works*, ed. Keynes, II, 122.]

However, Addison (*Spectator* Paper 191) writes of travelers who report the iron coffin to be in "perpetual suspense" by the equal attraction of magnets.

longer, if the Destinies had not spun his Thread of Life too strong. He is sure never to come to an untimely End; for by the Course of Law his Glass was out long before. He calls Rebellion and Treason laying out of himself for the Public; but being found to be false unlawful Coin, he was seized upon, and cut in Pieces, and hanged for falsifying himself. His espousing of Quarrels proves as fatal to his Country, as the *Parisian* Wedding[4] did to *France.* He is like a Bell, that was made of Purpose to be hanged. He is a diseased Part of the Body politic, to which all the bad Humours gather. He picks straws out of the Government like a Madman, and startles at them when he has done. He endeavours to raise himself, like a Boy's Kite, by being pulled against the Wind. After all his Endeavours and Designs he is at length promoted to the Gallows, which is performed with a Cavalcade suitable to his Dignity; and after much Ceremony he is installed by the Hangman, with the general Applause of all Men, and dies singing like a Swan.[5]

A CITY-WIT

Deals in a foreign Commodity, that is not of the Growth of the Place, and which his Neighbours have so little Judgment in, that he may put it off, how bad soever, at what Rate he pleases. His Wit is like a Piece of Buckram made of old Stuff new gum'd, and stiffened with Formality and Affectation, and rubbed into a forced Gloss; and he shews it to the best Advantage, as far as Impudence and Lying, the Virtues of his Education, can enable him. He can do nothing, if he has not somebody of less Confidence to play it upon, as a Boy does his Ball against a Wall, and as long as the dull Creature will endure it never lets it fall: But when he strikes too hard his Wit is returned upon him again, and has its Quarters beaten up with Cuffs and Knocks over the Pate, which is commonly the Conclusion of his Horse or rather Ass-play. His Jests are so slight and apt to break, that like a Tilter's Lance, his Antagonist scarce feels them, and if he did not

---

[4] The Parisian Wedding: the massacre on St. Bartholomew's Day, which took place (August 24, 1572) during the festivities at the marriage of Henri of Navarre and Margaret of France. [*Brewer's Dictionary of Phrase and Fable.*]

[5] "The swan sings before death": a fable and often-used expression from antiquity, doubted by Pliny and Sir Thomas Browne. [See *Pseudodoxia Epidemica,* III. 27, in *Works,* ed. Keynes, II, 290–91.]

laugh at them himself, nobody would imagine by any Thing else what they were meant for; for he does it to make others laugh too, as those that gape set all that see them a gaping—But his Way is too rugged to provoke Laughter by any other Means; for he, that tickles a Man to make him laugh, must touch him gently and softly, not rub him hard. His Wit has never been observed to be of the right Breed, but always inclining to the Mungrel, whether his evil Education, the bad Customs of the Place, or a Kind of secret Fate be the Cause of it; for many others, that have had as great Disadvantages, have nevertheless arrived at strange Perfections: But as his Behaviour, which he learns insensibly from those he converses with, does plainly distinguish him from Men of freer Educations: so his Understanding receives that Alloy from the Reason and Judgment of those he has to do withal, that it can never become considerable. For though many excellent Persons have been born and lived in the City, there are very few such that have been bred there, though they come from all Parts and Families of the Nation; for Wit is not the Practice of the Place, and a *London* Student is like an *University* Merchant.

A SUPERSTITIOUS MAN

Is more zealous in his false mistaken Piety than others are in the Truth; for he that is in an Error has further to go than one that is in the right Way, and therefore is concerned to bestir himself, and make the more Speed. The Practice of his Religion is, like the Schoolmen's Speculations,[1] full of Niceties and Tricks, that take up his whole Time, and do him more Hurt than Good. His Devotions are Labours, not *Exercises*, and he breaks the Sabbath in taking too much Pains to keep it. He makes a Conscience of so many Trifles and Niceties, that he has not leisure to consider Things, that are serious, and of real Weight. His Religion is too full of Fears and Jealousies to be true and faithful, and too solicitous and unquiet to continue in the Right, if it were so. And as those, that are Bunglers and unskilful in any Art, take more Pains to do nothing, because they are in a wrong Way, than those that are ready and expert, to do the excellentest Things: so the Errors and Mistakes of his Religion engage him in perpetual Troubles and Anxieties, without any Possibility

---

[1] See p. 29, n. 4.

of Improvement, until he unlearn all, and begin again upon a new Account. He talks much of the Justice and Merits of his Cause, and yet gets so many Advocates, that it is plain he does not believe himself; but having pleaded *not Guilty* he is concerned to defend himself as well as he can; while those that confess, and put themselves upon the Mercy of the Court have no more to do. His Religion is too full of Curiosities to be sound and useful, and is fitter for a Hypocrite than a Saint; for Curiosities are only for Show, and of no Use at all. His Conscience resides more in his Stomach than his Heart, and howsoever he keeps the Commandments, he never fails to keep a very pious Diet, and will rather starve than eat erroneously, or taste any Thing that is not perfectly orthodox and apostolical; and if Living and Eating are inseparable he is in the Right; and lives because he eats according to the truly ancient primitive Catholic Faith in the purest Times.

A DROLE

Plays his Part of Wit readily at first Sight, and sometimes better than with Practice. He is excellent at Voluntary[1] and Prelude; but has no Skill in Composition. He will run Divisions upon any Ground[2] very dextrously; but now and then mistakes a *Flat* for a *Sharp*. He has a great deal of Wit, but it is not at his own disposing, nor can he command it when he pleases, unless it be in the Humour. His Fancy is counterchanged between Jest and Earnest; and the *Earnest* lies always in the *Jest*, and the *Jest* in the *Earnest*. He treats of all Matters and Persons by Way of Exercitation, without Respect of Things, Time, Place, or Occasion; and assumes the Liberty of a freeborn *Englishman*, as if he were called to the long Robe with long Ears.[3] He imposes a hard Task upon himself as well as those he con-

---

[1] Voluntary: extempore piece; a piece or movement performed spontaneously or of one's free choice, especially as a prelude to a more elaborate piece, song, etc. [*O.E.D.*]

[2] To run division: the common old term for executing variations on a musical theme.

Ground: the plain-song or melody on which a melodious accompaniment is raised. [*O.E.D.*]

[3] I.e., "called to be a preacher."

Long robe: the dress of the legal or clerical profession.

Long ears: donkey's ears. See the illustrations by Hans Holbein for Erasmus' *The Praise of Folly*.

verses with, and more than either can bear without a convenient Stock of Confidence. His whole Life is nothing but a Merry-Making, and his Business the same with a Fidler's, to play to all Companies where he comes, and take what they please to give him either of Applause, or Dislike; for he can do little without some Applauders, who by shewing him Ground make him outdo his own Expectation many Times, and theirs too; for they, that laugh on his Side and cry him up give Credit to his Confidence, and sometimes contribute more than half the Wit by making it better than he meant. He is impregnable to all Assaults but that of a greater Impudence, which being Stick-free puts him like a rough Fencer out of his Play, and after passes upon him at Pleasure; for when he is once routed, he never rallies again. He takes a View of a Man as a skilful Commander does of a Town he would besiege, to discover the weakest Places, where he may make his Approaches with the least Danger and most Advantages; and when he finds himself mistaken draws off his Forces with admirable Caution and Consideration; for his Business being only Wit, he thinks there is very little of that shown in exposing himself to any Inconvenience.

AN EMPIRIC[1]

Is a Medicine-Monger, Probationer of Receipts, and Doctor Epidemic. He is perpetually putting his Medicines upon their Tryal, and very often finds them guilty of Manslaughter; but still they have some Trick or other to come off, and avoid burning by the Hand of the Hangman.[2] He prints his Trials of Skill, and challenges *Death* at so many several Weapons; and though he is sure to be foiled at every one, he cares not; for if he can but get Money he is sure to get off: For it is but posting up Diseases for Poltroons[3] in all the public Places of the Town, and daring them to meet him again, and his Credit stands as fair with the Rabble, as ever it did. He makes

---

[1] One who practiced physic or surgery without scientific knowledge; a quack, a charlatan.

[2] A mark was burned into the left hand, upon the brawn of the thumb, by a hot iron, so that if an offender was again picked up, the mark would reveal that he had been arraigned for a felony before. [William Harrison, *Elizabethan England*, p. 244.]

[3] Spiritless cowards.

nothing of the Pox and running of the Reins, but will undertake to cure them and tye one Hand behind him, with so much Ease and Freedom, that his Patients may surfeit and be drunk as oft as they please, and follow their Business, that is, Whores and him, without any Inconvenience to their Health or Occasions, and recover with so much Secrecy, that they shall never know how it comes about. He professes *no Cure no Money*, as well he may; for if *Nature* does the Work he is paid for it, if not, he neither wins nor loses; and like a cunning Rook lays his Bet so artfully, that, let the Chance be what it will, he either wins or saves. He cheats the Rich for their Money, and the Poor for Charity, and if either succeed, both are pleased, and he passes for a very just and conscientious Man; for, as those that pay nothing ought at least to speak well of their Entertainment, their Testimony makes Way for those, that are able to pay for both. He finds he has no Reputation among those that know him, and fears he is never like to have, and therefore posts up his Bills, to see if he can thrive better among those that know nothing of him. He keeps his Post continually, and will undertake to maintain it against all the Plagues of *Ægypt*. He sets up his Trade upon a Pillar, or the Corner of a Street—These are his Warehouses, where all he has is to be seen, and a great deal more; for he that looks further finds nothing at all.

THE OBSTINATE MAN

Does not hold Opinions, but they hold him; for when he is once possest with an Error, 'tis, like the Devil, not to be cast out but with great Difficulty. Whatsoever he lays hold on, like a drowning Man, he never loses, though it do but help to sink him the sooner. His Ignorance is abrupt and inaccessible, impregnable both by Art and Nature, and will hold out to the last, though it has nothing but Rubbish to defend. It is as dark as Pitch, and sticks as fast to any Thing it lays hold on. His Scull is so thick, that it is proof against any Reason, and never cracks but on the wrong Side, just opposite to that against which the Impression is made, which Surgeons say does happen very frequently. The slighter and more inconsistent his Opinions are the faster he holds them, otherwise they would fall asunder of themselves: for Opinions that are false ought to be held with more Strictness and Assurance than those that are true, otherwise they will be apt to betray their Owners before they are aware. If he takes to Religion, he has Faith enough to save a hundred wiser Men than himself, if it were right; but it is too much to be good; and though he deny Supererogation,[1] and utterly disclaim any Overplus of Merits, yet he allows superabundant Belief, and if the *Violence* of Faith will *carry the Kingdom of Heaven*,[2] he stands fair for it. He delights most of all to differ in Things indifferent, no Matter how frivolous they are, they are weighty enough in Proportion to his weak Judgment, and he will rather suffer Self-Martyrdom than part with the least Scruple of his Freehold; for it is impossible to dye his dark Ignorance into a lighter Colour. He is resolved to understand no Man's Reason but his own, because he finds no Man can understand his but himself. His Wits are like a Sack, which, the *French* Proverb says, is tied faster before it is full, than when it is; and his Opinions are like Plants that grow upon Rocks, that stick fast though they have no Rooting. His Understanding is hardened like *Pharoah*'s Heart, and is Proof against all Sorts of *Judgments* whatsoever.

A ZEALOT

Is a hot-headed Brother, that has his Understanding blocked up on both Sides, like a Fore-Horse's Eyes, that he sees only streight forwards, and never looks about him; which makes him run on according as he is driven with his own Caprich.[1] He starts and stops (as a Horse does) at a Post, only because he does not know what it is; and thinks to run away from the Spur, while he carries it with him. He is very violent, as all Things that tend downward naturally are; for it is impossible to improve or raise him above his own Level. He runs swiftly before any Wind, like a Ship that has neither Freight nor Ballast, and is as apt to overset. When his Zeal takes Fire it cracks and flies about like a Squib, until the idle Stuff is spent, and then it goes out of it self. He is always troubled with small Scruples, which his Conscience catches like the Itch, and the rubbing of these is both his Pleasure and his Pain: But for Things of greater Moment he is unconcerned; as Cattle in the Summer Time are more pestered with

---

[1] See p. 85, n. 15.
[2] Matthew, XI. 12.
[1] Caprice.

Flies, that vex their Sores, than Creatures more considerable; and Dust and Motes are apter to stick in blear Eyes than things of greater Weight. His Charity begins and ends at Home, for it never goes further, nor stirs abroad. *David* was *eaten up with the Zeal of God's House*;[2] but his Zeal quite contrary eats up God's House; and as the Words seem to intimate, that *David* fed and maintained the Priests; so he makes the Priests feed and maintain him—And hence his Zeal is never so vehement, as when it concurs with his Interest; for as he stiles himself a Professor, it fares with him as with Men of other Professions, to live by his Calling, and get as much as he can by it. He is very severe to other Men's Sins, that his own may pass unsuspected, as those, that were engaged in the Conspiracy against *Nero*,[3] were most cruel to their own Confederates, or as one says,

> *Compounds for Sins he is inclin'd to*
> *By damning those he has no Mind to.*

THE OVER-DOER

Always throws beyond the Jack,[1] and is gone a Mile. He is no more able to contain himself than a Bowl is when he is commanded to rub[2] with the greatest Power and Vehemence imaginable, and nothing lights in his Way. He is a Conjurer, that cannot keep within the Compass of his Circle, though he were sure the Devil would fetch him away for the least Transgression. He always over stocks his Ground, and starves instead of feeding, destroys whatsoever he has an extraordinary Care for, and like an Ape hugs the Whelp he loves most to Death. All his Designs are greater than the Life, and he laughs to think how *Nature* has mistaken her Match, and given him so much Odds, that he can easily outrun her. He allows of no Merit but that which is superabundant.[3] All his Actions are superfæta-

---

[2] Psalms, LXIX. 9.

[3] For accounts of the many conspiracies, civilian and military, see Tacitus, *Annals*. Probably the conspiracy referred to here is the one called Piso's Conspiracy [*Annals*, trans. Jackson, XV. xlviii ff.], which ended in betrayal by one of its members.

[1] See p. 58, n. 16.

[2] Ibid.

[3] Cf. p. 85, n. 15.

tions,[4] that either become Monsters or Twins, that is, too much, or the same again: for he is but a Supernumerary, and does nothing but for Want of a better. He is a civil *Catholic*, that holds nothing more stedfastly than Supererogation[5] in all that he undertakes; for he undertakes nothing but what he overdoes. He is insatiable in all his Actions, and, like a covetous Person, never knows when he has done enough, until he has spoiled all by doing too much. He is his own Antagonist, and is never satisfied until he has outdone himself, as well as that which he proposed; for he loves to be better than his Word (though it always falls out worse) and deceive the World the wrong Way. He believes the Mean[6] to be but a mean Thing, and therefore always runs into Extremities, as the more excellent, great, and transcendent. He delights to exceed in all his Attempts; for he finds that a Goose, that has three Legs, is more remarkable than a hundred, that have but two apiece, and has a greater Number of Followers; and that all Monsters are more visited and applied to than other Creatures that Nature has made perfect in their Kind. He believes he can never bestow too much Pains upon any Thing; for his Industry is his own, and costs him nothing; and if it miscarry, he loses nothing, for he has as much as it was worth. He is like a foolish Musician, that sets his Instrument so high, that he breaks his Strings for Want of understanding the right Pitch of it, or an Archer, that breaks his Bow with over-bending; and all he does is forced, like one that sings above the Reach of his Voice.

A JEALOUS MAN

Is very unsettled in his Mind and full of Doubts, whether he should take his Wife *for better*, or *for worse*. He knows not what to make of himself, but fears his Wife does, and that she made him and his Heir at a Heat:[1] His Horns[2] grow inward, and are very uneasy and painful to his Brain. He breaks his Sleep in watching Opportuni-

---

[4] Superfetation: a second conception occurring after (especially some time after) a prior one and before the delivery; the formation of a second foetus in a uterus already pregnant. [*O.E.D.*]

[5] See p. 85, n. 15.

[6] See p. 197, n. 3.

[1] Sexual excitement, as animals are said to be *in heat*.

[2] See p. 209, n. 4.

ties to catch himself Cuckold in the Manner. He fancies himself regenerate in the Body of his Wife, and desires nothing more, than with *Cardan* and *Gusman*³ to know all the Particulars and Circumstances of his own Begetting. He beats his Brains perpetually to try the Hardness of his Head, and find out how the Callus improves from Time to Time. He breeds Horns, as Children do Teeth, with much Pain and Unquietness; and (as some Husbands are said to be) is sick at the Stomach and pukes when his Wife breeds. Her Pleasures become his Pains, and, by an odd Kind of Sympathy, the Bobs she receives below break out on his Forehead, like a Tobacco-Pipe, that being knocked at one End breaks at the other. He seeks after his Honour and Satisfaction with the same Success as those do, that are robbed, who may, perhaps, find the Thief, but seldom or never get their Goods again. He throws Cross and Pile⁴ to prove himself a Cuckold or not, and as the World is always apt to side with the worst Sense, let his Chance prove what it will, he plays *at Cross you loose, and Pile I win*. The Remedies he takes to cure his Jealousy are worse than the Disease; for if his Suspicion be true it is past Cure; if false, he gives his Wife just Cause to make it true; for it is not the Part of a virtuous Woman to suffer her Husband knowingly to continue in an Error.

AN INSOLENT MAN

Does Mischief, like a Person of Quality, merely for his Sport, and affronts a Man voluntarily of his own free Inclination, without any Merit of his, or Advantage of his own, or Expectation of Return, merely to please himself. The meaner his Condition is, the more barbarous his Insolence appears; for Vices in the Rabble are like Weeds, that grow rankest on a Dunghill. He has no Way to advance his own Pride, or Worth as he takes it, but by treading with Contempt and Scorn upon others. If he is in Authority, he does it not

---

³ Cardan: see especially Chapter II, "My Nativity," in his autobiography, *De Vita Propria Liber*. See also p. 58, n. 17 of this volume.

Gusman: for the details, even to Guzman's claim of having two fathers, see Aleman, *Guzman de Alfarache*, Chapters I and II. See also p. 139, n. 5 of this volume.

⁴ Heads or tails. Cross: the face of a coin (on which was a figure of a cross); pile: the reverse side.

by the Virtue, but Vice of his Place; and the more odious his Carriage is the more he supposes it becomes him and his Authority. It is more notorious in base Persons than others, and most in Slaves, as Dogs, that use to be tied up, are fiercer when they are let loose. He raises himself as high as his Pride and Vainglory will bear him, that he may light the heavier upon those that are under him; for he never meddles with others, unless he is sure of the Advantage, and knows how to come off. He treats Men more rudely than the Hangman, and wants his Civility to ask them Pardon for the ill Accommodation they are like to have from him. He uses Men the best Way that he understands, and the worst that they do; for when he thinks to appear bravest[1] they esteem him the veriest Wretch in the World. He is a small petty Tyrant, and in that is so much the worse; for the meanest Tyrannies are always the most insufferable, as the thinner the Air is, the more it pierces. He is a dissenting Brother to Humanity, and as zealously barbarous in civil Affairs, as others are made by their Churches. His Composition is nothing but Pride and Choler, and he is hot in the fourth Degree, which is the next Door but one, on the left Hand as you go, to Poison. The only Way to deal with him is to despise him; for no wise Man will be mad, if he can help it, because he is bitten by a mad-Dog.

THE RASH MAN

Has a Fever in his Brain, and therefore is rightly said to be hot-headed. His Reason and his Actions run down Hill, born headlong by his unstaid Will. He has not Patience to consider, and, perhaps, it would not be the better for him if he had; for he is so possest with the first Apprehension of any Thing, that whatsoever comes after loses the Race, and is prejudged. All his Actions, like Sins, lead him perpetually to Repentance, and from thence to the Place from whence they came, to make more Work for Repentance; for though he be corrected never so often he is never amended, nor will his Haste give him time to call to mind where it made him stumble before; for he is always upon full Speed, and the Quickness of his Motions takes away and dazzles the Eyes of his Understanding. All his Designs are like Diseases, with which he is taken suddenly before he is aware, and whatsoever he does is extempore, without Premedita-

---

[1] At his best in making a fine show or display.

tion; for he believes a sudden Life to be the best of all, as some do a sudden Death. He pursues Things, as Men do an Enemy upon a Retreat, until he is drawn into an Ambush for Want of Heed and Circumspection. He falls upon Things as they lie in his Way, as if he stumbled at them, or his Foot slipped and cast him upon them; for he is commonly foiled and comes off with Bruises. He engages in Business, as Men do in Duels, the sooner the better, that, if any Evil come of it, they may not be found to have slept upon it, or consulted with an effeminate Pillow in Point of Honour and Courage. He strikes when he is hot himself, not when the Iron is so, which he designs to work upon. His Tongue has no retentive Faculty, but is always running like a Fool's Drivel. He cannot keep it within Compass, but it will be always upon the Ramble, and playing of Tricks upon a Frolic, fancying of Passes upon Religion, State, and the Persons of those, that are in present Authority, no Matter how, to whom or where; for his Discretion is always out of the Way, when he has Occasion to make Use of it.

A PIMP

Is a Solicitor of Love, a Whore's Broker, Procurator of the most serene Commonwealth of Sinners, and Agent for the Flesh and the Devil. He is a Bawd's *Legate a latere*[1]—His Function chiefly consists in maintaining constant Correspondence and Intelligence, not only domestic, that is, with all Houses profest, but also foreign, that is, with all *Lay-Sisters*, and such as are *in voto*[2] only. He disguises himself in as many Habits as a *Romish* Priest,[3] from a Person of Honour to the Person of a Footman; but most commonly (as those others do) in that of a Gentleman; for among such his Business chiefly lies. He is the Bawd's Loader, that brings Corn to her Mill: But he never thrives considerably in his Vocation without the Assistance of some accessary Profession, as Medicine, Astrology, silenced Ministry,[4] &c. which are wonderful Helps both for Disguise and Access. But if

---

[1] An ecclesiastical deputy of the highest class, whose acts are virtually those of the Pope himself.

[2] See p. 202, n. 3.

[3] Some priests moved from house to house, mixing with the world by way of disguise, risking imprisonment or death. [Trevelyan, *England Under the Stuarts*, p. 69.]

[4] See p. 59, n. 24.

he want[5] these Advantages, and be but a mere Pimp of Fortune, he endeavours to appear, as if he did it for his Pleasure, out of a generous Freedom to communicate his own Diversions with a Friend, and talks much of one Gentleman for another: nevertheless he suffers many dishonourable Indignities from the Ladies he relates to, who very well knowing his Calling to be but ministerial and subordinate to their own, fail not upon all Occasions to insult most tyranically over him. Between these and the Justice he lives under an arbitrary Government, much subject to Tribulation and Oppression, unless he happen to be in Commission himself (as it sometimes happens) and then he suppresses all others, and engrosses the whole Trade into his own Hands. Nothing renders him so accomplished as curing of Claps; for then the one Operation assisting the other he is sure never to be out of Employment. His Profession is of great Antiquity and Renown, and has been honoured by Emperors and great Philosophers, that have been free of his Company: for *Caligula* kept a Bawdy-House[6] himself, and *Otho* and *Seneca*[7] were Pimps to *Nero*. He is a Squire by his Place; for if Matrimony be honourable, Fornication is at least worshipful. He is a perpetual Brideman,[8] and by his Privilege may wear Garters in his Hat. He is a Settler of Jointures,[9] and the Devil's Parson, that joins Man and Woman together in the unholy State of Incontinence. His Life is a perpetual Wedding, and he is curst as often as a Matchmaker. He is a great Friend to Mountebanks; for where his Work ends the others commonly begins, and they gain more by him than the Plague, and he brings them in more Custom than their Bills. He is the Whores Jackal, that hunts out Treats for them all Day, and at Night has his Share in a Tavern-Supper, or a Treat at the *setting Dog and Partridge*,[10] a very significant Sign, like the Brokers *Bird in Hand*. He is the *Sylvan* to the Dryades of *Lewkner's Lane*, and

---

[5] Lack.

[6] See Suetonius, "Gaius Caligula." For the purpose of taxes for the treasury, Caligula set up stews and brothelhouses in the palace itself and invited by name old men and young.

[7] Partners of Nero's "dissipation and of his questionable secrets" were two handsome youths: Marcus Otho (the future emperor) and Claudius Senecio. [Tacitus, *Annals*, trans. Jackson, XIII. xi, and elsewhere.]

[8] Bridegroom.
In *Hudibras*, I. ii. 525 there is a reference to wedding garters worn in the hat.

[9] See p. 134, n. 2.

[10] A well-known ordinary in Fleet Street, mentioned in *The Country Wife* of Wycherly (Act I) and Shadwell's *The Sullen Lovers* (Act II).

Hamadryades of *little Sodom.*[11] He fastens his Plough to the Tail, as the *Irish* do, and when one is rendered unserviceable he gets another. He is the Foreman of a Bawd's Shop. He is Remembrancer of Opportunity, and a Doorkeeper in the House of the Devil. He is a Conjunction copulative, that joins different Cases, Genders, and Persons,

——A Pimp
Is but a Whore's Familiar, or her Imp.

THE AFFECTED OR FORMAL

Is a Piece of Clockwork, that moves only as it is wound up and set, and not like a voluntary Agent. He is a mathematical Body, nothing but *punctum, linea & superficies,* and perfectly abstract from Matter. He walks as stifly and uprightly as a Dog that is taught to go on his hinder Legs, and carries his Hands as the other does his Fore-feet. He is very ceremonious and full of Respect to himself, for no Man uses those Formalities, that does not expect the same from others. All his Actions and Words are set down in so exact a Method, that an indifferent Accomptant may cast him up to a Halfpenny Farthing. He does every Thing by Rule, as if it were in a Course of *Lessius*'s Diet,[1] and did not eat, but take a Dose of Meat and Drink, and not walk, but proceed, not go, but march. He draws up himself with admirable Conduct in a very regular and well-ordered Body. All his Business and Affairs are Junctures and Transactions;

---

[11] Lewkner's Lane: a street of low repute covered by small houses and tenements in the neighborhood of Drury Lane or St. Giles's, infamous for its brothels and poor lodging-houses.

Little Sodom: probably what Clement Walker refers to as the "new Statesmen, and their new erected *Sodomes* and *Spintries* at the Mulbury-garden at *St. James.*" [*The History of Independency* (London, 1661), Pt. II, p. 257. Referred to in *Hudibras,* ed. Gray, II. i. 368 n.]

[1] Great abstinence or at best a moderate diet. Leonard Lessius (d. 1623) was a physician who prescribed very strict rules for the amount of food to be consumed. [*Brewer's Dictionary of Phrase and Fable*; also Bailey, *Universal Etymological Dictionary.*]

See Burton's *Anatomy of Melancholy,* I. 2. 2: "Some again are in the other extreme, and draw this mischief [melancholy] on their heads by too ceremonious and strict diet, being over-precise, cockney-like, and curious in their observation of meats, times, as that *medicina stitica* [regimen of diet] prescribes, just so many ounces at dinner, which Lessius enjoins. . . ." [London: Everyman's Library, 1964, I, 230.]

and when he speaks with a Man he gives him Audience. He does not carry, but marshal himself; and no one Member of his Body politic takes Place of another without due Right of Precedence. He does all Things by Rules of Proportion, and never gives himself the Freedom to manage his Gloves or his Watch in an irregular and arbitrary Way; but is always ready to render an Account of his Demeanour to the most strict and severe Disquisition. He sets his Face as if it were cast in Plaister, and never admits of any Commotion in his Countenance, nor so much as the Innovation of a Smile without serious and mature Deliberation; but preserves his Looks in a judicial Way, according as they have always been established.

A FLATTERER

Is a Dog, that fawns when he bites. He hangs Bells in a Man's Ears, as a Carman does by his Horse, while he lays a heavy Load upon his Back. His Insinuations are like strong Wines, that please a Man's Palate till it has got within him, and then deprives him of his Reason, and overthrows him. His Business is to render a Man a stranger to himself, and get between him and Home, and then he carries him, whither he pleases. He is a Spirit, that inveighs away a Man from himself, undertakes great Matters for him, and after sells him for a Slave. He makes Division, not only between a Man and his Friends, but between a Man and himself, raises a Faction within him, and after takes Part with the strongest Side, and ruins both. He steals him away from himself (as the Fairies are said to do Children in the Cradle)[1] and after changes him for a Fool. He whistles to him, as a Carter does to his Horse, while he whips out his Eyes, and makes him draw what he pleases. He finds out his Humour and feeds it, till it will come to Hand; and then he leads him whither he pleases. He tickles him, as they do Trouts,[2] until he lays hold on him, and then devours and feeds upon him. He tickles his Ears with a Straw, and while he is pleased with scratching it, picks his Pocket, as the Cutpurse served *Bartl. Cokes*.[3] He embraces him and hugs him in his Arms, and lifts him above Ground, as Wrestlers do, to throw him

[1] See p. 59, n. 23.

[2] See p. 171, n. 1.

[3] In Ben Jonson's *Bartholomew Fair*, III. v, Bartholomew Cokes, a simpleton, is tickled twice in the ear with a straw by Edgworth to draw his hand out of his pocket.

down again, and fall upon him. He possesses him with his own Praises like an evil Spirit, that makes him swell, and appear stronger than he was, talk what he does not understand, and do Things that he knows nothing of, when he comes to himself. He *gives* good Words, as Doctors are said to *give* Physick, when they are paid for it, and Lawyer's Advice, when they are fee'd beforehand. He is a poisoned Perfume, that infects the Brain, and murthers those it pleases. He undermines a Man, and blows him up with his own Praises, to throw him down. He commends a Man out of Design, that he may be presented with him, and have him for his Pains, according to the Mode.

A PRODIGAL

Is a Pocket with a Hole in the Bottom. His Purse has got a Dysentery, and lost its Retentive Faculty. He delights, like a fat overgrown Man, to see himself fall away, and grow less. He does not spend his Money, but void it, and, like those that have the Stone, is in Pain till he is rid of it. He is very loose and incontinent of his Coin, and lets it fly, like *Jupiter*, in a Shower.[1] He is very hospitable, and keeps open Pockets for all Comers. All his Silver turns to Mercury, and runs through him as if he had taken it for the *miserere*, or fluxed himself. The History of his Life begins with keeping of Whores, and ends with keeping of Hogs,[2] and as he fed high at first, so he does at last; for Acorns are very high Food. He swallows Land and Houses like an Earthquake, eats a whole dining-Room at a Meal, and devours his Kitchen at a Breakfast. He wears the Furniture of his House on his Back, and a whole feathered-Bed in his Hat, drinks down his Plate, and eats his Dishes up. He is not cloathed, but hung. He'll fancy Dancers Cattle, and present his Lady with Messuage and Tenement.[3] He sets his Horses at *Inn and Inn*,[4] and throws himself out of his Coach

---

[1] The story of Danae, who became the mother of Perseus by Zeus. Danae was visited by Zeus after he became metamorphosed into a shower of gold and came down through the roof of the prison in which her father had placed her.

[2] Recall the story of the prodigal son.

[3] See p. 82, n. 4.

[4] Inn and Inn was a game very much used in an ordinary, played by two or three persons, with four dice. "Inn and Inn" occurs when a player throws all doublets, whether all of a sort or otherwise, viz., four aces, four deuces, or four sixes, or two aces, two deuces, two treys, two sixes, etc. [Chapter XXXIII in Charles Cotton, *The Compleat Gamester* (London, 1674).]

at *come the Caster*.[5] He should be a good Husband,[6] for he has made more of his Estate in one Year, than his Ancestors did in twenty. He *dusts* his Estate, as they do a Stand of Ale in the North.[7] His Money in his Pocket (like hunted Venison) will not keep; if it be not spent presently it grows stale, and is thrown away. He possesses his Estate as the Devil did the Herd of Swine,[8] and is running it into the Sea as fast as he can. He has shot it with a *Zampatan*,[9] and it will presently fall all to Dust. He has brought his Acres into a Consumption, and they are strangely fallen away, nothing but Skin and Bones left of a whole Manor. He will shortly have all his Estate in his Hands; for, like *Bias*, he may carry it about him. He lays up nothing but Debts and Diseases, and at length himself in a Prison. When he has spent all upon his Pleasures, and has nothing left for Sustenance, he espouses an Hostess Dowager, and resolves to lick himself whole again out of Ale, and make it pay him back all the Charges it has put him to.

A PETTIFOGGER[1]

Is an under-Coat to the Long-robe,[2] a Kind of a coarse Jacket, or dirty daggled Skirt and Tail of the long-Robe. His Business is, like a Spaniel's, to hunt and spring Contention for the long-winded Buzzards to fly at. He is a fast Friend to all Courts of Justice, but a mortal Foe to *Justice* herself; as some Catholics have a great Reverence for the *Church*, but hate the *Court* of *Rome*. He is a Kind of Law-Hector,[3] that lives by making Quarrels between Man and Man, and prosecuting or compounding them to his own Advantage. He is a constant Frequenter of country Fairs and Markets, where he keeps the Clowns in Awe with his Tricks in Law, and they fear him like a Conjurer or a cunning Man. He is no Gentleman, but a Varlet

---

[5] A term in gaming. The time when the dice are thrown?

[6] Husbandman.

[7] "Dusting a Stand of Ale is a Set of jolly Tapers agreeing to purchase a Barrel of Ale, and each one being provided with a Cup, to turn the Cock, and continue successive drinking till all is run out. This is a Custom in some Parts of *Lancashire*." [Thyer's note. See Thomas Shadwell, *Epson Wells* (1672).]

[8] See p. 195, n. 1.

[9] *Zampatan*: variation of *Sumpitan*, a blow-gun made by the Malays from a hollowed cane, from which poisoned arrows are shot. [*O.E.D.*]

[1] See p. 111, n. 1.

[2] Here, the robe of a lawyer.

[3] Hector: see p. 106, n. 2.

of the Long-robe, a Purveyor of Suits and Differences, most of which he converts to his own Benefit, and the rest to the Use of those he belongs to. He is a Law-seminary, that sows Tares amongst Friends to entangle them in Contention with one another, and suck the Nourishment from both. He is like a Ferret in a Coney-Borough, that drives the poor silly Animals into the Purse-Net of the Law,[4] to have their Skins stripped off, and be preyed upon. He has a Cloud of Witnesses always in a Readiness to obscure Truth, and swear Things into any Shape he has Occasion for, as Men fancy they see Armies fighting in the Air. He propagates the Law as Jesuits do the Gospel, and with much the same Integrity and Uprightness: for his Business is to debauch and pervert the Law, and make it act quite contrary to its own Conscience and Understanding, and like an Hypocrite say one Thing and do another. When he is engaged on one Side he has his Choice of both, and can take either as he finds it serve best to his own Advantage. His ablest Performances are to help a Cause out at a Pinch for Want of Evidence; this he atchieves by Virtue of his Intimacy and Correspondence with *Knights of the Post, common Bayl* and *Affidavit-Men.*[5] He is a tame Beast of Prey, an Animal that lives both by Land and Water; for when he walks afoot through the Dirt, he is paid for Boat and Coach-hire by his Clients, as if he never went without a Train to attend him. He instructs the Council to instruct him; and very justly gives them the one half of the Clients Fees for their Advice, and keeps the other himself for his own.

A BANKRUPT

Is made by breaking, as a Bird is hatched by breaking the Shell, for he gains more by giving over his Trade, than ever he did by dealing in it. He drives a Trade, as *Oliver Cromwel* did a Coach,

---

4 An image from hunting: the ferret, an animal of the weasel family, was kept for hunting rabbits and rats, which he drove out of their lurking places.

Purse-net: a bag-shaped net, the mouth of which can be drawn together with cords; used especially for catching rabbits.

5 Knights of the Post: see p. 186, n. 5.

Common Bayl: used in actions of small prejudice, or slight proof, called common, because any sureties in that case are taken: whereas upon cases of greater weight, or apparent specialty, special bail or surety must be taken. [Johnson, *A Dictionary of the English Language*.]

Affidavit-Men: see p. 75, n. 7.

till it broke in Pieces.[1] He is very tender and careful in preserving his Credit, and keeps it as methodically as a Race-nag is dieted, that in the End he may run away with it: for he observes a punctual Curiosity in performing his Word, until he has improved his Credit as far as it can go; and then he has catched the Fish, and throws away the Net; as a Butcher, when he has fed his Beast as fat as it can grow, cuts the Throat of it. When he has brought his Design to Perfection, and disposed of all his Materials, he lays his Train,[2] like a Powder Traytor, and gets out of the Way, while he blows up all those that trusted him. After the Blow is given there is no Manner of Intelligence to be had of him for some Months, until the Rage and Fury is somewhat digested, and all Hopes vanished of ever recovering any Thing of Body, or Goods, for Revenge, or Restitution; and then Propositions of Treaty and Accommodation appear, like the Sign of the *Hand and Pen* out of the Clouds,[3] with Conditions more unreasonable than Thieves are wont to demand for Restitution of stolen Goods. He shoots like a Fowler at a whole Flock of Geese at once, and stalks with his Horse to come as near as possibly he can without being perceived by any one, or giving the least Suspicion of his Design, until it is too late to prevent it; and then he flies from them, as they should have done before from him. His Way is so commonly used in the City, that he robs in a Road, like a Highwayman, and yet they will never arrive at Wit enough to avoid it; for it is done upon Surprise; and as Thieves are commonly better mounted than those they rob, he very easily makes his Escape, and flies beyond Persuit of Huon-cries,[4] and there is no Possibility of overtaking him.

---

[1] Perhaps an exaggeration of the episode where Cromwell, a lover of good horses, was presented by the Count of Oldenburg a team, which ran away in Hyde Park while Cromwell was driving them. Cromwell was knocked off and got entangled in the harness, but was not seriously hurt. [Charles Firth, *Oliver Cromwell* (London and New York, 1901), pp. 456–57.]

[2] A line of gunpowder or other combustible substance laid so as to convey fire to a mine or charge so as to explode it. [*O.E.D.*]

[3] Evidently an emblem. A hand from the clouds denotes God the Father. An emblem such as the one Butler seems to refer to here, where a hand is reaching out of the clouds for a feather (pen) is labeled *ulterius ne tende odiis*, "abstain from invectives." It may be found on Chart XXVIII (P. Q.) of *Emblems for the Entertainment and Improvement of Youth ... Hieroglyphical and Enigmatical Devices relating to All Parts and Stations of Life*. Sold by R. Ware at the Bible and Sun in Warwick Lane at Amen Corner (1750?).

[4] Hue and cries. This was the old legal name for the official outcry when calling for assistance in the pursuit of a criminal escaping from justice.

THE INCONSTANT

Has a vagabond Soul, without any settled Place of Abode, like the *wandering Jew*.[1] His Head is unfixed, out of Order, and utterly unserviceable upon any Occasion. He is very apt to be taken with any Thing, but nothing can hold him; for he presently breaks loose, and gives it the Slip. His Head is troubled with a Palsy, which renders it perpetually wavering and incapable of Rest. His Head is like an hour-Glass, that Part that is uppermost always runs out until it is turned, and then runs out again. His Opinions are too violent to last; for, like other Things of the same Kind in Nature, they quickly spend themselves, and fall to nothing. All his Opinions are like *Wefts* and *Strays*, that are apt to straggle from their Owner, and belong to the *Lord of the Manour*, where they are taken up. His Soul has no retentive Faculty, but suffers every Thing to run from him, as fast as he receives it. His whole Life is like a preposterous Ague, in which he has his hot Fit always before his cold one, and is never in a constant Temper. His Principles and Resolves are but a Kind of Moveables, which he will not endure to be fastened to any Freehold, but left loose to be conveyed away at Pleasure, as Occasion shall please to dispose of him. His Soul dwells, like a *Tartar*, in a Hoord,[2] without any settled Habitation, but is always removing and dislodging from Place to Place. He changes his Head oftner than a Deer, and when his Imaginations art stiff and at their full Growth, he casts them off to breed new ones, only to cast off again the next Season. All his Purposes are built on Air, the Chamelions Diet,[3] and have the same Operation to make him change Colour with every Object he comes near. He pulls off his Judgment, as commonly as his Hat, to every one he meets with. His Word and his Deed are all one; for when he has given his Word he has *done*, and never goes further. His Judgment being unsound has the same Operation upon him, that a Disease has upon a sick Man, that makes him find some Ease in turning from Side to Side, and still the last is the most uneasy.

---

[1] The famous medieval legend holds that a Jew who treated Christ contemptuously as He bore the cross to Calvary was condemned to wander on the earth until the Second Coming.

[2] Obsolete form of *horde*.

[3] See Sir Thomas Browne, *Pseudodoxia Epidemica*, III. 21, in *Works*, ed. Keynes, II, 257 ff.

A HORSE-COURSER[1]

Is one that has read Horses, and understands all the Virtues and Vices of the whole Species by being conversant with them, and how to make his best Advantage of both. He makes his first Applications to a Horse, as some Lovers do to a Mistress, with special Regard to her Eyes and Legs, and passes over other Parts with less severe and curious Scrutiny. He understands all Diseases incident to the Body of a Horse, and what to abate in the Price for every one, according as it is capable either of Cure, or Disguise. He has more Ways to hide Defects in Horse-flesh, than Women have Decays in Faces, among which Oaths and Lies are the most general; for when they are applied warm they serve, like an universal Medicine, to cure all Infirmities alike; for he that affirms or denies any Thing confidently is sure to gain some Belief, though from an equal Obstinacy; as two Stones of equal Hardness rubbed together will tear something from one another; and false Wares will not be put off, but by false Means, as all Things are maintained and nourished by that which is agreeable to their own Nature. All his other Operations are nothing to that of Quacking, with which he will put off Diseases as fast as a Mountebank does Cures. He understands the Chronology of a Horse's Mouth most critically, and will find out the Year of his Nativity by it, as certainly as if he had been at the Mare's Labour that bore him. All his Arts will not serve to counterfeit a Horse's Paces; but he has a lere[2] Trick, that serves instead of it, and that is, to cry down all those Paces which he wants, and magnify those he has. When he is lame of one Foot he has a very fine Expedient, by pricking the other over-against it, to make him go right again. He is a strict Observer of Saints Days, only for the Fairs that are kept on them, and knows which is the best Patron for buying, and which for selling: For Religion having been always a Traffic, the Saints have in all Ages been esteemed the most fit and proper to have the

---

[1] See John Fitzherbert, *The Boke of Husbandry*, 1534, f. 50: " 'A corser is he that byeth all rydden horses, and selleth them agayne' as distinct from the horse-master, who 'bieth wilde horses or coltes, and bredeth theym, and selleth theym agayne wylde, or breaketh parts of theym tame, and then selleth them.' " [Quoted in n. 19 to "The Persons of the Play" in *Bartholomew Fair. Ben Jonson*, ed. C. H. Herford and Percy Simpson, X, 172.]

[2] On lere-sense see p. 132, n. 8.

Charge of all Fairs, where all Sorts of Trades are most used; and always where a Saint has a Fair he has a Church too, as *St. Peter's* in *Westminster*, *St. Bartholomew* in *Smithfield*, &c.[3]

A GLUTTON

Eats his Children, as the Poets say *Saturn* did,[1] and carries his Felicity and all his Concernments in his Paunch. If he had lived when all the Members of the Body rebelled against the Stomach,[2] there had been no Possibility of Accommodation. His Entrails are like the *Sarcophagus*,[3] that devours dead Bodies in a small Space, or the *Indian Zampatan*,[4] that consumes Flesh in a Moment. He is a great Dish made on Purpose to carry Meat. He eats out his own Head and his Horses too—He knows no Grace, but Grace before Meat, nor Mortification but in fasting. If the Body be the Tabernacle of the Soul, he lives in a Sutler's[5] Hut. He celebrates *Mass*, or rather *Mess*, to the Idol in his Belly, and, like a *Papist*, eats his Adoration. A third Course is the third Heaven to him, and he is ravished into it. A Feast is a good Conscience[6] to him; and he is troubled in Mind, when he misses of it. His Teeth are very industrious in their calling; and his Chops like a *Bridewell* perpetually hatcheling.[7] He depraves his Appe-

---

[3] At Westminster on St. Peter's day, as in London and other places on St. Bartholomew's, from ancient Christian times tradesmen brought wares to sell, even in Church yards. [Brand, *Popular Antiquities*.]

On Bartholomew's Fair see p. 117, n. 14.

[1] Saturn was identified by the Romans with the Greek Cronus, leader of the Titans, who ruled over the Golden Age in Italy. Having been warned that one of his children would overthrow him, he swallowed them when they were born. However, Zeus was saved by a scheme of his mother's and later overthrew his father.

[2] See p. 160, n. 4.

[3] A coffin or tomb made of a limestone used by the Greeks because it disintegrated within a few weeks the flesh of the bodies deposited in it.

[4] See p. 240, n. 9.

[5] Sutler: a small vendor, especially one who follows an army or lives in a garrison town and sells provisions to the soldiers.

[6] See p. 168, n. 1.

[7] Combing flax or hemp with a *hatchel*, an instrument for the purpose. The combing or beating of hemp was a common occupation in *Bridewell*, a famous house of correction for pickpockets, harlots, and vagrants. Ned Ward (*The London Spy*, Pt. VI) describes wretched women who beat hemp and who were

tite with Haut-Gousts,[8] as old Fornicators do their Lechery, into Fulsomness and Stinks. He licks himself into the Shape of a Bear, as those Beasts are said to do their Whelps.[9] He new forms himself in his own Belly, and becomes another Thing than *God* and *Nature* meant him. His Belly takes Place of the Rest of his Members, and walks before in State. He eats out that which eats all Things else, Time; and is very curious to have all Things in Season at his Meals, but his Hours, which are commonly at Midnight, and so late, that he prays too late for his daily Bread, unless he mean his natural daily Bread. He is admirably learned in the Doctrines of Meats and Sauces, and deserves the Chair in *Juris-Prudentia*, that is in *the Skill of Pottages*.[10] At length he eats his Life out of House and Home, and becomes a Treat for Worms, sells his Cloaths to feed his Gluttony, and eats himself naked, as the first of his Family, *Adam*, did.

A RIBALD

Is the Devil's Hypocrite, that endeavours to make himself appear worse than he is. His evil Words and bad Manners strive which shall most corrupt one another, and it is hard to say which has the Advantage. He vents his Lechery at the Mouth, as some Fishes are said to engender. He is an unclean Beast that chews the Cud; for after he has satisfied his Lust, he brings it up again into his Mouth to a second Enjoyment, and plays an After-game of Letchery with his Tongue much worse than that which the *Cunnilingi*[1] used among the old *Romans*. He strips Nature stark-naked, and clothes her in the most fantastic and ridiculous Fashion a wild Imagination can invent.

---

whipped as they were observed by onlookers on particular days. See also Plate IV of Hogarth's "Harlot's Progress."

The name *Bridewell* was used for any house of correction or, as here, for a prisoner in a jail.

[8] Probably *haut-goût*, strong seasoning.

[9] See Browne, *Pseudodoxia Epidemica*, III, 6, in *Works*, ed. Keynes, II, 196 ff. "That a Bear brings forth her young informous and unshapen, which she fashioneth after by licking them over, is an opinion not only vulgar, and common with us: but hath been of old delivered by ancient Writers."

[10] A pun based on two meanings of *juris*: (1) broth or soup; (2) right or law. Pottage: a thick soup.

[1] Cunnilingus: stimulation of the vulva or clitoris with the lips or tongue. [*Webster's Third New International Dictionary* (Springfield, Mass., 1961).]

He is worse and more nasty than a Dog; for in his broad Descriptions of others obscene Actions he does but lick up the Vomit of another Man's Surfeits. He tells Tales out of a vaulting School.[2] A leud baudy Tale does more Hurt, and gives a worse Example than the Thing of which it was told; for the Act extends but to few, and if it be concealed goes no further; but the Report of it is unlimited, and may be conveyed to all People, and all Times to come. He exposes that with his Tongue, which Nature gave Women Modesty, and brute Beasts Tails to cover. He mistakes Ribaldry for Wit, though nothing is more unlike, and believes himself to be the finer Man the filthier he talks; as if he were above Civility, as *Fanatics* are above Ordinances, and held nothing more shameful than to be ashamed of any Thing. He talks nothing but *Aretine*'s Pictures,[3] as plain as the *Scotch* Dialect, which is esteemed to be the most copious and elegant of the Kind. He improves and husbands his Sins to the best Advantage, and makes one Vice find Employment for another; for what he acts loosely in private, he talks as loosely of in public, and finds as much Pleasure in the one as the other. He endeavours to make himself Satisfaction for the Pangs his Claps and Botches put him to with vapouring and bragging how he came by them. He endeavours to purchase himself a Reputation by pretending to that which the best Men abominate, and the worst value not, like one that clips and washes false Coin, and ventures his Neck for that which will yield him nothing.

AN ANTISOCORDIST[1]

Renounces his Christianity,[a] and gives himself a fantastic name, as witches do their imps.[2] He is a profest enemy to idleness,

---

[2] Vaulting School: a brothel or bawdy-house [*O.E.D.*]

[3] Pietro Aretino, or the Aretine (1492–1556), born in Italy, was the author of five comedies and a tragedy as well as of satires and other poems of a scandalous or licentious character. In *Areopagitica* Milton refers to "that notorious ribald of Arezzio, dreaded, and yet dear to the Italian Courtiers."

[1] See p. 124, n. 12.

[a] Christianity] Xtianity

[2] Imp: the familiar; the familiar spirit, a little animal assigned by Satan to do the Witch's evil commands: a dog, cat, mouse, polecat, etc. Curious names of "familiars" appear in trial records. The frontispiece of the 1647 edition of Matthew Hopkins' *The Discovery of Witches* gives the names of such imps as: Ilemanzor, Pyewackett, Pecke in the Crowne, Griezzel Greedigutt, Jarmara, Sacke and Sugar, Newes, Vinegar Tom, and Holt.

though he loses perpetualy by the contest, and always comes off with the worst; for the enemy is too strong for him, and holds intelligence with his own party, which renders all his attempts unsuccesful. He is perpetualy falling out with ignorance; but the quarrel is always taken up and compounded to his own disadvantage. He flys from it as a horse does from the spur, which he carrys along with him, or a dog from the madness, that he carrys in his brain. All his attempts upon knowledge are to no purpose; for it is too heavy for him, and he does but render himself weaker by spending his little strength in vain. He is a student only for his pleasure, but makes a horrible toil of it, like a country fellow that dances very laboriously. He sticks to all arts and sciences like pitch, only to lessen himself and defile that he takes to. He has not ingenuity enough to master one knowledge, and yet attempts all, like an ill marksman, that shoots better at a flock than one single fowl; or the nobility of Rome, that subdued the Tribunes of the people by increasing their number, whom they were not able to contend with when they were but few. He casts away much pains upon study, to as much purpose as the *Indians* sow gunpowder in the earth, and believe it will grow.[3] He does not read books to improve his knowledge, but only to say he has read; and the more strange and less known names they have, the more he glories in them. And as amongst gamesters those that lose most always love play best; so the more unfortunate he is in his studies, the more delight he finds in them. Fields that lye fallow recompense the loss of time by bearing nobler crops; but he wears the heart of his barren ground out with perpetual tilling.

A BANKER

Is both usurer, broker, and borrower, a triple cord that is easily broken. He borrows with one hand and lends with the other; and having as much to do as he can turn both to has never a third to pay. He lives by use upon use, or taking up usury upon interest; for he borrows of *Peter* to pay *Paul* five in the hundred, and lends it to

---

[3] Samuel Purchas reports (*Hakluytus Posthumus, or Purchas His Pilgrimes*, XIX, 163–64) that American Indians of Virginia in 1621 sowed gunpowder: "as Fame divulgeth (not without probable grounds) their King hath . . . caused the most part of the Gunpowder by him surprized, to be sowne, to draw there-from the like increase, as of his Maiz or Corne, in Harvest next."

John for fifteen. He undertakes to pay extempore, but as all things of that kind commonly prove slight, and, if they hit once by chance, yet fail for the most part, so do his performances: howsoever he is very just to the king; for he takes up his money at his own rates, and pays him back again at the very same. He is like a merchant's book of accompts, nothing but debtor and creditor; and he charges and discharges himself as fast as a gun that shoots nine times in a minute. He borrows the king's money and lends it him again, like the fellow that pawn'd the vintner's own cloak at the bar for the reckoning,[1] and breaks his laws into the bargain by taking extortion and double interest for keeping his own money from him. He forestals the kings money to raise the price of the interest, and then lends it to him back again upon security of the next that he shall forestal. He borrows the kings money of his officers to break his laws with, as *Chaucer*'s fryar borrow'd money of a merchant to corrupt his wife with, and makes him pay for his own injury.[2] He intercepts all taxes and royal aids that are sent up, and makes the king pay, instead of the county, where the robbery was committed.[3] He hires the public money, as they do farms in *Wales*, for half the profits, pays the one moiety to the collectors and receivers, and keeps the other himself: For the public cheats of the kings money are like the mystery of coining it in the tower, where every piece passes through many hands before it is finished, and every cheat through many offices, before it is brought to perfection. He turns and winds the public stock, and lives by the loss of it; for he has no other way to make himself a saver: for if he should pay as much for the use of money as he receives for it, he would lose by that which always lyes by him, which must of necessity be very great sums; and therefore he must either use very great exactions, or make himself whole by breaking in the end. He does not live by his own faith like a righteous man, but the faith of others like the unrighteous, and is sav'd, like sinners in the church of *Rome*, out of the public stock of merits.[4] The whole mystery of his iniquity is only this, to raise the value of money, (quite contrary to the custom of *France*) when the king is to receive his, and bring it down again, when he is to pay it out. His trade is but a kind of mart; for he takes

---

[1] I have found no further word on this incident.

[2] See "The Shipman's Tale."

[3] For an explanation of that county's having to pay in which the robbery was committed see p. 31, n. 10.

[4] See p. 85, n. 15.

all men's money (but the kings) that is brought him, to be paid back again at his return from some other world, (for that will be the case in the end) and by that time it will become 1000 for one; and in the mean while stills them, as thieves do mastives,[5] with small pittances for present occasions, untill he has pack'd up all, and then he breaks his own bank, like a burglarer, and steals away himself.

A BOWLER[1]

Turns the wheel of his own fortune, but trusts it out of his own hands, and sometimes he lights on the top of it, and sometimes under. His bowl is the very same with that which *fortune* is drawn standing upon,[2] and as that turns under her feet, his own fortune proves either good or bad. He is like a conjurer of the sieve and sheers;[3] for as that is said to turn with words; he uses all manner of conjurations, to make his bowl rub or run, as best suits with his own advantages, and when it fails reviles the poor innocent creature, with many bitter curses, for not doing that which was not in its power to do, when the thing is very true and faithful, and goes punctualy according to its first directions, and, if those err'd, is not bound to take notice of others, and if it should would be as much damn'd and curs'd by the other side; just as men, that are turn'd into the world by nature, are commanded and adjur'd by the cunning gamesters of the times to do things, not only against the first impression and force they receiv'd from the hand of nature, but contrary to one another, and if they fail, as it is impossible not to do, are damn'd and confounded by one side, or both. When he mistakes the measure of his cast, inclination of his ground, or has turn'd his bias the wrong way, he lays all the fault upon his bowl, and blames it for not going to one place when it was sent to another. His bowl is much wiser than himself; for when it has receiv'd orders from his hand, it is not so silly to alter it upon a verbal command, as he would have it. When words

---

[5] Mastiffs.

[1] For the game of bowls, see p. 58, n. 16.

[2] The wheel which, in fable, is turned by Fortune, as an emblem of mutability.

[3] Sieve and shears: a mode of divination; used for the recovery of things lost. [Skeat and Mayhew, *Glossary of Tudor and Stuart Words.*]

A sieve was put on the point of a pair of shears and was expected to turn around when the person or thing inquired about was named. [See Scott, *The Discovery of Witchcraft*, p. 148.]

fail he puts his body into postures, and cringes as if his bowl saw him, and being a dumb creature understood dumb signs better than language. He runs after his bowl, as fools do after conjurers, to see what his fortune is, but to no purpose; for it would have been the same, if he had staid where he was, and all his curiosity has no power to make it better or worse when it is once thrown out of his hand. He observes the method of all courts, where the weakest gamesters lead, and the best follow and come behind. He runs after his cast and turns the bias of his bum, as if it had a magnetic force to sway the bias of his bowl, and steer it which way he pleases to hang an arse: for, like a dog, he expresses his inclinations most of all by the motion and demeanor of his nether parts, as if he carried a rudder in his breech, as birds and fishes do. He talks to his wooden emissaries as Hocus-pocus does to his; but the one does it sillily in earnest, and the other cunningly in jest, as fools and knaves always use to do. He has heard, that a bowl in motion, (according to the doctrine of some late philosophers) is an animal,[4] and when it lyes still and rests becomes inanimate again; and that is the natural reason why very discreetly he never speaks to his wooden creature but when it is in motion, that is, alive, and in a capacity to understand what he says, otherwise he would be thought to be the verier blockhead of the two.

A BRISK MAN—PERT

Knows nothing of himself, but guesses by the company he keeps (which are the best in his opinion that he can be admitted into) that he is one of the same rate, or at least ought to be esteem'd so; and like a simple Catholic puts his trust in other men's superabundant merits,[1] which he believes he has right (as being one of the same society) to a share in. He has nothing in him, that is properly his own

---

[4] "The atomic philosophers, Democritus, Epicurus, etc., and some of the moderns likewise, as Des Cartes, Hobbes, and others, do not allow animals to have a spontaneous and living principle in them but maintain that life and sensations are generated out of matter, from the contexture of atoms, or some peculiar composition of magnitudes, figures, sites, and motions, and consequently that they are nothing but local motion and mechanism. By which argument tops and balls, whilst they are in motion, seem to be as much animated as dogs and horses. Mr. Boyle in his Experiments, printed in 1659, observes how like animals (men excepted) are to mechanical instruments." [Nash, ed., *Hudibras*, I. ii. 56 n.]

[1] See p. 85, n. 15.

but confidence, all the rest of him is borrow'd from several persons, like a citizens riding equipage. He is as familiar with the names of authors and titles of books as a stationer, and knows just as much of their insides, unless it be by hearsay, in which he is for the most part either misinform'd or mistaken, as men that rely upon tradition usualy are. He commonly pretends most to that in which he is most defective, as cowards do to valour; and the more he is wanting in any thing the more affects it (as men use to understand the worth of things by the want of them); and where he may be bold assumes it with the more confidence, and like a plover is most concern'd when he is furthest off[a] his nest. He is like a rook, that bets upon other men's hands, and when they throw out,[2] has no way to make himself a saver but by wrangling and judging on the wrong side. He is a carnal and prophane fanatic, that is gifted with opinion and confidence, as the other is with light and ignorance, and believes all mankind in an error but himself and some few of his own Church.

A BROKER

Is a taylor's antiquary, that preserves the memory of all his acts and monuments,[1] and keeps the annals and records of his proceedings in all ages, that posterity may not be to seek what customs have been in ancient times, and what innovations since introduc'd, merely arbitrary, against the fundamental usage of freeze-jerkins, trunk-hose and codpieces.[2] A snake when he casts his skin is said to eat it, and so do the one half of his customers their cast cloaths. Among these the hangman is his most constant customer; for as the keeper of a park claims the skins of all bucks he kills as his fee, so does he the cloaths of all those, he serves a warrant upon from the higher powers. The best bargains he buys are from thieves and housebreakers, with which he turns Merchant adventurer both by sea and land; for if they be discover'd before he has sent them to the plantations, he is

---

[a] off] of

[2] See p. 49, n. 17.

[1] Monuments: works, sayings, deeds, etc. worthy of record or of enduring. Note the serious use in the title of John Foxe's *Actes and Monuments* (1563).

[2] Freeze-jerkin: a jacket, often sleeveless, worn over a doublet (a kind of undergarment). Here made of a napped woolen cloth (frieze).

Trunk-hose: see p. 61, n. 5.

Codpiece: a triangular piece of cloth, often padded, that covered the front fork of the hose.

truss'd up in his calling, and his good friend the hangman gives him a quick dispatch for old acquaintance sake, and takes the cloaths he sold him back again for his pains. He furnishes bawds, as upholsterers do rooms, by the week, and lets out hackney gowns and petticoats, with which she accomodates the hackney gentlewomen, and receives hire for both, and all three in their several ways and callings live comfortably by one another, and pay the Justice and Constable *scot and lot.*[3] He finds by experience that those who have to do with necessitous people have a greater freedom of conscience than others, and can make a little go further, and therefore the greater their wants are of whom he buys, the less he gives them; and when he sells a bargain sets his price, not according to the worth of the thing, but the ignorance or necessity of the buyer. If it were not for hanging he would not change his trade for a better; but the perpetual dread of dangling makes him slip many a good bargain, to the great trouble of his conscience, and the hanging out of his frippery[4] is no better than a memento, that always puts him in mind of his latter end.

A BUFFOON

Is a tavern-Terraefilius,[1] a Pudding[2] impropriate without cure of puppets.[3] He pretends to the long-robe a fool's coat,[4] and enjoys the privileges of it, to say what he pleases. He stains his impudence with scurrility, and a very little wit, that makes it sparkle briskly, and pass well enough with those that want judgment. He is a land-pug,[5] that has commonplaces of ribaldry for all persons and occasions, and has something to say to every one he meets to please the fare he carries in his scull. His calling is to play upon somebody

---

[3] A parish assessment laid on subjects according to their ability to pay.

[4] Cast-off clothes, especially tawdry finery.

[1] The Terrae Filius was an orator at Oxford University privileged to make humorous and satirical speeches at university ceremonials. See L. H. Dudley Buxton and Strictland Gibson, *Oxford University Ceremonials* (Oxford, 1935), pp. 92–93 and 97.

[2] See p. 44, n. 44.

[3] The analogy is made between a jack-pudding and his puppets, a priest and his spiritual charge of parishioners (cure), with perhaps a play on the "cure" not effected by a quack.

[4] He wears his fool's coat as if he were a lawyer wearing the long-robe. See also p. 227, n. 3.

[5] Pug: an imp, a dwarf; a small demon; a sprite.

in the company, where he is like a fidler; but his greatest skill consists in the right choice of his instrument, for if he chance to mistake, he has his fiddle knock'd about his pate, and is kick'd down stairs. He vaults upon a man like a wooden horse to shew tricks and the activity of his insolence and illnature. His buisiness is to gain ill-will, and his pleasure to displease any man that he dares. He is a mortal enemy to all those, that have less, or more impudence than himself; as if his own forehead were the only seal'd measure, that had the mark burnt in it.[6] His calling is to be rude and barbarous, and he is free of all companies where he comes. He is bound to his ill behaviour, and if he should be civil it is more than he can answer. He spares nothing that comes in his way, but whether it be true or false, right or wrong, sacred or profane, he is very impartial. Sometimes he meets with those, that break his privilege and his head, and then he is put out of his play, but never out of countenance; for his impudence is impenetrable. He is commonly a coward, but his want of shame supplies his want of courage, and makes him run himself into perpetual dangers, without considering how he shall get off. He will sometimes hit upon things to the purpose; for as all great wits are said to have something of madness,[7] so all great madnesses have something of wit. His tongue runs before his courage, as well as his wit, and betrays him into quarrels before he is aware, which he is glad to undergo with much passive valour, or compound with miserable and wretched submissions. He will often take occasion to abuse himself for want of a better. He breaks jests, as man do glasses, by mischance, and before he is aware, and many times pays for them against his will. He is like *Harry* the 8th, spares no man in his railing, nor woman in his ribaldry, for which he frequently incurrs the curse of the Devil, and has his head broken.

A CATCHPOLE[1]

Is a journeyman sheriff, a minister of justice and injustice, right or wrong. He is a man of quick *apprehension*, and very great

---

[6] Branding was commonly administered to criminals; perjurers, for example, were burned in the forehead with the letter *P* and rogues burned through the ears. [Harrison, *Elizabethan England*, p. 241.]

[7] Great wits to madness near allied, a commonplace from antiquity. [See Seneca, *On Tranquility of Mind*, XVII. 10, following Aristotle, *Problems*, XXX. I; also Dryden's "Absalom and Achitophel," ll. 163–64.]

[1] A contemptuous term for a constable, who apprehended criminals.

judgment, for it seldom begins or ends without him. His business is to have and to hold the bodies of all those he has in his warrant—These are his tenements, no more in their own occupation, but his, till he delivers them over to *Satan*, that is the jailor. He lays his authority, like a knighthood on the shoulder, and it presently possesses the whole body, till bail and mainprise[2] bring deliverance. He fears nothing like a rescue, with which he is sometimes grievously afflicted, and beaten like a setting-dog, that springs the game. This never falls so heavy upon him, as when he does his business too near home, (like an unskilful cur that runs at sheep) for then the Lawyers, that set him on work, pump[3] and shave him for his pains. His greatest security is in his knavery, when he takes money off both sides, and is paid for not seeing, when he has no mind to it. His whole life is a kind of pickeering,[4] and, like an *Indian* cannibal, he feeds on those he takes prisoners. His first business is to convey their bodies to a tavern, or an alehouse, where he eats and drinks their heads out. He is a greater enemy to liberty than Mr. *Hobb* and would reduce all men, if he could, to *necessity*.[5] He eats his bread, not with the sweat, but the blood of his brows, and keeps himself alive, like those that have issues, by having holes made in his skin; for it is part of his vocation to be beaten, when it falls in his way, and sometimes kil'd if occasion serve.

A CLAP'D MAN

Has bred that in his bones, which will never out of the flesh. He pays for his sins in specie; for as the flesh committed the fault, so it endures the punishment. He has spent all the forenoon of his life in catching of diseases, as men do fish, and the greatest part of the afternoon in pickling them up in tubs,[1] to keep them from purtifying and stinking. He melts his grease like a candle in a paper-lanthorn, and consumes and wastes himself down to a stinking snuff, and goes out with a noisome vapour.[2] The pox takes him by the nose, as *Saint*

---

[2] Mainprise: the act of procuring the release of a prisoner by becoming surety for his appearance in court at a specified time.

[3] See p. 115, n. 17.

[4] Marauding, pillaging, plundering; also, privateering or piracy. [*O.E.D.*]

[5] See *Leviathan*, Pt. II, Chap. 21.

[1] Treatment for the pox by "suffumigation with cinnabar in a meat-pickling vat" was common. [Alban H. G. Doran, "Medicine," in *Shakespeare's England*, I, 438–39.]

[2] Sweating treatment and a low diet were prescribed for the pox. [Ibid., 439.]

Dunstan did the Devil with a hot pair of tongs,[3] and it vanishes and leaves nothing but a stink behind. He has layd so long abed, that his bones ake, and has broken his shins with groping in the dark. He is blasted, like a miner, by digging among unwholesome vapours. What he loses by *Venus* he thinks to recover by *Mercury*,[4] but catches his cure as an after-clap, that commonly proves the worse disease of the two. He takes the height and declination of the sun in his bones, and finds the aequinoxes there more certain than in the almanac; and if there were a new emendation of times to be made, he is a better judge than all the mathematicians to reform the calendar; for certainly his aches give a better account in nature of the measure of time, than all their pendulums. He knows more of the course of the moon than all the astronomers, and is like to lay a new and more certain foundation for astrology, and to cast nativities[5] nearer home by his own pains and predictions; and does not doubt but in time to give a shrewd guess at the longitude; for he finds by experience, that his pox goes truer than all their pendulum clocks. Napier's bones[6] are ridiculous to his for true casting of accompt; for by them he will undertake to tell exactly when the sun enters into the first scruple of *Aries* or *Libra*, and consequently how much it has varied since the creation, and how long the world will last—As for comets and meteors, he is like to give the world better discoveries than ever it has made yet; for his clap is a kind of lightning, that pierces the bones and never hurts the skin, and in all probabilitie[a] will give a better accompt of the motion of the earth than all comets or[b]   or all the spots in Saturn's belt.

A COFFEE-MAN[1]

Keeps a coffee market, where people of all qualities and conditions meet, to trade in foreign drinks and newes, ale, smoak, and

---

[3] See p. 147, n. 33.

[4] Mercury was widely used for the treatment of venereal disease, both in the form of mercurial ointment and through the prescription of mercurial pills. For a recurrence of gonorrhea in a patient, for example, Sir Thomas Browne prescribed "mercuriall" pills. [*Letters*, in *Works*, ed. Keynes, IV, 119.]

[5] See p. 110, n. 4.

[6] Pieces of bone, wood, or ivory with certain numbers on them used to facilitate arithmetical and geometrical calculations. The inventor Lord Napier (1550–1617) was the first to discover the use of logarithms in trigonometry.

[a] probabilitie] probalitie

[b] A blank space appears here in Thyer's edition.

[1] Coffee was introduced into England about 1652, by a Turkish merchant, a

controversy. He admits of no distinction of persons, but gentleman, mechanic, lord, and scoundrel mix, and are all of a piece, as if they were resolv'd into their first principles. His house is a kind of *Athenian* school, where all manner of opinions are profest and maintain'd to the last drop of coffee, which should seem, by the sovereign virtue it has to strengthen politic notions, to be, as some authors hold, the black porrige of the *Lacedemonians*,[2] and the very same *Lycurgus* himself us'd when he compos'd his laws, and among other wholesome constitutions hit upon that, which enjoins women to wear slits in their petticoats[3] and boys to steal bread and butter,[4] as *Plutarch* writes in his life. Beside this their manner of conversing with strangers and acquaintance, all in one company, agrees perfectly with the custom of the *Spartans*, that made their city but one family, and eat and drunk all together in public. He sells burnt water and burnt beans as puddle, and of as pure a race, and though not altogether so delicious upon the palate warmer in the stomach, that never stirs the blood with wanton heates, nor raises idle fancies in the brain, but sober and discreet imaginations, such as black choler, like it self, produces. It is a kind of drink, as curses are a kind of prayers, that neither nourishes, nor quenches thirst. *Dives*[5] would hardly endure a drop of it on the tip of his tongue. He is a *Barbarian* brewer of *Mahometan Taplash*,[6] that tempers his decoction according to the *Alcoran, and skinks in*

Mr. Edwards, and the first coffee house opened in the early 1650's. [D' Israeli, *Curiosities of Literature*, I, 344–45, and Traill, ed., *Social England*, IV, 323.]

[2] Plutarch mentions a Laconian "kothon" or drinking cup used by soldiers because its color concealed the disagreeable appearance of the water they often had to drink. The curving lips of the cup held back the muddy sediment. ["Life of Lycurgus," in *Plutarch's Lives*, trans. Perrin, ix. 4–5.]

[3] In the program for regulating birth and marriage, women were required to firm up their bodies so as to produce healthy children. To free them from softness and effeminacy maidens as well as young men were to wear only tunics in processions and at certain festivals. Scant clothing was worn to attract youths to marriage. [Ibid., xiv. 2–xv. 2.]

[4] To develop boldness and cunning, boys were encouraged to be adept at stealing food and at setting upon people who were asleep or off guard. However, careless thievery by the unskillful led to a flogging. [Ibid., xvii. 1–4.]

[5] *Dives* is commonly taken as the proper name of the rich man in the parable of Lazarus (Luke, XVI. 19 ff.) who, tormented in the flame of hell, begged for a cool drop of water on his tongue.

[6] Taplash: the "lashings" or washings of casks or glasses; dregs.
Coffee was used at first in connection with the long religious services of the Muslims, but the conservative section of the priesthood believed coffee to be

earthen goblets to his guests. If it were not for news and the cheapness of company he would be utterly abandon'd: for that, with the freedom to vapour, lye, and loiter upon free cost, draws more company than his coffee, or the *Turk* that drinks it on his sign,[7] though that be the better of the two. Coffee, though the vilest of liquors, carries away the name of the house from chocolate and tea drinks of better quality, that are equally sold there and of better reputation, even as mean thieves are only call'd so, and great ones taken no notice of.

A COINER

Is a prince incognito, and tributary to the prince of darkness, under whose protection he lives. He is the chief of all forgers; for he counterfeits that, for which all other forgeries are practised; and therefore when his actions are considered, he has all his members erected, like a trophy, to his memory, and his head, like an old *Roman* emperors, plac'd on his standard; while others of his quality leave no monument behind them but their ears.[1] He coins nothing but his own *pole-money*;[2] for when he is detected he pays his head for his money, as other men do money for their heads. He publishes a false impression of the Kings money, without licence, full of scandalous and treasonable practices. He begins commonly, a great way off his business, in chymistry, which is for the most part but an introduction to coining, in which having spent his time and fortune unprofitably, he finds himself not so properly qualify'd for any other course of life as that of coining: for having attempted in vain to make true metals (as a broken vintner sets up an alehouse) he resolves to try the experiment, what he can do with false ones. There is no man, that uses more in-

---

intoxicating and prohibited by the Koran. However, the drinking of coffee spread among Arabian Muslims and was used in Arabia to a large extent. Until the end of the seventeenth century the supply of coffee came almost entirely from the province of Yemen in southern Arabia. [*Encyclopaedia Britannica.*]

[7] Probably the painted board which advertised the house or shop. Usually such a sign was an easily recognizable emblem. It might be noted that Sir John Harrington's Rota Club met at the Turk's Head.

[1] See p. 206, n. 3.

[2] Poll tax, with a play on *poll*, a head?

dustry, art, and ingenuity to render himself a person of ability and merit to be hang'd than he does; and, like a devout christian, he makes the whole business of his life nothing but a preparation for death. He lives in perpetual hazard of life and limb, which always stand and fall together with him: for the law, in his case, is like the *Zampatan*,[3] that never touches but it kills. When he is discover'd he has one way to save himself, by procuring justice to change a life or two, and accept of two or three of his companions in exchange for his own, which is sometimes allowed of as a valuable consideration, and then he is repriev'd, until he is taken in the next matter of fact; and then he preaches repentance and newness of life to the rabble, as *Hacket*[4] did, out of a cart, and is gather'd to his fathers at the gallows. He cloaths his base metals in a thin vehicle of silver, such as spirits take of air, that serves it to pass up and down in the world until it is worn off, and then they are stop'd, and go no further. He never eates but *out of a diabolical instigation*, nor cloaths himself but *against the crown and dignity of the king*; nor does any thing but *with a felonious intent*: for his character is nothing but an inditement, of which he is always found guilty.

A CONJURER

There is nothing that the general ignorance of mankind takes to, but there is some cheat or other that always applies to it, especially where there is anything to be gain'd, and where that amounts to little they will rather play at small game than sit out. Hence some cunning Impostors observing that[a] the generality of mankind, like Beasts, do soon arrive to their height, and never outgrow the customs of their childhood (which being, for the most part brought up among all women, and imbued with stories of spirits and the Devil, that stick by them ever after) have found out this horrid way of cheat, to abuse their weakness and credulity. The his-

---

[3] See p. 240, n. 9.

[4] William Hacket (d. 1591), a religious fanatic (converted to religion after a riotous life), proclaimed both that he was immortal and that he was Christ and warned people to repent. He and a friend preached from a cart in Cheapside. Hacket was condemned to death for declaring that Elizabeth was not the queen of England and for defacing her picture. [*D.N.B.*]

[a] observing that] observing, that

tories of *Frier Bacon*,[1] *Doctor Faustus*[2] and others of that nature are canonical enough to make them believe, that there is such a thing as they call the *black art*, (mistaking *Negromancy* for *necromancy*)[3] and those that profess it cunning men. These are all that is left of the Devils oracles, that give answers to those that[a] come to consult him, not as their forefathers did by being inspir'd and possest, but as if they posses'd the Devil himself, and had him perfectly at command: for if they were not intrench'd in their circles, he would serve them as they did Chaucer's Sumner for daring to cite him to appear.[4] He is the desperatest of all Impostors next a hypocrite; for the one makes God and the other the Devil a party in all his practises. He calls himself a Magician, and derives himself from the Persian Magi, when the story of him that was chosen emperour by the neighing of his horse,[5] and him that continued himself so by concealing the loss of his ears[6] (which is all we know of them) proves clearly, that they were but cheats and impostors. He keeps the rabble in very great awe, who are persuaded he can do very strange things, which they are wonderfully delighted to hear of, and had rather believe, than try or disprove.

---

[1] See p. 150, n. 56.

[2] The wandering conjurer who lived in Germany, c. 1488–1541. The medieval legend of a man who sold his soul to the devil became associated with the sixteenth century necromancer. See the play by Marlowe.

[3] The art of revealing the future by communication with the spirits of the dead: (OF. *nigromance*, from L. *necromantia*, fr. Gr. *nekromanteia*, fr. *nekros*, a dead body, + *manteia*, divination. The old spelling is due to a confusion with L. *niger*, black; hence the name *black art*). [*Webster's Seventh New Collegiate Dictionary* (Springfield, Mass., 1963).]

[a] those that] those, that

[4] The summoner was swooped off to Hell by the Devil (see "The Friar's Tale").

[5] The story is about Darius, one of the seven princes who, having destroyed the usurper of the Crown of Persia, were competitors for the crown. They agreed to meet on horseback at a particular time, and the man whose horse neighed first was to be acknowledged emperor. The groom of Darius made sure that his master succeeded. [Herodotus, *History*, III. 84–87, in *Herodotus*, trans. A. D. Godley (Cambridge, Mass. and London, 1946–50).]

[6] The pseudo or Magian Smerdis, who, knowing that the true Smerdis, son of Cyrus, was dead, took his place in succession to the Persian throne. The Magian Smerdis having had his ears cut off by Cyrus, the son of Camlupes, for a grave offense was exposed when it was ascertained that he had no ears. [See Herodotus, *History*, III. 69, in *Herodotus*, trans. Godley. For the full story, see 61 ff.]

A CONSTABLE

Is the secular prince of darkness, as the Devil is the spiritual, and both divide equal empire, and haunt their several stations by night, and vanish when day appears. He walks with his lanthorn, not as *Diogenes* did to seek an honest man by day, but a knave by night, in which he is often at a loss, and perpetualy mistaken in seeking after that which he always carries about him. He is very gracious to those that give him money or good words, which he takes as tribute or homage, but implacable to those that rebel, or dispute his authority, which he will not endure to be scanted, as those that have but little of any thing ought to be thrifty, and make as much of it as they can; and therefore small Officers are always most imperious and arrogant. The first thing he never fails to do at his entrance into his office is to forswear himself, and be drunk with his neighbours, who to do him honour the first night trail rusty bills and halberts under his command, who being mounted on his throne a stall, (like a Prince at the beginning of his reign) most graciously grants his general pardon to all offenders during that night. He encroaches upon the ecclesiastical courts in laying fines upon sins and taxes upon bawdy-houses, that pay him contribution for taking their gentlewomen and their windows into his protection, and securing them against the invasion of the Hector and Scourer.[1] He is never admitted to reign in the street as constable until he has been swabber or scavenger, and made them clean. He is never severe in his office till after one at night, at which time all that walk the streets are his vassals, and he their natural Liege Lord, which they must either submit to, or, if they are not able to give battle, be led into captivity. The greatest and most criminal accusations he commonly charges delinquents with is for being sober too late, or not drunk in due season. The upper end of his staff and his face are the ensigns of his authority and his wisdom; and it is a question in which both are most apparent and eminent, but neither ever so much as by owl-light.[2] He makes drunkards pay him custom for

---

[1] Hector: see p. 106, n. 2.
Scourer: roisterer or night thief.
[2] See p. 136, n. 3.

the drink they are fraught with and impost,[3] and tell[4] for their heads like cattle, and the less considerable they are they amount to the more.

A COURT-WIT

Certainly court-wit must be very slight, when every man professes it, and that trade very frivolous, which all sorts of talents learn of themselves, and every one has a stock to set up with. Tis not unlike the subtle mystery of linkboys, whose business is to obtrude themselves upon all men in the dark, and walk before them with more smoke and vapour than light. Howsoever, what they want of real ingenuity they abundantly supply with confidence; and because that virtue is commonly a great support to wit, they believe it to be much its betters, and that it ought to take place of it, as all men are greater than their dependants: although as confidence is but the wit of the face, like painting, it may impart an artificial flourish to the outside, but cannot alter lineaments, nor mend those features, which nature has contriv'd amiss. It is true, he that ventures at wit wholly upon the accompt of confidence has one great advantage, that though his fortune be ever so bad he can never lose; for he throws at every man that sets him and has nothing about him to pay, if he should happen to fling out; while he that has reputation and credit, if it be his ill luck to throw out,[1] must be sure to pay his losses; and this is the true foundation of all his confidence; for cowards are most couragious when they are secur'd from danger. He despises one that does but look wise as formal and pedantic, while he does not only do the same thing himself, but much more; for he lays his pretences the most arrogant way, which the other does the most innocent and inoffensive, as one that is very drunk thinks all others so, and himself sober. Beside the authority of the place is sufficient to justify any thing that is not very lewd, and to give a man a protection for having no wit as well as no money to pay: For as in the universities wit goes by colleges, even so here it is measur'd by ordinary and extraordinary, and that which is call'd greatest here is understood to be the least every where else. They have agreed upon a mode of repartees, as well as a de-

---

[3] Tax (especially customs duty).
[4] Give an account; make a report.
[1] See p. 49, n. 17.

meanour of faces, legs, and elbows; and he that is unaccomplished that way is as ridiculous as he that wears the colours of his garniture[2] out of season, or is trail'd by an old fashion'd scent. The muse that inspires lampoons is very powerful here, where they admit of no other poesy; and for pleasant conversation nothing but raillery or pudding-sayings,[3] with which they play upon one another like the battery on a gittar, and make as sensless a noyse. There us'd to be but one heretofore of the faculty in ordinary, but since the place was retrenched, they all share the service among them, and every man claims the privilege to say any thing as part of his allowance and his vayles.[4] He[a] has a monstrous wit; for a monster is nothing else but a thing to be shown, and he does nothing but endeavour to shew his; and if he would but take money for going in, it would get him as much as a calf with five legs. His wit is like a watchman's bill with a chalk'd edge, that pretends to sharpness only to conceal its dull bluntness from as dull discerners.

A COWARD

Is as tender as the sensitive plant, the least touch makes him shrink. His valour is a fortification not tenable, that surrenders upon the first summons without articles. He wants ammunition, and is as ill mann'd. He is a merchantman, that carrys no guns, and strikes sail, rather than any thing else, to every man that hales him. He is an anvil, that men try their valours and their swords upon, a drum that makes a warlike noise, yet made of purpose to be beaten. He turns his back when he fights, like an ass, that he may not see the blows he gives and takes, and, like a Parthian, fights flying. He weares a sword as a stag does horns, for ornament only, not to fight, but run away with. He affects nothing so much as valour, but dare not go to the price of it. *He brags, and vapours, and makes a noise,*[a] but is charg'd with powder only, not lead. He is very magnanimous against a cudgel,

---

[2] The trimming of a suit with ribbons, precious stones, etc.

[3] I have found no definition of *pudding-sayings.*

[4] Vails: occasional profit or emolument in addition to salary or regular payment.

[a] The final two sentences in the Character are preceded by a note in the manuscript: "*Added afterwards* as appears by the difference of the ink."

[a] *He brags, and vapours, and makes a noise*] alternate wording in the manuscript: *His brags and vapours are but musters*

and despises bruises, but cannot endure to have any breach made in his skin. He brought his action of *Quare clausum fregit*[1] against one that broke his head. He has a great deal of comparative valour, but no positive, and is the most puissant man in the world over all those, that are greater cowards than himself. His skin is like a drum-head, moderate beating does it no hurt, but if you make a hole in it, it is spoil'd for ever, and therefore he cannot endure that. He is very skilful in the theory of fighting, and can exercise all the postures of quarelling, but when he is upon service forgets all, but only makes ready, and faces about. He is as tender of his foreparts as a crocodile is of his belly, but bold enough of his back, which makes him despise kicks and bastinados with wonderful fortitude, and sometimes cuts, because they are out of his sight. He is so bashful, as the Scots say, in the face of an enemy, that he cannot endure to see a sword naked. He hates no sight in the world so much as cold iron, and his own blood. He is but a standing tuck,[2] a foyl with a blunt edge, and a leathern poynt. The glittering of a sword kills him like lightning, and never hurts the skin. If he be heroical he will hold in his fear, as a man does his breath under water, untill he comes to the very nick of danger, and then it breaks out with the greater violence.

A CREDULOUS MAN

Has a gentle, easy, complacent belief, and will not deny any man the civility of his faith to any thing, especially if it be false; otherwise it is no courtesy, for if it be true every man ought to believe it: And that's the reason, though true or false be all one to him, why he always inclines to the wrong rather than the right, unless, as there are innumerably more lies than truths in the world, he always takes the strongest as the surest side. He is the same thing to a lyar, as a thief is to a receiver; what the one comes dishonestly by, the other entertains and disposes of, and in that appears to be the worse of the two; for if it were not for easy believers, liars would be at a loss, and either leave that vanity, or use it to no purpose. Every man's word is canonical with him, and he never questions the authority of

---

[1] *Quare clausum fregit*: *Clausum fregit*—a law term: "He broke into my enclosure." An act of trespass committed on lands or tenements. *Quare*: why; wherefore.

[2] Rapier.

it, but believes as the church-porch believes. He is very free of his faith because he comes easily by it; for it costs him no *consideration* at all, and he is sure he can hardly part with it for less than it is worth. He esteems it generous to be persuaded freely, and not to stand with any man for such a trifle as a lye is. His faith is of a very strong constitution, that will swallow and digest any thing, how crude, raw, and unwholesome soever it be. He has a worse opinion of himself than the rest of the world; for he cannot believe any man will lie and forswear himself, though he has done it himself never so often. He finds most delight in believing strange things, and the stranger they are, the easier they pass with him; but never regards those that are plain and feasible, for every man can believe such.

A CRUEL MAN

Has nothing of a man but the outside, as *Perillus's* bull[1] had of a beast; the insides of both are fill'd with horror, torture, and destruction. He is a creature of all speciese's; for man and beast are all one to him, and he has as much compassion for the one as the other. He approves of no law but the *forest law*,[2] and would make all men *feræ naturæ*,[3] because he is one himself. He is a Renegade to humanity, and being a proselyte[a] . . . . is very cruel to those of his former persuasion. He has no sympathy with mankind but that their afflictions are his delight, and he endures his own pleasures with less patience than they do their pains. He loves a widow of his own making better than a virgin, to whom he professes love as he does friendship to men, only to destroy them. He is more delighted with ruins, like an Antiquary, than a standing fabric, and, like a zealous catholic, worships the reliques more than the Saint. He is a kind of a leech, that relishes no part of a man but his blood. He is a rebel against the law of nature; for he always does what he would not be done unto, which is the privilege both of a Saint and the Devil, as

---

[1] Perillus invented for Phalaris (ruler of Argentum in Sicily and well-known as a cruel tyrant) a brazen bull in which the tyrant is said to have burnt alive the victims of his cruelty, the first victim being Perillus himself.

[2] Laws applicable to those woodland districts, usually belonging to the king, set apart for hunting wild beasts and game, etc.

[3] Of a wild nature; not domesticated.

[a] Ellipses appear here in the manuscript.

iron in the extremities of cold or heat does equally burn those that touch it. Nothing enables him more in his cruelty than religion; for the fire of his zeal and dull coldness of his ignorance renders his temper, like a piece of iron, proof against humanity, and that's the true reason why he's said to be hardhearted. The worse condition he can put any man into, the better he thinks of his own; flatters himself with other mens miseries, and will endure no parasites but hangmen and torturers. He is very humble in one thing, and desires men should take place of him and go out of the world before him, and he cares not how far he comes behind.

A CULLY[1]

Is a gibbet for all manner of cheats and rogues to hang upon; a Bridewel,[2] where pickpockets and rooks are set on work and kept. These, like Turks, make him believe he is a person of greater quality than he is, that they may set a greater fine and ransom on his head, and make him pay for it a great deal more than it is worth. He is fall'n among the wild Arabs, that make him buy himself over and over, and pay custom for his cargo, that is his ignorance and folly. Whores and cheats throw dice and rifle for him, win him of one another, and still he is anybodys but his own. Gamesters knap him with a whore, and throw what chance they please with him over a quart pot. He is a tenement in the occupation and possession of cheats and impostors, and rooks build in him like a tree. They have more ways to feed upon him, than ever dish of meat was drest; and, when they have eat out his head, they leave the rest of him (as a spider does by a fly) as good for nothing. They eat him out of house and home, as an oyster is out of his shell. When he proves stubborn and disobedient to his rulers they engage him in a war, which his Second prosecutes with all seeming hostility, until both parties are drawn up in the field ready to give battle, and then a cessation is propos'd, and accomodation concluded at a supper, which he pays for, and his honour declar'd to come off in a whole skin. He roasts his estate whole, like the ox at St. James's fair, and, as many mouths make a quick dispatch, he is devour'd in a moment. All the flies in the town flock about him, like a scab, and blow maggots into his head, which

---

[1] A dupe or gull.
[2] A prison. See p. 245, n. 7.

no medicine in nature can ever get out again. As soon as he is arrested, they all leave him, as the Devil is said to do witches, when they fall into the hands of justice.[a] Flatterers use him like a dish of meat, that is said to be best commended in being eaten, and they never praise and cry him up so much, as when they feed upon him and devour him.

A CUTPURSE[1]

Puts his life in his hand, and both into another man's pocket, out of which he picks his living, or his death. He quarters all his members upon his neck, and when he is surpriz'd that pays for all. The hangman is his landlord, of whom he holds in chief, and, when he fails, is serv'd with a *distringas*,[2] by virtue whereof he seizes upon *his very cloaths*.[b] He ventures choaking for his meat before he eats, and the outside of his throat stands engag'd for all that goes down the inside. He runs the very same fate with a seaman, that is said to be remov'd but three fingers from drowning, and just so many is he from hanging; for upon those his life and death perpetually depend. Every man he deals with carries his destiny in his pocket, out of which, like a lottery, he draws his chance, either to live, or dangle. His chiefest qualifications are the same with those of a surgeon, to have the hand of a lady, and the heart of a lion; for if either fail his life lyes at stake, and he swings out of one world into another, as seamen use to do from ship to ship. The sign is with him always in *Taurus*[3] neck and throat; and Mercury is his ascendant[4] with Saturn, which argues that he will in time be burnt in the hand,[5] or mount a cart,[6] which, if

---

a "N. B. The same character is continued further, but it rather seems incorrect and partly a repetition of what is said before. The following sentence may be properly added." [This note appears here in the manuscript.]

[1] See p. 165, n. 6.

[2] The name of a writ bidding the sheriff distrain (constrain or force by the seizure and detention of a chattel or thing) in certain cases. [*O.E.D.*]

b *his very cloaths*]alternate wording: *all his moveables*

[3] Taurus the bull, the second sign of the zodiac, governs the neck and throat.

[4] The horoscope, or, more technically, the degree of the zodiac which appeared on the eastern horizon at the moment of birth. The house and lord of the Ascendant is said to exercise great influence on the future life of the child. Mercury is the god of merchants and of thieves.

[5] See p. 228, n. 2.

[6] The victim was carried from prison to the place of execution in a sled or cart.

the Sun interpose, is inevitable, for he thrives best in the dark. He differs from a highwayman as a thief does from a cheat; for the one does the same thing privately, which the other does openly in the face of the King's authority and his highway, and both in the end meet in the same hemp.[7] He gives himself a commission of treasure-trove,[8] to sound for hidden money in the bottoms of pockets, and when he lights upon his prey he handles it very gently, that it may go quietly along without making any noise; otherwise as spirits are said to keep hidden treasure and hurt those, that attempt to take it away, that dreadful hobgoblin the hangman takes possession of him.

A DANCING-MASTER

Is a live Punchinello incarnate, professor of the tactics of balls and masques, and a dance-driller. He teaches to tread musick, as they do wine at a vintage. His kit is the hornbook, and the stick the fescue,[1] with which he instructs his scholars to spell and read a coranto.[2] He ties his puppets to his leg, and makes them skip and frisk how he pleases. He teaches the postures of the coranto, jig, and saraband, and instructs his pupils how to order, not their arms, but their legs. Perpetual skipping, hopping, and capering have jog'd all his wit down into his legs, and his feet are much better accomplish'd than his head—This makes him call making of legs making of honours, as intimating the leg to be the most honourable member of the body. The dancing horse and he are fellow collegiates, have both all their paces, and tell money with their feet, only the horse has the advantage of him as having four legs to his two. He gets his living by the labour of his legs, and lives by the sweat of his toes. He expounds upon his enchiridion[3] kit, the constant inhabitant of his pocket, that squeaks like a kitten, and his pupils apprehend and improve at the wrong end. He is an expert foot-commander, very skilful at em-battling a breach, and leads up a dance with admirable conduct. He is very just, does all things in measure, keeps his time exactly, and

---

[7] That is, in prison, where the combing or beating of hemp was often an assignment for inmates. See p. 245, n. 7.

[8] Treasure-trove: treasure (gold or silver, money, plate, or bullion) found hidden in the ground or other place, the owner of which is unknown.

[1] A teacher's pointer.

[2] Courante: a dance with quick running steps.

[3] Handbook or manual.

carries himself uprightly in his life and conversation. He wears wings on his feet like Mercury, but needs none on his head, for that is light enough of it self.[a]

A DETRACTOR

Is a briar, that lays hold on every thing, that comes within its reach, and will, if it can, tear off something that it is never the better for, or tear it self in pieces. He has no way to make himself any thing but that of a leveller,[1] by bringing down other men to an equality with himself, which he does his unchristian endeavour upon all occasions to perform; and, like a needy thief, cares not how great a loss of credit he puts another man to, so he can make but ever so little of it to himself. He makes his own construction, that is the worst he can, of every man's actions; and when any thing appears doubtful, the worst sense always with him takes place of the better. He deals pretty fairly in one thing, and that is he never attempts to rob any man of his reputation, that has not much to lose, and can best spare it: as for those that have none, they are of his own rank, and he lets them pass freely. When he has depriv'd a man of his good name, he knows not what to do with it, like one that steals writings which he can claim nothing by. He is a kind of common cryer; for his business is to cry down a man's reputation, till he believes it is lost; and yet if he can but produce marks to the cryer that it is his, he shall have it again with all submission, otherwise he has the law on his side and takes it for his own. His general design is to make as much of himself as he can, and as little as he can of another man, and by comparing both together to render himself something: but as all comparisons and emulations are ever made by inferiors on the wrong side, after all his industry of himself and others he is but where he was before, unless he be worse, that is more contemptible. For as nothing enables the poor to endure their wants with greater patience than finding fault and railing at the rich; so nothing supports him more in his ignorance and obscurity than detracting from those, that either deserve more, or are believ'd to do so than himself.

---

a "N. B. A sentence or two more are added, but imperfect." [This note appears here in the manuscript.]

1 There is apparently a suggestion here of the Levellers, an extreme group in the army, led by John Lilburne, who in the 1640's worked for republicanism, universal suffrage, and religious toleration.

A DUELLER

Measures his life by the length of his weapon, and sends it back to his adversary as the measure of his resolution to join issue, and come to tryal. All his challenges are but passes to carry his antagonist into another world; or himself, if the uncertain hazard of the war will have it so. He sets a very low value upon his life, because by his manner of living he is like to have term in it, but is very careful to prolong his honour, as far as the course of nature will give it leave. He encounters his enemy most commonly at two weapons, single rapier, and civility; and is as careful not to be vanquished at the one, as the other; for he passes upon him with singular courtship, and does his endeavour to kill and slay him most obligingly; and will by no means be persuaded by his good will to take place, and go out of the world before him. There is nothing of unkind in all the quarrel but only the beginning of it, and the rest of the proceedings are managed as civilly as any other treaty; and in the end, when one falls, they part with extraordinary endearments. He encounters his principal as if he did but salute and compliment him, desires to wait upon him into the field, and have the honour to cut his throat, and protests to take it as a very great favour, and be ready to serve him in a greater matter, whensoever he shall please to command it—that the hangman, who uses to ask pardon of his customers before he presumes to break their necks, cannot do it in a more civil and obliging way. He is a man of mettle, and his sword and he are of the same family, and very near of kin; but he is chief, and the weapon a poor dependant or hanger-on. His second espouses his quarrel, and matches into his family, takes it to have and to hold, for better or for worse, till death them do part. The law is very favourable and indulgent to him, if he has but a care to dispatch his business with expedition, and kill his man without consideration; but if he delay it and lapse his time the case alters, and he is hang'd up for a sluggard, like one that rides post with a halter about his neck, and fails to come within his time. To avoid this inconvenience therefore, they agree by consent to make it a rencounter, that is appoint to meet by chance; and then the law is satisfied that there is no diabolical instigation, nor malice prepense in the business, but the proceedings have been legal; and if he can but read a hard old hand, his learnings and manners are approv'd of, and he has his degree under hand and seal deliver'd him by the hangman.

A DUNCE

Is so slow of apprehension, that every thing escapes and gives him the slip. He is very thick of understanding, and apprehends nothing that is not often and loud repeated over and over again, and then commonly he mistakes something too. His dull blunt wit is like a hammer, that will rather break things in pieces, then pierce into them; and all knowledge to him is like some late philosophers[a] definition of body—*impenetrable but discerpible.*[1] He has lost the use of his understanding, and is taken with a lameness in his brain, that he is not able to stir himself, but as he is help'd by those that are about him. He is commonly compos'd of two different tempers, strong inclinations and as feeble abilities, both which pulling contrary ways he stands stock still, unless, as all things are up hill to him, every strain he makes, his weight being more than his strength can master, does but set him backwards. He loves learning, but it does not love him; for it always lies crude and undigested upon his stomach, and he is much the worse for it. His judgment is lighter than his fancy, which renders him like a goose; for his feet are better than his wings, and he swims much better than he flyes. With much drudgery and long time he gets something by rote, which he always carrys about him, and produces like a watch, when he is askd what a clock it is. If he hit upon any thing that is not amiss, 'tis by chance, like the oyster, that catch'd a bird, that thrust his head into his mouth when he gap'd. The thickness of his scull renders it very able to keep out any thing. All his study and industry does but render his understanding duller and stiffer, as hard labour does mens hands. As soon as his capacity is full, which is long because slow in arriving to, he stops there, and whatsoever he meets with after runs over and spills.

AN ENVIOUS MAN

Is sick of another man's surfeits, and, like a *catholic* penitent, whips himself for another's enjoyments. He kickes and spurs himself like a jade, because another man outgoes him, and torments himself for want of a better. He turnes another man's happiness into his own

---

[a] philosophers] philosopers
[1] Henry More, *The Immortality of the Soul,* (London, 1659), Bk. I, Chap. 3.

misery. As love wounds the heart through the eye[1]; so hate does his at the sight of anothers perfections; and, like a lover, he pines away with the hate of that, which he fain wou'd, but cannot enjoy. Envy is like the common friendship of the world, that only waits on those whom fortune smiles on, and, when she leaves them, gives them over too. Envy persues the living like a beare, but leaves them, when th'are dead, to their own fame, that then flyes higher than it did before; as men are taller dead than when they liv'd. He hates himself, because he is not what he would be, and would be that he hates, because he is not it. He bears another man's prosperity more heavily than his own misfortune. He is so senseless, that he takes part against himself with that which he abhors, and like a drunkard, when his humour is crost, falls foul on the next man, that is himself. He is a great reformer of providence, and is very much concern'd, that things are not carried on as he would have them, which he believes would be much better than they are, at least for himself. This is sufficient to make him a rebel against his prince, as he would against God, if he durst own it. He racks himself when he sees another man taller, not out of design to add to his own stature, but because he cannot cut him shorter, as *Procrustes* us'd to do, by his own standard. When one ship outsails another, Seamen call it *wronging*; and he has translated that term to land, and believes, all those that outdo him in any thing do him an injury.

A FENCER

Is a fighting-master, that expounds upon a foyl, and instructs his pupils in the rudiments of blows, thrusts, and broken heads, and reads upon the subtlest point of a rapier. He teaches the theory of killing, wounding, and running through, and with the privilege of a Doctor professes murder and sudden death. His calling is previous to a Surgeon's, and he tutors his pupils to make wounds, that the other may cure them, and sometimes to the hangman's, when they venture to break the laws of the land, (instead of breaking heads) which he

---

[1] The idea that a lover is wounded (or slain) through his eyes is a familiar one in literature. This idea, more than a conceit of poets, was based on an old scientific hypothesis than an effluence, as either a spear or an arrow, passed from the eyes of the lady through those of the lover into his heart. [Cf. Plato, *Phaedrus* and Sophocles, *Antigone*, 795. Also, "The Knight's Tale" of Chaucer, ll. 1096-97.]

breaks y[ou]r necks for.[a] He wears a parapet upon his breast, to which he directs the points of their weapons, till by often repeating their lessons upon it, they can hit him where he pleases, and never miss a button, at least that on the end of the foyl. He instructs them, as the Professors of liberal arts do in schools, to practise that which is only useful upon the place, and no where else, as to stamp when they make a thrust, which makes a noise sufficient to terrify the foe upon boards, but is of no service at all in the field. He presses his documents upon his pupils with all vehemence, and they improve wind and limb. He infuses his precepts into them till they are quite out of breath, and their lungs profit more than their brains: But as no art can improve a man beyond his natural capacity; so no practise can raise his skill above his courage. He lays about him like another Orbilius[1] in his school, where his disciples con nothing but blows, and cuts, and bruises. He instructs them how to carve men, as they do wooden fowl, with a good grace, to slay in mood and figure,[2] without any illogical inferences, and to run a man through correctly and accurately, which he calls masterly strokes. He teaches the discipline of duels, to beat up quarters back and side, charge a body through and through, and dispute a pass with the greatest advantage. He is a duel-Doctor, and professes to help nature by art, and his prescriptions, like those of other doctors, destroy as many as they preserve.

A FIDLER

Commits a rape upon the ear, like *Tiberius's Spintrias*.[1] He is a Bouley[2] that sets men together by the ears, enchants them with

---

[a] y[ou]r yr.; he breaks y[ou]r neck for] alternate wording: he is fain to heal

[1] The schoolmaster of Horace and a teacher who flogged. See Horace, *Epistles*, II. i. 69–71: "Mark you! I am not crying down the poems of Livius.—I would not doom to destruction verses which I remember Orbilius of the rod dictated to me as a boy. . . ." [In *Satires, Epistles and Ars Poetica*, trans. Fairclough.]

[2] Mood and figure: terms in logic.

[1] According to Suetonius, Tiberius Nero Caesar devised a room with seats and benches in it for the purpose of his secret wanton lusts. He had gathered from all over young persons whom he termed *Spintriae*, experts in all kinds of "libidinous filthiness," who "abused and polluted" on one another's bodies before Tiberius, so that he might stir up his failing courage and fainting lust. ["Tiberius," in *Lives of the Caesars*, trans. Rolfe, III. xliii.]

[2] Bouley: a burly?

his magical rod, his fidlestic, out of themselves, and makes them skip as if they were bit with a *tarantula*. He inflames and blows them up like *Bel and the Dragon*[3] with rozen and hair. He tickles their ears, as the cutpurse did *Bartlemew Cokese's*,[4] while he picks their pockets. The ancients held, he could charm beasts (that is the rabble) and make them follow him,[5] and force stones to build themselves into a wall,[6] that is draw a crowd about him, which is no such strange thing. The ancient *Romans* us'd to torment men with fiddlestrings, and he retains and observes the custom most exactly[a] to this day. The roughness of his bow makes his strings speak, which otherwise would be silent and unuseful, and when he grows humorous himself, (which is not seldom) and will not play, he is us'd as niggedly till he does. He is an earwig,[7] that creeps into a mans ear and torments him, until he is got out again. The scrapings of his fiddle and horse-tail (like horse-radish) with white wine and sugar, or brandy make excellent sauce for a whore. He scratches and rubs the itch of lovers upon his fiddle, to the wonderful delight of those that have catch'd it, till it turns to a worse disease: for his fiddlestic is but a rubber made of a horses tail to carry sinners with, and he scrubs and firks them till they kick and fling, as if the Devil were in them. The noise of cats-guts sets them a caterwauling, as those, that are bitten with a mad dog, are said to foam at the mouth and bark. He is free of all taverns, as being as useful to relish a glass of wine as anchovies of caviare, serves like stum to help of bad wine, and conduces wonderfully to over-reckoning. He is as great a provocative, as a Romance, to love, and at weddings is a prime *ingredient*,[b] and takes place of the sack-posset.[8] The scrapings of his fiddle steep'd in wine make excellent love-powder. 'Tis like the spring of a clockwork-motion, that sets all the puppets a dancing, till 'tis run down, and then they are quiet. He does not live but rub out, spends time while he keeps it, is very expert in his way, and has his trade at his fingers ends.

---

[3] See p. 63, n. 2.

[4] See p. 238, n. 3.

[5] Suggestive of musicians in mythology, such as Orpheus: see p. 90, n. 41.

[6] See p. 93, n. 51.

[a] exactly] alternate wording: punctualy

[7] See p. 138, n. 2.

[b] *ingredient*] alternate wording: *officer*

[8] A drink composed of hot milk curdled with sack, often with sugar, spices, etc.—considered a delicacy.

A FOOL

Is the skin of a man stuff'd with straw, like an alligator, that has nothing of humanity but the outside—He is utterly unfurnish'd within, nothing but bare walls, and those so thin and full of chinks, you may see through them. His head is like a nut with a maggot in it, or a rotten egge, not worth the cracking. He is not actuated by any inward principle of his own, like an animal; but by something without him, like an engine; for he is nothing of himself, but as he is wound up, and set a going by others. Tho' he be no black swan, he is a grey one, that eates grass, and lives as much on the land, as water. His inward man is a monster, born blind, without brain or heart; and his mind nothing but a *mola*,[1] or false conception. He is a *Soland-Goose*, that's neither fish nor flesh, but between both, for you know not what to make of him.[2] He was born with a wither'd brain, like *Richard* the third's arm, an abortive brought forth, before its[a] time, imperfect.[3] His soul and his body are not of the same grass; for the one was calv'd before the other was ready to be put into it, which makes them agree so ill together. If the soul dwell in the body, or be imprison'd in it, his is very ill accomodated, and is lodg'd in a dungeon; and it does not live in him, but is clap'd up close. His parents, that are asham'd of him give out, (to save their credit) that he is a foreigner, native of *Fayry-land*, and chang'd in the cradle,[4] like a cloke at a tavern. The little wit he has tends naturaly to knavery, and he is dishonest by instinct. As a little rain makes the streets dirty, and a great deal washes them clean; or as a little wine is apter to pall and grow sour, than a great quantity: So his little understanding inclines him still to the worse; for he mistakes fraud and perfidiousness for wit and wisdom. He is like a building cover'd with lead—He is like the man in the fable, that carried his asse upon his back.[5] He will sometimes

---

1 Mola: a fleshy mass occuring in the womb, and thus a false conception.

2 Soland-Goose: the gannet, a large sea-fowl resembling a goose. The sentence seems to be an echo of the exchange between Falstaff and Mistress Quickly (*Henry IV, Part I*, III. iii. 140–50).

a its] it's

3 Cf. Shakespeare, *Richard III*, especially the opening soliloquy.

4 See p. 59, n. 23.

5 The fable from Aesop is of a miller, his son, and the ass they take to a fair to be sold. Each group of people they meet makes a suggestion which is

speak to the purpose; but that is but like a little mercury in a lead-mine. A knave and he are like a bow and arrows, that can do nothing without one another. He is a flat-bottom'd boat built of purpose to sail in shallow waters. His head is like the garret of a house, altho' uppermost, yet worst built, worst furnish'd, and design'd for the meanest lodging of all the rest.

A FORGER

Is a Master of the pen, that professes to write any man's usual hand, and draws and ingrosses all sorts of business with such admirable care and secresie, that he does it without the knowledge of those, that he undertakes for. He has an art to bloat parchment, and make a spick and span new deed look old before its time. His chief dealing consists in importing mens last wills and testaments out of other worlds, and raising apparitions of hand and seal out of the grave, that shall walk and appear in the likeness of the deceased so perfectly, that their nearest friends shall hardly be able to distinguish. He has as many tricks to cheat the Devil and his own conscience, as he has to abuse the world, as by writing with a pen in a dead man's hand, or putting a scroll of written paper in a dead man's mouth, and swearing those were the last words that came out of it, as if plain downright perjury were not more pardonable than that, which is meditated and prepar'd with tricks and finesses. He will bind a man's hands behind his back in a bond, before he is aware, and make him pay before he is loose again. He endeavours to oblige as many as he can by giving their names as much credit as he is able, though without their knowledge. He does all his feats with other mens hands, like the monkey that scratch'd with the cat's paw.[1] As soon as he is detected all his devices fall upon his own head, which is presently laid by the ears in the pillory,[2] where his lugs are set on the tenters,

---

followed: that at least one man should ride, that the old man should be the rider, that both should ride, that they should carry the ass. As they try to carry the ass over a bridge leading into town, the ass kicks and falls into the river. Trying to please everyone the miller pleased no one and lost the ass in the bargain.

[1] The fable tells of a monkey who wanted to pull some roasted chestnuts from the fire and used the paws of the cat, his friend, for the job.

[2] See p. 206, n. 3.

and suffer wrongfully for the fault of his fingers, unless holding his pen be sufficient to render them guilty as receivers. If he be toward the Law, he only does the summersault over the bar, and is forbidden all other practise during life, that he may apply himself wholly to his own way, in which his abilities are capable to do his country better service than in any other. He is the Devil's Amanuensis, that writes what he dictates, and draws up his deeds of darkness.

A GAMESTER

Is a merchant adventurer, that trades in the bottom of a dice-box—Three bales of *Fulhams*[1] and a small stock in cash sets him. He seldom ventures but he insures beforehand. He is but a juggler of the better sort; for the one's box and dice, and the other's box and balls are not very unlike; and the slight of hand in managing these is the mastery of both their arts. He throws dice for his living, as some condemn'd to be hang'd do for their lives. He pays custom to the box for all he imports; and an ordinary is his port. He shakes his dice like a rattlesnake; and he that he fastens upon is sure to be bitten, and sometimes swells till he breaks. He takes infinite pains to render himself able in his calling, and with perpetual practise of his hand and tools arrives at great perfection, if the Hangman do not spoil his palming with an untimely hot iron.[2] His box and dice are his horn-ring[3] and knife, with which he will dissect an insufficient gamester's pocket alive, and finger his money before his face. He never cuts the cards, but he cuts a purse, and when he deals the cards he sells them. He never stakes anything but his conscience, which is none of his own; for the Devil has the keeping of it, and he ticks with him for it upon reputation. He trusts his false dice to themselves, but never ventures a true one without a slur or topping. The rook is his affidavit-man,[4] and he lets him go half a crown now and then, that he may swear it out upon occasion, and judge always on his side right or wrong. Besides this is business is to fancy for him, for he is superstitious that

---

[1] A cant term for false dice, which ran high or low, depending on how they were loaded.

[2] See p. 228, n. 2.

[3] Horn-ring; also, horn-thumb: a thimble of horn worn by cutpurses on the thumb, for resisting the edge of the knife in cutting purses. See also p. 165, n. 6.

[4] See p. 75, n. 7.

way, and will rather bar his own cast than go against the conscience of his fancy. He differs nothing from a common pickpocket, but that he does the same thing by another method, and so much a worse, as he picks a man's reason and reputation as well as his pocket. After he has spent all his own time and a great deal of other mens money he becomes known, and so avoided; or else new tricks come in play, which he is too old to learn, and so dwindles to a rook, and at last leaves the world as poor as almes-ace.[5] The cheat and gull with equal hope for one anothers money cope; but the former being of confederacy with the dice, they and he easily run down the other.

AN HECTOR[1]

Is master of the noble science of offence and defence, a mungrel Knight[a]-errant, that is always upon adventures. His calling is to call those to accompt, that he thinks have more money, and less to shew for their valour than himself. These are his tributaries, and when he is out of repair, he demands reparation of them. His skill consists in the prudent conduct of his quarrels, that he may not be drawn to fight the enemy but upon advantages. He is all for light skirmishes and pickeering,[2] but cares not to engage his whole body, but where he is sure to come off. He is an exact judge of honour, and can hit the very mathematic line between valour and cowardise. He gets more by treaties than fights, as the French are said to have done by the English. When he finds himself overpowr'd he draws up his forces as wide in the front as he can, though but three deep, and so faces the enemy, while he draws off in safety, tho' sometimes with the loss of his baggage, that is his honour. He is as often employ'd as a Herald,[3] to proclaim war, defy the enemy, and offer battle, in which desperate service he behaves himself with punctual formality, and is secur'd in his person by the law of nations. He is *Py-powder*[4] of all quarrels, affronts, and misprisions of affronts, rencounters, rants, as-

---

[5] Almes-ace: ames ace or ambs-ace—i.e., two aces, the smallest throw at dice.
[1] See p. 106, n. 2.
[a] Knight] Kn^t.
[2] See p. 255, n. 4.
[3] See p. 115, n. 1.
[4] Variation of piepowder, a traveling man, a wayfarer, especially an itinerant merchant or trader. [*O.E.D.*]

saults and batteries, and invasions by kick, cudgel, or the lye, that fall out among the sons of Priam,[5] the brethren of the hilt and scabbard, that have taken the Croysade upon them, to fight against the Infidel, that will not trust; and he determines whether they are actionable, and will bear a duel, or not. He never surrenders without flying colours, and bullet in mouth. He professes valour but to put it off, and keeps none for his own use, as Doctors never take physic, nor Lawyers go to law. When he is engag'd in a quarrel, he talks and looks as big as he can, as dogs, when they fall out, set up the bristles of their backs, to seem taller than they are. It is safer for a man to venture his life than his conversation upon him.

AN HIGHWAYMAN

Is a wild Arab, that lives by robbing of small caravans, and has no *way* of living but the King's *highway*. Aristotle held him to be but a kind of huntsman;[1] but our sages of the law account him rather a beast of prey, and will not allow his game to be legal by the forest law.[2] His chief care is to be well mounted, and, when he is taken, the law takes care he should be so still while he lives. His business is to break the laws of the land, for which the hangman breaks his neck, and there's an end of the controversie. He fears nothing, under the gallows, more than his own face, and therefore when he does his work conveys it out of sight, that it may not rise up in judgment, and give evidence against him at the sessions. His trade is to take purses and evil courses, and when he is taken himself the laws take as evil a course with him. He takes place of all other thieves as the most heroical, and one that comes nearest to the old Knights errant, though he is really one of the basest, that never ventures but upon surprizal, and where he is sure of the advantage. He lives like a Tartar always in motion, and the inns upon the road are his hoordes, where he reposes for a while, and spends his time and money, when he is out of action. These are his close confederates and allies, though the common interest of both will not permit it to be

---

[5] Butler apparently plays on the term *hector* as a degeneration of the name of that magnanimous Trojan chieftain and eldest son of Priam.

[1] I have found no source for this view of Aristotle's.

[2] See p. 265, n. 2.

known. He is more destructive to a grasier than the murrain,[3] and as terrible as the Huon-cry[4] to himself. When he dispatches his business between sun and sun he invades a whole county,[5] and like the long Parliament robs by representative.[6] He receives orders from his superior officer the setter, that sets him on work and others to pay him for it. He calls concealing what he takes from his comrades *sinking*, which they account a great want of integrity, and when he is discover'd he loses the reputation of an honest and just man with them for ever after. After he has rov'd up and down too long he is at last set himself, and convey'd to the jail, the only place of his residence, where he is provided of a hole to put his head in, and gather'd to his fathers in a faggot cart.

AN HOST

Is the greatest stranger in his own house of all that come to it; for, like an *Italian* Cardinal, he resigns up the whole command of himself and his family to all that visit him.[1] He keeps open house for all comers to entertain himself. His sign and he have one and the same employment, to invite and draw in guests, and what the one does by dumb show without doors the other interprets within. He bids a man welcome to his own table, and invites him with hearty kindness and all freedom to treat himself. There is no ability so requisite in him as that of drinking, in which the whole manage of his affairs consists; and the larger his talent is that way the more he thrives in his trade: for his materials cost him nothing, and he is paid for his pains, beside the many opportunities he lights on to cheat and misreckon, and turn and wind the business of his cellar with a quicker trade. His hostler is both host and chamberlayn to the horses; and his province is to cheat and misreckon them in their meat, as the other does their masters in their drink. He is like the old Philosopher or Statesman choose ye

---

[3] A wasting disease among cattle; the rot.

[4] See p. 242, n. 4.

[5] See p. 31, n. 10.

[6] On the Long Parliament see p. 84, n. 9. To pursue the Civil Wars the Houses of Parliament, fighting in the name of the king, "used against him the revenues which he had enjoyed, as well as the taxes which they had the power to levy in their own right." [Trevelyan, *England Under the Stuarts*, p. 199.]

[1] I have found no explanation to amplify this simile.

whether, that was never less at home than when he was at home, that is when he had fewest guests;[2] for being nothing of himself, the more he is of that, the less he is of any thing else. He is like the catholic church, to which all men are welcome for their money, and nobody without it. He is the only true instance of that old saying—*nusquam est qui ubique est*;[3] for by being the same to all people that come from all places, he is nobody himself, and of no place. He is a highwayman, for he lives upon it, but in a regular way, yet holds intelligence with all interlopers, and if there were no more that rob'd upon the kings highway it were well for the nation. He pays nothing for his lodging, that brings a horse into his stall, as rooks pay nothing that bring chouses to ordinaries, for the poor dumb creature pays for all.

AN IGNORANT MAN

Has his opinions contracted within a narrow compass, which renders them the more intense and violent. He is one half of all the vexations of mankind, which the knave and he divide equaly between them; and though[a] his ignorance be the mother of devotion (as the church of *Rome* very ingenuously confesses) all the rest of the kindred are the basest breed and generation in the whole world, and obstinacy is ever of the elder house and chief of the family. The extremity of his defects (as contraries do in nature) produces the same effects with other mens abundance; for he believes himself sufficiently qualified, because he does not understand his own wants. His understanding is hidebound and straitlac'd, which makes it more stiff and uneasy than those that are free and active. And as among beggars he that is most maim'd, and can shew most sores is esteem'd the ablest man in his calling: so he, that is most voluble in expressing and shewing his ignorance and confidence, is esteem'd by the rest of his own latitude for the most excellent and incomparable person. The

---

[2] Cicero, *De Officiis*: "Cato, who was of about the same years, Marcus, my son, as that Publius Scipio who first bore the surname of Africanus, has given us the statement that Scipio used to say that he was never less idle than when he had nothing to do and never less lonely than when he was alone." [Trans. Walter Miller (London and New York, 1913), III. I. 1.]

[3] "The man who is everywhere is nowhere." [Seneca, *Epistles*, trans. Gummere, II. 2.]

[a] and though] and: though

less he understands of any thing, the more confident he is of it; and because he knows no better himself believes nobody else does. His dull ignorance has the same operation with the wiser part of the world as lead has in the test of metals, that being apply'd to gold carries away all the baser metals that are mixt with it, and leaves only the pure behind. He makes more noise with his emptiness, like a tub, than others do that are full; and some late philosophers, that have found out a way by knocking at a door to find how many persons are in a room,[1] may much more easily discover by his noise how little is in him. His dull temper, like lead, is easily melted into any passion, and as quickly cold again, whereas solider metals are the more difficult to be wrought upon.

IMPERTINENT

Is one that straggles always from the purpose, and goes about every thing he undertakes, and fetches a compass, as if he meant to attack it in the rear, but never comes near enough to engage. He will make as many doubles as a hare, to render those at a loss, that would willingly know what he would be at. He is a weft and stray, that is always taken up far from home, or a child, that has lost it self, and knows not whence it came, nor whither it would go. He is always losing of his way and fain to go back again, and round about to get into it again. He is an outlyer that will not be confin'd by any thing that is to the purpose. He omits no circumstance, though it be far enough out of his way, but expatiates, not as if he went about his occasions, but rambled for his pleasure. He is like a watch out of order, though he be ever so often set right, he will be sure to go wrong again. He never comes near the mark, but always carries too high, or too low, or wide. Men are finer upon holidays when they do nothing than on other days when they follow their business; and he believes himself a much finer man when he talks impertinently and to no purpose, than if he came directly to the matter, and fell close to the business; for, for one man that is impertinent out of downright ignorance, ten are so out of affectation and conceipt, and believe they please others, because they please themselves; for this folly is more frequently found in overdoing of things than any other mistake. As a

---

[1] See p. 124, n. 11.

lyar is never believ'd when he tells truth; so an impertinent person is never regarded when he speaks to the purpose: howsoever though he observes, that nobody attends to what he says, yet he goes on and talks to himself as fools and madmen use to do in public; for he is resolv'd to hear himself out, though nobody else will.

AN IMPOSTOR

Is a great undertaker, and as great an under-performer; for his business being only to profess, he believes he deals fairly with the world in having done that, and is not engag'd to proceed any further; for he takes so much pains to get opinion and belief, that it is not to be expected he should be able, or at leasure to do any thing else; as shopkeepers, that sell and put off their wares, and study how to get custom, have no time to work and labour themselves, and commonly understand nothing of the manufacture of that which they deal in, for to profess much and perform too is more than the business of one man. He is so prodigal of his promises, that of so many thousands, which he has made, he was never known to keep one: for they are the only commodity he deals in, and he gets his living by putting them off; and the quicker trade he has, the better he thrives; for they drive no mean trade, that live by turning and winding of their words. All the force of his art and knowledge lyes in his face, as *Sampson's* strength did in his hair; for it is proof against any impression whatsoever: and though he finds himself detected by the wiser part of the world he disdains that, and fortifies himself with the better judgment of the ignorant, which he is sure will never fail him. All his abilities consist in his impudence; and the instrument, with which he does all his feats, like an elephant's proboscis, grows on his face: for he gets employment and credit by giving himself countenance, which he esteems more honourable than to receive it from another. He never goes without some dull easy believer and under-cheat, whose office is to cry him up and lye for him, and with him he stalks as a fowler does with his horse. He will offer great advantages for such slight and trivial consideration, that the very cheapness of his undertakings argues they are counterfeit, or that he never came honestly by them, otherwise he could not part with them upon such terms. He never shows his judgment more than in his choice of those he has to deal with; for the impostor and gull, when they are fitly match'd, draw in one another like the male and female screw; and the one contributes as much as the other to the business.

AN INCENDIARY

Blows fire out of his mouth like a jugler, as the *Roman* slave did, when he set all Sicily on a flame.[1] He lays a train[2] at men's ears to blow them up with like the powder-plot.[3] He is like *meum and tuum*,[4] that sets all men together by the ears. His whole business is to break the peace wheresoever he finds it, and cancel all obligations between friends. He is an Immoderator of controversies and promoter of contention. He makes quarrels, as others end them, by intercession; and as things of different natures commonly agree in a third, those of the same kind differ in him. He is like the clapper of a bell, that hangs in the middle, and yet makes both sides clamour against one another. He is a pimp and procurer of malice and hatred between party and party, which in the end commonly falls all upon himself. All his endeavours are so foolish, that they beget nothing but an ill understanding between those he has to do with; and when he is discovered the bastard is laid at his own door. He sets men at a distance, that they may encounter with the greater force, as rams and tilters use to fight; and divides them, that they may meet with the greater fury. He takes part with both sides till the quarrel is determined, and then he is always found to be for the strongest, and was so really from the beginning, before he knew how it would fall out, which argues him to be a man of great prudence and foresight, and no less integrity; for he was for the prevailing side, before any body else knew which it was.

---

[1] Eunus incited the slaves in Sicily to arms for the cause of liberty in the Servile War, beginning 135 B.C. To prove the divine inspiration which he claimed, Eunus secretly placed in his mouth a nut filled with sulphur and fire and, by gentle breathing, shot forth a flame as he spoke. [Lucius Annaeus Florus, *Epitome of Roman History*, trans. Edward Seymour Forster (London and New York, 1929, II. vii.]

[2] See p. 242, n. 2.

[3] A suggestion of the Gunpowder Plot, in which some Roman Catholics planned to blow up the House of Parliament, November 5, 1605, while the King and the houses of Lords and Commons were meeting. Robert Catesby and Guy Fawkes were central figures in this plot, which was revealed by one of the members before its execution. See also p. 242 for mention of "Powder Traytor."

[4] Mine and thine: used to express the rights of property.

AN INFORMER

Is a wolf held by the ears, that no sooner gets loose but he flys at the throat of those that held him. He has a licence to say what he pleases, that others may do so too that have none, and betray themselves first for him to do it afterwards: for perfidiousness in him, like faith in others, comes by hearing. He usurps the same liberty that public fame does, to alter and add to what he hears, until it become fit to his purpose. If he can but catch a man by the tongue, as the mastif dog did the lion,[1] he will easily destroy him, though he has ten times his own abilities. He has a subtle way of destroying with a whisper, and like a serpent blasts with his breath; it is as dangerous to talk with him, as it is to eat with a poysoner. The most frequent places where he plys at present are coffee houses, where he has free admission into all companies, and as freely undiscover'd sets what covey he pleases, while they perceive nothing, until the net is drawn over them. He blows up a man before he is aware like white gunpowder, that is said to make no noise when it is fir'd, and he never knows from whence it comes. He makes it his business, like the Devil, to accuse as many as he can, and does it with the very same secrecy, without appearing to make good his objections; for neither of them will endure to be seen in the matter. He is very careful to conceal himself, and so are those that employ him; for when he is once discover'd he is disabled from doing them any further service in his occupation, which is so odious to all men, that it is never pardonable but when it is done for some public good, and yet he is never after thought fit to be trusted. Nevertheless he is useful in all governments; for without him no conspiracy would be so apt to miscarry as we find it is, and consequently no government so securely subsist; so naturally wicked is the world, that the best things of it are forc'd to depend upon the evil.

A JAILOR

Is a keeper of the liberties, for he keeps them safe enough from all those that are in his custody. He is a kind of secular Devil, for when the sentence of the law is past upon a man, he is deliver'd

---

[1] I have found no source for this fable.

over to him, until he is reconcil'd to the civil power. When men have run out of all, and 'tis too late, he keeps them in, secures them from themselves, as the poet says, and from the foe, that is their vices; for vice, like other dependances, will forsake those that are not able to maintain it. He is like a raven, that picks out the eyes, and feeds upon those poor creatures only that are fast in the briars, and never meddles with those that are at liberty. His stone walls, and iron grates, and himself are all of a piece, and all equaly sensible of compassion. He makes those of his captives that have any money to buy sleep of him at his own rates, whether they use it or not, and pay him rent for a hole to be buried alive in, otherwise they are remov'd to the common hole, and tumbled in all-together, as they use to do the bodies of poor people in the time of a great mortality. There they live, as they do at ordinaries, upon scraps of broken meat and the revenues of the box. He keeps his doors always shut, as if the house were visited, as indeed it is with a malady not much inferior to the pestilence. He has a trick to commit one leg prisoner to the other, that they may not combine to run away together. His mansion is a kind of civil *Bedlam*, where those, that run out of their estates, which is all one with running out of their wits, are shut up, or whip'd, to be cur'd; and he compels those to keep within compass, that would not be persuaded to do so before. He keeps a live lumber-house, where decay'd men are pawn'd and laid up under lock and key, until they become forfeit to be ex- pos'd at the grate, or are in a condition to be redeem'd, or hang'd out in public like frippery. As for criminals, he delivers them over to *Satan* the hangman, to wear hempen cravats, or in exchange to have their hands held up with a hot iron[1] to pray for the King. As thorns and brambles, though they are the curse of the earth, are yet the fittest to make hedges of; so the worst of men are most proper to be made Jailors.

A JUROR

Is a sworn officer, that takes his oath to measure other mens oaths by like a standard; and if they agree not perfectly, they will not pass for good and lawful perjuries, but are void and of none effect. He plys at a court of justice as a rook does at a gaming ordinary,

---

[1] See p. 228, n. 2.

that though his name be not in the list, if any that are *make default*, he may come in with a *tales*,[1] and do a job of justice on the bye. His business is to pass on mens lives and fortunes, in which he might make himself considerable advantages, if it were not for his conscience, but chiefly his ears, which he knows not well how to preserve, or be without: for if they were lost he were incapable of dealing any more in his profession, and while he keeps them they lose him more than his head is worth. His employment is a kind of work of darkness; for, when he is upon service, he is shut up without fire or candle, (as Cardinals are at the election of a new Pope) that his conscience may play at *blindman's-buff* with the rest of his fellows, until they are all tie'd into the right or wrong, and *agreed among themselves*, whose fortune it is to be hang'd, and whose but undone, which, if they had but been allow'd light, they might have done as well by casting lots, or throwing *cross or pile*.[2] His jurisdiction extends but to *matter of fact*, in which words are included by a figure in law: for words, that will *bear an action*, are held sufficient to make one, as the law makes no difference between *bearing* of witness and *making* of it. His oaths, though of less bore, are found to do greater execution than those of common swearers; for wheresoever they hit they either kill or maim.

A LAMPOONER

Is a moss-trooping[1] Poetaster, for they seldom go alone, whose occupation is to rob any that lights in his way of his reputation, if he has any to lose. Common fame and detraction are his setters, and as those describe persons to him he falls upon them; but, as he is for the most part misinform'd, he often comes off with the worst, and, if he did not know how to conceal himself would suffer severely for doing nothing. He is a western-pug[2]-poet, that has something to say to everyone he meets, and there go as many of them to a libel, as there do slaves to an oar. He has just as much learning as to tell the

---

[1] See p. 64, n. 3.

[2] See p. 233, n. 4.

[1] Mosstrooper: one of a group of seventeenth-century freebooters who infested the border country between England and Scotland, an area called the *mosses* because of its mossy or boggy character.

[2] Western pug: a man who navigated barges down the Thames to London. [Skeat and Mayhew, *Glossary of Tudor and Stuart Words*.]

first letter of a man's name, but can go no further,[3] and therefore makes a virtue of necessity, and by selling all makes it pass for wit. His Muse is a kind of owl, that preys in the dark, and dares not show her face by day, a Bulker[4] that plys by owl-light, and he dares not own her for fear of beating hemp,[5] or being beaten and kick'd down stairs. He is a Jackpudding[6] Satyr, that has something to say to all that come near him, and has no more respect of persons than a Quaker. His Muse is of the same kind of breed with his that rimes in taverns, but not altogether so fluent, nor by much so generous and authentic as a Ballad-makers; for his works will never become so classic as to be receiv'd into a Sive,[7] nor published in the street to a courtly new tune. He loves his little tiny wit much better than his friend or himself; for he will venture a whipping in earnest, rather than spare another man in jest. He is like a witch that makes pictures according to his own fancy, and calls them by the names of those, whom he would willingly do a mischief to if he could, without their knowing from whence it comes. He hears himself often call'd Rascal and Villain to his face, but believes himself unconcern'd, because having abus'd men behind their backs he thinks he is only liable in justice to a punishment of the same nature.

A LIAR

Is a crooked gun, that carries wrong, and his bore is a great deal too big for his bullet. He is an ill bowler, that never comes near the jack,[1] but is always wide or narrow, or gone a mile. He dreams waking, and talks in his sleep, disguises everything he sees or hears, and, like the *Devil* his father, makes it take what airy shape he pleases. He has a natural antipathy to truth, as some have to cheese and cats,

---

[3] I.e., the lampooner writes the first letter of a name and a line, when the victim is mentioned.

[4] A prostitute.

[5] Petty rogues, in Bridewell, pound hemp; and possibly the product of their work may be used for rope with which greater criminals are hanged. [Nash, ed., *Hudibras*, II. iii. 370–71 n.]

[6] See p. 44, n. 44.

[7] Sive: obsolete form of *sieve*—here a figurative use, suggesting that only classic works remain after the process of judgments through time filter out lesser works.

[1] For the game of bowls, see p. 58, n. 16.

but can give no reason for it, or if he could, would not, except it were a false one. He is like a glass, that represents that left which is right, and right left, or a screw'd gun,[2] that will carry a bullet bigger than his bore. He is a false medium, that represents things otherways than they are. He suits his protestations proportionable to the size of his narratives, and the larger they are, the more oaths he allows to make room for them. Nothing delights him so much as to find himself believ'd; for as he cannot lye alone, so he, that seems to credit him, blows the bellows of his organ, and then he pleases himself so much with his own voluntary,[3] that at length he swallows his own lyes, and believes himself. He is so just as to do no more to another, than he would have done to himself; for he will believe any mans legends, that will allow of his, and though he knows himself to be a lyar, he is not apt to suspect another man to be so. When he meets with unbelievers he endeavors to convert them to the faith by swearing and damning himself; for oaths with him are but the vehicles of lies; and if that will not do, he gives them over for reprobates. His discourse is a kind of microscope, that represents things much bigger than they are, but not so true to the object. He is a great forger, clipper, and counterfeiter of truth, and like the *Dutchman* that coin'd old groats rather than fail,[4] will quote authority for his own imaginations. If his faculty be only narrative he seldom means any hurt, but only lyes to please himself, and because he does so, believes he pleases others; and when they laugh at his indiscretion, believes they do it at his wit. When he lyes earnestly he commonly puts his face into a posture, and looks about him to see who is most like to believe, as bowlers screw their bodies that way they would have the bowl run. If his talent tend to bragging and vapouring, you will find the biass of all his narrations turn'd that way; and as archers, that shoot with a side wind, take their aim wide of the clout, so does he, that the wind of vainglory may convey his arrow to the mark. This makes him sally into many impertinent circumstances, to no purpose, but that of his own vanity, and if he can but make you believe in him, he will afterwards believe in you, and conclude himself to be really what you take him for. He that will humour him may screw him up, like a fiddlestring, to any pitch, and make him speak higher and higher, till

[2] See p. 195, n. 2.
[3] See p. 227, n. 1.
[4] I have not discovered a source for this reference.

he cracks. They say he draws a strong bow, but never comes near the clout; But as an arrow shot from a bow makes an arch in the air like that of the bow, from which it was shot; so all his narratives are, like himself, false, that never hit point blank but only fly at rovers. No man is a lyar, that does not pretend to tell truth, as a player deceives nobody, because he professes to do it, and he deserves best when he does it most. If he should tell truth he would be false to himself, and deceive as many as when he lyes. He allows London measure[5] to all his stories, but stretches them so unmercifully, that they always prove scant upon the tryal.

A MERCHANT

Is a water-spaniel that fetches and carrys from one country to another. Nature can hide nothing out of his reach from the bottom of the deepest seas to the tops of the highest rocks, but he hunts it out and bears it away. He ransacks all seas and lands to feed his avarice, as the old *Romans* did their luxury; and runs to the end of the rainbow to find a bag of gold, as they persuade children. He calls all ships that are laden good ships, and all that are rich good men. He forsakes the dry land, and betakes himself to wind and water, where he is made, or mar'd, like a glass either blown into a good fortune, or broken in pieces. His trade being upon the sea partakes of the nature of it; for he grows rich no way so soon as by devouring others of his own kind, as fishes use to do, and gains most by losing sometimes to make others do so, that are not able to bear it, and thereby leave the whole trade to him. He calls newes advice, which he and his correspondent make by confederacy, to terrify with false alarms of ships lost or cast away, that are safe and out of danger, those, that have ventures[1] upon them, to insure at excessive rates, and pay 30 per cent[a] for taking a commodity of lies off his hand; for he always gains more by false newes, as well as false wares, than by true, until he is discover'd, and then he must think of new ones. The more ignorant and barbarous people are, the more he gets by dealing with them;

---

[5] It was a practice of London drapers in that day to allow something above the standard yard in measurements. [*O.E.D.*]

[1] Dangers or hazards; especially commercial enterprises in which there is considerable risk of loss as well as chance of gain.

[a] per cent] 'p cent

glass beads and copper rings pass for jewels among the *Indians*, and they part with right gold for them. He studys nothing (beside his own books) but almanacs and weathercocks, and takes every point of the compass into serious consideration. His hopes and fears turn perpetualy with the wind, and he is sea-sick after a storm, as if he had been in it, and runs to a conjurer to know how the Devil has dealt with him, and whether he may be confident and put his trust in him. His soul is so possest with traffick, that if all churches had not made souls a commodity and religion a trade, he had never been of any; but if the Pope would but give him leave to farm purgatory, he would venture to give more than ever was made of it, and let no soul out, how mean soever, that did not pay double fees. One of the chiefest parts of his ability in his profession consists in understanding when to break judiciously, and to the greatest advantage; for by that means, when he has compounded his debts at an easy rate, he is like a broken bone well set, stronger than he was before. As for his credit, if he has cheated sufficiently and to the purpose, he rather improves than lessens it; for men are trusted in the world for what they have, not what they are.

THE MODISH MAN

Is an orthodox gallant, that does not vary in the least article of his life, conversation, apparel, and address from the doctrine and discipline of the newest and best reform'd modes of the time. He understands exactly to a day what times of the year the several and respective sorts of colour'd ribbands[1] come to be in season, and when they go out again. He sees no plays but only such as he finds most approv'd by men of his own rank and quality, and those he is never absent from, as oft as they are acted, mounts his bench between the acts, pulls off his peruque, and keeps time with his comb and motion of his person exactly to the music. He censures truly and faithfully according to the best of his memory, as he has receiv'd it from the newest and most modish opinions, without altering or adding any thing of his own contriving, *so help him God*. It costs him a great deal of study and practise to pull off[a] his hat judiciously and in form,

---

[1] Great loops of ribbons decorating the outer side of the loose breeches and garters were quite fashionable in the time of Charles II.

[a] off] of

according to the best precedents, and to hold it, when it is off, without committing the least oversight. All his salutes, motions, and addresses are, like true *French* wine, right as they came over, without any mixture or sophistication of his own, *damn him upon his honour.* His dancing-master does not teach, but manage him like a great horse; and he is not learnt, but broken to all the tricks and shews. He is as scrupulous as a *Catholic* of eating any meat that is not perfectly in season, that is, in fashion, and drest according to the canon of the church, unless it be at a *French* house, where no sort of meat is at any time out of season, because the place it self is modish, and the more he pays for it and is cheated, the better he believes he is treated. He is very punctual in his oaths, and will not swear any thing but what the general concurrence of the most accomplisht persons of his knowledge will be ready, upon occasion, to make good. He omits no occasion to insinuate his pretences to the pox, and would not willingly be thought so rude and ill-bred, as to be unfurnish'd of a clap at any time, although, as modesty makes men commit many faults, if that would give him leave to confess the truth, he is far enough from deserving it, though he wears his hand always in his codpiece,[2] and a syringe[3] in his pocket to produce like a certificate, if he should have occasion to be question'd; and, rather than fail, will give his instrument injection before sufficient and credible witnesses, to clear his reputation in the opinion of the world: for he endeavours to appear an honest man, that makes a conscience of his ways, and would not willingly assume any thing, that is not his right. But if this will not do, rather than be thought to have got it, *Needham's* way,[4] by popular contagion, he will name some Lady, that sent it him for a present; for it is ten to one they never come to a personal treaty; and if there be any thing in it, he got it by proxy from some common sinner, that dealt in the name of a person of quality; for those do frequently lye with cullies, as embassadors do with queens,[5] in the names of great ladies and persons of quality.

---

[2] The codpiece (see p. 252, n. 2) served as a pocket in which purse, handkerchief, etc. could be put.

[3] Ned Ward (*The London Spy,* Pt. IV) makes reference to a doctor's use of a "water-syrenge" for the cure of gonorrhea and other venereal diseases.

[4] The common way; need, poverty, beggary, by a punning allusion to *need,* from the small town of Needham, near Ipswich in Suffolk.

[5] In the sense of "queans," or harlots.

A MUSITIAN

Is his own *Syren*,[1] that turns himself into a beast with musick of his own making. His perpetual study to raise *passion* has utterly debas'd his *reason*; and as music is wont to set false values upon things, the constant use of it has render'd him a stranger to all true ones. *David* play'd an evil spirit out of *Saul*, but he plays one into himself, that is never to be got out again. This puts him into the condition of a traytor, whom men hate but love the treason; so they delight in music, but have no kindness for a musitian. The *scale* of music is like the *ladder* that *Jacob* saw in a dream, reaching to heaven with angels ascending and descending; for there is no art in the world that can raise the mind of man higher, but it is but in a dream, and when the music is done, the mind wakes and comes to it self again.

> Music is beauty to the ear,
> That charms the souls of all that hear.

And therefore a musitian, that makes it his constant employment, is like one that does nothing but make love, that is half mad, fantastic, and ridiculous to those that are unconcern'd. *Cupid* strings his bow with the strings of an instrument, and wounds hearts through the ear. He winds up souls, like watches, with a lute-string, and when he sets church music and mollets[2]

> Attracts devotion with his airs and words
> To string her beades upon his charming chords.

THE NEGLIGENT

And his business are ill matcht, for they can never agree, but are always falling out and leaving one another. He is never in perfect mind and memory; for he forgets every thing, though it be ever so near to him, if he be not perpetualy put in mind and prompted. He does not love to be beholden or troublesome to himself of all men living, and had rather be dispos'd of by any other person. He is a

---

[1] See p. 139, n. 4.
[2] Mallets?—i.e., plucks or strums?

bird of the air, that neither sows nor reaps, nor gathers into barns.[1]
He delights in nothing but his ease, and yet is so ill an husband of it,
that he will make it away before it falls to him for a very small trifle
in hand. Every mans tongue runs before his wit; for while he listens
to one thing he thinks of another, and forgets both, and then asks
what was that you were saying. His scull has sprung a leak, and whatsoever is put in it runs out again faster than it went in; and he does
not hear at his ears but a crack, like one that listens at a chink. He
keeps no accompt of anything, but trusts to his memory for no other
reason but because it always betrays him. He is indifferent to all persons, times, and occasions, and whosoever lights upon him first has a
right to him, like a thing lost, and may keep possession of him as long
as he pleases. He lays his time and all things else that concern him
out of the way, and when he has occasion to make use of them, he
knows not where to find them. He lives windbound all the days of
his life, and has nothing to do but to wait for a fair gale to carry him
into another world. All his thoughts interrupt one another, and will
not give him leave to attend to any thing, but rambles like one that
dreams waking, or talks in his sleep. He makes even with the world,
and neglects it just as much as it does him; so that there is no love
lost between them both. He does all his business according to the
order and process of nature, conceives and grows big of it, is brought
to bed and lyes in, but has a very hard labour, as it commonly befalls
all abortions and miscarriages. He is a man of happy memory, as the
dead are said to be; for he remembers just as much as they. He
neglects his own affairs as if they did concern him less than other
mens, like the lawyer, that could not endure to trouble himself with
his own affairs, because he took no fees for them.

AN OFFICER

Is a mungrel of a mixt generation—Nature meant him for a
man, but his office intervening put her out, and made him another
thing; and as he loses his name in his authority, so he does his nature.
The most predominant part in him is that in which he is something
beside himself, which renders him so like a madman, that some be-

---

[1] Cf. Matthew VI. 26: "Behold the fowls of the air: for they sow not, neither
do they reap, nor gather into barns."

lieve he is within a straw of it. He was nothing of himself, but had a great ambition to be something, and so got an office, which he stands more upon than if he had been more of himself; for having no intrinsic value he has nothing to trust to but the stamp that is set upon him, and so is necessitated to make as much of that as he can. This makes him take more upon him than his authority will bear, which he endeavours to relieve like the country fellow, that rode with a sack of corn on his own back to ease his horse. The meaner his authority is, the more insolence he allows to make it up, like the hangman who has the basest of all, and yet it extends to life and limb, and has power to hang and draw within his own territories. He bears himself and his office very untowardly, and kicks and flings like a horse, that has not been us'd to carry double. If his place be of profit he plays high, and takes all that is set him, but rams his bags so full, that they will not tye, but are apt to scatter what they hold; for when he is taken himself he departs his politic life, and as he brought nothing into it, so he carries nothing out of it. He is a person of a double capacity public and private, and that may be one reason, why he is said to deal doubly with all men that have to do with him. He is but a pimp to his place; for any man that will give him money may do what he pleases with it, but nothing without it.

AN OPPRESSOR

Is said to grind the faces of the poor, because he holds their noses to the grindstone. He is like the Spaniards of Potosi, that make their sheep bear burdens, as well as fleeces, on their backs, and supply him by extraordinary ways more heavy than those they were design'd for. He lays the heaviest weights upon those that yield easiest to them; like the foundation of London bridge upon woolsacks,[1] that rests upon a soft cushion for its ease; and, therefore, the poorer and weaker men are, the fitter and easier he always finds them for his purpose. Where Fortune has begun to oppress a man he presently strikes in and seconds her, and like a right bloodhound hunts none but a wounded deer. He is as barbarous as those inhuman people that

---

[1] "London Bridge was built upon woolpacks": a saying stemming from the fact that in the reign of Henry II the new stone bridge over the Thames was paid for by a tax on wool. [*Brewer's Dictionary of Phrase and Fable.*]

dwell upon the coasts of rugged seas, and live by robbing all those, whom the less cruel sea has spared and cast upon them; for he makes other mens wrecks his returns, and ships that are cast away bring him a prosperous voyage. He is a Hun, that when he is thirsty opens a vein and sucks the blood of the poor beast that bears him. He loves his neighbour's goods better than his own, and rejoices more over one pound that he comes sinfully by, than ninety nine that are righteously gotten, and need no repentance. He believes a man gains nothing by that which is his due, and therefore is not at all the better for it; but that which comes, where nothing could be expected or demanded, is like a present that he makes himself, and how mean soever ought to receive a value from the good will of the giver. He is so kind and goodnatur'd, that he loves to have something of every mans to remember him by; but does not care to put any man to the trouble of preserving any thing that is his. Tis natural for gamesters to love other mens money better than their own, else they would never venture to lose that which they are certain of to win that which is uncertain; and as the philosopher said, of all wines another mans wines are[a] ever the best, he is confident it is much more true of another man's money.

A PARASITE

Feeds himself by feeding another man's humour. His tongue keeps his teeth in constant employment, and he lives by eating in praise of the founder. He quarters his gluttony upon another man's vainglory, and pays him with praises which he has no right to; for if he had, he needs not pay for that which is his due. *Thus one vice lives upon another*, and all support themselves by mutual commerce and trade, as well as men in civil societies. He feeds upon him that treats him, as fire does upon fuel, and consumes him by making him shine bright for a while. He that praises a man deservedly gives him nothing but his own, but he that extolls him without merit, presents him with that which he wants. He is a guest by his calling, and his occupation is to eat upon free cost and flattery. He victuals himself, as our merchants do at *Madagascar*, for glass-beads, which he hangs in the ears of those that feed him. He is of a wild and savage kind naturaly, but being fed at hand becomes very tame and fawning,

---

[a] are] is

especialy to those that give him meat. He eates to all that love and
honour them, and devours all the prosperity in the world to their
inclinations. He expresses a singular devotion to a person by dining
with him, as the ancients did to *Jupiter* by eating with his statue.[1]
He *deifies*[a] that which feeds him, as the Ægyptians did their leeks,[2]
tastes all his humours, as well as his dishes, and magnifies both with
admirable judgment—He goes as true to all his humours, as the
weather-glass[3] rises and falls in warm or cold weather, and like a
puny[b] setting-dog is glad to sett his meat, and creep upon his belly
on the ground, before he is allow'd to touch it. He does not dine, but
baites, and like a *Spanish* mule carries his provender about his neck,
and his rider, that feeds him, on his back—at the same time. He is
every man's domestic, that keepes a good *house*.

THE PERFIDIOUS MAN

Lives by his faith as well as a righteous man, but is like one
that spends out of the main stock, until he is run out of all. His word
is a cobweb, very frail of itself, yet strong enough to catch flyes, and

---

[1] Reference to *epulum Iovis*, or feast of Jupiter, in which three deities (Jupiter, Juno, and Minerva) seem to have been present in the form of their statues, Jupiter having a couch and each goddess a *sella*, and to have shared the meal with the senate and magistrates. [*Encyclopaedia Britannica*.]

[a] *deifies*] alternate wording: *adores*

[2] Cf. Juvenal, *Satires*, XV. 1–2, 8–11:

> Quis nescit . . . qualia demens
> Ægyptus portenta colat? . . .
> . . . . nemo Dianam.
> Porrum et caepe nefas violare, aut frangere morsu.
> O sanctas gentes, quibis haec nascuntur in nortis
> Numia!

("Who knows not . . . what monsters demented Egypt Worships? . . . None adore Diana, but it is an impious outrage to crunch leeks and onions with the teeth. What a holy race to have such divinities springing up in their gardens!") [In *Juvenal and Persius*, trans. Ramsay.]

See also the quotation from Macrobius in Burton's *Anatomy of Melancholy*, Part III, Sect. IV, Memb. I, Subsect. 3 (Everyman's Library edition, III, 353), on the gross idolatry and superstition of Egyptians; and the passage from the *World*, No. 45 (November 8, 1753), p. 246 in Vol. XXVI of *British Essayists*, ed. Berguer.

[3] See p. 137, n. 2.

[b] *puny*] alternate wording: *student*

such simple creatures as will suffer themselves to be entangled in it. He that believes him has an erroneous faith, and is in the state of perdition: for he is not so unthrifty in his calling to spare any man, whom it is in his power to betray. He is like a false religion, that damns all those that believe in it. His oaths and vows are like granados[1] made to blow men up with, and when they are broken, destroy all that are within their reach; for he will say and swear any thing that another man pleases, that it may be in his power to do what he pleases himself. When he appears most kind, he always proves most treacherous, and with *Judas* never kisses but when he intends to betray. He finds no engine so useful to his designs as flattery, that with little force and less pains will carry things of greatest weight; and therefore he always plys that to insinuate with, conforms himself to all mens humours and inclinations, and when he has got the word, passes for a friend, although among the enemies guards. He will work himself into secrets like a mole under ground, to feed on the wormes of those he finds fit for his purpose to undermine. He that would surprize a guard must first kill the sentinels; and so does he begin with a mans reason and understanding, and when he has possest himself of any of his fortifications, sets up his own colours, and puts on for the rest. He finds pretences of friendship the best expedients to convey treachery, as poysons are easiest given in meat and drink, that are taken for preservation. He embraces and hugs a man like a wrestler, when he intends to overthrow him, and break his neck if it be in his power.

A PLAGIARY

Is one, that has an inclination to wit and knowledge, but being not born nor bred to it takes evil courses, and will rather steal and pilfer, than appear to want, or be without it. He makes no conscience how he comes by it, but with a felonious intention will take, and bear away any man's goods, he can lay his hands on. He is a witsharke, that has nothing of his own, but subsists by shifting, and filching from others. He comes by his wit, as some do by their money, that are said to live by their wits, that spend at a high rate, and no body knows how they come by it. He is a spirit, that steals the chil-

---

[1] Grenades.

dren of other mens brains, and puts them off for his own; a witcaper,[1] that will venture upon any thing he can master, and bear it away as lawful prize. He knows not what invention means, unless it be to take whatsoever he finds in his way, which he makes no scruple to do, because very few will enquire, whether he came honestly by it, and no action of *trover*[2] lyes against him. He accounts invention and thievery all one, because *Mercury* is equally Lord of both,[3] and in that he owns him for his ascendant,[4] but in nothing else. As soon as he has lighted upon a purchase, he presently commits it to writing, and to that purpose always carrys pen and ink-horn about him, which are his horn-thimble[5] and knife, with which he dispatches matters neatly, and conveys them away without being discover'd. Notwithstanding all his industry he never prospers; for as goods ill gotten never thrive, so his cheats being so inconsiderable, that they are neither allow'd, nor punish'd by the laws of the land, they never amount to any thing; and commonly he leaves the world, like imposters of the same quality, with beggary and infamy: for tho' the world be but an ill judge, yet it is so just, as in process of time to see its error, and cast off that with contempt and scorn, which it at first admir'd. For all impostures pass, till time and truth bring in evidence against them; and then they vanish of themselves, and never appear, till they are forgotten, and put on them some new disguise. For of so many bastards, as have in all ages been laid at the world's door, we find nothing surviving, but only the names of some few branded with infamy; while those that are legitimate and true born last from age to age; as the stomach sometimes receives unwholesome food with an appetite, but afterwards finding it hard of digestion, grows sick of it, and casts it off of its own accord, and retains only that, which is agreable to its own nature. He is like an Italian thief, that never robs, but he murthers, and endeavours to de-

---

[1] Caper: a privateer.

[2] An action at law to recover the value of personal property illegally converted by another to his own use.

[3] As the herald of the gods Mercury was considered the god of eloquence. He was also the god of prudence and cunning, and even of fraud, perjury, and theft. His shrewdness and sagacity made him regarded as the inventor of a variety of things.

[4] The degree of the zodiac which at any moment is just rising above the eastern horizon.

[5] See p. 277, n. 3.

stroy the reputation of those he steals from, that it may not rise up in judgment, and bring in evidence against him. He is not taken, but apprehended for a wit, merely upon suspicion, though wrongfully enough, for his own conscience knows he is innocent enough that way. He commits all manner of thieveries from the King's high way to petty larcenies; and as he that came off for stealing two horses; because the statute made it felony to steale a horse, that is one horse, the more thieveries he committs, the better he thrives and prospers. He steals mens wit, which the law setting no value on, it will not bear an inditement, and so he comes off clear, without putting himself to the hazard of God and his country. He adopts other mens writings for his own, especially orphans, that have no body to look after them, having no issue legitimate of his own. All his works are like instruments in law; what other men write he owns as his own act and deed. He is like a cuckow, that lives by sucking other birds eggs.[6]

A PLAYER

Is a representatif by his calling, a person of all qualities; and though his profession be to counterfeit, and he never means what he says, yet he endeavours to make his words and actions always agree. His labour is to play, and his bus'nes to turn passion into action —The more he dissembles, the more he is in earnest, and the less he appears himself, the truer he is to his profession—The more he deceives men, the greater right he does them; and the plainer his dealing is, the less credit he deserves. He assumes a body like an apparition, and can turn himself into as many shapes as a witch. His buisness is to be somebody else, and he is never himself, but when he has nothing to do. He gets all he speaks by heart, and yet never means what he says. He is said to enter when he comes out, and to go out when he goes in. When he is off the stage he acts a gentleman, and in that only makes his own part himself—When he plays love and honour in effigie, the Ladies take him at his word, and fall in love with him in earnest; and, indeed, they may be truly said to fall in love, considering how much he is below them. This blows him up with so much vanity,

---

[6] It is said that the cuckoo makes no nest of its own but rather lays its eggs in the nest of some other bird that hatches the chicks and feeds them.

that he forgets what he is, and as he deluded them, so they do him. He is like a Motion[1] made by clockwork, the Poet winds him up, and he walks and moves till his part is run down, and then he is quiet. He is but a puppet in great, which the poet squeaks to, and puts into what posture he pleases; and though his calling be but ministerial to his author, yet he assumes a magistery over him, because he sets him on work, and he becomes subordinate accordingly. He represents many excellent virtues, as they light in his part, but knows no more of them than a picture does *who it was drawn for*.[a] His profession is a kind of metamorphosis, to transform himself out of one shape into another, like a taylors sheet of paper, which he folds into figures.

It is not strange that the world is so delighted with fiction, and so averse to truth, since the mere imitation of a thing is more pleasant than the thing it self, as a good picture of a bad face is a better object than the face it self—All ornament and dress is but disguise, which plain and naked truth does never put on. Whores and cutpurses flock to him to ply for employment; and he is as useful to them as a mountebank is to an applewoman. He is an operator of wit and dramatic poetry, and Jan Gricuss[2] to the Muses. His prime qualifications are the same with those of a lyar, confidence and a good memory; as for wit he has it at second hand, like his cloaths. The ladies take his counterfeit passions in earnest, and accompany him with their devotions, as holy sisters do a gifted hypocrite at his holding-forth,[3] and when he gives the false alarm of a fight they are as much concern'd, as if he were in real danger, or the worst were not past already. They are more taken with his mock love and honour, than if it were real, and, like ignorant dealers, part with right love and honour for it. His applause and commendation is but a kind of manufacture form'd by clapping of hands; and though it be no more than men set dogs together by the ears with, yet he takes it as a testimony of his merit, and sets a value on himself accordingly. His harvest is the spring and winter, when he gets that which maintains him in the summer and autumn. A great plague is terrible to him,[4] but a

---

1 Puppet. See p. 128, n. 6.

a *who it was drawn for*] alternate wording: *whom it resembles*

2 Possibly a pretender to classical learning.

3 Preaching.

4 Theatres were ordered to be closed during times of plague. Plagues occurred in 1625, 1630, 1636, and 1637, and the Great Plague occurred in 1665–66.

thorough[5]-reformation much more; in the one he is but suspended, but by the other abolish'd[6] root and branch.[7]

A PROUD LADY

Swells and grows big with a false conception, a mooncalf[1] of vanity, which she will never be deliver'd of. She is made like a glass by being blown up and puft into a thin, brittle, empty, hollow piece of pride and vanity. She sets so great a value upon her precious self, that she can allow nobody else any at all. She needs no flattery; for she can do her self that service without being beholden to any other; for all her[a] vices are of her own growth, and lye so conveniently within themselves, that they need no outward support. She loves humility in others as much as she hates it in herself; and endures nothing with more impatience than to miss of it any where but at home. Her original sin is the same with the Devil's, pride and arrogance; and she derives it rather from his fall, than the fall of *Man*. She has a strong faith in her own superabundant merits,[2] and treats all people as if they were to be saved by them. She agrees with the Devil most exactly both in the doctrine and discipline of pride and insolence, according to the custom of the most ancient and primitive times of his apostasy. She is a secular *Whore of Babylon*,[3] and believes herself to be as good a woman as *Pope Joan*,[4] no disparagement. She is

---

[5] See p. 87, n. 21.

[6] The Puritans, once in power, by ordinance in 1642 closed the theatres, which remained closed until 1660. They believed that the theatre was immoral in itself (especially as it was conducive to frivolity and idleness). Note the details of argument in William Prynne's long work *Histrio-Mastix: the Players Scourge or Actors Tragedie* (1636).

[7] Suggestive of the Root and Branch Petition brought to the House of Commons in December, 1640, signed by 15,000 citizens, the object being abolition of Episcopacy "with all its roots and branches." Such a position on church matters was thereafter known as Root and Branch. [Trevelyan, *England Under the Stuarts*, p. 170.]

[1] An abortive, shapeless, fleshy mass in the womb; a false conception (regarded as influenced by the moon.) See p. 275, n. 1.

[a] all her] all, her

[2] See p. 85, n. 15 (supererogation).

[3] The Church of Rome was often compared to the Whore of Babylon (mentioned in Revelation, XVII).

[4] A mythical female pope, who supposedly succeeded Leo IV and preceded Benedict III in the ninth century. Born in Germany, she is said to have fled to

very conscientious in one thing, and that is in keeping of state and distance; for happy are they that never come near her, or are soon deliver'd from her; for there is nothing tolerable of her, but that she is vain and perishable. Her mind is swell'd with a tympany of vicious humours, that render her a monster of a kind, that Nature never purpos'd, nor design'd. She is cloath'd in jewels, but they all look upon her as if they were ill set, and were the very same with that which Æsop's cock found in a dunghill.[5]

A PUBLICAN[1]

Is as able a sinner, as any of his forefathers the *Jewes*[2] was, under the *Devil*. He pretends the kings' pressing occasions, when he exacts, and grates upon the people, and the people's pressing wants, while he delays, and endeavours to defraud the king; and very artificaly makes both cheates confederate to relieve one another by turns, and support him in the abuse of both king and people too. He finds that the public money is like a common woman, which every man may make free use of, that can get her in his hands, and that when he can keep her no longer, it will be time enough to part with her, and before too soon. If he took no more than his allowance, he would gain nothing by his delays; but he has a chymical trick of projection to multiply it by putting it out, as the eel-bouts in the Thames are more than maintained by the growth of the eels, when they lie upon their hands, and will not go off at a considerable rate.[3] As soon as he

Greece, disguised as a man, to follow her lover, a Benedictine monk. She is said to have moved on to Rome, where her great learning led eventually to the papacy. Her sex was discovered as she gave birth to a child during a procession. The whole story has long been disproved. [See Grey, ed., *Hudibras*, I, iii. 1249–50 n.]

[5] As a cock was scratching in the farmyard in search of food for the hens, he hit upon a jewel that by chance was there. He said that the jewel was undoubtedly fine for those who saw the great worth in it, but for himself a barley-corn was to be preferred to all the pearls in the world. [A fable from Aesop.]

[1] One who keeps a public house (alehouse or tavern).

[2] The publicans mentioned in the Bible were tax-gatherers.

[3] "If he took . . . a considerable rate": evidently the Publican sent out bills late, so as to charge interest, and thus gained by his delays.

Projection and multiplication: final stages in the transmutation of base metals into gold and augmentation of the elixir.

"Putting it out": lending the "allowance" for interest as a usurer. Further, in

receives the public money he lets it out to the bankers, like a common hackney, to earn more: for nothing breeds money like money; and when it is well husbanded, and lights in a fruitful soil, yields a very great increase, as all seeds multiply their own kind. When he has receiv'd money and given a discharge for it, if the acquittance happens to be lost, (as among so many some cannot but miscarry) he demands it again, and pretending his own forgetfulness makes them pay it over again for theirs; to which purpose he keepes several books, that if one be crost, like a christian, and will not bear false witness, he may have another ready, in which his own hand will not, like *Sodom* and *Gomorha*, rise up in judgment against him. He understands the law as learnedly as one that has been thrice in *Newgate*, and mooted in his own case.[4] He has a slight[5] to pass the ordeal trial bare-handed, and comes off without the least visible singe to appear against him the next time.[6] He cures the kings-evil by wearing his money about his neck,[7] and finds it the only preservative against all hard swellings thereabout.

A QUARELLER

Picks a quarrel, as a cutpurse does a pocket, to rob a man of his reputation, and get it to himself. He is a false interpreter of another man's words and actions, and wrests them always against sense and himself, expounds them against their true meaning to his own injury, and picks a quarrel with himself, as many things are

---

the passage, usury is compared to the breeding of eels, which reach the point of overpopulation when they are retained by the owners ("lie upon their hands") and bring no good price on the market.

Concerning "eel-bouts" see Ben Jonson, *The Staple of News*, III. ii. 84. Eel boats lay at Brook's wharf during Lent. These boats from Holland had gained a free mooring place off the Custom House Quay by virtue of a charter given by Charles II in 1666 for the assistance they gave during the Great Fire of London. [Herford and Simpson, eds., *Ben Jonson*, X, 275, n. 84.]

[4] Tried to defend his own case.

[5] Trick.

[6] See p. 228, n. 2.

[7] Scrofula was called the king's-evil because it was supposedly cured by the touch of the monarch. Henry VII introduced the practice of presenting a person who had been "touched" a small gold or silver coin, called a touch-piece. [Edwin Radford and M. A. Radford, *Encyclopaedia of Superstitions* (London, 1948).]

made witty by the apprehenders, that were never meant so by them that spoke them. He sets so great a value upon himself, that no man is able to come up to it; and therefore whatsoever is said or done to him he expounds as an undervaluing and disparagement of his high and mighty merits. He interprets every thing, not as he is pleas'd, but as he is displeas'd, and does not take, but snaps occasion, before it is offer'd him. The more his adversary gives way to his heat, the more averse he is to pacification; and the more intercession is us'd, the more violently he prosecutes his pretences. He shews his antagonist the length of his tongue, as a dog, when he quarrels, does the length of his teeth; but forbears to commit any act of open hostility, unless he finds he has the advantage, and is sure of present accomodation. He is as jealous of his honour as if it had plai'd false with him, and were no better than it should be; or were so ticklish, that it will not endure to be touch'd ever so gently. He is so tender and nice of his reputation, as if it were sore and so full of pain, that it is impatient of any thing that comes near it. He stands upon his punctilios, as if he were embassador from some foreign prince, and were to answer and make good every scruple of *his* honour, whom he represents, with his life. If the enemy be formidable he is very cautious of proceeding to the lye, which is alway the signal of giving battle, otherwise the sooner the better; for he that calls *Son of a whore* first is eldest hand, and has the advantage, in all equal chances, of the encounter. He complains much of a strange face, and can no more endure it than a cur can a stranger, but always quarrels at first sight, as the ancient *Latins* call'd strangers and enemies by the same name.[1] His punctilios of honour are as subtle as the point of his sword, which he disputes them with; and he will rather be run through with the one than suffer the other to be contrould. He is an espouser of quarrels, and will marry any living thing that lights in his way.

A ROOK

Is an under-gamester, that frequents ordinaries, where dice are cast, as other rooks do fields, where corn is sown. There goes a great deal of art and Science to render a man compleat in his calling,

---

[1] Probably *barbari* or *barbarian*: the name was given by the Greeks to all foreigners whose language was not Greek. The Romans applied the name to all people who spoke neither Greek nor Latin.

that is able by cunning observation of the running of the dice to lay his wager judiciously on the race, and discover who slurs or tops, though he does it ever so dextrously, and who plays fair, and consequently is like to lose; for all betters lay on the cheat's hand, never on his that has no tricks; in consideration whereof he claims as his right of the gamester to go a small snip with him, when his hand is in, for which he is bound by his order to swear and judge on his chief's side, right or wrong, when any controversy falls out about a cast, to the best of his skill and cunning, which he never fails to perform with more fidelity and integrity too than persons of honour and employments commonly use. He can do nothing of himself, but drives a trade, like a Judge's favourite, by having the good graces of the court—This brings him into a kind of pettifogging[1] practise, which, being always in the way, he improves by setting of gulls that are every way qualified to be cheated, and have not only abilities and parts, but great natural inclinations to be chous'd. When he has lodg'd game at a tavern, his bus'ness is to stand by and give aim, to fill glasses and tobacco-pipes, begin healths and tell stories, and with wine and smoke and newes divert the silly animal that he may stand fair, and not startle, till he fall in the place. Beside this it is his duty to assist at changing the dice, and help to convey away the *Fulhams* and *bucklers*,[2] when there is danger of discovery, that they may not appear to give in evidence at the sessions, and tell tales out of the school how they were palm'd, and have justice done with an untimely hot-iron,[3] in the place where the crime was committed.

A SAILOR

Leaves his native earth to become an inhabitant of the sea, and is but a kind of naturaliz'd fish. He is of no place, though he is always said to be bound for one or other, but a mere citizen of the sea, as vagabonds are of the world. He lives within the dominions of the water, but has his protection from the contrary element fire, without which his wooden castle were not tenable. He is confin'd within a narrow prison, and yet travels further and faster than those that are at liberty can do by land. He makes his own way by putting

---

[1] See p. 111, n. 1.
[2] Fulhams: false dice.
Bucklers: small round shields.
[3] Branded. See p. 228, n. 2.

a stop to the wind's, that drives his house before it like a wheelbarrow. The waves of the sea are both the road and wheels of his carriage, and the horses that draw it, without all question, of the breed of the wind. He lives, like Jonas,[1] in the belly of a wooden whale, and when he goes on shore, does not land, but is vomited out as a crudity, that lay on the fishe's stomach. How far soever he travels he is always at home; for he does not remove his dwelling, but his dwelling removes him. The boysterous ruggedness of the element he lives in alters his nature, and he becomes more rude and barbarous than a land man, as water dogs are rougher than land spaniels. He is a very ill neighbour to the fishes he dwells among, and, like one that keeps a gaming house, never gives them a treat, but with a design to feed upon them, like a sea canibal that devours his own kind; and they, when they catch him out of his quarters, use him after the same manner, and devour him in revenge. A storm and a calm equally annoy him, like those that cannot endure peace, and yet are unfit for war. He ploughs the sea, and reaps a richer crop than those that till the land. He is calk'd all over with pitch and tar like his hull, and his cloaths are but sheathings.[2] A pirate is a devil's bird to him, that never appears but before a storm. He endures a horses back worse than foul weather, and rides as if he rod at anchor in a rough sea, and complains the beast heaves and sets uneasily. The land appears very dry to him,[a] having been us'd to a moister element, and therefore he is fain to keep himself wet, like a fish that is to be shown, and is drunk as oft as he can, as the founder of his order *Noah* was, when he came ashore, and he believes himself bound to conform to the practise of his fore-grandfather.

A SCOLD

Is a *Syren*, against whom there is no defence, but by fortifying of ears, as *Ulysses* and his mates were fain to stand upon their guard.[1] *Armed* and *langued*,[2] as heralds call it are all one to her; for

---

[1] Jonah.

[2] The covering of a ship's bottom and sides.

[a] dry to him] dry him

[1] *Odyssey*, XII.

[2] Armed (heraldry): having the claws or talons of a different tincture from that of the adjoining parts; also, represented with claws, teeth, etc.

Langued (heraldry): of a charge: represented with a tongue of a specified tincture.

her tongue is her weapon, artillery, and ammunition, with which she defyes the enemy, and holds out with admirable resolution. There is nothing so odious as the noise she makes compos'd of all manner of discords, and with her tongue she will put the teeth of those that hear into a shivering, like a knife cutting upon a plate. When she is heated she fans the air with her tongue, as a dog does when he is hot, to cool himself. She does not speak, but break silence and the sculls of those that are within the reach of her clamour. Her elocution is so powerful, that nothing is able to hold out against it but deafness, or a drum. Nothing troubles her more than to gain a victory ingloriously, without any resistance of the foe, which she interprets contempt of her forces; and she is most implacable, when having planted her battery the enemy surrenders upon the first playing of the cannon. She is a vehement declaimer, and is stor'd, though not with flowers, with all manner of weeds of eloquence, that either sting, stink, or poyson. She has her commonplaces as common as the kennel, from which she is furnished upon all occasions with all sorts of dirty oratory; and is never at a loss for matter or expression. She has evil words enough to corrupt all the good manners of the civilest nation.

A SCRIVENER

Is a writer of great authority, and one whose words are for the most part authentic; for if he be discover'd to have committed a fault he expiates the offence with his ears, as *Caligula* made the bad writers of his time do theirs with their tongues.[1] He dashes the latter end of *Latin* words always, and the middle of *English*.[2] He puts out other men's money and his own to nurse together, takes brokage for both, and if either miscarry knows how to secure his own, and with *Solomon*'s harlot to lay claim to the live child.[3] If he be dextrous at *Shorthand*, his pen is like the tongue of a ready speaker, as *David*'s tongue was of a ready writer.[4] He is the usurer's pimp, that *procures*

---

[1] Cf. Suetonius, "Gaius Caligula," in *Lives of the Caesars*, trans. Rolfe, XX. Caligula held a contest in oratory, in which some of the least successful participants were ordered to erase their writings with a sponge or with their tongues.

[2] On "dashing the latter end of Latin words" see p. 113. He "dashes" the middle of English words perhaps because he is a poor speller.

[3] I Kings, III. 16 ff.

[4] See Psalms, XLV. 1.

statute, bond, and mortgage to satisfy his insatiable desire of getting. One of his chiefest talents is to discover exactly and readily how able any man is to be trusted, and upon a good occasion to help him pass muster with the usurer for a valuable share in the purchase, and to cast up suddenly, according to the desperation of the debt, what is justly due for procuring, as the present rates go. He has a table of use upon use in his memory, and can tell readily what a penny let out in the *Conqueror's* time would amount to this present year. He is very skilful at his weapon, and has most certain and excellent guards against the sword of Justice; and knows how to defend his money and his ears against all penalties of the law, in despight of all it can do or say to the contrary. When he deals with a small usurer, whose custom he does not greatly care for, he will let his money lye dead in his hands, until he admits of such security, as he can be best paid to approve of. His employments should be virtuous, for they lye between two contrary vices, Avarice and prodigality, both which he serves in their several ways, until the lean one has devour'd the fat, and he had his share of both. He stretches parchment with his tongue, as shoemakers do leather with their teeth, and multiplies words to no purpose, but to increase the bulk of the instrument; this he calls drawing, that is drawing it out at length.

THE SELF CONCEITED OR SINGULAR

Is a separatist from the rest of mankind, that finds nobody fit for him to comply with but his own dearly beloved self. He is rather an owl than a phoenix; for though there be many of his kind they never mix together. He likes no man's humour, judgment, or opinion but his own, nor that as soon as he finds any man else concur with him. He endeavours to render himself a phoenix[1] as he very well may in one sense; for he is bred out of a maggot, and is burnt with love of himself, as a lover is with his Mistresse's eyes. He is a man of a most singular understanding; for he will allow of nobodys but his own. He sets a high value on the meanest trifle that comes from himself, as a lover does on any toy he receives from his mistress; but dis-

---

[1] For a very full discussion of the sources of the legend of the phoenix see Browne, *Pseudodoxia Epidemica*, III. 12, in *Works*, ed. Keynes, II, 219 ff.

esteems any thing else how good soever, because it is not his. All his parts are curiosities, and he values them the more as the owners of rarities use to do, because he believes nobody has them but himself. He never approves of any thing that comes from another man, how well soever he likes it; but will pretend to have known it before, and esteem'd it not worth his notice, though afterwards, when he thinks it will pass for his own, he will value himself highly upon the account of it. He cries down all mankind but only two or three at a time, that he may not be thought to approve of nobody, and those he will afterwards cry down as much, when he has no need of them to save him from the inconvenience of being shown to disdain all men but his dearest self. The like he will do by books, condemn all, and reprieve only two or three, that he may not be thought too cruelly critical; and yet those he will afterwards make away in private. He never commends anything unless it have relation to himself, but that which nobody else will, and then it is in opposition to something else, that he has a design to undervalue, and partly to preserve the humour of singularity; for he believes himself nobody, if he be not that which is nearest to it, that is utterly unlike any man else. He admires his own defects, as those that are born in poor and barren countries do their native soil, only because they have the least reason to do it. He has a strange natural affection for all his own conceptions, as beasts have for their young, and the rather because they are like him, that is vain and idle. He wonders that all men do not concur with him in the opinion he has of himself, but laughs to think it is their ignorance, and not his own. He prefers, very philosophically, a known evil before an unknown good, and would not change his own familiar ignorance for all the strange knowledge in the world, which he is utterly unacquainted with; and in that he does wisely; for it would but make him think worse of himself. He enjoys all the felicities which[a] the poets fancy of a country life, and lives and dyes content on his own dunghill,[2] with a convenient neglect of all the rest of the world. He likes nothing but what he does, or would be thought to do himself, and disapproves of every thing, not because it is not well, but because it is not his. He envies no man, for envy always looks upward, and he believes all men below him, and fitter for his contempt, than emulation.

---

[a] which] w^h

[2] Recall the proverb "Every cock crows on its own dunghill."

A SHARKE

Lives upon freequarter like a *Dane* heretofore among the *English*.[1] He invites, treats, and welcomes himself with all freedom and dearness imaginable which he may well do; for being his own guest he is oblig'd to nobody but himself for his entertainment. All his acquaintances are his tenants, and pay him, like a *Welch* lord, with provisions, and a little in money when he can get it. He goes to a tavern as a horse does to water, and carries him that is to give him drink. The old *Romans* us'd to give money to be invited to great mens tables; but he saves himself that trouble and charge wherever he comes and makes open house where he pleases, which is something more than to keep it. He revives the old *English* hospitality as much as in him lyes, and makes those entertain him freely that never intended it. He is very officious and free in offering his services, but he that accepts it takes a begging present, and never comes out of his debt; for he values his pains like a *Dutch* host, not according to the worth of the business, but the quality of the person he does it for. He is very sagacious at hunting out of public treats, and will wind a tavern dinner further off than a fidler. He grows familiarly acquainted with all persons of quality as soon as they are dead, and will intrude at funerals to condole with their relations, and perform the last offices to the memory of a friend so extraordinary, that he never saw him in all his lifetime. He takes tunnage and poundage[2] of all tradesmen for customers which he brings them, and at tavern-reckonings has his own share return'd, and so much more out of the money, which the company he brought have spent, as is due to him according to agreement, for which he is to allow of all cheats and over-reckonings as very reasonable, and vouch all bad wine to be the best in the town.

---

[1] Probably a reference to the region of the "Dane-Law," a district where (in Saxon England) the Danish Law, not the Common Law, prevailed. The "five boroughs" of the Danes were: Lincoln, Stamford, Leicester, Derby, and Nottingham, serving both as military garrisons and as trading centers.

[2] Tunnage and poundage: taxes commonly considered together. The former was a tax upon wine imported in tuns or casks, at a set rate per tun. The latter was an impost, a subsidy granted by Parliament on all imports and exports except bullion and the commodities paying tunnage.

A SILENC'D PRESBYTERIAN[1]

Is a seminary Minister, a Reformado reformer, and a *Carthusian*[2] *Calvinist*; that holds two things by his order, seditious opinions, and his tongue. He was very pernicious to the government, till his tongue was bound to the peace, and good behaviour; ever since he breaks the king's laws, as he does God's, in private. He makes proselites as coyners do false money, in hugger-mugger. The handkerchief, he wore about his neck at the institution of his order[3] here, was a type, that in process of time, he should be troubled with a sore throat,[4] and since it is fulfill'd. His gifts are found to be contagious, and so are shut up, that they may not infect others. His doctrine is a prohibited commodity, and seiz'd upon as unlawful. He finds there is more to be got in dealing in prohibited commodities, than such as are allow'd, and therefore prefers that way of traffic before all others. He cares not for holding forth aboveboard, as long as he can get more by foul-play underhand. He gains more by having an embargo laid upon his holding-forth,[5] than if he had free and open trade. He is in pension with his conscience, that maintains him for maintaining it, and he grows rich by the bargain. He left his living for a better Church preferment; for he finds persecution better than a fat diocess, and had rather have an Officer lay hands on him than a Bishop. His offerings come to more in the year than the revenues of any church, and his gifts bring him in more now without trouble, than when he was a painful Teacher. The pity of his suppos'd sufferings works

---

[1] See p. 59, n. 24.

[2] Carthusians: an austere order of monks founded in the mountainous region (Chartreuse) near Grenoble in 1086. Thus, by analogy, Carthusian Calvinists are strict Calvinists.

[3] Reference to the Presbyterian Settlement voted by Parliament 1644–45, whereby Presbyterianism was established as the state religion.
On the handkerchief, cf. *Hudibras*, I. iii. 1165–70:

> The handkerchief about the neck—
> Canonical cravat of smeck,
> From whom the institution came,
> When church and state they set on flame,
> And worn by them as badges then
> Of spiritual wayfaring-men—. . . .

[4] I.e., silenced.

[5] Preaching.

much on the tender sex the sisters, and their benevolence is as duly paid as the husbands; for whatsoever they are to their spouses, they are sure to be his helpers, and he as sure to plow with their heifers. Since he was silenc'd he finds the proverb true, and catches more fish than he did before[6] with all his talking and holding-forth. He takes money, like a lawyer, for his opinion in religion, and is retain'd to be of council against the government. He prays himself above ground, as *Appollonius* and *Iamblicus*[7] are said to have done. His devotion may be truly call'd in a strict sense *religio adversus Deum*.[8] He parted with his benefice, as gamesters discard a suit that is dealt them, to take in better out of the stock, and mend their hands.

A SOLDIER

Pawns his life to get his living. He is a merchant adventurer, that trades in lives and limbs, and will engage to lay down his own, at any time, for him that will lay down most money for them. He exposes life and blood to sale, and is willing to consign his body over to death or slavery for any man, that will advance most upon it. His pay is the price of his own blood, as well as his enemys; and what he receives he does but take up beforehand upon the credit of his own slaughter, to be paid down, whensoever there shall be occasion to demand it. He is a gamester, that stakes his life to try, whether it be his own or not, not to gain another or more lives if his good fortune be to win, but a price of a living, and a small byc of honour, that is not current, but among a few of his own profession, and which he hedges in and thinks he is sure of whether he wins or loses. He is one of the lifeguard of government, and without him it is impossible either to rule or rebel. He takes money to throw dice for his life upon a drum; for fighting and that is all one; and has no way of slurring but running away, and, if he be taken in the manner, is hang'd for foul play. He is the last determiner of all controversies divine or human,

---

6 Probably "the fish is caught when the net is laid aside."

7 Apollonius Tyaneusis or Tyanaeus—i.e., of Tyana in Cappadocia, a Neo-Pythagorean philosopher born about four years before the Christian era, who pretended to have miraculous powers.

Iamblichus (died c. A.D. 330), a Syrian mystic, a pupil in the school (of Neoplatonism) of Porphyry.

8 Religion against God.

though he understands nothing at all of them; and passes a fine and recovery[1] upon all the curious disputes of mankind without knowing so much as what they are. He takes plunder for his vails,[2] and honour instead of the old donative that soldiers us'd to receive from their princes, since they left off that custom, and made choice of the other way, as more easy and less chargeable. He has no way to mend his condition of life but by despising it; and the less value he sets upon it, the better it proves to him: for he is never thought fit to have the charge and command of other mens lives, until he has made it appear, that he cares not a straw for his own; for he that contemns his own life is said to have any man's else in his power.

A STATIONER

Is one that lives by books, and understands nothing of them but the prices. He gets his living by learning as hypocrites do by religion, that neither know, nor care to know any thing of it, further than serves their interest, or conduces to their profit; and as the corruption of the best things is always the worst, so he is just so much a verier knave by dealing in the best things, than others are that deal in worse. He abuses those most (like other cheats) that he gains most by, and, like a disease, destroys those that feed him. He is a kind of a paper-worm that breeds in books, and maintains himself by feeding upon other mens writings. He lives by other mens wits, and his own impudence, which is all he has to shew for his title. He insults over the printer and binder as but ministerial, and expects suit and service from them as if he were Lord of the soyl. His conscience is no part of his calling, in which he regards nothing but his profit, and therefore desires most to deal in contraband goods, which he buys cheapest and sells dearest, and ventures nothing but his ears. He had rather have a good bargain of blasphemy and treason, than the most lawful and warrantable ware, that stands him in more: By this means he spreads more treason and sedition than ever was reveal'd in a conventicle, or whisper'd under the rose.[1] He is a *sower* of sedition,

---

[1] The fact or procedure of gaining possession of some property or right by a verdict or judgment of the court.

[2] Vail: A casual or occasional profit or emolument in addition to salary or other regular payment, especially one accruing or attached to an office or position. [*O.E.D.*]

[1] Under the rose: privately, in secret, in strict confidence; *sub rosa*.

and stitches up all his traiterous pamphlets himself, which he dares
not trust his servants with—These he vends according as he finds men
inclin'd, to some as horrid things which he lighted upon by chance,
and was willing to get, to show the villany of those people, and to
others as his faithful endeavours to serve his country and *the good
old cause*.[2] When a book lies upon his hands and will not sell, notwithstanding all his lies and forgeries of known mens approbation,
his last remedy is to print a new title-page, and give it a new name, (as
mercers do by their old rotten stuffs) and if that will not do it is
past cure, and falls away to waste paper. He makes the same use of
mens names as forgers do, and will rob the living and the dead of
their reputation by setting their hands to the frauds and impostures
of false and counterfeit scriblers, to abuse the world, and cheat men
of their money and understanding. To these he falsifies the date (as
those virtuosi use to do) and begins and ends the year, like a *Jew*,[3]
at pleasure, which is commonly in November, after which all he
prints bears date the year following. His chief ability consists in putting off his ware and his creditors, and when he has done with the one
he begins with the other, and does his endeavour to the uttermost of
his power, as far as lying and impudence shall enable him. He commonly sets up in a churchyard like a malefactor that takes sanctuary,
and justifyes that proverb in his life and conversation, which proves
him to be the further off God. He values nothing but as it is vendible,
and would not greatly care what becomes of his own soul, but that
he finds it will sell; for he believes the joys of heaven to be but dull
sport, to taking of money. He cares for no more learning than will
serve, upon a good occasion, to secure his throat against twelve good
men and true, and by his own reading prevent the Judge's reading
of sentence;[4] and accounts him a fool, that will trouble himself any
further with it. He lives by learning, but never cares to know what
it is, more than a horse does the grass he feeds upon; for he has no
thoughts, like a beast, beyond his own private concernment.

---

[2] See p. 45, n. 2.

[3] The Jewish calendar combines solar years with lunar months, an additional
month being intercalculated in each of seven years in every cycle of nineteen
years. The new year begins on the first day of the month *Tishri* (the first month
of the civil year and the seventh month of the ecclesiastical, corresponding to
parts of September and October).

[4] Benefit of clergy: originally the privilege allowed to clergymen of exemp-
tion from trial by a secular court; it was modified and extended to everyone who
could read.

A TENNIS-PLAYER

Is a very civil Gentleman, that never keeps a racket, but a racket keeps him. He is always striking himself good or bad luck, and gains, or spends what he has with the sweat of his brows, and makes, or undoes himself with the labour of his hands. He is a great critick, of profound judgment in a ball, and can tell by seeing it fly where to have it at the rebound, as the Frenchman did where the late comet would be three months after.[1] He gains more by losing than by winning; for when he makes a confederate match, which is commonly for some very great sum of money, he allows a fortnight or three weeks time, to spread the news abroad, that the gulls may have notice to provide their money, and be ready against the day—When that comes, he has an officer with an unknown face, that appears with his pockets full of gold, that lays against him, and takes all bets that are laid on his hand. When that is done the set is up; for he has nothing to do but to dissemble losing, and share the bets with his confederate, between whom and him the match goes for nothing. He strips himself of his cloaths first, and then of his money, and, when he has done his business is rub'd like a Presbyterian Holder-forth, until he is a clean gentleman—This is supposing him a gamester for his pleasure, that neither uses, nor knows tricks, but is to lose by his place. When he misses his stroke he swears, and curses the ball, as if it understood him, and would have a care to do so no more; and in that, indeed, he makes it plain, that the thing has as much reason as himself. The marker is register of the court, and more righteous than the register of a court of justice; for he crys what he sets down, and cannot commit iniquity, but with a forked chalk.

AN USURER

Keeps his money in prison, and never lets it out but upon bail and good security, as *Oliver Cromwel* did the *Cavaliers*, to appear again upon warning. Lords and Courtiers are apocryphal with him,

---

[1] Observation of comets was of particular interest at this time, as evidenced by accounts in the Philosophical Transactions of the Royal Society. I have found no word on this particular reference.

but Aldermen and Country Squires canonical, but above all statute and mortgage—though he is often cheated with a butter'd bun,[1] and lays out his money a day after the fair; when land-security proves under age, and elder mortgage goes away with all. He abhors a Member of parliament as a malefactor, that takes sanctuary in the temple, and lurks in his Ram-alley-privilege,[2] against which varlets[3] and bumbailifs are void and of none effect. He undoes men by laying obligations upon them, and ruins them for being bound to them. He knows no virtue but that of an obligation, nor vice but that of failing to pay use. He makes the same use of mens seals, as witches do of images in wax, to make the owners waste and consume to nothing. A man had better be bound to his good behaviour, than to him; for he that is bound to him is bound prentise to a prison, and when he is out of his time is sure to be in. He curses the bones of those, that made the act against extortion, as too great an imposition upon liberty of conscience—He ventures to break it out of zeal; and though he lose his principal, is contented, like a Fanatic, *to suffer persecution for righteousness.* He delights most of all to deal with a rich Prodigal, who maintains *his* avarice, as *he* does the other's luxury. These two vices, like the male and female viper, keep together until the one has spent all, and then the other devours it—until the one bites off the other's head.[4]

THE VAINGLORIOUS MAN

Has perpetual designs to cheat the world of a little reputation that he has no right to at all, but always takes a wrong course, and misses of his aim; for he endeavours to put off a little counterfeit merit, that might pass among some easy observers in private well enough, but being expos'd every where in public the trick is discover'd, and renders him ridiculous. He makes his applications to the good opinion of the world, not as if she were an honest woman, but

---

[1] A mistress or a harlot. [Partridge, *Dictionary of Slang and Unconventional English.*]

[2] Ram Alley led from Fleet Street to the Temple and, at the time, provided immunity from arrest and thus was the habitat of sharpers and various men and women of ill reputation. See L. Barry *Ram-Alley* (London, 1611), in Dodsley's collection of Old Plays.

[3] See p. 70, n. 1.

[4] See p. 204, n. 2.

a common whore, and were to be accosted with vapouring, ranting, and lying: for he pretends to every thing, how weak soever his title be, as some gallants use to do to the enjoyment of ladies, they have only seen at a distance, or perhaps but heard of. He courts fame as unfortunately as some *squires of dames*[1] do women, who by making general applications to all are receiv'd into the good graces of none, but disdain'd as paltry vagabond makers of love-tricks, that, like pedlars, open their packs of passion at every market, where any thing is to be gotten. All his actions and words are like the epilogues of plays, that always either insinuate, or beg applause. He sets off himself always to the best advantage that he possibly can, like a horse that is to be sold in a fair, with his mane and tail trim'd with ribbands, though that does not all mend his shape, nor his pace. He endeavours to appear upon all occasions he can possibly lay violent hands on, and by main force draw in to serve his purpose, a person of extraordinary merit and renown; and though it will very seldom pass, yet he finds the flattery, which he receives from himself (though no man is apt to be mov'd with the tickling of his own fingers) so pleasant, that he does not altogether lose his labour, though he gains nothing else by it. He has that natural affection for all his own actions and concernments, that, how ridiculous and contemptible soever they appear to others, he believes they deserve to have no mean value set upon them, and with the tenderness of a parent caresses whatsoever comes from him, how deform'd soever it appear to others. He is a gut stuff'd with the wind of vain glory, that makes a filthy noise and offensive stink to others, but gives it self ease when it is vented, and deliver'd of the nasty vapour.

THE VOLUPTUOUS

Is very hard to be pleas'd; for he makes it the whole business of his life to give himself content, but cannot possibly bring it to pass, for still he is either sick or weary of his employment; for he mistakes one thing for another, and makes that his business, which nature meant for his recreation, and therefore the more he uses it, the less he enjoys of it, as too much drink instead of quenching thirst makes it greater. He devours his pleasures so greedily, that he neither tastes nor digests them; for he swallows and voids them by turns, as

---

[1] See the Character of A Squire of Dames.

fast as a cormorant does an eel. Perpetual surfeits have so destroy'd his stomach, that it does not concoct but putrify his meat; and wine by perpetual running up into his head has engendred a stone in his brain, as well as his bladder. He is like a froward child, that must always have some foolish toy or other to still it with, or else it will be peevish and unquiet; and, therefore, his flattering pimps and parasites have found out as many devices to apply to his humour, as the engineers, that work to baby-shops, have rattles to appease children. He lives, like Adam, in a paradise of pleasure, but eats himself out of it as he did; for perpetual surfeits fill him as full of diseases as meat, and he devours the personal estate of his *health*,[a] as well as that of his fortune. When he drinks he cools his wine with ice, and himself with women, and has all sorts of both, which his pimps keep always in a readiness, whensoever he is pleas'd to call for them. Fidlers, Pimps, and flatterers are his caviare, anchovies, and tongues, which he uses to relish his pleasures with, and provoke his gusto to a new appetite, and when it grows dull and tir'd, these are, as the rabble says, his right hands and the keys of the work, that can keep out, or let into him whom and whatsoever they please. His buffoon is master of the revels, a principal favourite, that has command of more than his smile, his laughter, a very weighty charge; for it is all that he has left to shew for his humanity that he is *animal risibile*,[1] the only property of man that he is able to produce: but as a man that has lost one eye, is said to see better with the other than he did before; so what he has lost of his rational distinction he has doubly repaid in the ridiculous. His valet de chambre or pimp, if he be but a person of any abilities in flattery, is his minister of state, chiefly his pimp, who has a double capacity; for his very employment is flattery, and if he have a gift the other way, is esteem'd (as the Turks do one that is both Eunuch and mute) above any of the single faculties; for he is always of the junto, and admitted into all private consultations.

A SELF-CONCEITED MAN

Is a very great man with himself, and reposes all trust and confidence in his own extraordinary abilities. He admires his own

---

[a] *health*] alternate wording: *body*

[1] Risible: disposed to laugh; exciting laughter (even "ridiculous"). For a discussion of man as a laughing animal see Cureau de la Chambre, *The Characters of the Passions* (1650).

defects, as those that are born in poor and barren countries do their native soil, only because they have the least reason to do it. He takes his own natural humour for better or for worse, though it be within the prohibited degrees,[1] and forsakes all others to cleave to that. The worse opinion the world has of him, the better he has of himself, and, like a disguised Prince, is pleas'd with the mistakes of those, who he believes have not cunning enough to decypher him; though he is as transparent as a cobweb. He envies no man, for envy always looks upward, and he believes all other men below him, and fitter for his contempt than emulation. He likes nothing but what he does, or would be thought to do himself, and disapproves of every thing not because it is not well, but because it is not his. He has a strange natural affection for all his own conceptions, as beasts have for their young, and the rather because they are like him, that is vain and idle. He wonders that all men do not concur with him in the opinion he has of himself, but laughs to think it is their ignorance, and not his own. He confines himself to his own latitude and never looks further, which renders him so erroneous in his judgment of himself; for wanting occasion to measure himself with others, he has no way to understand his own true dimensions. He prefers, very philosophically, a known evil before an unknown good, and would not change his own familiar intimate ignorance for all the strange knowledge in the world, which he is utterly unacquainted with, and in that he does wisely; for it would, at best, but make him think worse of himself. He enjoys all the felicities which the poets fancy of a country life, and lives and dyes content on his own dunghill,[2] with a convenient neglect of all the rest of the world.

A BAWD

Is mother of the no-maids, the Devil's Nuncia[1] resident with the flesh, an agent for incontinence, a superintendant of the *family of*

---

[1] The number of steps in the direct line of descent (which determine the proximity of blood of collateral descendants) within which marriage is prohibited.

[2] See p. 310, n. 2.

[1] Feminine of *nuncio*, a permanent official representative of the Pope at a foreign court or seat of government.

love,[2] a siminary sister with mission to reconcile those that differ, and confirm the weak. She manages all treaties of amity, league, and alliance between party and party, and engages to see conditions performed. She is a publick envoy employ'd to maintain correspondence and good understanding between confederates. She does very good offices in her way, intercedes, mediates, and compounds all differences between the well affected, though under several forms and dispensations. She is judge of the spiritual court, and gives sentence in all matters of fornication and incontinence, that fall within her jurisdiction. She keeps an office of address, where all mens occasions may be serv'd with trust and secresie. She is very industrious in her calling, takes great pains in brandy, and gets her living by the labour of her drinking, which swells her till she becomes a just dimension for a cart, and grows a B. of the first magnitude. Her sins and her bulk increase equally together, till she becomes the badge of her profession, to signify she belongs to the flesh. After she has perform'd all her exercises, both public and private, she has her grace at the sessions, is advanc'd to the cart,[3] and ever after is stil'd *right reverend mother in the Devil*. She is the whore's learned council, and a person of great chamber-practice; for she is very skilful in conveyances and settlements, and like a great Practiser, takes fees on both sides. She is excellent at actions of the case. She lives under the canonical obedience of the Justice and the Constable, to whom as her superiors she is subordinate, and in case of contumacy is suspended *ab officio et beneficio*,[4] till satisfaction be made, in default of which she is depriv'd, degraded, and deliver'd over to the secular power. She deals in prohibited commodities and contraband goods, which she puts off in secret, other she and all become forfeit to the Law, and are secured to forge hemp[5] on a wooden anvil, *till death them do part*. Next this the greatest visitation, that commonly falls upon her, is breaking of her windows, which she endures with unchristian patience, rather than venture to seek reparation of the common enemy Law and Justice.

---

[2] Probably suggestive of such a group as the Familists, a continental sect of the sixteenth century, of which there may have been a secret English version in the seventeenth. One reference to the group says that it was a "wild development of Anabaptism." Masson [*Life of Milton*, III, 152] refers to the "esoteric mysteries . . . of the Family of Love."

[3] See p. 267, n. 6.

[4] From office and benefit (privilege).

[5] See p. 245, n. 7.

AN AMBITIOUS MAN

Is a mortar-piece that aims upward always. He is one that flies in a machine, and the engines that bear him are pride and avarice. He mounts up into authority, as a coachman does into his box, by treading upon the wheel of fortune;[1] and gets up to preferment, though it be on the wrong side. He leaps over hedge and ditch, like a hunting nag, and like a vaulter, will throw himself over any thing he can reach. He will climb like the cripple, that stole the weather-cock off Paul's steeple.[2] He rises, like a meteor, from corruption and rottenness, and, when he is at his height, shines and dispenses plagues and diseases on those that are beneath him. He is like a hawke, that never stoops from his height, but to seize upon his prey. He is like the north pole to his friends, the nearer they are to him, the higher he is above them; and when they steer by him, unless they perfectly understand their variation from him, they are sure to find themselves mistaken. He is never familiar with any man in earnest, nor civil but in jest. He is free of nothing but his promises and his hat, but when he comes to performance, puts off the one as easy as the other. He salutes men with his head, and they him with their feet; for when he nods at one end, they make legs at the other. He is a great pageant born upon men's shoulders, that pleases those that only look upon him, and tires those that feel his weight. He sells offices at the outcry of the nation, and has his brokers, that know where to put off a commodity of justice at the best rates. He is never without a long train of suitors, that follow him and their bus'ness, and would be glad to see an end of both. He is commonly rais'd like a boy's paper-kite, by being forc'd against the popular air. His humility is forc'd like a hypocrite's, and he stands bare to himself, that others may do so too. His letters of course are like charms for the tooth-ache, that give the bearer ease

---

[1] See p. 250, n. 2.

[2] Possibly a reference to a performance such as the one in 1553 before Queen Mary on her way through London to Westminster, described by Holinshed: Peter, a Dutchman, stood upon the weathercock of St. Paul's steeple, holding and waving in his hands a streamer five yards long. He stood on one foot, shook the other, and then kneeled. [Joseph Strutt, *The Sports and Pastimes of the People of England*, ed. William Hone (1876), p. 304. See also the reference to Dutchmen who stood on weathercocks in Arthur Bryant, *The England of Charles II* (London, 1935), p. 127.]

for the present, according as he believes in them, for which he pays the Secretary, and after finds himself cheated both of his money and his expectations too.

A VAPOURER

Is one that vapours over every thing he does, like a hen that cackles when she has laid an egg. He overvalews all his own performances, which makes them lie upon his hands; for nobody will take them off upon such terms. Whatsoever he treats upon of himself begins, like a small poets work with his own commendation; and the first thing you meet with is *in laudem authoris*:[1] But as no man's testimony is valid in his own case, no more in reason ought his word to pass in his own praise. He blows up his own concernments, as a butcher does his veal, to make it appear larger and fairer; but then it will not keep. He does as ridiculously, as if he gave himself his own certificate, or thought to be received with letters of his own recommendation; yet the rabble is very apt to believe in him, which he takes for their approbation; and though he receives no more from them than they had from him, yet he believes himself a gainer, and thinks he has more reason to believe in himself than he had before. He that praises himself and his own actions does like a beast, that licks himself and his own whelps with his tongue. It is natural to all men to affect praise and honour; but very few care to deserve it: for as stol'n pleasures are said to be most delightful, so undeserv'd glory cannot but be more pleasing to some men, than that which is earn'd with the drudgery or danger of merit. He that gives himself praise, if it be due, is no more the better for it, than if he gave himself that which he had before; but if it be undue he loses by it, as he that takes that which is not his own forfeits that which is. All his brags tend only to cloath and cover his defects, as Indians wear feathers about their breeches; for commonly he does but vapour in his own defence. Glory is nothing but a good opinion which many men hold of some one person; and if he will take that into his own hands, it is no longer to be expected from others. He that braggs and vapours is but his own Pudding,[2] and shews himself to the worst advantage; for it is a pitiful monster, that is fain to wear its own livery. His extolling of himself

---

[1] In praise of the author.
[2] Jack-pudding; see p. 44, n. 44.

does but forbid others to do so; for it is a vain superfluous office to commend one that can commend himself. His success always falls out quite contrary to his design, which is nothing else but to take up reputation upon his own word; but being known not to be responsible, he always comes off with repulse, and loss of credit; yet that does not at all discourage him, for he is never told of it but in some quarrel, and then he imputes it to anger, malice, or revenge, and so it goes for nothing. Some will not vapour downright, but by circumstances and insinuations on the bye will hedge in their own praises, as if it were not meant, but only fell out by chance: others by undervaluing of themselves will hunt after their own vainglory, like tumblers, by seeming to neglect it, and lay a necessity upon men's modesties to flatter them merely out of shame and pity. They undervalue themselves, that others may overvalue them as much, like rooks at tennis, that win by losing, and gain by betting against themselves. There is no vice so odious, and yet so harmless, for it hurts nobody but its owner, and many times makes pleasant sport to others: But as all civility is nothing but a seeming submission or condescension to others, and is grateful to all men; so whatever appears contrary to that must be incivility, and consequently as much hated.

It appears he came easily by all his pretences, by the large measure he allows, and the willingness he expresses to put them off upon any terms. He is his own broker. All the noise he makes is but like that of a trumpet, a mere blast of wind. He is like the moon, that looks bigger the wider sphere of vapours she appears through. He is like those that cry things about the streets, who make more noise and take more pains to put off a little stinking rotten stuff, or trash, than those that have their warehouses stor'd with the richest merchandises. He never obliges a friend, but it is in the nature of an obligation, which all men are to know.

A MOROSE MAN

Is like a piece of knotted wood, every thing goes against the grain with him. He is impatient of every thing but his own humour, and endures that no longer than it is in opposition to something else. He approves of nothing but in contradiction to other men's opinions, and like a buzzard, delights in nothing more than to flutter against the wind, let it be which way it will. He is made up of cross-crosslets,[1]

---

[1] Crosslets: small crosses, especially as a heraldic bearing.

and always counterchang'd; for when he is join'd with white he is
sure to be black, and black with white. He esteems all men extravagant
and intolerable but himself, as those that have the jaundice think all
objects yellow, because their own eyes are so. He is a strict observer
of his own humour, and would have every man else so too, otherwise
he retires to solace himself with his own complacence; and as great
men keep natural fools to please themselves in seeing somebody have
less wit than themselves (which they would never do unless they kept
such of purpose) he delights in his own folly, and the more ridiculous
it is the better he is pleas'd with it. He is very nice and thrifty of his
conversation, and will not willingly afford it, but where he thinks to
enjoy the greatest share of it himself, in which he is often mistaken;
for none endure him better than those, that make him their sport, and
laugh at his folly, when he thinks they do at his wit. He abhors a
stranger, because having no humanity he takes him for a thing of
another kind, and believes it too difficult a task ever to bring him to
his humour. He hates much company though it be ever so good; for
the more there are, the less share he has of his own humour, which is
all he[a] values or looks for. He rolls himself up in his own humour, as
a dog does with his nose in his breech, and pleases himself with that
which offends all others. The choice of his humour supposes his
ignorance, as empty boats sail best against the stream. He is like a
windmill that never moves, but when it is planted directly against
the wind.

A RAILER

Is a stout man of his tongue, that will not turn his back to
any man's reputation living. He will quarrel by natural instinct, as
some wild beasts do, and lay violent language upon a man at first sight,
and sometimes before. His tongue is his weapon, which he is very
skilful at, and will pass upon any mans credit as oft as he pleases. He
seldom charges, but he gets the crupper of his enemy, and wounds
him behind his back. He was born to a clan with all the world, and
falls out with all things (as spirits are said to converse) by intuition.[1]
His violence makes him many times hurt himself, instead of his enemy,
and he blunts the point of his weapon upon some, that go so well
arm'd, that their credit is impenetrable. He is as lavish of his own

[1] See p. 108, n. 1.
[a] he] she

reputation, as he is of another mans; for to set his tongue against some-bodys back parts (as he usually does) is not much for his credit. He is like a leech that sucks blood out of a man's reputation behind his back. He destroys more learning and arts than the Goth and Vandal ever did; and talks more mischief than the long-parliament.[2] He is most unmerciful to a man in his absence, and blows him up like sympathetic gunpowder,[3] at any distance. He is an ill orator, for he never speaks well of any thing. He bites any thing that comes in his way, like a mad dog, throws his foam about, and runs on, he cares not whither, so he do but infect somebody with his own venom. Serpents lay by their venom when they drink, but he retains his, and all his nourishment turns to gall, and he spits it out, as men in consumptions do their lungs. His words are like an ill wind that blows nobody good, and he carrys a cudgel in his mouth, like a water-dog. He is an Ismaelite,[4] his tongue is against every man, and every mans against him. He ploughs upon men's backs, as David complains he was used; and destroys all he encounters with a jaw-bone of an ass. He fights with his mouth, as wild beasts do. He carries his bullet in his mouth, and chaws it, to make it poison the wounds it gives.[5] He stings men like a bug; and, when he is destroyed for it, offends them as much with the stink. He is said to have a foul mouth, and whatsoever comes out of it is the fouler for having been there. He is a man of integrity, and may be believ'd to mean what he says; for no man will counterfeit that, which is bad enough of itself.

A DRUNKARD

Was conceived, like Orion, in a beast's hide[1] and—. He is an animal amphibium, that lives in two elements, but most naturally in the moist; for like a beaver's tail he would gangrene, if he were kept

---

[2] See p. 84, n. 9.

[3] A play on the idea of powder of sympathy, for which see p. 194, n. 1.

[4] See Genesis, XVI. 11–12.

[5] Possibly an extension of the idea of the powder of sympathy. See p. 194, n. 1.

[1] The legend of Orion's birth is based on a false etymology which derives Orion from the Greek *ouron*, "urine."

Hyrieus, a bee-keeper and farmer, who was old and impotent, kindly entertained Zeus and Hermes, who visited him incognito. The gods gave him a chance to have whatever he wished, and his desire was for a son. Hyrieus was directed to sacrifice a bull, make water in its hide, then bury it in his wife's grave. Nine months later a child was born to him, whom he named Urion—"he

dry.[2] He has sprung a lake, and sucks in faster than nature can pump out, till at length he founders and sinks. His soul dwells in a fenn, stifled with perpetual fog and Scotch mist. His drink and tobacco render him more like a smoaky house and a rainy day than *Solomon's* scold.[3] He sucks in his liquor like a spunge, which the learned say is a kind of live plant, and such he becomes when he has taken his dose. He is a coronation conduit, an ale-commanding engine, an overtaker. He is like an *Irish* bog, if you do not run quickly and lightly over him, you will be apt to sink in him, and find it harder to get, than keep out of him. He takes his drink as a medicine to procure another man's health, as *catholic* penitents whip themselves for other men's sins. A beer-glass is his divining cup, with which he swallows good or bad fortune, as the country fellow did a potion to find his asses;[4] and happiness and prosperity, or confusion and destruction ensue according as the spirit of the drink disposes him. He conjures his reason to go out of him, as the *Greeks* do their souls when they drink wine,[5] and this he does so oft, that at length it cannot find the way in again, and then he turns sot, and is drunk for term of life. He is never valiant but in his drink, as a madman, that has lost his wits, has double his strength. He is not given to drink, but thrown away and lost upon it. When

---

who makes water." The rising and setting of the constellation Orion do bring rain. [Robert Graves, *Greek Myths*, (reprint edition, Baltimore, 1957), I, 151–53.]

[2] Pliny [*Natural History*, VIII. xlvii. 109] says that the beaver has a fish's tail, while the rest of its conformation resembles an otter's.

Cf. Butler in "Nature" in *Poetical Thesaurus*:

> As some Affirme a Bever, and his Taile,
> Is each a Different Sort of Animall,
> And tho they seem by Nature of one Piece,
> The one is Perfect flesh, the other Fish:
> And therefore in his House, The Beast do's ly
> Above the waters Top one Story high,
> Altho his Tayle would mortify, and Gangreen
> Without a Constant Watry Cell to hang in.

[In *Samuel Butler: Satires and Miscellaneous Poetry and Prose*, ed. Lamar, p. 196.]

[3] Probably a reference to the harlot in Proverbs, V. 1–9.

[4] Cf. Butler in "Astrology," in *Poetical Miscellany*:

> Hee that tooke Pills for finding-out his Ass
> Altho by Accident, it came to pass.

[In *Samuel Butler: Satires and Miscellaneous Poetry and Prose*, ed. Lamar, p. 202.]

[5] Perhaps a reference to the ecstasies of the wine orgies in the Mysteries of Dionysus.

Noah had escap'd the waters he presently[6] found out wine, which drown'd and destroy'd as many sinners since, as the waters did before.

A MASTER OF ARTS

Is commonly an ill master, and as ill serv'd. The arts are his menial servants and followers, but he keeps them so short, that they are forc'd to cheat and outwit him; for as *Tacitus* says of *Nero*, he has *infra servos ingenium*.[1] He is as proud as a Pharisee of the title of *Master*, and his learning is like the other's righteousness, that consists in straining of gnats and swallowing of camels.[2] He wears the greatest part of his learning on his back (as a needy gallant does of his estate); for his gown is the better part of his knowledge, and all he has to shew for his degree. It is but the livery of his learning, and a loose garment that fits all sizes equally. He has been a prenticeship in breaking his natural reason, and putting it out of its pace into an artificial shuffle, that makes no progressive advance at all. He melts down all his learning into abstruse notions, that destroy the use and lessen the value of it, and by too much refining loses much of its weight;[3] for the finer any mettal is, the more unuseful it becomes, and is only capable of a greater alloy. His understanding is weak and consumptive (like those that have the dog-hunger) with oppressing his capacity with more than it is able to digest.

---

[6] Immediately.

[1] The remarks by Tacitus followed a discussion of the overbearing pride of Agrippina, Nero's mother, who destroyed her husband Claudius to make way for Nero to succeed to the throne: "Sed neque Neroni infra servas ingenium." ("But neither was Nero's a disposition that bends to slaves.") [*Annals*, trans. Jackson, XIII. ii.] The phrase from Tacitus, as quoted by Butler only in part and out of its context, means the very opposite of what the original passage says about Nero.

[2] See Matthew, XXIII. 24: "Ye blind guides, which strain at a gnat, and swallow a camel."

[3] Cf. p. 29, n. 4.

APPENDIX:

A Character from Manuscript Commonplace Book

SCHOOLMASTER

is a kind of Lord of Misrule[1] that has Absolute Dominion in his Territories & (like ye King of Macassa) is Party Judge & Executioner[2] Himselfe. Authority is a great Corrupter of good Manners & His perpetuall Dominion over Children makes him not know How to continue[a] Himselfe in a private condition & as Countrey Sqrs become stark fooles by being always ye wisest in the Company So does hee among his Pupills. The utmost of his Jurisdiction extends but to ye Breech only & hee does Justice on that Part for ye whole outward Boy. Hee carryes his Rod before Him like a Roman Consull & is both magistrate & Lictor[3] for himselfe & is no lesse proud & Cruell than both together. His perpetuall concernments in Boyes play makes him . . .[b] but in Trifles & always a Truant in Serious things. Hee never takes down a Boy but hee takes him upp as a Grave Statesman sayd of ye Army that was preferd to disbanding. Hee finds that to say the Same thing over & over ever so many times is not so dangerous as ye Ancients held it & Hee is a small magistrate in ye Comon Wealth of letters, that has his office for terme of Life & never rises Higher. He

---

[1] See p. 191, n. 1.

[2] Perhaps a reference to the King of Macassar's poison, referred to by Sprat and in other places by Butler:

Sprat's remarks follow:

"Q. *What Poyson is it the King of Macassar in Colebees is said to have peculiar to himself, which not only kills a man immediately . . . but also within half an hours time, make* [sic] *the flesh . . . fall . . . from the Bones . . . ?*

A. That there is such a Poyson in this Kings possession is most certain; but what it is no *Christian* hitherto ever knew right. . . ."

[*History of the Royal Society*, ed. Cope and Jones, pp. 164–65.]

[a] continue] alternate wording: behave

[3] The officer who bore the fasces as insignia, whose duty was to clear the way for the chief magistrates in public.

[b] Illegible word(s) in the manuscript.

practises oratory as Demosthenes did, who is sayd to put stones in his Mouth to mend his Pronunciation, & hee is very Industrious to use words every way at Hand. Ffor hee teaches his Schollars as they doe Birds to sing by Keeping them Darke with his insignificant terms that they may not understand what they are doing.